THE NATION'S NATURE

THE NATION'S NATURE

HOW CONTINENTAL PRESUMPTIONS GAVE RISE TO THE UNITED STATES OF AMERICA

JAMES D. DRAKE

UNIVERSITY OF VIRGINIA PRESS

Charlottesville and London

University of Virginia Press
© 2011 by the Rector and Visitors
of the University of Virginia
All rights reserved
Printed in the United States of America
on acid-free paper

First published 2011

9 8 7 6 5 4 3 2 1

Library of Congress
Cataloging-in-Publication Data
Drake, James David, 1968–
　　The nation's nature : how continental presumptions gave
rise to the United States of America / James D. Drake.
　　　　p. cm.
　　"Winner of the Walker Cowen Memorial Prize for an
outstanding work of scholarship in eighteenth-century
studies."
　　Includes bibliographical references and index.
　　ISBN 978-0-8139-3122-7 (cloth : alk. paper)
　　ISBN 978-0-8139-3139-5 (e-book)
　　1. United States—Historical geography. 2. Geographical
perception—United States—History—18th century.
3. United States—History—Colonial period, ca. 1600–1775.
4. Nationalism—United States—History—18th century.
5. United States—Territorial expansion. 6. United States—
History—Revolution, 1775–1783—Causes. I. Title.
　　E179.5.D827 2011
　　973.3′1—dc22

2010051962

For Haley, Hanna, and Monique

Every continent has its own great spirit of place.

Every people is polarized in some particular locality,

which is home, the homeland. Different places on

the face of the earth have different vital effluence,

different vibration, different chemical exhalation,

different polarity with different stars: call it what you

like. But the spirit of place is a great reality.

— D. H. Lawrence,

   Studies in Classic American Literature

CONTENTS

ACKNOWLEDGMENTS

Over the past decade, I have leaned heavily on countless friends, scholars, and institutions to help bring this book to fruition. Unfortunately, my debts to individuals are so numerous, and my memory so faulty, that I fear I have forgotten someone in the thanks that follow. If so, please accept my apologies.

I am grateful for the assistance of librarians at the American Antiquarian Society, the Boston Athenaeum, the British Library, the British Museum, Harvard University, the Historical Society of Pennsylvania, the Library Company of Philadelphia, the Library of Congress, the Library of Virginia, the Louisiana State Museum, Metropolitan State College of Denver, the National Gallery of Art, the National Gallery of Canada, the University of Georgia, the University of Pittsburgh, and the Yale University Art Gallery. The Metropolitan State College of Denver provided funding for short research trips, paper presentations, and a year's sabbatical. The American Philosophical Society funded a month at its magnificent library. There I found the assistance of Rob Cox, Valerie Lutz, and Roy Goodman unfailing. Roy, in particular, took pity on me as a new father who was far from home and family, taking me to lunches and dinners where, undoubtedly, he heard more than he cared to about continents. A fellowship from the National Endowment for the Humanities (NEH) paid for an essential year of writing. Of course—and in compliance with NEH requirements—I must state that any views, findings, conclusions, or recommendations expressed in this publication do not necessarily reflect those of the NEH.

The book has benefited from the input of participants at the History of Science Society Conference in 2001; the Front Range Early Americanists Conference (the FREACs) in 2002 and 2006; and the Metro Unpublished Papers and Extended Thesis Seminar (the MUPPETS) on multiple occasions in 2008. Virginia Anderson, Joyce Appleby, Kyle Bulthuis, Vincent C. de Baca, Dolph Grundman, Woody Holton, Ben Irvin, Kim Klimek, Susan Lanman, Todd Laugen, Matt Makley, Holly Mayer, Laura McCall, Kris Mitchener, John Monnett, Andrew Muldoon, Tish Richard, Paul Sidelko, Brian Weiser, and Jennifer Wynot all read drafts, usually crude, of portions of the manuscript. Holly Mayer, Paul Mapp, and Peter Silver generously shared their work in progress with me.

Portions of chapters 1 and 6 appeared in the *Journal of World History* 15 (2004). I received apt suggestions from the journal's editor, Jerry Bentley, and its anonymous reader. The judges for the University of Virginia Press's Walker Cowen Prize offered shrewd suggestions on how to improve the manuscript as a whole, as did a subsequent anonymous reader. At the press, Angie Hogan, Penny Kaiserlian, Mark Mones, and Morgan Myers deftly guided me through the publication process. Susan Deeks did a superb job of copyediting. At a critical time, the press also granted me temporary access to *The American Founding Era,* a remarkable digital collection under its Rotunda imprint.

Paul Mapp has served as both an intellectual inspiration and a model of generosity, sharing drafts of his remarkable book and critiquing my early chapters. Tom Ingersoll, Gary Nash, Fred Anderson, and Steve Leonard all slogged through the first draft of the entire manuscript. I also owe special thanks to both Gary and Fred for the wisdom and support they offered on several occasions and, in the case of Fred, for some wild boar. Steve Leonard painstakingly took one of the sharpest pencils I've ever seen to my prose. If there is a decent sentence in the book, he probably deserves credit for it.

My greatest debt—and affection—goes to my family. Haley, Hanna, and Monique have influenced and supported me more than anyone else.

THE NATION'S NATURE

INTRODUCTION

THE HISTORICAL
ROLE OF AN IMAGINED
PLACE

Frayed and fading documents—the Declaration of Independence, the Constitution, and the Bill of Rights—embody Americans' most prized principles. For decades the nation has carefully guarded those six pages, going so far as to move them to Fort Knox during World War II and storing them in a bomb shelter at night during the Cold War. Today, they sit enshrined under the great rotunda of the National Archives building in Washington, D.C., encapsulated in glass cases to protect them from the air we breathe. The rotunda viewing area pays homage to the "Charters of Freedom," which rest on an altar-like platform, framed by an arch and flanked by marble columns. To the sides loom large murals portraying the men who, more than two centuries ago, signed the very names that appear under the glass. Lines of visitors waiting to get a quick look at the texts pass under the murals like communicants shuffling to the front of a cathedral. Millions have made the pilgrimage; if the secular nation has a sacred space, surely this is it.[1]

With good reason, Americans tend to think of their country as founded on the enlightened ideals displayed in their founding documents rather than on territorial claims or crass geopolitical ambitions. The Louisiana Purchase, which sits a few paces from the Declaration of Independence, garners nowhere near the reverence enjoyed by the declaration. New citizens swear they will "defend the Constitution and laws of the United States" instead of promising to protect their new homeland, the 3,537,438 square miles that constitute it. Yet land, lots of land, has always been a touchstone of American identity, a source of national pride, an object of diplomacy, war, and even civil war. By the mid-eighteenth century, geographical sensibilities had already developed to a point that they became major tributaries to the great flow of ideas and aspirations that animated the Revolutionary generation in its quest for independence.

The men portrayed on the rotunda's murals and many of their contemporaries were well aware of the continental division of the earth and its ramifications. Their geographical perceptions, in turn, guided their actions and provided one of the most significant and potent justifications for the nation's founding. In 1776, for instance, Thomas Paine's popular *Common Sense* made the most trenchant argument for independence British colonists had ever seen. In one of his most ringing phrases, Paine declared it "absurd" for "a continent to be perpetually governed by an island." Mainland colonists had already created a Continental Congress, a Continental Association, and a Continental Army to resist British tyranny. But Paine believed such steps, which did not fully embrace America's separateness from Europe, to be inadequate half-steps, for "in no instance hath nature made the satellite larger than its primary planet, and as England and America, with respect to each other, reverse the common order of Nature, it is evident they belong to different systems: England to Europe, America to itself."[2] Paine had good company in equating the British mainland colonies with an entire continent. His words, coupled with powerful ideas, spurred the drive for independence.

Although instrumental in turning resistance into revolution, and foundational for early American diplomacy, Paine's propagandistic appeal to geography and natural order suffered from obvious defects. Britain occupied only a fraction of North America, and the division of the world into continents was then, as it is now, not a matter of simple common sense. Britain's eighteenth-century mainland colonists had only a limited knowledge of North America's contours and characteristics. Few Europeans had ventured far into its interior, the Rocky Mountains were virtually unknown, and coasts and waterways awaited exploration. With limited knowledge of North America, colonists and the founding generation made presumptions about the continent's contours, nature, and potential. They developed a "geography of the mind" that saw the continent as a natural geographic phenomenon, a discrete entity with an underlying coherence and unity.[3] And since they believed in a fundamental connection between geography and politics, this geography of the mind guided much of their political thinking and shaped their diplomatic goals.

This is a book, then, about our nation's founding and the historical role of an imagined place. It seeks answers to the question of how a wide and diverse swath of Americans pulled together to form a nation, how they came to see themselves as enough of a coherent political group to create an expansive state. It traces, first, how British mainland colonists developed an array of perceptions about their continent that were preconditions to thinking about independence. Then it argues that when some of these colonists decided to latch onto these ideas by defining and referring to themselves as the continent, it crystallized and nurtured their independence movement. After the Revolution, the Constitution's backers invoked the same continental perceptions when they argued for ratification. They used them to defuse their opponents' arguments that the Constitution ran counter to conventional wisdom and cherished principle. Trends in geographic thought allowed them to rein in the Revolution's more radical tendencies and solidify rule by elites. Thus, during the formative years of the United States, continental presumptions colored political views, permeated political rhetoric, and gave shape to political action.[4] Imaginings of the continent made American independence compelling, and the Constitution conceivable.

GEOGRAPHICAL understandings are inseparable from imagination, which, in turn, reflects the cultural influences that inform it. Close your eyes and picture a deserted island. Which describes your vision best: a warm place with sandy beaches and perhaps some palm trees and a blue lagoon, or a windswept mass covered with ice and snow? When I ask the students in my classroom to perform this exercise, nineteen out of twenty pick the former. Their islands come almost entirely from their imagination, their minds swayed, perhaps, by Golding's *Lord of the Flies,* Shakespeare's *Tempest,* Defoe's *Robinson Crusoe,* or, more likely, reruns of *Gilligan's Island* and *Survivor,* and commercials encouraging escapes to sunny getaways.[5] Maybe my sample of students is atypical. They all live in one of the big, squarish states with no coastline, much less an offshore island, in sight. A majority of them have never left the continental United States. Yet for seventeenth-century English colonists to imagine a continent was akin to my students' trying to imagine a tropical island. These English stood on the edge of a continent, but they had few resources to help conceptualize its extent, topography, or features. Uncertainty created a void that they filled with preconceptions or imaginative speculation.

Asia, Africa, Australia, Antarctica, Europe, North America, and South America—today, schoolchildren memorize the continents as if they were timeless entities fixed by a creator who divided the land from the sea. But this taxonomy is largely the imperfect, shifting product of the past three hundred years, during which scholars and statesmen struggled, or simply failed, to define what they meant when they spoke of continents. Such change over time should not be surprising, because continental categories stem not so much from natural geographical phenomena as from social, political, and intellectual developments. Modern dictionaries typically define "continents" as the principal landmasses of the earth, usually comprising Africa, Antarctica, Asia, Australia, Europe, North America, and South America. It is easy to question the logic of this scheme. Why, for example, is Europe a continent, India a subcontinent, Australia a continent, and Greenland an island? Continental taxonomies also often have little bearing on the development of flora, fauna, or human societies. Creatures on the American side of the Bering Strait often have more in common with those just across the water than with those near the Isthmus of Panama, and the regions to the north and south of the Sahara Desert are virtually distinct ecological regions.

Though its logic and relevance is questionable, we allow the continental taxonomy to frame how we conceive the world. Ask most Americans to close their eyes and imagine an Asian or an African, and few would immediately picture a Russian or a Libyan, or even an Indian or an Afrikaner. The historians Martin Lewis and Kären Wigen note that global geographical conceptions lead to gross oversimplifications: "We talk of African wildlife as if it constituted a distinct assemblage of animals, and we commonly compare it with the fauna of Asia or South America." More pressing, we have a "tendency to let a continental framework structure our perceptions of the human community. Thus Africans become a distinct people who can be usefully contrasted with Asians or Europeans, and we imagine Africa's problems to be unique to its landmass, as though tied to it by some geographical necessity."[6]

Geographical assumptions functioned similarly in the minds of many eighteenth-century North American colonists, even though they experienced space and distance differently from Americans today. Since the eighteenth century, much of humanity has witnessed the demise of distance and the shrinking of space. We read news with bylines recording the hour and minute of a story's publication. New Englanders make guacamole with avocados, and Californians pour maple syrup on pancakes, without much thought. But in the mid-eighteenth century, roads in North America were few and poor. Years might pass before Spaniards in New Mexico learned of events in New England. When news did arrive, it might well have come via Europe instead of overland. To travel from England to the Chesapeake often took nine weeks and sometimes much more. The postal system for British North America, though a marvel for its day, linked only the major ports along the Atlantic seaboard. High rates meant that ordinary people rarely used its services, magazines rarely reached beyond a local audience, and printers produced for a small region. It took until 1766 to establish regular stagecoach service between New York and Philadelphia, for those willing to suffer the three-day journey.[7]

That the natural world literally loomed large presents paradoxes: how was it that Paine and others could envision themselves as a continental society, and how did this vision become widely shared? During the sixteenth and seventeenth centuries, it would have been unfathomable that a single polity could control an expanse the size of North America. True, European powers longed for the spread of Christendom and a "universal monarchy"; still, it was a distant dream. Europe, North America, and Africa were each divided into roughly five hundred polities.[8] The English, in particular, struggled just to establish a colonial foothold in the Americas. It took until 1607—one hundred and fifteen years after Columbus's first voyage—for them to plant their first lasting settlement at Jamestown.

At the time that the English settled Jamestown and, later, Plymouth and Boston, North America was not consistently thought of as a continent. When many Anglo-Americans thought of the "continent" in the seventeenth century, they often referred to what we think of as something less than the whole. A New England merchant might speculate that the messiah would make his return in "the Mexican Continent," or a report from Virginia might explain that "the Governour of that Continent" faced a rebellion in 1676.[9] Colonists did not use continental labels consistently, for they did not live in a world where continents had standard definitions or appeared on maps as stable, timeless entities.

Determining what colonists later, in the eighteenth century, meant by "continent" thus presents interpretive challenges. At times when colonists referred to themselves as the "continent," they undoubtedly did so as a manner of speaking, a trope, or a way to distinguish themselves from colonists in the West Indies. But oftentimes when they referred to themselves as the "continent," they meant all of North America, and sometimes all of the Americas. They might make this clear by referring to their continent and themselves as stretching "sea to sea" or "pole to pole." Although I have attempted to distinguish among the different usages, it is important to recognize that, at times, contemporaries slipped among them, as if such distinctions mattered little.

Given that people's imagination of geographic space has varied over time, one must be careful not to project modern understandings of geography on the past. Making such a case, one historian calls even the colony a "fabricated region," arguing that political units such as New York, Virginia, and Massachusetts were not nearly as important to eighteenth-century Americans as they have been to modern historians. Migration, economics, social relations, and foreign relations all transcended colonies' boundaries, which were themselves at times fluid and contested. Nor could these boundaries even contain provincial politics. William Penn promoted political peace and stability in other proprietors' colonies to prevent within them any imperial intervention that might endanger his own Pennsylvania. At the imperial level, British policymakers often treated the American colonies as the "Plantations General," instead of distinguishing among local political units, and the same policymakers periodically flirted with plans to form unions among the colonies that would obliterate borders.[10]

Broader units of analysis, such as regions, would seemingly provide historians with a way out of their colonial cells, but "regionalism" has its own problems. Michael Zuckerman argues that although a "regional paradigm" has "acquired an absolute primacy," this new paradigm is one more of form than content. A consensus exists that early America comprised a variety of geographic regions, each with a local society and often a coherent culture, but it comes apart when it comes time to define them. Sure, most see the United States divided into North and South between the drafting of the Constitution and the end of the Civil War (with the West somehow lurking on the fringes), but historians might posit anywhere from three to six regions before the Revolution in the British North American mainland. Differences stem largely from historians' emphasizing different periods or giving primacy to different variables in their analyses.[11] A current trend to see the American colonies as part of an "Atlantic world" and efforts to incorporate the West into colonial American history can be seen as new regional conceptualizations and backlashes against traditionally constructed regions. Yet these newer frameworks pose some of the same problems of anachronism as any others used by historians.

Thus, the question arises as to how eighteenth-century British North American colonists actually related to space. The only safe thing to say is that there was no single way. People living in different places, plying different trades, and differing in race, religion, national background, class, and gender undoubtedly had varied experiences of space that changed over time. A backcountry farmer's ties to the land and quotidian concerns affected his perceptions, as did a mariner's life on the seas. At times a colonist in North America might well have had a strong provincial identity, thinking of Massachusetts or Virginia as his "country." In the presence of imperial agents or British military officers, the same individual might have sensed his place in a larger British Empire yet, at the same time, be made starkly aware that he was different, that he was American. Context, culture, and geographical imagination could give colonists an almost kaleidoscopic perception of their spatial identity.

That said, a host of British imperial reforms in the 1760s and 1770s drew many British mainland colonists into, as it was often phrased, a "common cause." Shared grievances fueled popular mobilization. Successful popular mobilization, whether through the rejection of British goods or, eventually, the creation of an army, reflected shared interests. And these actions and these interests contributed to the process by which colonists came to imagine themselves a people. But what were these new people? Stratification and fragmentation still characterized colonial America. Ethnicity, race, class, gender, religion, political traditions, and provincial loyalties sliced through the common cause, affecting the trajectory of resistance. Were Revolutionaries a people glued together simply by what they opposed? How could they define themselves as part of a broad community? What were the geographic contours of any community they might have envisioned? How did this geographic understanding, in turn, shape their resistance movement and help turn it into one for independence? And how did it affect their parley in Paris and their formation of a new federal union? In short, what role did their geographical imagination play in their emerging nationalism, the success of the Revolution, and the ratification of the Constitution?

WHEN it comes to the emergence of nationalism in the Americas, the work of Benedict Anderson has been more influential among historians than most. He defines the nation as "an imagined political community." It is "imagined as both inherently limited and sovereign," and it is one where "most of its members will never know each other." Precipitating the rise of such communities, according to Anderson, was the advent of widely available printed material. In the Americas, the rise of newspapers and print culture in general, he argues, helped large numbers of people think about themselves and their relationships to others in new ways, creating new senses of social space. Anderson speaks to the importance of print culture in fostering a sense of community among the "original Thirteen Colonies." He argues that their compact nature and the accessibility of their market centers—such as Boston, New York, and Philadelphia—to one another allowed their populations to be closely connected by print and commerce. This "print-capitalism" thus allowed colonists to imagine themselves as a political community.

Anderson's argument has plenty of pitfalls. Among them, he does not pay heed to the British colonies in Canada and the West Indies. Nor does he grapple with the transatlantic flow of print-capitalism. Anderson also fails to demonstrate that colonists on the mainland shared a common print culture instead of living in a fragmented world where local printers served local readers. The social space framed by print-capitalism on the eve of the American Revolution simply did not provide a blueprint for the nation that emerged. Yet despite these shortcomings, Anderson's argument is still one to be reckoned with, especially his notions on the role of imagination.[12]

Instead of accepting Anderson's position wholesale or delving into shifting scholarly debates over how to define a "nation," I argue that imaginings of space paved the way for American nationhood. I suggest that prevailing "metageographies" bore heavily on the character of early American nationalism and facilitated the institutionalization of an "American" community. "Metageography," as defined by Martin Lewis and Kären Wigen, is "the set of spatial structures through which people order their knowledge of the world: the often unconscious frameworks that organize studies of history, sociology, anthropology, economics, political science, or even natural history." Examples of metageographies that have shaped recent Americans' understanding of the world include the division of its nations into First, Second, and Third World countries, or into east and west. For eighteenth-century British North Americans, the most influential metageography was the emerging division of the earth into continents.

Many in the Revolutionary generation viewed themselves as acting on a global stage, promoting a cause beneficial to all humankind. And, as Lewis and Wigen argue, "every global consideration of human affairs deploys a metageography." Metageographical understandings underlay a cognitive framework akin to a national identity well before the formal declaration of an independent nation. Indeed, the word "nation" was slippery and vague in the late eighteenth century. Sometimes "nation" referred to formal political entities; at other times, it referred to a group of people who usually shared some combination of culture, language, and lineage. But nationalism does not need a nation for its existence. In the absence of a nation, nationalism can take the form of an aspiration, a blueprint, or, in this case, a geopolitical vision for the future.[13]

Metageographical categories coexisted with multiple and changing forms of political identity, whether expressed as loyalty to an empire, a colony, a state, or the new nation. A colonist could simultaneously profess loyalty to Britain, the continent, and Virginia, or to the United States, the continent, and New York. The continent, even if not precisely defined, provided one of many communal foundations and aspirations, within and then outside the British Empire. As an imagined geographical community, it lent the colonists an embryonic or incipient political destiny, and after independence, it would continue at the heart of an institutionalized political community, the foundation for a federal state.

FOR at least a hundred years, the writing of the history of the American Revolution has largely taken a two-pronged approach. The historian Carl Becker put it best, early in the twentieth century, when he explained that two struggles shaped the conflict: one over home rule, and the other over who should rule at home and how. Less examined have been definitions and conceptions of "home"—in this case, the continent—and how they bore on the two struggles.[14] Though not as obviously contentious as the issues of independence or the distribution of political power, they unfolded in an equally contingent way and played an essential role in the Revolution. They have a history.

The Nation's Nature does not provide a comprehensive narrative of the Revolutionary era or even of the evolution of spatial conceptions and nationalism in eighteenth-century British North America; no single volume could accomplish either task. Instead, the book traces some of the more important ways in which spatial identity changed over time and altered many North Americans' political consciousness. The result is synthetic, and I have relied heavily on the work of historians from a variety of specialties.

To get at eighteenth-century geographic conceptions, I have cast a wide net for sources. As one might guess, maps provide an essential body of material, but only one of many. People learned about, interpreted, and communicated geographical notions in myriad ways. Geographic thought, like political thought, permeated geographies, travel narratives, newspapers, almanacs, cartoons, plays, personal correspondence, political tracts, sermons, songs, poems, paintings, rituals, and rebellions. For this reason, *The Nation's Nature* draws on geographic vernacular as expressed in a wide array of documents, maps, and other images.

Although I have tried to include the thoughts of ordinary people, many readers will note that, unfortunately, entire segments of the colonial population, including Native Americans, African Americans, and women, have little voice in the book. Indians defending their land, slaves fighting for their freedom, and women seeking a greater political voice all made the Revolution a truly radical movement. Indeed, their views on who shall rule at home threatened the political visions for North America held by many of the learned, literate, patriot white men who appear disproportionately on the pages that follow, often under the imperfect shorthand of "colonists" or, after independence, "Americans." Nonetheless, I have emphasized the thoughts and views of a number of white men—prominent intellectuals, political leaders, and diplomats—not just because my choice of scale and detail precludes comprehensive treatment of all colonists, or because these men wrote the most. Instead, focusing on them sheds light on a persistent topic in American history: whether the Constitution embodied the central principles of the American Revolution or represented a conservative reaction of elites against them.

Ironically, the same metageographical thinking of elite white men that had such radical implications in the context of North America's relation to Britain was used to conservative effect during the debate over the Constitution and helped rein in the Revolution's more radical impulses. Nationalism founded on continental constructs helped these elites define who belonged to the nation, "the people," in a way that excluded African Americans, Native Americans, and, politically, the majority of ordinary whites. Highlighting this strand of continuity and consistency does not justify the contradictions, self-deception, or even hypocrisy of many of the founders, but I hope it renders their thoughts and actions more comprehensible.

BECAUSE the book is fairly long, and its argument is sometimes subtle, I feel obligated to briefly outline what follows. *The Nation's Nature* proceeds in two parts; it begins in the late seventeenth century and concludes with the ratification of the U.S. Constitution. Part 1 traces intellectual and political developments up to the eve of the American Revolution. The opening chapter explains how ideas about continents developed such that thinkers in the 1760s and 1770s could imagine an independent, viable, and cohesive American polity. They posited critical relationships among geographic features, cultural traits, and political organizations. North American space appeared suitable for control by one power: large enough to hold the bulk of a growing nation-state, yet small, porous, and yielding enough to be manageable. Britons also came to see themselves as having the ideal character to thrive in the North American environment and, at the same time, to see the native inhabitants as ill placed. I argue that these new continental notions served as an intellectual precondition for independence; without them, rebellious North Americans would have found breaking away from Britain far less compelling.

Chapter 2 illustrates how such intellectual trends went beyond abstractions and became the grist of imperial rivalries, war, and diplomacy. Events leading up to and surrounding the Seven Years' War in North America saw the emergence of continental thinking as a guiding force. Perceiving the continent as a unified entity meant that if politics were to conform to nature—an ideal held by many—North America ought to be inhabited by one people, under a single power. By the mid-eighteenth century, many British colonists feared that France stood on the verge of becoming that power, leading to shrill rhetoric that an entire continent was at stake. When the British prevailed spectacularly in the Seven Years' War (1756–63), they took control of the mainland east of the Mississippi River, and France ceded its holdings west of the Mississippi to a patently weak and overextended Spain. Though Britain did not claim the entire continent on paper in 1763, the ouster of its archrival France from North America led many colonists to assume it was only a matter of time. Victory heightened the colonists' attachment to the continent and their patriotism toward the empire; imperial patriotism and continental affiliation went hand in hand. Yet by recognizing themselves as an embryonic continental society within the British Empire, colonists unintentionally came closer to making independence plausible.

The years between the Seven Years' War and the American Revolution—and the link between the two conflicts—form the subject of chapter 3. The ostensible acquisition of a continent well suited for a polity gave Britain unprecedented potential power and made France and Spain look for opportunities to restrain it. At the same time, Britain's vast spoils made it difficult for it to maintain the consent of its governed. Parliament appeared as the source of disappointed expectations of prosperity and continental grandeur. Taxes and regulations raised issues of both political representation and, as a matter of course, geography, because in the British tradition, representation rested on geographically defined communities. British North Americans' views of representation often focused on constituents' physical location. In a tension that would remain unresolved until the ratification of the Constitution, colonists cast themselves as members of an expansive continental community while somewhat awkwardly rejecting the possibility of representation at vast distances. When colonists made such arguments, they often declared that geography made them unique among Britons. In so doing, they reinforced their habit of thinking of themselves as a geographically distinct people, a practice that, in time, prepared them to declare independence.

Part 2 of the book focuses on the early United States as a budding continental empire and the relationship between Americans' metageographies and the development of their national institutions. Chapter 4 argues that the perception that the continent was ideal for a political community turned into the prescription for one's establishment. Metageographical ideas transformed into Revolutionary action when patriots resorted to geography to define their community. Patriots enacted their status as a people through the use of continental language. When the Continental Congress convened in 1774, the delegates came from colonies fragmented along lines of distance, economic interest, administrative tradition, and religion. At their first meeting, they agreed to call themselves simply "the Congress." Not only was the "Continental" descriptor initially absent from the institution's formal title, but a close analysis of the *Journals of the Continental Congress* and *Letters of Delegates to Congress* reveals that it only gradually percolated into common use.[15]

The "continental" label emerged in a contingent, piecemeal way through everyday practice rather than careful deliberation and decision making. Herein lay one of its great strengths: the term did not appear to be created by any particular individual or interest group. It thus allowed for mass-mobilization and trust over vast distances. The imagination or creation of a natural community based on prevailing understandings of global geography also meshed with the colonists' rejection of their rights as Britons. Colonists came to see their rights as every bit as natural as their community's presumed boundaries. Finally, further analysis of the *Journals of the Continental Congress* and *Letters of Delegates to Congress* shows that, as the Congress's shortcomings became apparent, the "continental" label faded from use.

As the Congress failed to fulfill prophecies, war both revealed and helped sustain Americans' continental identity, as discussed in chapter 5. Memories during the Revolutionary War recalled the sacrifices of the Seven Years' War. Many came to see the Revolution, in part, as a war to defend the legacy of the earlier conflict. As such, the Revolution, too, became a war for North America. Americans, in turn, liked to think that theirs was the fight of, and for, an entire continent, and their diplomats tried to implement Paine's vision of a continental society. In reality, economic difficulties and aversion to standing armies meant that states' support for the war in men and materiel was often tepid, at best. Adding to the reluctance to contribute was the belief that geography worked to Americans' advantage; that Britain's army—though the most powerful in the world—simply could not conquer a continent. The continent appeared as one of the patriots' greatest military assets, and war thus enhanced Americans' attachment to it, even as this attachment helped rationalize starving the army. Paradoxically, then, the apparent wealth of the continent allowed many patriots to eye the army warily and withhold support materially, and it heightened patriots' optimism and commitment—abstract though it often was—to the Revolutionary cause. It allowed the Revolution to succeed even as support for the army withered.

Chapter 6 focuses on the social and historical roots of Americans' appropriation of the continent. These serve as a reminder that the emergence of a political collectivity in British North America that rested heavily on meta-geographical conceptions should not be taken for granted. The chapter returns to the intellectual debates over the nature of the Americas and their ability to support a society that could rival those of Europe. It analyzes at length Thomas Jefferson's *Notes on the State of Virginia* (1785) and a similar work by a Spanish American, Francisco Clavigero. By comparing the history and social structure of the British mainland colonies to British colonies in the West Indies, Atlantic Canada, and India, as well as to Spanish America, the chapter argues that the unique character of British mainland society created the optimum conditions for Jefferson's distinctive intellectual approach, and for a geographically expansive, nationalist view to take root in general.

After the Revolution, Americans experienced disappointments similar to those felt by colonists in 1763; prognoses of continental grandeur foundered on the problems of military demobilization, economic depression, and lingering foreign powers. The Constitutional Convention tackled this hornets' nest and, in so doing, brought under greater scrutiny the unresolved tension between Americans' appropriation of a continental realm seemingly destined for rule by one nation and their rejection of representational rule at a distance. The Constitution challenged traditional views of representation and local sovereignty in ways that many thought ran counter to Revolutionary ideals. Against the backdrop of a generation of metageographical assumptions about the continent as a naturally unified entity, however, this shift appears in a new light. The decision to extend the national government's sphere at the expense of traditional notions of representation makes more sense when we understand how, among other things, those men on the rotunda's murals drew on geographical understandings to refute inconvenient political principles.

PART I

CONTINENTAL
PRECONDITIONS
TO AMERICAN
INDEPENDENCE

CHAPTER I

SCIENTIFIC TRENDS,
CONTINENTAL
CONCEPTIONS,
REVOLUTIONARY
IMPLICATIONS

Of the founding generation, George Washington would not rank at the top of anybody's list for his abilities as a scientist. Benjamin Franklin's scientific experiments assured him of an honored place in the pantheon of Enlightenment scientists, and Thomas Jefferson's *Notes on the State of Virginia* (1785) put him among those select savants. Nor did Washington think of himself as a scientist. Though an accomplished surveyor, he sometimes fretted about lagging behind many of his contemporaries in formal education.[1] Still, Washington, like so many colonists, took an interest in scientific debate, at least when it related to one of his core concerns: the nature and fate of his continent.

Washington revealed his interest on a number of occasions. Just before Christmas in 1780, the general and several of his officers took a break from the war to enjoy a sleigh ride from their winter headquarters to a farm in New Windsor, New York, where the Reverend Robert Annan had unearthed fossil remains. Two-pound teeth, from what we now know to be a mastodon, drew Washington's attention. He explained to Annan that at Mount Vernon he had some similar specimens found in the Ohio River valley. In another instance, during a relatively quiet period in Washington's life, after he chaired the Constitutional Convention and while he awaited news of the resulting document's fate in the hands of the states, he wrote a letter in which he explained what prospective immigrants to America might profitably read: "As to the European Publications respecting the United States, they are commonly very defective." Among the most misinformed, in Washington's opinion, was the Abbé Raynal's *Histoire philosophique et politique, des établissemens et du commerce des Européens dans les deux Indes* (1770), which denigrated Americans and their natural environment. Better, Washington argued, to consult "Mr. Jefferson's 'Notes on Virginia,'" which "will give the best idea of this part of the Continent to a Foreigner."[2]

In examining prehistoric remains and in dismissing Raynal, Washington became a minor participant in what one historian has called the "Dispute of the New World."[3] For more than a century, a group of leading European thinkers had been trying to explain the Americas' human history in light of their natural history, an effort that was part of a larger attempt to build a comprehensive and systemic knowledge of the world. Through the second half of the eighteenth century, European intellectuals, including not just the Abbé Raynal but also Cornelius de Pauw, William Robertson, and others influenced by the great French naturalist Georges-Louis Leclerc, Comte de Buffon, took jabs at the Americas. Based on their reading of natural history, they posited the region was either a new continent or one that had undergone a geologic catastrophe. As a result, its environment was putrid, filled with dangerous miasmas, and colder and wetter than other parts of the world. The noxiousness of the "New World" made its species, including humans, degenerate and effete. If those conclusions were true, the grandiose aspirations of the colonists and the subsequent new nation would be for naught. The nature of the continent would prevent them from ever rivaling Europe on the world stage. Like the Soviet Union's launching of Sputnik in 1957, almost two centuries later, the doubts raised by Buffon, Raynal, and others cast a worrisome shadow over Americans and their geopolitical visions. Science and national pride had become intertwined, and scientists in the late-eighteenth-century British colonies worked vigorously to disprove the aspersions cast on their continent, just as those of the twentieth century committed their energy to the space race.

This "Dispute of the New World" may seem almost amusing today. After all, one might easily confound Buffon by sending him on a trek across the hot, arid portions of the American West. Yet contemporaries took Buffon's theories seriously. Books on American degeneracy made for good reading. They sold well, and they were reprinted in a number of languages and excerpted in newspapers. Even many of Buffon's critics made similarly sweeping generalizations about the Americas and the other continents. Scientific trends in the seventeenth and eighteenth centuries led inhabitants of the British mainland colonies to comprehend their world through a continental filter. Colonists came to assume that continents—and their people—had inherent traits because they were natural geographic phenomena. A continent constituted an interdependent system (a popular term in eighteenth-century science) of creatures and environments that formed a complex unity. A continent could comprise pockets of variation, but these nested within the larger assemblage and shared traits that ran throughout the whole. This view meshed with a general Enlightenment quest to harmonize politics with nature. In Britain's North American colonies, debates over the continent's nature—and scientific discourse in general—helped foster widespread rhetoric to defend the American landmass and the colonists' place in the world and in human history. Science provided some of the grammar and habits of the mind necessary for these colonists to view themselves as a people who shared a naturally unified land.

American Revolutionary thought sprang in part out of these intellectual developments. Geographic presumptions, demographic projections, and racial constructions provided British colonists with cogent arguments in support of a grand continental society, initially within and, after 1776, outside the British Empire. British North Americans could conceive of independent nationhood only after they saw several criteria as met. First, North American space had to be suitable for a nation-state: large and coherent enough to hold a viable polity and small, porous, and yielding enough to be manageable and facilitate trade and communication. Second, the inhabitants of such a nation had to have a character well suited to North American space. Third, the continent had to be intellectually separable from its original Indian inhabitants. Finally, the colonists' population needed to be able to spread over the continent without becoming too diffuse. Land had to be plentiful enough to allow expansion as the population grew so that farmland would be readily available. Otherwise, the society would become increasingly urban and the economy more dependent on manufacturing, trends widely believed to lead to political corruption.[4] Over the course of the eighteenth century, developments in geography and science created a perception that fulfilled these criteria. Sensing this, many leaders of the Revolutionary era began to create a society, as they saw it, in harmony with geography and nature.

POLITICS, GEOGRAPHY, AND SCIENCE

Educated colonists, like their European counterparts, were fascinated by geography and its relationship to politics. By the mid-eighteenth century, a transatlantic intellectual tradition had developed that posited critical connections linking geographic features, cultural traits, and political organizations. In particular, many Enlightenment thinkers saw ties between natural boundaries and a people's character. The French philosopher Charles de Secondat, Baron de Montesquieu, for example, argued that despotism reigned in Asia because it "has broader plains; it is cut into larger parts by seas . . . and its smaller rivers form slighter barriers." Europe, by contrast, had "natural divisions" that created "many medium-sized states in which the government of laws is not incompatible with the maintenance of the state." Jean-Jacques Rousseau, too, emphasized the importance of nature in shaping the international order: "The lie of the mountains, seas, and rivers, which serve as boundaries of the various nations which people it, seems to have fixed forever their number and size. We may fairly say that the political order of the Continent is in some sense the work of nature." Other French geographers expressed visions of a future where, should polities be divided along natural boundaries, greater harmony would prevail. The Scotsman David Hume even suggested—in contrast to Montesquieu—the possibility of a non-despotic continental society when he argued that a national character could permeate a large area as long as the people lived contiguously—that is, not divided by impassable mountain ranges, deserts, or rivers. The British author William Doyle perhaps summed up this outpouring of theory best when he argued that it was "geography, on which should ever be built all political systems"—the corollary being that "no man can possibly be qualified for the ministry, who has not the first a considerable knowledge in geography."[5]

In the mainland colonies, well-to-do men amassed impressive libraries loaded with geographies, travel narratives, and maps. Within William Byrd's four-thousand-volume library, "History, Voyages, Travels, &c." filled three and a half bookcases. According to Thomas Jefferson's own classification system, geographies constituted one of the largest categories in his library, and he subdivided it by continent. George Washington's relatively modest library included sixty-two volumes of "Geography and Travels" and thirty-five volumes of "Science" at the time of his death. John Adams, known more for his legal and political thought than his scientific inclinations, held numerous atlases and geographies published before the Revolution, as well as at least a dozen volumes by Buffon and men who echoed the Frenchman's theories. Beyond their libraries, fashionable gentlemen displayed globes or hung maps in their parlors or dining rooms, partly for their guests' perusal, but also to demonstrate their own familiarity with geography. Sometimes they even carried a trendy fashion accessory: the pocket globe.[6]

Interest in geography, and in science in general, extended beyond the salons of Europe and the parlors of colonial gentlemen to a wide swath of Britain's North American colonists, particularly in the urban seaports. Colleges offered courses in geography. Newspapers advertised sales of "maps of the world, and of each quarter, Europe, Asia, Africa and America." In some cases, they offered estimates of the populations of each of these quarters. Periodicals were rife with inexpensive reprints of maps that most people otherwise would never have seen. Almanacs, newspapers, cartoons, songs, and sermons spread geographic and scientific information among ordinary folk.[7]

Perhaps nowhere was geographical and scientific knowledge more widespread than in Philadelphia. There, Benjamin Franklin and members of the Junto founded the Library Company of Philadelphia, a subscription library in which members jointly owned the books. As the Library Company's premier historian notes, it had a collection "made by and for a group of merchants, tradesmen, and artisans struggling to gain wealth and position." The books chosen by the Library Company's directors departed from the theological bent of early colleges such as Harvard, William and Mary, and Yale. Histories, broadly defined to included geographical books and travel literature, made up roughly a third of the holdings through the eighteenth century, and science made up nearly a fifth.[8]

The Library Company's subscribers could enjoy large folio geographies, lavishly illustrated atlases, and maps printed in London with copper plates, all by some of England's premier geographers and engravers, such as Peter Heylyn, Emanuel Bowen, John Senex, and Thomas Jefferys. Subscribers could also leaf through the century's best selling and relatively inexpensive geography by Patrick Gordon, *Geography Anatomiz'd,* first published in 1693 and reissued in nineteen more editions by 1754. Or they could learn about the parts of the world by reading articles in periodicals, which increasingly included simpler, woodcut variations of the maps made by England's master cartographers. The Library Company had complete runs of the *London Magazine* and the *Gentleman's Magazine,* the most influential English periodicals of the eighteenth century. The *Gentleman's Magazine* alone published fifty maps before the outbreak of the Seven Years' War. The Library Company thrived because it catered to the tastes of its intellectual yet non-elite membership. Similar libraries sprang up in Albany, Boston, New York City, Philadelphia, Newport, and Charleston before the Revolution.[9]

Those who were unable or unwilling to pay the fees for one of these subscription libraries—it cost £10 to initially join the Library Company of Philadelphia, followed by small annual fees—could readily access travel literature, geographies, and scientific tracts elsewhere. Circulating libraries—privately held collections from which one rented books—opened in six cities before the Revolution. To be sure, many of these proved short-lived; still, the holdings of these libraries likely indicate what their owners thought customers would want to read. Although works of fiction constituted the largest percentage of books, the number of volumes on geography, travel writing, and science generally exceeded by far those on government and politics. For those who could not afford the annual fee of these circulating libraries (usually around £1), coffeehouses typically provided patrons with access to newspapers, periodicals, almanacs, and occasionally books for the price of their beverage. For Philadelphians, James Logan, who had advised the Library Company of Philadelphia on its selection of books, bequeathed his massive private library of nearly three thousand books to the city at his death. This public library opened in 1760 and remained available to readers until the British occupied the city in 1777.[10]

As a newcomer in 1774, Thomas Paine rhapsodized about Philadelphia's intellectual ferment. His first words written as the editor of the *Pennsylvania Magazine* described "America" as "a country whose reigning character is the love of science."[11] Benjamin Franklin and other colonists of scientific renown constituted only a minuscule portion of the colonies' population. But their ideas, as the historian Richard Brown argues, "by a trickle-down process, seem to have influenced common belief." The leading intellectuals of British North America belonged to and helped create a sizeable and expanding learned class that shaped much of the public discussion and brought scientific thought to bear on colonial and imperial politics.[12]

Colonists devoted to science often served as go-betweens, linking curious Europeans to diverse Americans who gathered the specimens and the data that the Europeans craved. To gather bark and beetles and the other stuff of natural history, white elites often relied on Native Americans, African Americans, and women. As the historian Susan Scott Parrish explains, these exchange networks, "though influenced by hierarchies of gender, class, institutional learning, place of birth or residence, and race, were nevertheless accessible to such a range of people in the colonies because they could supply novel information or specimens from the American side of the Atlantic." Scientific investigation created sinews of communication that wound through Britain's mainland colonies. Perhaps the best demonstration of the extensive communications networks among scientists in American and in Britain came in 1769 when men from Pennsylvania, Rhode Island, and Boston coordinated to perform a series of measurements studying the transit of Venus at the behest of astronomers in England.[13]

At the same time that scientific inquiry bound disparate colonists together, learning gave them a chance to advance socially, particularly because British North America's intellectual elite was more willing to accept newcomers than were the savants of Europe. At the beginning of the century, the colonies counted only three institutions of higher learning; that number had increased to nine by 1770. Added institutions and relative prosperity led to a tripling in the number of matriculants between 1740 and 1770.[14] The typical Harvard graduate in the years just before the Revolution came from a yeoman background and was the first and only member of his family to attend college. William Eustis, the son of a housewright, for example, studied medicine before serving as a surgeon in the Continental Army and, later, as state legislator and member of Congress. Not all Harvard graduates went on to such prominence, however. Sixteen percent spent their careers as clerks, scribes, or schoolmasters.

To the south, in Philadelphia, a cohort led by Benjamin Franklin formed the American Philosophical Society (APS). Called by one historian "one of the first truly intercolonial organizations in colonial America," the APS dedicated itself to the pursuit of scientific knowledge, and its membership eventually included many of the nation's founders: John Adams, Alexander Hamilton, Thomas Jefferson, James Madison, Thomas Paine, and George Washington, to name a handful.[15] Alongside these luminaries, the APS ranks included many learned artisans and tradesmen. The carpenter Samuel Rhoads of Philadelphia taught himself architecture, developed a friendship with Franklin, and actively participated in the society. The colonies' premier astronomer, David Rittenhouse, made a living as a clockmaker but eventually succeeded Franklin as president of the society.

Though of ordinary means, Eustis, Rhoads, Rittenhouse, and most other APS members were atypical in that they lived in cities, something that fewer than one in twenty colonists did. Their urban status allowed them to become catalysts of change, because cities were cauldrons of social, political, and economic innovation. Printing presses and taverns spread scientific and political information. Members of Franklin's Junto and similar clubs, along with political organizations such as the Sons of Liberty, flourished in urban seaports. Most members of the APS lived in Philadelphia, and two-thirds of Harvard graduates from 1772 to 1774 remained in or near Boston. Almost half from each institution pursued careers in law, medicine, or religion. These men shaped the eighteenth-century mainland colonies, and many of them participated in the Revolution. A majority of APS members held political office. Harvard graduates were as outspokenly patriotic as the population at large, if not more so, with only 17 percent loyalists.[16]

These men and their less educated counterparts passionately embraced geography. Benjamin Franklin enthroned it as a core scientific pursuit of the APS. When he formed the society in 1743, he believed its seven members should include a physician, a botanist, a mathematician, a chemist, a mechanician (roughly an engineer in modern parlance), a natural philosopher (a physicist would be today's closest approximation), and a geographer. The natural sciences dominated Franklin's list, and geography provided the most suitable way to inject what we now call the social sciences into the society's scientific mission, because geography implied, among other things, the scientific study of social affairs.[17]

Recognizing that knowledge of home fostered love of home, John Adams echoed a common sentiment when he urged Americans to study geography. He wrote to his wife, Abigail, in the summer of 1776, "America is our Country, and therefore a minute Knowledge of its Geography, is most important to Us and our Children," and he preached the need to "turn the Attention of the Family to the subject of American Geography. Really, there ought not to be a State, a City, a Promontory, a River, an Harbour, an Inlett, or a Mountain in all America, but what should be intimately known to every Youth, who has any Pretensions to liberal Education."[18] Knowledge of geography had become a political imperative.

THE "SCIENCE" OF CONTINENTAL TAXONOMIES

For minds steeped in eighteenth-century geographic thought, formulations of modern continental taxonomies, along with uncertainty about the contours and topography of North America, rendered the continent suitable for control by one power. North America appeared large, yet at the same time it seemed coherent and manageable. Geographic ignorance did not dampen such views, for despite the debatable utility and logic of continental designations, the geographers of the seventeenth and eighteenth centuries who helped create what would gradually develop into our modern system wrote in definitive tones, even describing their work as a science.

Granted, the term "science" had broader connotations then than it does now; nevertheless, writers touted geography for the wide-ranging, immutable, and precise knowledge of nature that it offered readers. The geographer Peter Heylyn celebrated geographical knowledge for its use to physicians, "who are hereby acquainted with the different temper of mens bodies, according to the Climes they live in; the nature and growth of many Simples and Medicinall Drugs, whereof every Country under Heaven hath some more natural and proper to it self." Another geographer, William Pemble, deemed his *A Brief Introduction to Geography Containing a Description of the Grounds and General Part Thereof* (1675) "very necessary for young Students in that Science." In an eighteenth-century geography text widely studied by British American students, Patrick Gordon described his work as an "exact analysis" in the subtitle. His preface urged students to apply themselves "to this most useful and diverting science." Another popular author, William Guthrie, opened his text with reference to "the science of Geography." The first edition of the *Encyclopaedia Britannica* (1771) concurred with this assessment, defining geography as "the science that teaches and explains the properties of the earth, and the parts thereof."[19]

One respect in which geographies departed from modern conceptions of science was that they rested heavily on descriptive travel writings. Geographers were essentially armchair travelers, writing with authority about distant lands they had never seen. They rendered the disparate, often anecdotal, details and minutiae in the narratives and journals of actual travelers into coherent, concise, and readily comprehensible portrayals of the entire world, all with a tone of objective detachment. Travelers to distant continents might write for pages on end about squirrels, birds, snakes, or trees that geographers in places like London had never seen. These geographers then collated available texts, passed judgment on which were most reliable, and condensed them to make sweeping generalizations about the various parts of the world. Complicating matters, travelers either relayed or generated an inordinate number of tall tales. Or, in a reciprocal twist, travelers who read geographies often echoed what they had read rather than witnessed, their writings guided and constrained by geographic theory as much as personal observation. Such travelers tried to relate their local and particular observations to the templates of geographers. Having seen an unusual squirrel, a traveler might generalize about all of the continent's squirrels, including the non-existent ones that he or she had never seen, because the continent was the geographers' unit of analysis.[20]

This unit of analysis had such primacy because much of the bone and sinew of geographical studies during this era, like science as a whole, was composed largely of taxonomies and nomenclature.[21] Geographers were system builders. Atlases and geographies often began with rigid definitions of the parts of the earth and then broke big categories into subcategories, sometimes including diagrams resembling the brackets in a modern sports tournament (fig. 1). They usually divided the earth into water and land. The land, in turn, included continents, islands, peninsulas, isthmuses, promontories, and mountains. Erratic variations in these systems show that geography, though considered science, had not reached the precision to which its practitioners aspired. In the mid-seventeenth century, Peter Heylyn referred to Europe, Asia, and Africa as a single continent. But he also referred to the "Continents of France, Spain, [and] Germany." The Americas constituted a single continent, "naturally divided into two great Peninsulas," but "Mexicana, or the Northern Peninsula, may be most properly divided into the Continent, and Ilands."[22]

Geographers continued to produce equally slippery taxonomies for the rest of the seventeenth century. The author Peregrine Chamberlayne began from the premise that "the Earth, it may most properly be divided first into Islands and continents." From there, "Continents are of two sorts: First a Continent properly so called, is a large quantity of Land having little or no

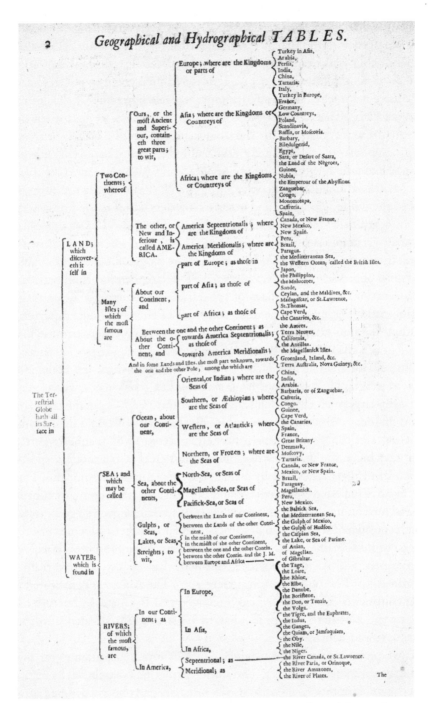

FIGURE 1. Diagram from Bernhardus Varenius, *Cosmography and Geography in Two Parts . . .*, trans. and ed. Richard Blome (1682). Courtesy Library of Congress

Sea near it; as Muscovy, Poland &c. The other sort of Continents, are those which are almost environed with Water, to which the name of Peninsula, or Chersonesus, is more fitly applied; such is Morea, the South part of Greece."[23] John Ogilby, the king's official "Cosmographer" and "Geographick Printer," wrote separate tracts describing Africa, America, Europe, and Asia. Introducing his volume on Africa, he explained that the "Earth is divided into three parts, or rather Islands, remoted from each other by Circum-ambient Sea, though their Largeness nominates them Continents. The first Contains Europe, Asia, and Africa, the second America, and the third Isle, Magellanica."[24] John Seller, the king's hydrographer, minimized his use of the term "continent," calling Europe, Asia, Africa, and America the "four parts" of the world. When referring to Africa, he deemed it a "peninsula," as he did with North and South America, which he also called Mexicana and Peruana.[25]

To be sure, some questioned the accuracy of prominent taxonomies. In 1680, the atlas author Moses Pitt observed, "The division seems not so rational; for Asia is much bigger than both of the others; nor is Europe an equal balance for Africa."[26] In his popular *New Voyages to North-America* (1703), Louis A. de LaHontan described the "vast Continent" of North America. In doing so, he thought it "a Paradox" that Canada "comprehends a greater extent of Ground, than the half of Europe." He editorialized that, "since we are wont to measure Provinces, Islands, and Kingdoms by the space of Ground, I am of the Opinion, that we ought to make use of the same Standard, with respect to the four parts of the World." Instead, geographers "parcel out the Earth in their Closets, according to their fancy."[27]

Pitt's and LaHontan's admonitions had little effect, and geographers and travel writers continued to conceptualize continents inconsistently. When Woodes Rogers, an English privateer who later became the first royal governor of the Bahamas, wrote in 1712 of his circumnavigation of the world, he described the "Continent of Chili." Yet he did not think California deserved continental status. Instead, it was either an island or it "joins to the continent"—this despite there being "no certain Account of its Shape or Bigness." At midcentury, the physician and historian William Douglass of Boston published a monumental history of the British settlements in North America. On some pages he referred to the "continent of America," and on others to the continents of North America, South America, or Greenland.[28]

Such travel writers and historians might be excused, given that in 1755 the dictionary most commonly used by British colonists still did not clarify what constituted a continent, defining one simply as "land not disjoined by the sea from other lands," and the *Encyclopaedia Britannica* was equally vague.[29] Prominent geography texts and atlases of the eighteenth century, too, provided little guidance and continued to employ inconsistent classification schemes. Whereas Patrick Gordon's *Geography Anatomiz'd* treated the Americas as a single continent, William Guthrie's *A New Geographical, Historical, and Commercial Grammar* persisted in referring to North and South America both as separate continents and as one taken together. So, too, did Thomas Salmon in his *A New Geographical and Historical Grammar*.[30] Atlases likewise split on the issue of whether the Americas constituted one or two continents. They usually contained maps of two hemispheres with different colorings for Europe, Asia, and Africa, but they divided almost equally on whether the Americas should be in one or two colors to signify distinct continents.[31]

Although agreement had not yet been reached on whether North and South America constituted one or two continents—that would have to wait until the twentieth century—inconsistency did not lead to quarrels. More often than not, the disparate views on continental taxonomies lay buried in slippery, silent assumptions. Writers who contradicted themselves rarely challenged the equally problematic formulations of others. Moreover, by the mid-eighteenth century, a consensus of sorts had emerged regarding Britain's littoral mainland American colonies. These came to be seen as sharing part of a continent, however that continent might be defined. For British North Americans of George Washington, Benjamin Franklin, and Thomas Jefferson's era, there were no continents of Delaware, South Carolina, or Virginia, as there had been the "Continents of France, Spain, [and] Germany" or "Muscovy, Poland &c" in the seventeenth century.[32] The inhabitants of all of these colonies could boast, so long as they did not ask inconvenient questions, that they lived on an American continent. And, as will be discussed in later chapters, boast they did.

CARTOGRAPHIC FRONTIERS

A close cousin of inconsistent continental taxonomies was geographic uncertainty. In the mid-eighteenth century, Europeans and European colonists still lacked familiarity with large swaths of the Pacific, the contours of North America's western coast, and vast areas west of the Mississippi River and Hudson Bay. Without thorough exploration of these regions—still decades away—the distribution of the world's continents and their shapes puzzled geographers and moved them to rely more on abstract theories than on precise measurement and consistent standards. Voids in geographic knowledge also allowed geographic assumptions, often bolstered by wishful thinking or paranoia, to guide mapmakers' pencils, explorers' routes, and merchants' investments. The North America such men envisioned often suited their aims more than it mirrored reality. They saw a landmass smaller than it really was, amenable to travel and trade, and without obstacles preventing one European power from easily controlling it. Gaps in geographical knowledge allowed geographers to speculate to their nation's advantage. Science and politics overlapped; knowledge of nature entwined with the desire for wealth and power.

For many influential Britons in the middle of the eighteenth century and through the Revolutionary era, North America seemed a region suitable for a non-despotic continental society, a place where a people of singular character could expand without adulterating their national spirit. Europeans and colonial Americans were ignorant of northwestern North America, the Rocky Mountains north of New Mexico, and the general aridity of the West. Indeed, most European powers hoped—or feared, depending on who they thought would control it—that the elusive Northwest Passage from the Atlantic to the Pacific would be found. Unaware of natural boundaries that would form obstacles to westward expansion, and influenced by Enlightenment thought regarding the relationship between political borders and nature, many saw potential for politically homogeneous, expansive polities that stretched across the continent.[33]

Just as geographers collated travelers' writings to present broad overviews, the men who produced maps of continents or the entire world extrapolated from the work of others. They took regional maps, voyagers' tales, presumptive theories, and imagination to present an expansive point of view. Their task was like that of solving a jigsaw puzzle with missing pieces, no box, and the ability to paint in the missing areas. "Cartography" and "cartographer," with their connotations of specialized, technical expertise and craftsmanship, did not enter the English lexicon until the 1850s and 1860s. A British mapmaker in the eighteenth century might come to the enterprise from a variety of backgrounds. Surveyors, explorers, or engravers all might make maps. One of the most influential engravers of the eighteenth century, Thomas Jefferys, for example, became the official mapmaker for George III more for his ability to sculpt copper plates than for his aptitude at delineating territory. Like most in London who made continental maps, he relied heavily on the work of a handful of colonists and other mapmakers—especially French—to create his broad perspectives.[34]

Lewis Evans produced the most influential and best-received map to emanate from the British mainland colonies in the eighteenth century, *A General Map of the Middle British Colonies* (1755), a significant piece in the puzzles of large-scale mapmakers. In 1737, Evans began surveying portions of Pennsylvania, New York, and New Jersey. Based on his own explorations and firsthand accounts from Indian traders he had met, Evans offered the most accurate English rendition of the Ohio River valley to date. On the surface, at least to the modern eye, it was just that: a rendition of a fraction of the eastern part of North America. Yet the map's reception indicates just how much viewers could extend their sights beyond its edges and make presumptions about the continent at large. Evans dedicated his map to Thomas Pownall, a future governor of Massachusetts and member of Parliament. On examining Evans's work, Pownall wrote that he had no reason to doubt that "all the continent of North America . . . is to the westward of the endless [Appalachian] mountains, a high level plain."[35]

In his review of Evans's map in the *Literary Magazine and Universal Review*, Samuel Johnson said that it, along with the establishment of libraries and Franklin's "electrical discoveries," so demonstrated the intellectual advancement of the colonies that he quoted Bishop George Berkeley's famous verse: "Westward the seat of empire takes its way." Evans had managed to "delineate the immense wastes of the western continent" and "enabled the imagination to wander over the lakes and mountains of that region, which many learned men have marked as the seat destined by providence for the fifth empire."[36]

With such unfettered imaginations, fixing the colonies' area and their boundaries to the west of the Appalachians in turn became a matter of debate, even after the Peace of Paris of 1763 ostensibly recognized the Mississippi River as the western limit of Britain's North American empire. One of Britain's premier geographers conceded that it was "difficult to ascertain the precise bounds of our Empire in North America. . . . If we might hazard a conjecture, it is nearly equal to the extent of all Europe." The statesman Edmund Burke expressed befuddlement, telling his readers that it "is somewhat difficult to ascertain the bounds of the English property in North America, to the Northern and Western sides." If the founding charters of some colonies were binding, that property might run "across the continent to the South-Sea [Pacific Ocean]." At the same time, "Others contract our rights to the hither banks of the Mississippi, . . . but upon what grounds they have fixed upon that river as a barrier, other than that rivers or mountains seem to be a species of natural boundaries, I cannot determine."[37]

Though unclear of the political boundaries of the colonies and the precise extent of the continent, armchair geographers and perambulatory travelers regularly gushed over North America's waterways. A British lieutenant stationed at Quebec wrote in a letter that those who had "made the tour of Europe" had seen nothing in the Rhine or the Danube, for these were "mere rivulets, when put in competition with . . . the Saint Lawrence."[38] Inducing from what they had seen or read about in the eastern portions of North America, writers touted networks of waterways as providing riparian highways throughout the continent's interior, including a quick passage to the Pacific. It did not matter that no one had yet navigated a route to the Pacific. Waterways made the continent seem—from sea to sea, for geographic ignorance facilitated the view that eastern rivers had equal counterparts in the West—coherent, porous, and manageable. "Without comparison," Burke wrote, "America is that part of the world which is the best watered." This would facilitate trade and the "intercourse of each part with the others." The political philosopher Richard Price saw in the continent's "vast rivers and widespread lakes" the potential for communication "unknown in any other region of the earth."[39]

Because the waters of the continent provided avenues of commerce and communication, statesmen recognized the continent as having tremendous unifying potential. Governor Arthur Dobbs suggested to William Pitt that control of the St. Lawrence and the Mississippi, together with "opening the Hudson Bay Trade[,] will give us the whole Trade of the Northern Continent to Mexico."[40] Thomas Pownall similarly celebrated the watersheds of the St. Lawrence and Mississippi rivers. Together, they provided "communication to every quarter and in every direction," drawing North America into "one mass, a one whole." Because the Great Lakes sat between the St. Lawrence and the Mississippi, they were the potential *"throne,"* with dominion "through all and every part of the continent."[41]

Such perceptions made sense, given that these Britons' knowledge of the western half of the Mississippi watershed stemmed almost entirely from Guillaume Delisle's popular *Carte de la Louisiane* (1718). In that map, North America's rivers appeared like the venation of a leaf, with the stem situated at the mouth of the Mississippi. The map became the foundation for most British maps of the region. The acclaimed mapmaker John Senex of London even went so far in 1721 as to make an English replica of the map without any acknowledgment of Delisle (fig. 2). It would not be until the second half of the 1760s that Britons would have any findings of their own to add to Delisle's portrayal of the Mississippi.[42] And even then, their additions did little to change Delisle's fundamental portrait.

Beyond interior waterways, many saw the Gulf Stream—which attracted the interest of British hydrographers in the 1760s, including Benjamin Franklin, who hoped that knowledge of it would help the Post Office—as aiding North American transportation. At least one traveler was struck by a Newport coffeehouse owner who, as early as 1744, talked "much of cutting

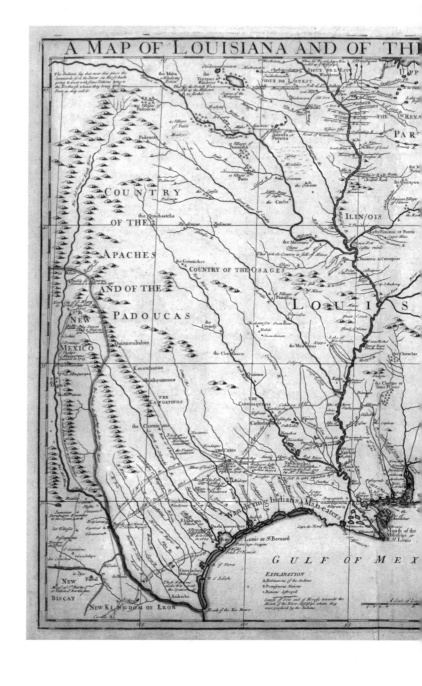

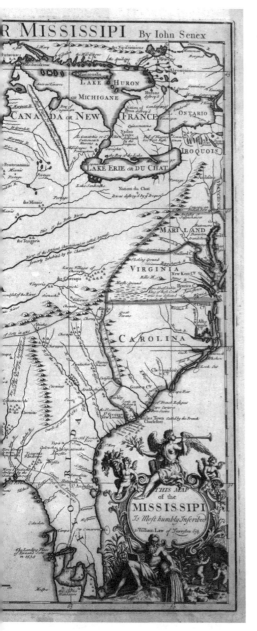

FIGURE 2. John Senex, *A Map of Louisiana and of the River Mississippi* (1721). Courtesy Library of Congress, Geography and Map Division

the American isthmus in two, so to make a short passage to the south seas." It was a possibility that travelers and prominent Anglo-Americans, such as Thomas Jefferson, still contemplated at least into the 1780s. North America, then, differed dramatically from Europe. Where Europe had natural subdivisions that chopped it into numerous peoples, North America's lakes, rivers, and surrounding waters—real and imagined—had the potential to draw people together.[43]

AMONG cartographers' theories, few had greater impact on exploration than the notion that the stability of the earth—or, at least, divine orderliness—required that its features be spread evenly over its surface. This idea led many European writers to assume the existence of an undiscovered continent between Chile and New Zealand to balance the landmasses in the Northern Hemisphere. Readers of the 1772 English translation of Peter Kalm's authoritative travel narrative would have learned from its editor that South America's native population sprang from this "unknown south continent," a mirror to the peopling of North America from Asia. Equilibrium also suggested that the Strait of Magellan in the Southern Hemisphere should have a counterpart in the Northern Hemisphere and that the Pacific Ocean separating the Americas from Asia should approximate the Atlantic. Besot with theory, many cartographers of the late seventeenth century and early eighteenth century showed North America as well removed from Asia. For them, there was no narrow Bering Strait; instead, as a counterbalance to the Strait of Magellan, a Northwest Passage connected the Atlantic with the Pacific through the northern reaches of Canada.[44]

When Dr. John Campbell revised John Harris's *Navigantium atque Itinerantium Bibliotheca: Or, a Compleat Collection of Voyages and Travels* (1744–48), he theorized that the passage must exist because "the Situation of the Streights of *Magellan* agrees perfectly with this Notion, and suggests according to the Analogy of things, a like Communication between the seas towards the North Pole." Nor would the passage from Atlantic to Pacific be long, because, given how far eastern Asia extended into the northern Pacific, balance dictated that the unexplored northern coast of the Americas must surely veer to the northeast, starting somewhere in California, to allow enough ocean to offset the vastness of Eurasia. Based on this reasoning, Campbell challenged the claim that Vitus Bering had discovered the coast of the North American mainland so close to Asia: "The Supposition of such an extended Continent would in a great Measure destroy that Proportion between Land and Sea, which . . . we have the greatest Reason to believe should always be preferred."[45]

Campbell wrote during a decade of renewed and fervent British interest in a Northwest Passage. Though the possibility of such a passage had drawn attention since at least the days of John Cabot and Jacques Cartier, geographic preconceptions, potential profits, curiosity, and imperial rivalry coalesced during the 1740s to spawn two of Britain's most aggressive attempts to find a navigable route from Hudson Bay to the Pacific Ocean. The Arctic was solidly frozen, so neither voyage accomplished the impossible. But that does not mean that the British lacked reason for trying. The British did not have firsthand knowledge about the northwestern parts of North America, but they had heard of an alleged Spanish voyage in 1592 that supposedly revealed an inlet leading deep into the interior of North America from the west, suggesting the possibility of a temperate waterway through the continent.[46]

What the British did not know was that such a report only masked Spain's woeful understanding of North American geography. The nation with the most extensive New World claims had only sporadically explored areas to the north beyond Florida, the Gulf of Mexico's coastline, and New Mexico over the course of the sixteenth, seventeenth, and early eighteenth centuries, and none of its explorers grasped the scope and scale of the North American West. From northern New Mexico in 1604, Juan de Oñate traveled west to chart a route to the Pacific but made it only to the Colorado River. Roughly a century later, Father Eusebio Kino explored the lower Colorado and Gila river valleys and convinced himself that the sea between Mexico and Baja California was a cul-de-sac, but he could only speculate about regions to the north and the proximity of the western coast of North America to Asia. Well into the second half of the eighteenth century, governors and naval explorers predicted that it would be easy to transport goods from New Mexico to the Pacific, the distances between it and the Rio Grande supposedly being short or the waterways plentiful. By the mid-1740s, some Spaniards still could not decide, despite Kino's thorough explorations of the Southwest, whether California connected to the mainland. As late as 1751, New Spain's Viceroy Revilla Gigedo referred to "the vast unknown continent of this northern America." In 1768, José de Galvez, the royal inspector-general in New Spain, fretted about the English being "very close to our towns of New Mexico, and not very far from the west coast of this continent." Only after hearing of Russian explorations and fur trading in Alaska did the Spanish urgently establish fledgling settlements and missions along the California coast as far north as San Francisco Bay. Had they known how remote the Russians and Alaska really were, they might not have been in such a hurry.[47]

Spanish geographic ignorance would have comforted Britons had they been aware of it. Instead, it remained shrouded in secrecy, allowing the British imagination to run wild. The Spanish, situated on the Pacific as they were, seemingly should have known more about North America's western coast than any other European power. French reports only compounded British befuddlement. French geographers, particularly Guillaume Delisle and J. B. Nolin, some of the best in the world and hailing from the European nation that had explored the trans-Mississippi West more extensively than any other, posited great inland seas and straits connecting to Hudson Bay (fig. 3). Within a decade, an English-language map of North America by Herman Moll also suggested such "Straits of Annian," just north of an insular California. Moll's *A New and Correct Map of the Whole World* (1719) also traced "the Tracks of the Bold Attempts which have been made to Find out the North East & North West Passages." Henceforth, British map-makers routinely included the straits on maps of North America, with interior rivers angling tantalizingly westward toward them. In 1725, John Senex's map of the world also hinted at the possibility of a waterway running through the continent by designating northern regions as a separate "Arctic Continent." Many thought the Northwest Passage would be much shorter if it reached the Pacific north of the Straits of Annian, based on the presumption that North America's west coast veered east as it headed north. News of Russian explorations disproving this view was slow in spreading. Russian authorities did not publish accounts of Vitus Bering's 1741 landfall in Alaska until 1758, and even then, many Europeans thought that he had landed on an island rather than on the North American mainland.[48]

Meanwhile, in Britain, Arthur Dobbs, a newly elected member of Parliament and soon-to-be surveyor-general of Ireland, lobbied vigorously for a voyage to discover the Northwest Passage. In 1731, he circulated copies of a seventy-page memorandum among influential officials, including his friend Prime Minister Robert Walpole. It argued, "There is the greatest probability of a Passage from our Atlantick Ocean into the Great Western & Southern Sea of America [Pacific Ocean], by the Northwestward of Hudsons Bay." Dobbs based his argument mostly on higher-than-expected tides and whale sightings in the western portions of Hudson Bay. If only one strait entered the bay from the east, tides should have decreased the farther one got from the Atlantic, but ship captains' logs seemed to report the contrary. Also, whales frequented the western shore of the bay, but none had been spotted entering from the Atlantic. Both the tides and the whales proved, Dobbs thought, the existence of a strait to the west and the relative proximity of the Pacific.[49]

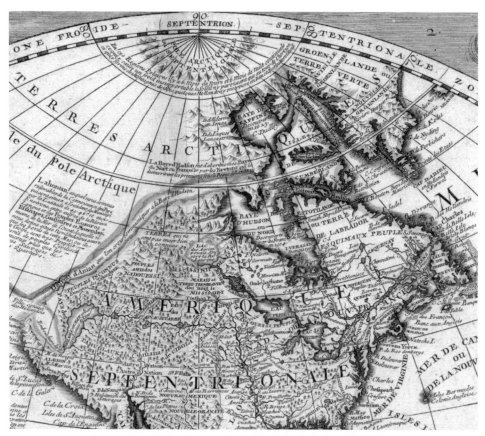

FIGURE 3. Detail from J. B. Nolin, *Le globe terrestre représenté en deux plans-hémisphères* (1708). Courtesy Library of Congress, Geography and Map Division

Passage through the strait would allow for a three- to four-month trip to California from Britain and, beyond that, the unexplored realms of the South Pacific. Once there, British ships could trade and intercept Spanish commerce, most tantalizingly the galleons laden with Asian riches sailing out of Manila.[50] After receiving royal patronage, Dobbs hired Captain Christopher Middleton of Hudson's Bay Company to command two naval ships and ninety men to find and traverse the passage. Departing London in June 1741 and sailing across the Atlantic to Hudson Bay, the crew wintered on its western shore, at the mouth of the Churchill River. There the ship's surgeon spent much of his time tending to cases of scurvy and "Country Distemper," or sawing off toes "Mortify'd with being froze."[51] In 1742, they spent the narrow window of opportunity provided by the weather futilely probing any semblance of a route heading west from the bay's shore.

Trends, Conceptions, Implications (37

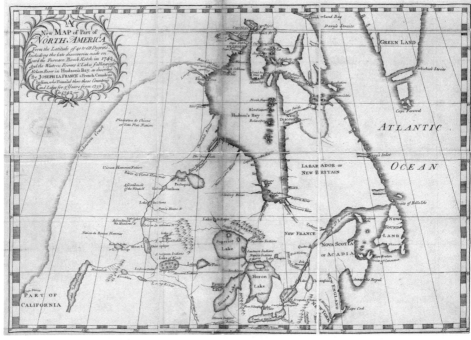

FIGURE 4. Arthur Dobbs, "A New Map of North America," *Account of the Countries Adjoining to Hudson's Bay* (1744). American Philosophical Society

Though Middleton and his crew concluded that no passage existed, Dobbs remained a booster and accused the seasoned Middleton of incompetence. Dobbs published *Account of the Countries Adjoining to Hudson's Bay* (1744), which accused the monopolistic Hudson's Bay Company of lethargy in exploiting the region's potential and portrayed the French as filling the void. He warned that the French stood to dominate the continent if they controlled the Northwest Passage, leaving the British, at best, with only littoral colonies. Beyond the evidence of tides and whales, he offered two phantasmal accounts allegedly proving the passage's existence. One came from a French fur trader whom Dobbs had met, who claimed to have met an Indian who had traveled across the continent and seen a strait that allowed whales and Pacific tides to roil Hudson Bay. The other was an equally imaginary story of a Spanish admiral, Bartholomew de Fonte, who allegedly had sailed inland far enough from North America's western coast to meet a Boston fur-trading vessel in 1640. Dobbs produced a map based on his conjectures that it would be easy to pass from the Atlantic to the Pacific (fig. 4). On it, the northern reaches of North America appeared almost as a pyramid honeycombed with lakes and rivers. The western coast angled sharply eastward, with an uncertain terminus near the north end of Hudson Bay, and unexplored rivers and straits point suggestively in its direction. Others echoed Dobb's optimism over the next few years. Campbell's edition of *Navigantium atque Itinerantium Bibliotheca* (1744), for example, foresaw British naval ships wreaking havoc on Spanish shipping in the Pacific without having to risk their own destruction in the long voyage around Cape Horn. In 1745, Parliament offered a gigantic £20,000 prize to anyone who could sail west from Hudson Bay to the Pacific.

It is not that merchants lacked incentive, for many hoped to crack the Hudson's Bay Company's monopoly and trade in areas such as California and Japan. Some even proved willing to back Dobbs; he garnered enough support to fund a private expedition in 1746. While it was away, Stephen Whatley edited a new edition of Herman Moll's popular *A Complete System of Geography,* which optimistically stated, "There has been no News of them, that we know of; but it is suppos'd they are gone thro' the Passage, and an Account of them is expected by the first homeward bound East-India Ships."[52] After suffering through a long winter and failing to find a passage in 1747, the starving, emaciated crew returned.

Though they fell far short of the Pacific, two prominent members of the voyage published books on their return, suggesting the likelihood that someone eventually would succeed where they had failed. The Irish-born Henry Ellis had plied his trade at sea for five years before joining the expedition at twenty-five. His *A Voyage to Hudson's-Bay* (1748) noted on its title page the inclusion of "A fair View of the Facts and Arguments from which the future finding of such a Passage is rendered probable," and it contained a map similar to Dobbs's in that the part of North America above 45° latitude appeared as pyramid honeycombed with waterways (fig. 5). Another man, who went by a number of names, including Theodore Swaine Drage and Captain Charles Swain, published his account at the same time; twenty years later, he wrote *The Great Probability of a North West Passage* (1768).

Dobbs, Ellis, and Swaine all spent significant parts of their lives in the colonies after these expeditions. There the supposition of a Northwest Passage effervesced, even as the quest for it became less fervent. Dobbs became the governor of North Carolina in 1752 and assumed his post in 1754. As he prepared to take that post, he had his portrait painted by William Hoare. Dobbs presented himself holding a map of North Carolina in his left hand and a compass in his right hand, with a globe near his right shoulder. On the globe, light bathed the northeastern portion of North America and the entrance to Hudson Bay (fig. 6). For the rest of his life,

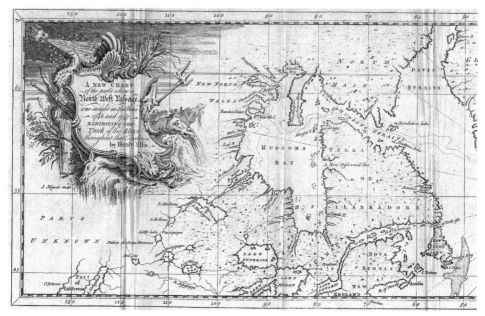

FIGURE 5. From Henry Ellis's map to accompany *A Voyage to Hudson's-Bay* (1748). American Philosophical Society

Dobbs clung to his belief in the passage. As governor, he warned against French power in North America, and when the French were excluded from the continent in 1763, he wrote that he had "nothing to wish for but the opening of the Trade to Hudson Bay and discovery of the passage to the Western American Ocean, which I have labour'd to obtain these thirty Years, and then I should die in Peace."[53] He died two years later. Henry Ellis went from seaman to captain of a slave ship to, like Dobbs, a fellow of the Royal Society—Britain's most elite scientific institution—and to the governorships of Georgia in 1758 and Nova Scotia in 1761. He continued to believe in a passable connection between Hudson Bay and the Pacific until the combined efforts of Captains James Cook and George Vancouver proved otherwise in the 1770s and 1790s.[54]

Captain Charles Swaine never rose to such high office as Dobbs and Ellis. He arrived in Pennsylvania in 1750 and sought support for another voyage in search of a Northwest Passage. He found subscribers from Maryland, New York, Boston, and Philadelphia, the home of his most illustrious supporter, Benjamin Franklin. These investors sponsored him and a crew of fifteen to sail the sixty-ton *Argo*. The voyagers failed to navigate the schooner even through Hudson Strait and into the bay after two attempts in 1753

FIGURE 6. Engraving of William Hoare's portrait of Arthur Dobbs (c. 1753).
Darlington Digital Library Images, Archives Service Center, University of Pittsburgh

and 1754. Franklin, nonetheless, remained a believer in both Bartholomew de Fonte's account of 1640 and the existence of the passage. He was only slightly deterred by the slow-to-spread revelation that Vitus Bering had allegedly found the North American coast much closer to Asia than many had believed. Franklin, like many, thought that Bering might have found a large island instead of the coast of North America.[55]

The failures to find the Northwest Passage in the 1740s and early 1750s might have temporarily snuffed interest in it, but neither the French nor the British dared dismiss the possibility of the passage's existence. Statesmen from both nations believed that, should one power discover and control it, the other would have a dismal future in North America and the East Indies. French geographers reinforced British fears. Joseph Nicholas Delisle and Philippe Buache published controversial maps in the 1750s that depicted an extensive system of straits, lakes, and inland seas in the northwestern realms of North America (fig. 7). Though some questioned the reliability of such maps, nervous Britons, especially American colonists, could not safely dismiss them.

Nor would British mapmakers let the empire's subjects forget the stakes. Drawing on published sources, Emanuel Bowen, geographer to George II, produced *An Accurate Map of North America* (1755) (fig. 8). He covered the northwestern, unknown part of North America with an inset detailing Hudson's Bay. An annotation read, "If there is a North West Passage it appears to be through one of these Inlets." Bowen's work reached a large audience when a simplified, seven-inch-by-eleven-inch version of his world map appeared in the December 1755 issue of *Gentleman's Magazine* (fig. 9). Because the small size of the map precluded including many details, a posited inland strait stood out, and the geopolitical implications were obvious. Tensions between France and Britain had been rising, and the French ostensibly stood well positioned to understand the northwest's features through their own efforts and through the assistance of their native trading partners who stretched west from the Great Lakes. The French, it seemed, threatened the very existence of Britain's littoral colonies.[56]

As the next chapter discusses in greater detail, continental conceptions structured much of the rhetoric and strategy of Britons when war finally did break out between the two powers. Since the Treaty of Utrecht in 1713, Britain had claimed control of the territory around Hudson Bay and the Nova Scotia-to-Georgia littoral, stretching west into at least the Ohio River valley. France also claimed the Ohio country, along with a vast crescent of territory extending from the mouth of the St. Lawrence River, through the Great Lakes, and down the Mississippi to New Orleans. The dispute over the Ohio River valley offered a necessary, though not sufficient, cause for the war that ensued in 1754. The American phase of the Seven Years' War (1756–63), sometimes referred to as the French and Indian War, revolved, in the eyes of most British mainlanders, around which power would gain control of not just the Ohio country but the entire continent. As the historian Paul W. Mapp has argued, uncertainty about the shape of North

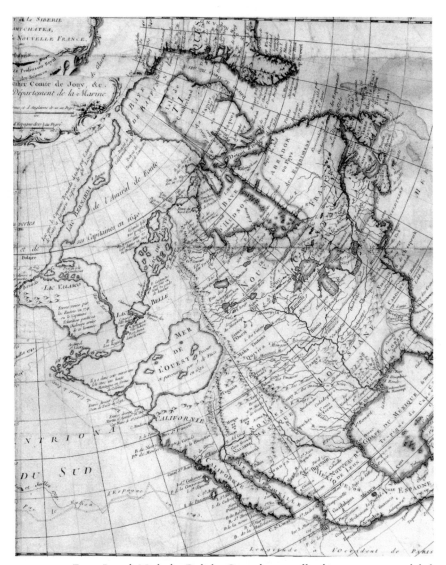

FIGURE 7. From Joseph Nicholas Delisle, *Carte des nouvelles découvertes au nord de la Mer du Sud* (1752). © British Library Board. Maps C.27.g.22.(1.)

America's western regions and the supposition that either the French or the British might control the Northwest Passage proved at least as important as the Ohio country in driving the two powers' statesmen, and eventually those of Spain, to decide on war.[57] The rhetoric of Britain's mainland colonists virtually ignored the Spanish presence, for on their geopolitical map, so to speak, Spaniards rarely appeared as an obstacle to continental control.

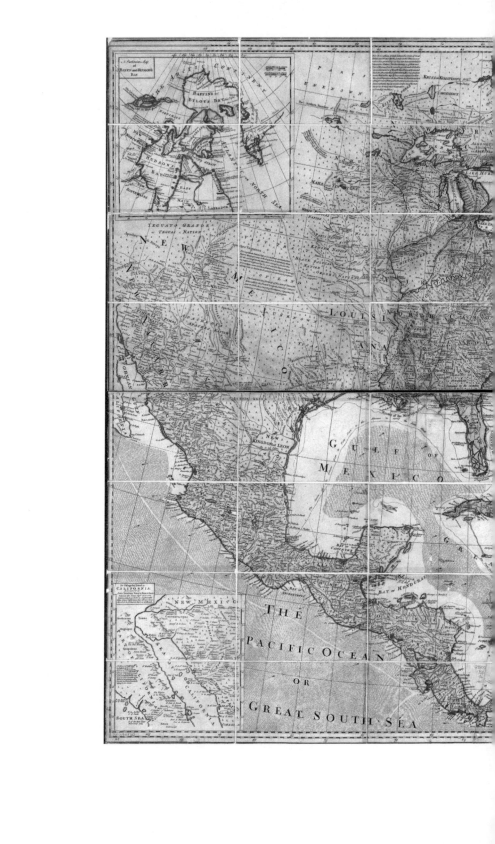

FIGURE 9. From Emanuel Bowen, "A Map of the World, on Mercators Projection," *Gentleman's Magazine,* vol. 25, Dec. 1755. Courtesy Library Company of Philadelphia

Instead, the Spanish North American empire seemed a speed bump on the way to the Pacific, where the truly lucrative holdings lay.

When Britain prevailed in the Seven Years' War, it took as its spoils, among other territories, France's holdings on the North American mainland. The nominal ouster of the French from the continent alleviated Britain's concerns that its archrival might control the main waterways and, eventually, the Northwest Passage. The British search for the Northwest Passage thus lost some of its urgency. But because curiosity and the quest for profits were not easily satiated, it continued. Robert Rogers, hero of the Seven Years' War, secured an appointment as commandant of Fort Michilmackinac partly to pursue the dream. His *Concise Account of North America* (1765) emphasized the potential of the passage and anticipated Britons' thriving along the Mississippi, as well. In 1778, his lieutenant, the Massachusetts militiaman Jonathan Carver, published a bestselling account of his travels that underscored the likelihood of the passage's existence, and he included a map to indicate its location. In the meantime, new editions of Emanuel Bowen's *An Accurate Map of North America* appeared into the 1770s and continued to indicate where a Northwest Passage might be found. The Yale graduate Timothy Dwight wrote a poem in 1772 celebrating the colonists' imperial future, when "Around the frozen shores thy sons shall sail." Britons still viewed North America as a tidy, manageable landmass unified by chains of waterways that would allow trade to flow both through and throughout it. North America had the natural unity often attributed to continents, and the power of a single empire could seep throughout.[58]

Though counterfactual history is impossible to prove, it is worth considering for a moment. Had geographers of the seventeenth and early eighteenth centuries known of the vast Rocky Mountain spine dividing the continent; had they known of the difficulties to be had crossing North America; or had they known that the ice-choked Northwest Passage was so far north that it was essentially useless, might they have been set on a road toward the construction of a continental taxonomy different from that which we have inherited? After all, they had dignified the minor appendage of Europe with continental status, separated from Asia, in part, by the entirely passable Urals. By 1770, some lonely voices, such as that of William Doyle, who doubted the existence of the Northwest Passage and believed the northern parts of North America to be vast, criticized prevailing taxonomies as irrational, arguing, "We consider only those divisions, which not princes or states, not geographers, or historians, but which nature itself has made between the several parts of this globe." For Doyle, this meant focusing on "the most natural of all boundaries, namely seas." He reverted to seeing the Old World and New World as continents, along with Australia as a third.

Yet Doyle's contrarian call went unheeded. Even if some had listened, however, they may have wondered why Doyle himself considered Australia a continent and Greenland not. How big did an island have to be to reach continental status? Doyle's work had little impact; the newly emerging metageographical habits of the mind were already well on their way to becoming entrenched. North America, and possibly even both Americas combined, had emerged as a region with the potential for control by one power.[59]

CONTINENTAL CHARACTERISTICS

In tandem with the evolving cartographic construction of North America as a coherent whole emerged British conceptions of their nation as the one best suited to inhabit it. Geographers may have differed on how to divide the world, but they all assigned essential attributes to its parts and their inhabitants. This tendency helps explain how Europe emerged as a continent distinct from Asia though physically attached to it. It is no accident that, despite significant variations in their work, geographers began creating the framework for the seven-part continental scheme during what is commonly called the "Age of Exploration." As European nation-states coalesced and encouraged overseas exploration and colonization, nationalism grew. Nationalistic rivalries pitted states against one another, but they simultaneously strengthened people's collective perception of themselves as Europeans. In the fifteenth and sixteenth centuries, "Europe" saw increasing use for self-reference at the expense of the term "Christendom." When Europeans began viewing themselves as inhabiting one of the world's continents, they tied their identity to their perception of the others. In the process, they began to attribute characteristics to the people in other parts of the world in ways that gave traction to notions of themselves.[60]

By the seventeenth century, English geographers had instituted an organizational convention that would last into the next century and beyond.[61] They divided their geographies into sections along continental lines and began them with sweeping generalizations about the people who inhabited these areas. John Seller's *Atlas Minimus* (1679), for example, introduced Europe with a brief paragraph explaining that, "though it be the least of the four grand Divisions of the Earth," it "is yet of most Renown" for its climate, its "fertility of the soil," the "flourishing of Arts and Sciences," and the "Purity and Sincerity of the Christian Faith." The introductory paragraph for Asia highlighted the region's size and, reflecting that most seventeenth-century English men and women thought of Asia as what we now think of as the Middle East, that it was the birthplace of Christ and home of the "most memorable occurrences mentioned in the old and new Testament" (fig. 10).

Other parts of the world did not fare so well. Seller offered a cursory description of Africa's boundaries and dimensions and then dismissed the region as "not very fruitful nor populous except in Monsters and Wild

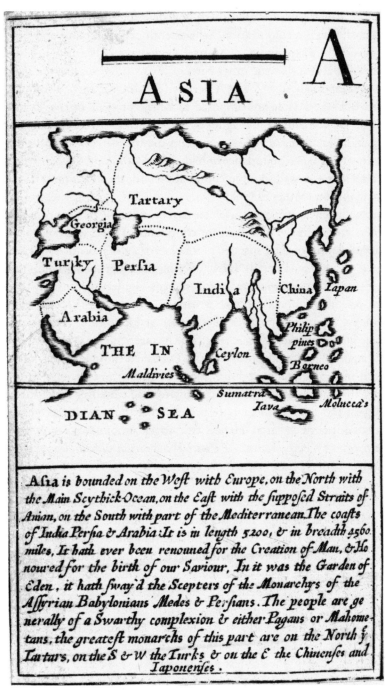

FIGURE 10. A summary of Asia's notable attributes according to John Seller's *Atlas Minimus* (1679). © British Library Board. Maps.c.7.a.16

Beasts." The Americas warranted the fullest description because they had seen successful English colonization. Seller mentioned Columbus and Amerigo Vespucci before explaining, "This large Region is very plentiful in Fruits and sundry Creatures that the other parts of the world never know; as also in Mines but especially silver." The Americas' "inhabitants are of a complexion swarthy. These People are supposed to be the progeny of the Tartars, with whose gross manners and ignorance they nearly agree."[62] Similarly, John Ogilby's discussion of Asia summed up the world's commercial prospects, stating that Asia's "abundance of high-valu'd Commodities . . . exceeds Europe also, and may well stand in competition with the new-found World America, with all its Mines of Gold."[63]

By the eighteenth century, travel narratives reflected this tendency of geographers to generalize about entire continents. To be sure, such narratives devoted most of their space to particulars of a given location. Writers expounded on mundane details, rarely offering the blunt metageographical overviews offered by geographers. In this respect, eighteenth-century travel literature resembles modern travel writing, readers of which are more likely to learn about the weather of a particular locale than encounter a treatise on global climate change. Even so, metageographical conceptions grounded many eighteenth-century works. Published travel literature often announced metageographical presumptions right on the title page. It did not matter that most travelers in North America had trod over very little of the landmass; they had a proclivity to project what they saw as representative of the continent at large. Hence, title pages announced *Travels into North America* (by Peter Kalm), *A Concise Account of North America* (by Robert Rogers), or *Travels through the Interior Parts of North America* (by Jonathan Carver).

A continental blueprint often structured the narratives that followed. Peter Kalm's work arguably had the greatest influence among colonists disposed to scientific study. No eighteenth-century work could match the array of flora and fauna he described, or his level of detail. On squirrels alone, he gave readers a dozen pages, making precise just how much variety he encountered (or, at least, he believed existed). Yet even though Kalm catalogued diversity, a fundamental order structured most of his findings: a comparison between Europe and North America. The poplar tree, for example, "grows to the greatest height and thickness of any in North America." It "vies in that point with our greatest European trees." He compared the life expectancy and health of Europeans and Americans. Despite the obvious variety he encountered in the different parts of North America, he treated the whole like an ecosystem, one whose basis of comparison was Europe.[64]

Even when travel narratives did not explicitly compare North America and Europe, authors expressed wonder at the novelty of the "natural curiosities"—to use a phrase common at the time—that they encountered. European writers were often stunned or enraptured by the newness, the foreignness of the natural phenomena they encountered. Yet taken together, the little details were like bricks in a wall, indicating that although the traveler was in a new land, it was a coherent land. By rattling off page after page describing exotic plants and animals, the net effect was to homogenize the whole. By cataloging the uniqueness of nearly everything they encountered, travelers suggested a line of commonality running through the entirety. In some cases, even those travel writers and diarists who carefully documented regional variation could not resist boiling their findings down to sweeping continental generalizations. Near the end of his journal, Nicholas Cresswell wrote a few summary sentences for each region he had journeyed through, from north to south. Immediately thereafter, he wrote, the "Continent of America, take it all in all, is undoubtedly one of the finest countries in the World. . . . Every part of the Continent abounds with large navigable Rivers. . . . The face of the Country is in general delightfully pleasing." This was just the kind of ordered extrapolation that armchair geographers had long made from London.[65]

The order imposed in the seventeenth and eighteenth centuries also included iconography personifying the parts of the world. Geographers and mapmakers built on a tradition established by Flemish graphic and decorative artists and practiced in many other parts of Europe. The frontispiece to Peter Heylyn's *Cosmographie,* for example, depicted both a man and a woman for Europe, Africa, Asia, and the Americas (fig. 11). Map cartouches, too, associated human figures with the parts of the world. Such images reflected Europeans' sense of superiority and their experiences, aspirations, and stereotypes regarding the world's other peoples. Though the images varied over time and with the artist, patterns emerged. Europe often appeared with crown, scepter, or sword signifying her power over the rest of the world. Or she might carry a small temple or orb symbolizing Europe's role in spreading Christianity. Depictions of Asia varied the most. They, like those of Europe, might include orbs, to represent Asia as the birthplace of Christianity, or riches in the form of silks, jewelry, and spices, signifying "Asiatic luxury" and wealth available for extraction. Africa, dark and mysterious, often connoted inferiority and danger, with sparsely clad individuals and exotic animals such as lions or reptiles. The Americas' persona appeared to come from tropical regions, in keeping with Europeans' first contacts in Central and South America. She often conveyed naked innocence as well as

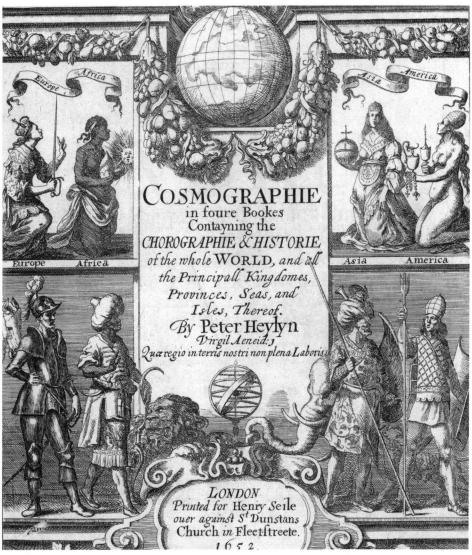

FIGURE 11. From the frontispiece to Peter Heylyn's *Cosmographie in Foure Books* (1652). Reproduced by permission of the Huntington Library, San Marino, California

material abundance, portraying the Americas as a land of primitives await-ing enlightenment and rich natural resources awaiting exploitation.[66]

These personifications and sweeping inferences ran counter to a prevail-ing belief that latitude strongly influenced a people's character. At times, this implicit challenge could even appear as an explicit contradiction within a geographer's work. Latitudinal determinism grew out of the notion that climate corresponded strictly to latitude. The most influential authors of the era's geographies typically defined climates as latitudes or circum-global rings. "Climates are those tracts of the Surface of the Earth, bounded by imaginary circles, running Parallel to the Equator," explained Patrick Gordon's highly popular *Geography Anatomiz'd* (1693).[67] Working on such an assumption, Richard Blome prefaced his translation of *Cosmography and Geography* (1682) by arguing that geography provided the key to understanding history. "Nature" had "not only diversly distinguished the Faces and Physiognomy, but also the Souls and Minds of Men." In turn, "Geographers have divided the World into Climates, and every Climate is distinctly Subject to the Dominion of some Planet, as the chief cause of this Diversity." More important, but still underpinned by latitude, was the "great and different effects of the Celestial Rays." For Blome, history had borne this out. "Northern People being remote from the Sun and by consequence inhabiting in cold Countries; are Sanguine, Robust, full of Valour and Animosity, hence they have always been Victorious and predominant over the Meridional or Southern Nations."[68]

Latitudinal determinism permeated early English colonizing endeavors, often with grave consequences. Puritans expected a winter like that in balmy parts of Spain or southern France when they migrated to New England. Promoters so believed in circum-global rings as climate that they could shamelessly sell colonizing ventures based on their latitude. In the early eighteenth century, Sir Robert Mountgomery spoke confidently, without ever leaving England, about the prospects of a settlement in what is now Georgia. Referencing only a map, he could describe the region as the "Most Delightful Country of the Universe," for it "lies in the same Latitude with *Palestine* Herself, which was pointed out by *God's* own Choice, to bless the Labours of a favourite People."[69]

Even firsthand experience had difficulty overcoming deeply ingrained ideas. Despite living far from Elysian Virginia, William Byrd II and Robert Beverley stubbornly clung to the preconception that climates remained constant at given latitudes around the world. This bode well for Virginia. Beverley believed that it "must be a happy Climate, since it is very near of the same Latitude with the Land of Promise." Moreover, "All the Countries in the World, seated in or near the Latitude of Virginia, are esteem'd the Fruitfullest, and Pleasantest of all Clymates." William Byrd II also believed that regions at a given latitude had similar properties. In a minor dispute over the value of Virginia as a wine-producing region, Byrd asserted that, because the colony shared its "latitude" with known wine-producing regions, any "difficulties may be overcome by good management."[70]

Byrd wrote at a time, however, when naturalists began to challenge the rigid link between latitude and climate and political theorists started to complicate and refine their views on the relationship between a people's character and the environment. The tension between latitudinal determinism and continental character subsequently and subtly shifted in favor of the latter. A revival of ancient Hippocratic medical thought emphasized the relationship between environment and the physical condition of both individuals and peoples. Chauvinistic Europeans touted their particular locales as shaping their nation's superior temperament. The English hailed their cool, northerly island as ideal, making them hardier than southern Europeans. Those who migrated to another climate either would perish or their physical condition and temperament would change. Such views disturbed promoters of colonization, who went to great pains to assure prospective settlers that American territories lay at latitudes conducive to good health.[71] Yet such arguments faced obvious limits, given the wide latitudinal span that colonizing ventures in the Americas eventually took. Observers, sometimes with promotional interests, began to place greater weight on factors besides latitude, such as soil, topography, plant life, and human population, as determinants of climate.

Travel narratives extolled the salubriousness of climates that, within a latitudinally deterministic framework, should have sickened Britons. John Lawson, the native Scot who was assigned the responsibility of surveyor-general of North Carolina, and the travel writer Thomas Nairne both reassured readers of Carolina's amenability to Englishmen. They pointed to brisk winters, "refreshing" rains that countered the effects of hot summers, and air that "is generally very clear and fine."[72] Even more pivotal in the shift from latitudinal determinism was the physician Sir Hans Sloane, a resident of the Caribbean for two years and eventual president of the Royal Society. His *A Voyage to the Islands* (1707–25) argued for the uniqueness of the Caribbean climate and its conduciveness to good health, despite the heat and malaria. Like Lawson and Nairne, Sloane emphasized the rejuvenating qualities of the air, as well as the wholesomeness of the water. Another Royal Society member, Stephen Hales, further challenged simplistic notions of climate by proposing that vegetation affected the temperature and moisture of a region. In North America, the naturalist Mark Catesby questioned the rigid relationship between latitude and climate, and he suggested a hemispheric component, something Buffon would emphasize and elaborate on.[73]

Such ideas undermined notions of links among people who shared latitudes. Work such as Montesquieu's political theory aided the process. His *Spirit of the Laws* (1748) presented a more comprehensive portrait of climate's influence, in conjunction with that of topography and terrain, on political systems. Montesquieu suggested that a wide array of factors, not just latitude, could give contour to a people's political possibilities. He also argued that an agricultural way of life tempered the effects of environments on polities.[74] The geographies that colonists read eventually reflected this general shift away from rigid latitudinal climate zones. Thomas Salmon could argue in the 1770s, without paying any regard to latitude, that inhabitants of East Asia differed from Europeans because they inhabited a different climate. He wrote of Asia that "the warmth of these Eastern climates has doubtless ever contributed to the indolence and effeminacy of its inhabitants." He doubted that Asians "ever had the industry and active spirits" of Europeans, "who found the necessity of labour for their support, which the Asiaticks had less occasion for."[75]

At the same time, no one, at least in the eighteenth century, completely denied that stark climatic variations existed within the various parts of the world. Thomas Jefferson compiled for the Marquis de Chastellux an extensive list of traits differentiating northerners and southerners in North America. "In a warm climate," for instance, "no man will labour for himself who can make another labour for him."[76] Climatic variations, Jefferson believed, functioned as a prism, refracting a relatively homogeneous population into one with diverse characteristics when it scattered along the North American coast. He did not, however, suggest consequences as dire for the temperament of white colonists as those predicted by early modern Hippocratic theory. Similarly, Hector St. John de Crèvecoeur, answering the question "What is an American?" had to concede that, because "men are like plants," they were shaped by environmental influences. Unlike Jefferson, though, he did not see the greatest change running from north to south; rather, Crèvecoeur emphasized the variation as one moved from the coast to the interior, from "those who live near the sea," to "those who inhabit the middle settlements," to those "near the great woods."[77]

Ironically, this shift away from latitudinal determinism corresponded with a rapid surge in Europeans' knowledge of Africa and the Americas, which comprise far more latitudes than Europe. Europeans began shifting away from latitudinal determinism at the very moment they were learning about and colonizing those parts of the earth where the effects of latitude were most striking. But rather than reinforce latitudinal determinism, colonization corresponded with its demise. Latitudinal determinism was eventually overshadowed by racial categories that transcended climates, mirrored the parts of the world, and paved the way for the belief that Britons might be the true Americans.

The "Enlightenment imagination," one historian explains, came to be "dominated by the picture of great continental land masses, each, apparently, with its own color of human."[78] Colonization's resulting intermixture of Africans, American Indians, and Europeans—and the widely diverging fates it delivered to these three groups—bolstered notions, which quickly became cloaked as science, of fundamental differences among the parts of the world. Racial and continental categories increasingly corresponded in the minds of many. Climate might still offer to British North Americans a partial explanation as to why their compatriots in other regions differed from themselves. But the variations appeared minimal compared with the deeply rooted differences distinguishing Europeans (who, in relative terms, thrived in America), from American Indians (who suffered horrendous death and dispossession), and from Africans (who appeared as a foreign commodity to import). Native Americans had been inappropriately placed on the continent and were destined for replacement.

The seventeenth-century colonizing experience of the English led them to believe that their bodies differed fundamentally from those of Indians. Witnessing the decimation of Indian populations from disease, the colonists eventually attributed this demographic collapse and the rise of the English population largely to physical differences between the two groups. They concluded, around the time of their most cataclysmic wars with Indians in New England and Virginia—King Philip's War and Bacon's Rebellion (1675–76)—that the English body had a constitution better suited to the American environment than that of the Indian.[79]

Wars in New England and Virginia reinforced a latent racial divide between English and Native Americans. King Philip's War was particularly important, because in its aftermath, printing presses spewed histories of the conflict, spinning it as one between Indian savagery and English civilization. Though this memory departed somewhat from the war's reality as a conflict among disparate groups of English and Indians where, relative to their respective populations, more Indians fought on the "English" side than Englishmen, it persisted. Just two years after the war's end, Samuel Nowell preached that Indians "will not joyn or mix with us to make one Body." Instead, they were thorns in the colonists' sides, and the task at hand was "to root them out." By the early eighteenth century, the historian Joyce Chaplin explains, "white Americans seemed to believe themselves more natural than the aborigines, as if English bodies (little changed in America) had always been meant to be planted in Virginia, or Plymouth, or Carolina. To colonists, the arrival of another population before them meant little if people in the first group had bodies that never truly acclimated." At times, English colonists might admire Indians' ability to survive harsh winters or their physically fit appearance, but these traits did not negate the Indians' high death rate from imported diseases, which the English did not understand as alien to North America's environment. It did not matter if one looked at New England or the Carolinas. Indians seemed to die throughout English-speaking America, suggesting conclusions applicable to all of the continent.[80]

The colonial population's growth against the backdrop of Indians' death created a fulcrum for emerging notions of continental difference. Debate, with the goal of revealing nature's underlying plan, ensued over who was best suited to occupy the world's regions. An important backdrop to this effort, and a milestone in the scientific expression of race, appeared in 1740 when the Swedish botanist Carolus Linnaeus published the second edition of *General System of Nature*. The first edition (1735) had focused exclusively on plants and animals. Now, to the consternation of some, Linnaeus applied the same crass scrutiny to humankind. Though not universally lauded, Linnaeus's revolutionary ideas permeated the tightly knit North American scientific community, where they received a more hospitable reception than in Europe. A prominent protégé of Linnaeus, Peter Kalm, visited North America from 1748 to 1751 seeking botanical data. A list of some of the men he met during his travels reads like an honor roll of eighteenth-century American science: John Bartram, Mark Catesby, Cadwallader Colden, Benjamin Franklin, and John Mitchell. Many of these men corresponded directly with Linnaeus, and his ideas would retain a prominent place in British North American thought through the Revolution. The efforts of these and other natural historians on both sides of the Atlantic focused on weaving discoveries into a presumed global order that emphasized differences among the world's landmasses.[81]

When it came to humans, Linnaeus initially developed four categories: "Europaeus albus, Americanus rubescens, Asiaticus fuscus, Africanus niger." This division marked an early effort to differentiate "scientifically" among humans according to skin color. The categories paralleled the frequent, somewhat arbitrary classification of people as white, red, yellow, or black. Lumping the myriad shades of human skin color into four categories masked complexity, as did the simultaneous division of the world into four continents or parts. Indeed, given the prefix of each skin-color category— Europaeus, Americanus, Asiaticus, and Africanus—it seems likely that a presumed four-part division of the world led Linnaeus to arrive at four rather than, say, forty categories of skin color. A pioneer in physical anthropology, Johann Friedrich Blumenbach, observed in 1795 that Linnaeus was "following common geography." Linnaeus and his followers saw their endeavor to systematize nature as one in which they would display essential underlying characteristics. The four parts of the world—often interchangeable with continental status at the time—may not yet have revealed their precise boundaries, but they provided a key to nature's plan. So, too, did the variations among their human inhabitants.[82]

In some ways, Linnaeus's systematic theory of nature rivaled that of the other great naturalist of the century. Georges-Louis Leclerc, Comte de Buffon, for his part, thought Linnaeus's approach of compartmentalizing nature within a totalizing taxonomy superficial, for it failed to explain how nature functioned or to account for change over time. Buffon sought, among other things, to illuminate relationships between organisms and climates and to reveal a set of laws governing nature.[83] Despite their differences, however, Linnaeus and Buffon shared assumptions. Both had systematized nature in ways comprehensible through a prevailing metageography. Buffon's observations of American flora and fauna led him to make generalizations about the Americas and speculate about their history, while Linnaeus's compartmentalization of humans into four categories stemmed from a belief that all life in the Americas shared characteristics unique to that part of the world. That said, Buffon's work went further than Linnaeus's by positing laws that regulated nature and by suggesting how organisms and observable phenomena interacted. Buffon's formulations had an implicit predictive capacity that Linnaeus's lacked. For example, the American climate, according to Buffon, helped determine the nature of species. Should a species from another part of the world migrate there, its nature would change over time.[84]

While Buffon's ideas evolved over time, most Americans who read his work focused on his most significant departure from Linnaean thought, the belief that species changed over time because of variations in climate, habitat, and diet. Buffon argued that higher humidity and lower temperatures in the Americas led to a degeneration of species there. Coming from the premier naturalist of the time, Buffon's theories seeped into other widely read works denigrating Americans, such as Cornélius de Pauw's *Recherches philosophiques sur les Américains* (1768–69) and the Abbé Raynal's *Histoire philosophique et politique des établissemens et du commerce des Européens dans les deux Indes* (1770). Predictably, Buffonian arguments created a backlash because they spelled trouble for colonizers. Although critics disagreed with Buffon's emphasis on environmental factors, they largely accepted the continental assumptions embedded in his arguments. Buffon viewed all of the Americas as a suitable unit of analysis, for he saw a "general contraction of animated nature throughout the whole Continent." Outside of Spain and Latin America, few of Buffon's detractors questioned either the epistemological foundations or the system-building tendencies of his arguments.[85]

Although many criticized Buffon, few Britons disagreed with his lumping of the peoples of entire continents into discrete, homogeneous categories. Like Linnaeus, Buffon saw four skin colors. White was the natural one, but environmental variables made people "yellow, brown, and black," as well. Henry Home, Lord Kames, challenged this assessment, not on the ground that it included only four hues, but by asking why Native Americans were "without exception . . . of a copper-colour, though in that vast continent there is every variety of climate." The effect of the environment on the human body was questionable, not the categorization of people. Similarly, when Benjamin Franklin noted that many North and South American Indians died from disease, he surmised that the natives had bodies that differed fundamentally from those of Europeans, particularly in their skin and their perspiration. Such differences, he thought, could not be attributed to climate.[86]

The government engineer and botanist Bernard Romans's *Concise Natural History of East and West Florida* (1775) argued that Indians and Europeans constituted two completely different stocks from the outset: "From one end of America to the other, the red people are the same nation, and draw their origin from a different source . . . God created an original man and woman in this part of the globe." Romans lumped all Indians together, because "throughout their own continent their wild manners are universally alike." Indians were inferior, whether culturally or bodily, and not best suited to occupy that part of the world. He essentially deprived Indians of their indigenous status: "We might call them Americans . . . but this would be confounding them with the other natives [British colonists]." British Americans were as American as their aboriginal neighbors, if not more so. Such thinking tacitly accepted the continental taxonomies of the Americas' critics. Reactions to Buffonian theories ended up reinforcing a burgeoning continental identity.[87]

Colonists cared about science not just out of curiosity, but also because it potentially foresaw their destiny. Buffon's sweeping claims about the stunted nature of the Americas' life forms gave them cause for worry about how their bodies would fare in their new environment. But seeing Indians die in droves while Europeans fared better—especially after a period of "seasoning" —and subscribing to Hippocratic theories that linked human health closely to place gave settlers, in Chaplin's words, "considerable psychological and corporate strength from the belief that, at the deepest physical level, they were the true and natural residents of America—the powerful, racist fiction that remains the basis of North American identity."[88] The colonizing experience had suggested to colonists in British North America that they were the more natural natives of the continent.

THE emerging racial categories and metageographies did not mean that all Europeans suddenly appeared equal. Even as racial categories became more entrenched over the course of the eighteenth century, national rivalries continued to help drive colonization. Britons stereotyped themselves as having the ideal national character for spreading settlements across North America. In a fairly typical observation made during the Seven Years' War— a period of obviously intense national rivalry—Edmund Burke found "a remarkable providence in the casting of the parts . . . of the several European nations who act upon the stage of America." Each European nation appeared to Burke to have colonized the part of America best suited to its temperament. Among the players, the "Spaniard, proud, lazy and magnificent, has an ample walk in which to expatiate; a soft climate to indulge his love of ease; and a profusion of gold and silver to procure him all those luxuries his pride demands, but which his laziness would refuse him." In contrast, the "French, active, lively, enterprising, pliable and politic . . . are notwithstanding tractable and obedient to rules and laws." Fortuitously, they had "a country where more is to be effected by managing the people than by cultivating the ground; where a peddling commerce, that requires constant motion flourishes more than agriculture or a regular traffic." Burke's English countrymen were "of a reasoning disposition, thoughtful and cool, . . . and lovers of a country life." They may have been dealt "a lot which indeed produces neither gold nor silver; but they have a large tract of a fine continent; a noble field for the exercise of agriculture, and sufficient to furnish their trade without laying them under great difficulties."[89]

National temperament could take on different shades as the geopolitical situation changed. With the French nominally eliminated from North America at the end of the Seven Years' War, the English started to see themselves as having the superior character for controlling even more of North America than that which they had obtained through their treaty with the French. The geographer Thomas Salmon admitted that Spain ostensibly controlled more of the Americas than did the British, but he thought Spain's North American empire moribund, leading him to claim that, "from the general character of nations, . . . Britain shall have a wider domain there."

England's "great spirit of discovery" would allow it to expand "to the Northern parts of the Pacific ocean."[90]

The Hippocratic emphasis on the importance of place to human physical condition still bore consideration, so writers took a variety of tacks to reconcile the character of the English with the vast diversity of climates they encountered in the Americas. Edmund Burke, for example, made sweeping generalizations about European nationalities, but he also saw important distinctions among the English at home. The variations among the English corresponded nicely with the different areas that they occupied in the Americas. Burke contrasted the West Indies with the more temperate parts of the North American continent, and he suggested corresponding differences between the inhabitants. Heavy rains, acidic air, and fiery temperatures made the West Indian climate "unfriendly and unpleasant to an European constitution." There were, however, a handful of Englishmen with "fiery restless tempers, willing to undertake the severest labour . . . who love risk and hazard." The West Indies were well suited for "characters of this sort," because otherwise they would be dangers to "a regular and settled community." The English Caribbean could serve as "a vent to carry off such spirits."[91] It could isolate England's vile elements, allowing the essentially healthy English character to thrive on the mainland.

A far more common approach to reconciling climatic variation with rigid notions of race and national character was to regard climate as a geopolitical or commercial factor instead of making it a fundamental determinant of human character. Important human differences could transcend climates, but one still could not grow sugarcane in New England or harvest thick furs in the Caribbean. Seen from such a perspective, the climatic diversity of the Americas appeared as a desirable asset and a source of economic unity, even autonomy. North America, in one 1758 almanac, was the "Garden of the World" because it was "capable of producing . . . all Things necessary for the Conveniency and Delight of Life."[92] The growth of intercolonial union drew sustenance from a willingness to embrace such diversity. Franklin's preamble to the proposal to form the American Philosophical Society explained that the "English are possess'd of a long Tract of Continent . . . extending North and South thro' different Climates, having different Soils, producing different Plants, Mines and Minerals, and capable of different Improvements, Manufactures, &c." He used climatic variety to demonstrate the need for centralized organization and the benefits it would accrue to science.[93]

In 1768, the APS published extracts in the *Pennsylvania Gazette* from a meeting in which it found that the American climate "seems capable of supplying almost all the Productions of the Earth." Some writers even seized on climatic diversity in defending colonists' rights against parliamentary violations. As early as 1766, George Mason asked London merchants if a people living in "a country abounding in such variety of soil and climate . . . will long submit to oppression?" The climatic variation in a vast tract of land meant that a continental society could produce all of the goods it needed and thus avoid the border wars that had plagued Europe for centuries.[94] Clearly, the economic security provided by occupying a "long Tract of Continent" made potential environmental risks to colonists' bodies palatable to some.

CONFORMING TO NATURE'S LAWS

By 1775, intellectual developments had made it possible for British colonists to see their continent as suited for rule by one power and to see themselves as best positioned to constitute that power. As soon as the schism between the mainland colonists and mother country ruptured, American Revolutionaries invoked readily available scientific justifications—or, at least, analogies—for a North America outside the British imperial framework. In the process, the English national character fell out of favor as an explanation for why the colonists were well suited for their part of the globe. Instead, many argued that even though the continent had varied climates, it could exert a unifying force on all of its European inhabitants. Thomas Paine believed that "all Europeans meeting in America, or any other quarter of the globe, *are countrymen;* for England, Holland, Germany, or Sweden, when compared with the whole, stand in the same places on the larger scale, which the divisions of street, town, and county do on the smaller ones; distinctions too limited for continental minds." Paine's scientific inclinations shone through when he used an astronomical metaphor wherein the natural state of "America" created a "necessity" that, "like a gravitating power, would soon form our newly arrived emigrants into society."[95]

Paine had plenty of company in expressing his vision of the future new world order as one that would follow natural forces, particularly those involving celestial mechanics. His was part of an Enlightenment quest to apply scientific principles to the understanding and ordering of human society. In Virginia, as part of a broader restructuring of college curriculums influenced by the Scottish Enlightenment, Thomas Jefferson drafted legislation that eliminated professorships at William and Mary in theology and rhetoric and replaced them with, among others, a chair in "the laws of nature and of nations." William Doyle, though he denigrated the logic of prevailing continental taxonomies, still thought geographical knowledge essential to sound politics. As mentioned earlier, he wrote, "These two parts of knowledge . . . Geography and the law of nature and nations are the two great, and comparatively speaking, almost only qualifications necessary for a prince, or a prime minister."[96] One of the more astute and influential observers of the British Empire, and now a member of Parliament, Thomas Pownall, used Newtonian imagery to explain the politics of the Revolutionary era. Substituting the spirit of commerce for the force of gravity, Pownall argued that North America was the "new primary planet" in the world.

Geographical conceptions lay at the heart of Pownall's arguments, the science within the science. Pownall's imagery hinged on the most common continental taxonomy of the day and the belief that continents constituted natural systems and sound political foundations. The "three parts of the old world, Europe, Asia, and Africa," he wrote, "seem to have a natural division in the natural scite and circumstances of their territory. They are also inhabited and possessed by three different and distinct species of the human being. They have, therefore, generally by the effect of principles of nature operating against the vigour of man, fallen, in dominion, into their natural division." North and South America also "naturally divided into two distinct systems." Eventually their politics would reflect this, and they would, "as naturally, divide into two distinct dominions." North American geography formed a natural, unified system that favored its commercial and political independence. The continent acted like a mass under a gravitational pull, "ADVANCING, TO GROWTH OF STATE, WITH A STEADY AND CONTINUALLY ACCELERATING MOTION, OF WHICH THERE HAS NEVER YET BEEN ANY EXAMPLE IN EUROPE."[97]

Pownall's image of "continually accelerating motion" drew on earlier scientific developments, just as his idea of the "growth of state" built on demography, a science whose rise has prompted one historian to see the "beginnings of the statistical mind."[98] Demography's practitioners saw their studies not just as simple census taking but as a quest to ascertain laws of nature. One of the most important arguments within many demographic writings, sometimes made implicitly, was that continents presented logical units of analysis. As with the Newtonian imagery of Thomas Pownall, arguments of demographers often rested on geographic assumptions; geography was again the science within the science, and, in turn, a foundation for political theories.

Benjamin Franklin's *Observations on the Increase of Mankind* (1755) and Ezra Stiles's *Discourse on Christian Union* (1760) best exemplify eighteenth-century Anglo-American demography. Franklin's wide readership and prophetic insight have prompted historians to spill much ink on *Observations*.

After its first publication, it appeared in a number of periodicals, and Franklin eventually appended it to the fourth edition of his *Experiments and Observations on Electricity* (1769). Buying into the grand myth of Euro-American expansion that the continent was either a virgin land or thinly populated by Indians who subsisted by hunting, Franklin viewed "America as fully settled as it well could be by Hunters." But North America contained plenty of land for agriculturalists. Plentiful farmland translated into more frequent marriages by young couples and a higher birthrate. This led Franklin to conclude that America's "people must at least be doubled every twenty years." Travel writers soon echoed Franklin in their formal tracts and private journals.[99]

Rarely did Franklin combine his scientific ideas with his political thought, but *Observations* was an exception, a scientific tract that doubled as a geopolitical roadmap. *Observations* argued that, by virtue of the colonies' rapid population growth, the future of Britain's transatlantic power lay in North America, not the British Isles. Many feared that Britain might overextend itself if it did not closely regulate and limit the manufacturing capacity of the colonies. Franklin argued, to the contrary, that the mainland colonies' population and territorial growth could strengthen the empire. He envisioned the expansion of such colonies within the British Empire. Plentiful land would ensure the possibility of expansion as the population grew, so farmland would remain available. The colonies would remain predominantly agricultural and thus complement the English economy, which was more dedicated to manufacturing. As late as March 1775, the month before the battles of Lexington and Concord, Franklin lamented that poor policy decisions had prevented Britons from "extending our Western Empire [by] adding Province to Province as far as the South Sea."[100]

The science of geography and one of its most common continental taxonomies underpinned Franklin's demographic work. A comparison between "old Countries, as Europe," and "new Countries, as America," served as the backbone of *Observations*. When Franklin wrote of "America," he meant not just the colonies pinned against the Atlantic, but also the "vast . . . Territory of North-America," which would "require many Ages to settle it fully." The continent might be populated "from one Nation only . . . for Instance, with Englishmen." To create an all-English population in North America, however, Britain must be careful to deal with the French in a way that would "secure Room enough, since on Room depends so much the Increase of her People." He hoped North America would become a "white" continent, since the world had relatively few "purely white People" and "All Africa is black or tawny. Asia chiefly tawny. America (exclusive of the new Comers) wholly so." Increased English colonization would make "this Side of our Globe reflect a brighter Light to the Eyes of Inhabitants in Mars or Venus," so why, he asked, should "we . . . darken its People?"[101]

Franklin's fellow demography pioneer, Ezra Stiles, also viewed continents as suitable units of analysis. Though he focused on New England, he extrapolated from his data to show how the political future could conform to the continent's nature. Stiles, like Franklin, thought New England would double its population every twenty years. Also in accordance with Franklin's views, Stiles saw no immediate territorial limits to this growth but those of the continent. Should Britain gain Canada through the Seven Years' War, "We may extend our settlements into new provinces . . . cross the continent to the pacific ocean."[102]

Franklin and Stiles had originally spoken of the colonies' growth as aggrandizing the empire as a whole. But for other, increasingly radical members of the Revolutionary generation, changing understandings of demography, climate, race, and global geography provided politically and emotionally useful science. Patriotic speakers rallied people to their cause with population projections. In 1774, Pastor Samuel Williams of Massachusetts plied a crowd with claims of an American past that foreshadowed a destiny: "So amazingly rapid has been our growth in a century and an half, we are become more than three millions of inhabitants. The period of doubling in these colonies, is not more than 25 years." Building on this theme, the physician and politician David Ramsay of Charleston claimed, "Where land is easily and cheaply obtained, the natural increase of people will exceed all European calculations."[103] If colonists could defend themselves against British tyranny, Americans could experience the "biggest part of that liberty and freedom that yet remains, or is to be expected, among mankind." In short, the "perfection and happiness of mankind" rested in their hands.[104]

Supporting such a future was the nature of the American continent. Embracing continental rather than latitudinal determinism, Williams pointed to "that vast extent of country which reaches from Labrador to Florida." Here could be found "a climate adapted to health, vigour, industry, liberty, genius, and happiness." The continent "never fails to give the labourer what neither Europe nor Asia will afford him, a comfortable support for the wages of his work." He pleaded with his listeners that, if they were "Americans any more than by name," they must struggle for their "country."[105]

AS Revolutionary patriotism gained sustenance from scientific claims, patriots hoped that their success would, in turn, advance scientific discovery. For David Ramsay, American independence would lend advantages in discerning nature's laws. In a 1778 speech celebrating the struggle of the United States for independence, Ramsay noted, "Little has been hitherto done towards compleating the natural history of America." Indicating that when he referred to "America," he meant in the broadest continental taxonomy prevalent at the time, he added, "Our Independence will redeem one quarter of the globe from tyranny and oppression, and consecrate it the chosen seat of Truth, Justice, Freedom, Learning and Religion." Thinking of Europeans beyond America's shores, Ramsay reminded readers that the "extent of territory westward, is sufficient to accommodate with land, thousands and millions of the virtuous peasants, who now groan beneath tyranny and oppression in three quarters of the globe." Under these new circumstances, free from constraints imposed by Britain or other European nations, the "Book of Nature" could be read: "The face of our country, intersected by rivers, or covered by woods and swamps, gives ample scope for the improvement of mechanicks, mathematicks, and natural philosophy."[106]

The truth that Ramsay and other patriots sought would put to an end the dispute of the New World. As a French traveler who was a friend to the Revolutionary cause explained, "America will render herself illustrious by the sciences. . . . The extent of her empire submits to her a large portion of heaven and earth. . . . Natural history and astronomy are her peculiar appendages." The patriots' vitriolic scientific rhetoric rested on an affinity for the land and strongly countered the aspersions of Georges-Louis Leclerc, Comte de Buffon. These North Americans, far from degenerating, would outdo the greatest scientists of Europe. They cared deeply about science as both its objects and its students. Indeed, this dual role led many to believe that they stood in the best position to expand the boundaries of scientific knowledge. Success in the Revolution would bring peace and "cause science once more to bloom, and the light of truth to rise with fresh lustre on the land."[107]

Geographic presumptions, racial constructions, and demographic projections had made the Revolution conceivable. Now, many thought, the Revolution would cause intellectual trends to accelerate. Arguably, they were right, as Thomas Jefferson wrote much of his *Notes on the State of Virginia* (1785)—the strongest rebuttal to Buffonian formulations to come out of the former British colonies—in the war's waning years, and he finished it shortly after he assumed Benjamin Franklin's role as the most famous U.S. citizen living in France.

CHAPTER 2

THE GEOPOLITICAL
CONTINENT, 1713–1763

Few, if any, American scientists in the past two hundred years have attained the international renown enjoyed by Benjamin Franklin in the eighteenth century. Yet Franklin was much more than a scientist, and his unfaltering commitment to public service garnered him as much celebrity as his intellectual pursuits. At forty-two, he gave up his successful printing business to sit on the Philadelphia City Council. Five years later, he assumed royal office as the deputy postmaster-general for North America. After that, he spent most of his time before the American Revolution in England, where he unsuccessfully lobbied to change Pennsylvania from a proprietary colony to one with a royal charter. He returned to the American colonies in 1775, a fervent patriot, saddened by his perception that British policymakers had blundered the empire to the precipice of a fratricidal war. Then he sailed almost immediately back to Europe, where, in France, he won the admiration of the cream of society, successfully negotiated an alliance, and helped shape the peace treaty that created the United States.

Franklin had devoted much of his public life before the Revolution to defining and defending North America as an integral part of the British Empire. Whether coming from the perspective of an Anglo-American, a Pennsylvanian, or a Briton, Franklin had many worries about the possible trajectories his continent might take. In the early 1750s, he was fearful that the growing German and African populations would somehow taint the cultural and racial purity of the colonies. By the middle of the decade, the threat of French and Indian attacks made him fret that the British colonies might not have any future at all. And by the 1760s, imperial reforms forced him to defend the political status of the colonists as coequals with inhabitants of the home country.

When defending his vision of the colonies, Franklin proved a master rhetorician. He constructed images and metaphors on a variety of scales to

FIGURE 12. "JOIN, or DIE," *Pennsylvania Gazette,* May 9, 1754. Courtesy Library of Congress, Prints and Photographs Division (LC-USZC4–5315)

illuminate the plights British North Americans faced. He asked readers to assume a celestial position and imagine how North America might reflect a brighter light toward inhabitants of Mars and Venus if settled by more Britons. To drive home the fate the French and their Indian allies presented to the colonies, he drew people to ground level with the image of a severed snake symbolizing the lack of unity among the colonies. Without unity, the far larger English population would not be able to resist an enemy it outnumbered thirty to one. Its fate would be the same as that of the snake, so the colonists must "JOIN, or DIE" (fig. 12). The snake image was pregnant with the potential of American independence, and after the Stamp Act raised taxes, a move decried by colonists as a violation of their rights, the image took on a life of its own as radical elements of the American resistance movement appropriated it and gave it seditious overtones. Franklin, still ever the patriotic and politically moderate Briton, countered with a new image of the colonies as limbs severed from a British body. "MAGNA Britannia: Her Colonies REDUC'D" suggested that, unlike a snake, the colonies could not survive detached from the empire, and in turn, the empire could not survive the loss of its colonies (fig. 13).[1]

Franklin and others frequently and consciously manipulated emblems

FIGURE 13. Benjamin Franklin, "MAGNA Britannia: Her Colonies REDUC'D" (c. 1766). Courtesy Library of Congress, Rare Book and Special Collections Division

and metaphors of American community to serve their political aims. Images and metaphors took on partisan overtones as weapons whose provenance could easily be traced. The North American colonies appeared in the guise of any number of animals, an Indian, or a child. But when done, the artificiality of the construct was obvious, for as persuasive as such images could be, North America was simply not a snake, a Mohawk, or a young boy. Presumably, it was a continent. Political debates, even when carried out with figurative representations, often swirled around the question of what exactly that meant geopolitically.

Over the first half of the eighteenth century, a geopolitical vision, anchored in the intellectual trends and modes of thought traced in the last chapter, guided the behavior of many British statesmen and colonists. As the colonies' population and economic and strategic importance grew, policymakers and theorists thought increasingly about how to better incorporate them into the empire. War with France, Indians, and, to a lesser extent, Spain, whether threatened or real, made security a central element in the resulting formulations. Assumptions about continents, and corollary notions about demography and race, made it necessary to drive others out of North America. Bit by bit, statesmen and colonists began to perceive Britain's littoral American colonies as part of a coherent whole. Such geopolitical logic and the unprecedented success of Britain in the Seven Years' War created a precondition for the American Revolution. Many mainland colonists came to see themselves as part of an embryonic but inevitably continental society, a distinct part of the British Empire capable of flourishing on its own.

UNITY, SECURITY, AND CARTOGRAPHIC CONTESTS

As metageographical notions of a coherent North American environment emerged, a number of British policymakers and colonists began to assess the potential of a commensurate political unity among the mainland colonies. These visions of continental unity developed slowly and departed drastically from the modest beginnings of the colonies in the seventeenth century. In fits and spurts, security concerns, more than anything else, gave metageographical constructs credence in political affairs. Still, the road toward conceptualizing a continental community—even vaguely—remained incomplete until the eve of the Seven Years' War.

Only fledgling seeds of grandeur can be found in the colonial charters. Those of Virginia and Massachusetts created two distant outposts by granting lands in North America between set latitudes. The original legal legitimacy of such claims rested largely on the theory that the English king, as head of the Church of England, had the power to authorize Christian subjects to enter the lands of infidels to facilitate the work of missionaries. Accordingly, early charters acknowledged the presence of the Spanish and French to the south and north, respectively, and prohibited colonists from settling areas "possessed by any Christian Prince or People."[2]

These distant settlements, then, were semiautonomous plantations founded by entrepreneurs and rightly seen as just some of the many footholds European nations had in the Americas. In the case of the New England charter of 1620, the narrow swath of land represented a "continent" but only in the narrow sense of the word sometimes employed by seventeenth-century geographers, wherein France, Spain, and Germany could also be continents. These grants nominally comprised lands that extended from "sea to sea," but such claims signified geographic ignorance as much as realistic intentions to settle a continent-wide band of territory.[3]

Under the seventeenth-century charters, the constitutional relationship between the crown and colony varied from case to case. Unions among colonies were, at most, ephemeral and local. The most famous, the New England Confederation, for example, provided for protection and harmony among the Puritan colonies and Rhode Island but had no role beyond New

England or after King Philip's War. As the colonies grew in population and economic importance, however, they gained strategic value, drawing more attention from policymakers who pondered the possibility and utility of colonial union. Between the Glorious Revolution and the Seven Years' War, a number of Englishmen on both sides of the Atlantic, including Pennsylvania's proprietor, William Penn; the economist Charles D'Avenant; the planter-historian Robert Beverley; and the Board of Trade member Martin Bladen, proposed plans of colonial union to improve economic regulation, military defense, and political control, especially over wayward proprietary and charter colonies.[4]

The desirability of union usually correlated with perceptions of French encroachments or the fear of war. At the same time, practical obstacles and fears that union might lead to colonial independence always made many dismiss it. The colonies had only irregular intercourse with one another along the coast and arguably had stronger commercial ties with Europe, Britain, and the West Indies than with one another. Politically, the colonies ordinarily operated independently from one another and were usually more absorbed by internal debates than relations with other colonies. Provincial separatism reigned supreme within the assemblies, while a handful of influential colonists and British officials' pleas for unity fell on deaf ears.[5]

Though unable to obtain formal unity among the colonies, apparent French encroachments led British officials to conceive of a continuous frontier, from Nova Scotia south to the Carolinas, at least as early as 1721. In South Carolina, Britain's claim to western regions hinged only on a fledgling Indian trade and portrayals on paper. Thomas Nairne's 1711 map of the region served both to alarm British policymakers about a lurking French, Indian, and Spanish presence and to assert British territorial claims (fig. 14). The fragility of Britain's position became all the more apparent in 1715, when Yamasee warriors attacked South Carolina, nearly destroying the colony. Further undercutting British claims, Guillaume Delisle, in his highly influential *Carte de la Louisiane* (1718), restricted "Caroline" to the eastern side of the Appalachians and asserted that the region was originally colonized by the French and named after Charles IX (fig. 15).

Delisle's map also alarmed colonists farther north. William Byrd II of Virginia fretted in a letter to Charles Boyle, fourth Earl of Orrery, that the French along the Mississippi might endanger the English colonies by capturing the support of the Iroquois and Cherokees. New York's Governor William Burnet wrote to the Lords of Trade in 1720, noting that "the last Mapps published at Paris . . . are making new encroachments." The French appeared to be claiming not only Carolina but "about 50 leagues all along

FIGURE 14. Thomas Nairne's map of southeastern North America as it appeared in an inset to Edward Crisp, *A Compleat Description of the Province of Carolina in 3 Parts* (1711). Courtesy Library of Congress, Geography and Map Division

the edge of Pensilvania & this Province."[6] By this time, Herman Moll had already raised alarms on his maps. His 1719 map of the world had depicted British charter claims stretching from sea to sea. Then, on *A New Map of the North Parts of America* (1720), he left Delisle's boundaries "inserted on purpose" so that those "interested in our Plantations" could decide whether they constituted "Incroachments."

Fear of more wars with Indians, along with the threat of French incursions and slave revolts, led Virginia's government to encourage settlement in gaps along the Blue Ridge Mountains by white, Protestant yeomen. Realizing that all of the mainland colonies shared security threats, Britain's Board of Trade argued for the need to build on Virginia's work on a larger scale. In the short run, a series of fortifications along the mountains, along with zones of settlement, would serve the colonies' security interests well, but such measures would not suffice indefinitely. The board reported to the king that, "altho these mountains may serve at present for a very good frontier, we should not propose them for the boundary of your Majesty's Empire in America." Instead, the board's members hoped "that the British settlements might be extended beyond them and some small forts be erected on ye great lakes." One of the authors, Martin Bladen, subsequently suggested a central government for the colonies, which he hoped would both enhance their security and strengthen imperial control over them. As if these benefits were

FIGURE 15. Detail from Guillaume Delisle, *Carte de la Louisiane* (1718). Courtesy
Library of Congress, Geography and Map Division

not enough, he added that his plan would enable the colonies "to drive all
other European Nations out of the North Continent of America, if it
should become necessary to attempt it."[7]

Bladen's plan was never implemented, but a number of men in England
began to propose similar reforms. A group of philanthropists, including
Member of Parliament James Edward Oglethorpe, saw an opportunity to
assist England's urban poor by shipping them to the region between South
Carolina and Spanish Florida, where they could work their own farms. In
addition to redeeming the indolent, the plan would bolster the empire's
defense against the Spanish. To procure financial assistance from Parliament
and the crown, and to lure migrants, Oglethorpe offered a romanticized
cartographic vision. He produced a map portraying the scheme in an expan-

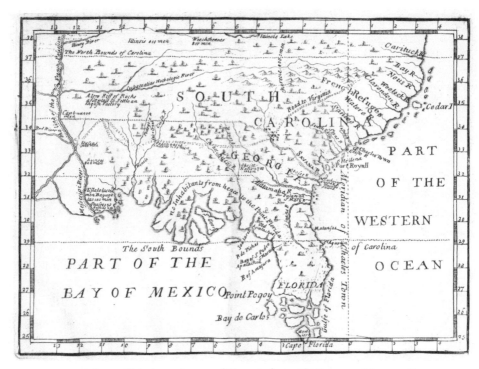

FIGURE 16. James Oglethorpe's map of Georgia (c. 1733). Courtesy Hargrett Rare Book and Manuscript Library, University of Georgia Libraries

sive and promising fashion, one that derived from Thomas Nairne's 1711 map of the southeast but that denied many of its geopolitical realities (fig. 16). Nairne had intended his map to provide a geopolitical overview of the region and serve as a warning of French encroachments in the interior. Accordingly, it included a number of inscriptions with estimates of available French, Indian, and Spanish fighting men; the positions of their forts, settlements, and trading posts; and routes taken by war parties. Oglethorpe conveniently eliminated this information from his promotional map. Spain vanished, despite its settlements in Florida and claims to regions as far north as Charleston. The French receded to the west side of the Mississippi, despite their settlements at Biloxi, Mobile, and New Orleans. In keeping with the proposed charter of Georgia and the existing one for South Carolina, dotted lines marked boundaries to these colonies extending beyond the Mississippi, to the edge of the map, and presumably to the Pacific.[8]

Notwithstanding Oglethorpe's geopolitical obfuscations, British policymakers found it increasingly difficult in the 1730s to ignore the French presence in North America. In 1726, the French had strengthened their claim to the Great Lakes, building Fort Niagara between lakes Ontario and Erie. Meanwhile, they continued constructing massive fortifications at Fort Louisbourg on Cape Breton Island, in the Gulf of St. Lawrence. Louisbourg cost 4 million livres to build, enough for King Louis XV to quip that its streets must be paved with gold. Massive stone walls and garrisons that eventually held thousands of soldiers made it appear a formidable barrier to any British assault on New France via the St. Lawrence River. Future wars would demonstrate Louisbourg's vulnerability and show that the geography of Quebec made it the superior stronghold guarding New France, but for nearly a quarter-century, the French and nervous New Englanders touted Louisbourg as an American Gibraltar, France's "key to America." Further inland, a fort at Crown Point, on Lake Champlain, helped guard the river from the south. Looking westward, the French also built forts on the shore of Lake of the Woods and the Red River near Lake Winnipeg.[9]

These French actions, and the British urge to respond, help explain the creation of Henry Popple's popular *Map of the British Empire in America* (London, 1733) (fig. 17). Popple's brother was the secretary of the Board of Trade, and Popple himself served on the board briefly in 1727, a time when it was busy responding to the French construction of Fort Niagara. The board commissioned the map with the hope of staking out an aggressive position in North America. Paper claims would have to substitute for formal occupation. In turning to Popple, the board found a man who valued cartographic ammunition as a way to forestall French and Spanish expansion.

As the first large-scale British map of North America, Popple's work grandly embodied Britain's desire to control more western lands. Printed using twenty copper sheets to imprint white paper with black ink and then sold in atlas format, the map measured seven feet and ten inches by seven feet and six inches when assembled. Often publishers applied watercolors by hand to the map according to the scheme "*Green—Indian Countrys. Red—English. Yellow—Spanish. Blue—French. Purple—Dutch.*"[10] Refusing to acknowledge France's and Spain's claims to vast swaths of territory, most publishers used blue and yellow minimally. Typically, the French received only narrow and unconnected stretches along the western bank of the Mississippi River; coastal Louisiana; the St. Lawrence River; and St. John's, Cape Breton, and Anticoste islands. Meanwhile, English red usually figured prominently all of the way from the Atlantic coast to the crest of the Appalachians and the southern edge of the St. Lawrence, even though British colonists had settled much of the area only thinly and unevenly. Shooting westward, straight across the blue, green, and yellow shadings, red

FIGURE 17. Henry Popple, *A Map of the British Empire in America* (1733). Library of Virginia

lines asserted colonial charter claims stretching to the Pacific, while other European colonies appeared as meager "settlements."[11]

The map's popularity surged with the outbreak of the Anglo-Spanish War (1739–44), sometimes known as the War of Jenkins' Ear, and the subsequent entrance of France into the conflict as part of King George's War (1744–48). Britain's declaration of war against Spain was the latest chapter in Albion's pursuit of Spanish silver and East Indian riches. Policymakers coveted key Spanish American territories, such as Darien at the Isthmus of Panama, Havana, Portobello, and Cartagena, a fortified harbor in present-day Colombia that sheltered bullion-filled galleons en route from Panama to Spain. The Caribbean proved an active theater in the conflict, and Britain sailed roughly 3,500 mainland colonists there to fight. More than half of them succumbed to Spanish defenses and tropical diseases in a dismal attempt to take Cartagena. Once France declared war, Britain left the colonists to defend themselves against French and Indian attacks on New England's frontier settlements. Unwilling to accept such attacks idly, four thousand New England soldiers, with the help of a British naval squadron, successfully laid siege to the French stronghold at Louisbourg in 1745. For all of their sacrifice at Cartagena and their success at Louisbourg, however, the colonists saw no improvement to their geopolitical situation; war with Spain ended in stalemate, and Britain returned Louisbourg to the French in order to retain territories in India.

The shadings on Popple's map thus remained the same, an irritant to colonists who felt their efforts marginalized. Such was true even in Pennsylvania, where the Quaker-dominated Assembly, to Benjamin Franklin's chagrin, had refused the Massachusetts governor's request for men and money for the assault on Louisbourg. As a clerk in the Assembly in 1746, Franklin requested that a friend in England send two sets of Popple's map—one to be hung in the Assembly (John Adams mentioned thirty years later seeing such a map in the Pennsylvania State House; he was impressed by its size but complained that it was "not very accurate"). When Franklin ordered the maps, he added, "There must be some other large Map of the World, or of Asia, or Africa, or Europe, of equal size with Popple's to match it; they being to be hung, one on each side the door in the Assembly Room."[12] Franklin had supported the New England expedition against Louisbourg as necessary to the defense of all British American colonies. Now he gave Assembly members a visual reminder of Pennsylvania's place in the larger world. Popple's map, suggesting Britain as the preeminent power on the continent but one that faced threats, argued for the interconnected fates of all the North American colonies, including the one dominated by Philadelphia's pacifist Quakers. Reminding the Assembly just how much was at stake, a large map of the world or its parts situated Popple's North America in broad metageographical context. The Assembly could not easily take a pacific, insular attitude with the fate of entire continent to be determined.

Franklin's jab at the Pennsylvania Assembly represented only one of his many attempts to convince others of North America's importance to the empire. He found help in members of an informal cohort steeped in political reform and natural science. In the 1740s and 1750s, a number of men from New England to South Carolina—William Douglass, John Bartram,

Cadwallader Colden, Lewis Evans, Archibald Kennedy, John Mitchell, and Henry McCulloh, to name a handful—produced a slew of tracts to educate their countrymen on both sides of the Atlantic about North American botany, geography, demography, history, Indian affairs, and economics. Disproportionately represented in these writings were the voices of well-educated Scots, the American voice of the Scottish Enlightenment. In the aftermath of the Anglo-Scottish Union of 1707, many Scots had migrated to North America, where they found a provincial culture that, like that of their homeland, was often scorned by the English. They also found a far more fluid social structure, with far more opportunities in science and politics, than at home. They took advantage of these avenues to present an imperial vision that countered the perception of both Scots and Americans as the degenerate and inferior stepchildren of the empire. Celebrations of the importance of the colonies to Britain and calls to incorporate them more fully within the British Empire permeated their tracts.[13]

In celebrating the progress of the colonies, these writers also argued for their strong defense. The Scottish-born physician William Douglass of Boston presented the most noteworthy effort. His magisterial first volume of *Summary, Historical and Political, of the First Planting, Progressive Improvements, and Present State of the British Settlements in North-America* (1749) appeared in the immediate aftermath of King George's War, when Douglass was likely unaware of the formal peace at Aix-la-Chapelle. Douglass's formula for a lasting peace was simple. The French, he argued, would continue to disrupt North America, just as they did Europe, until "fenced off from us by ditches and walls, that is, by great rivers and impracticable Mountains." Douglass lacked the long-term, prophetic vision of Franklin, who would soon predict that the colonial population would double every twenty years, and instead sought remedies to immediate problems. Although Britain had a right to all of North America by virtue of "discoveries and conquests," it was "not capable of settling inland countries in a short time." If it tried to claim more than it could "well improve and protect," Britain would overstretch itself like the "Phoenicians, Greeks, Venetians, Genoese, &c.," who had had "colonies in sundry places, but for want of people sufficient to maintain these possessions, they soon vanished."[14]

Like Bladen's blueprint for union, Douglass's prescription for colonial defense represented a geopolitical vision on the road toward conceptualizing Britain's mainland colonies as a continental society. Though a relatively small population meant that the society's boundaries could not yet be coterminous with the continent, he saw the need to treat the disparate colonies as part of a coherent whole, and he wished for policies that would draw them more tightly and prominently into Britain's imperial orbit. Boundaries with foreign powers needed to follow nature's dictates; colonial governments needed to be made uniform; and the colonial population needed to grow, but slowly and cautiously, since Great Britain had a smaller population than competing European powers. Instead of rapid settlement by Britons, the colonies might rely on the naturalization of foreigners. Fruitful Europeans could help Britain secure and expand its American possessions. Yet the naturalization of foreigners also presented a perilous path, as shown by Pennsylvania's sizeable German population, which had established "large separate districts," where for generations they might retain their "Language, Modes of Religion, Customs and Manners." Instead, foreigners "ought to be intermixed with the British settlers" and required to learn English.[15]

Douglass envisioned an American population that, if carefully nurtured, would become fully British yet remain distinctively American. Meanwhile, existing policies fell short. Britain had undercut its efforts to grow the colonies by simultaneously rounding up their men as enlisted soldiers and impressed sailors to serve far from home. Making matters worse, "Whites, Natives of America, do not well bear Transplantation." New Englanders in military expeditions to the Caribbean and even relatively nearby Louisbourg suffered horrendous casualty rates, and those who survived "came home with a habit of idleness, and generally consumed more than they earned, and consequently were worse than dead."[16] The new native Americans' bodies, whether the children of British or of naturalized European immigrants, had acclimated to their homeland, warned the Scottish American physician; prudent political policy demanded recognition of this fact.

When Douglass wrote, the idea of some sort of unity among the mainland colonies to enhance their security was on the ascendance, and Douglass himself thought it would be useful "to reduce them to some general Uniformity."[17] Yet too many forces still conspired to prevent the goal from approaching reality. Nevertheless, the totalizing classification of continental taxonomies had led many to think of imperial rivalries in metageographical terms and to conceive of the colonies as a coherent unit.

In his influential interpretation of early nationalism in the Americas, Benedict Anderson notes that, whereas thirteen British colonies came together to form the United States, the Spanish American empire rapidly split into eighteen separate states. To explain these diverging paths, he points, in part, to a geography that made communication among the Spanish colonies difficult. In contrast, the "original Thirteen Colonies" of the North American mainland benefited from their compact settlement and the interconnection of their urban market centers. "The total area of the Thirteen Colonies was 322,497 square miles. That of Venezuela was 352,143; of Argentina, 1,072,067; and of Spanish South America, 3,417,625 square miles," Anderson asserts with remarkable precision and without explanation.[18]

Although perhaps close to true, Britain's mainland colonists, with sea-to-sea charters in hand, would have disputed these figures, even if they could not offer precise alternatives. Their mental map of the world rested not simply on actual maps, such as Oglethorpe's and Popple's, but also on a half-century's worth of publications, public discourses, private conversations, imperial ambitions, and pressures from foes. These had, by a process akin to alchemy, begun to give the inhabitants of limited seaboard territories a continental consciousness. Colonists had the conceptual grammar to appropriate the continent if only it could overcome their countervailing language of provincialism. The continent could fall under the rule of one power, and many began to think it inevitably would.

A WAR FOR A CONTINENT

By midcentury, Britons' visions of a unified North America heightened their alarm at French actions. The Treaty of Aix-la-Chapelle (1748) that ended King George's War did not bring lasting peace between France and Britain. Instead, it set the stage for more conflict. The two powers soon began to contest the Ohio country in a dispute magnified by the weakening of the Iroquois Confederacy's influence over the region in the 1730s and 1740s.[19] By 1754, the ominous sense that it might be necessary to combat the French again and cries that British colonial disunity might prove fatal reached a fever pitch. Newspapers printed and reprinted governors' alarms of an imminent threat. Jonathan Belcher of New Jersey warned, based on letters from Massachusetts and New York, that the French "seem to be laying Schemes for a general Destruction and Ruin of the English Provinces on this Continent." North Carolina's Governor Arthur Dobbs—not far removed from his quest for a Northwest Passage—laid before his Assembly the details of the "Grand Plan of France, to ruin and distress all the British Colonies on this Continent."[20]

Periodicals similarly predicted that, if the French could secure a line stretching from the St. Lawrence River and down the Mississippi, they would be able to sever communication between the English colonies and Indians of the "inland Countries." Then, with the assistance of Indians, the French would have little trouble when they decided to attack the English colonies and "drive the Inhabitants into the Sea." The possibility endangered not just colonies on the empire's margins. Instead, the whole British Empire would suffer as it lost the American market for manufactured goods and the source of so many of the empire's raw materials. The mainland colonies' demise meant "our Merchants will be ruined, our Customs and Funds will sink, our Manufactures will want Vent, our Lands will fall in Value, and, instead of decreasing, our Debts will increase, without the least Prospect of the Nation's emerging."[21]

Because of North America's imagined geography, many colonists and policymakers in Britain viewed any war with France as one to decide which king would reign as "Master of North America."[22] The governor of Massachusetts said that once one realized the French were "Masters of the entire Water Communication throughout the whole Country," it would be clear "how firmly they hold the Command of the Continent."[23] Another writer admonished readers that the French would not rest until they had "stretched their Arms from one Sea even unto the other."[24] In one of his typically firebrand sermons, Jonathan Mayhew of Boston found the British colonies rapidly "encompassed by the French.... The Continent is not wide enough for us both; and they are resolv'd to have the Whole." John Mitchell, a Virginian living in England, saw at stake not just a strip of colonies along the coast, but "more than all Europe put together.... The result of this contest in America between the two nations must surely be, to gain a power and dominion, that must sooner or later command all that continent, with the whole trade of it, if not many other branches of trade."[25] Even more shrilly, one periodical argued that Britain's loss of its American possessions would be an "event of the most tremendous consequence to us,—to the Protestant religion in general,—to the peace of Europe, and even to the peace and happiness of all mankind."[26]

With the colonies seemingly the first teetering domino in the collapse of the entire British Empire, calls for unified and decisive action grew louder. In the past, the colonies had frittered opportunities away, "lopping off branches, when the axe should have been laid to the root of the tree." Now, "Canada must be demolished, or our colonies are undone."[27] Governor Arthur Dobbs expressed a common fear when he explained that it would not matter "that we outnumber the French colonies upon this Continent by above Forty to One."[28] Governor James Glen of South Carolina, too, pleaded for unity in a letter dated March 1754 to Virginia's Governor Robert Dinwiddie. He explained that the French recognized the "Superior Strength of the English Colonies on the Continent," but "they have too good Reason to consider us a Rope of Sand, loose and inconnected."[29] Dinwiddie, in turn, wrote to Pennsylvania Governor James Hamilton, concerned that if the French "are allow'd a peaceable Settlemt on the Ohio, I think the Consequence . . . will be Destruction to all our Settlemts on the

Continent."[30] It would be Dinwiddie who commissioned a young George Washington to confront the French threat.

THE epochal war broke with an ugly skirmish in an Allegheny glen on May 28, 1754. None of those involved—the Virginia troops under an inexperienced Major George Washington, the Iroquois loyal to the "Half King" Tanaghrisson, or the French diplomatic party led by Joseph Coulon de Villiers de Jumonville—anticipated or intended that their actions of that day would commence a chain of events leading to the expulsion of the French from North America. Washington, falling prey both to his own ambition and to the machinations of Tanaghrisson, attacked the French delegation in a clear violation of European rules of war. Expecting retaliation, Washington and his men retreated behind the poorly constructed, yet aptly named, Fort Necessity, where attacks forced their surrender on July 4, 1754.[31]

Meanwhile, the usual factionalism flourished between and within colonies. Virginia pleaded with Pennsylvania for assistance against the French, only to see Pennsylvania's pacifist-dominated Assembly vote, contrary to advice from a committee led by Benjamin Franklin, that the French presence did not violate Pennsylvania's boundaries.[32] Beginning in mid-June, representatives from the Iroquois Confederacy and seven English colonies—New York, New Hampshire, Massachusetts, Rhode Island, Connecticut, Pennsylvania, and Maryland—met at Albany, New York, to resolve differences over trade and land policies and to develop a plan to thwart French expansion. Although the Board of Trade in Britain had ordered the congress, the conflicting interests of the colonies and their internal factionalism prevented it from achieving many of its goals. But the colonial representatives did agree on some issues, such as increasing fortifications against the French, establishing a single superintendent of Indian affairs, and sanctioning greater royal control of future Indian land acquisitions.

More famously, however, Benjamin Franklin, representing Pennsylvania, ushered through the congress a proposal for colonial union. Under this plan, responsibility for the colonies' military defense would fall under the jurisdiction of a council of representatives elected by the colonial assemblies and a president appointed by the crown. Thomas Pownall, who attended the congress as a "stander-by," wrote that Washington's defeat at Fort Necessity "comes seasonably to convince the several assemblies of the necessity of their doing something."[33] Yet the colonial assemblies did not heed the call, and they rejected the "Albany Plan of Union." Though never implemented, the Albany Plan demonstrated an ongoing conceptual shift away from the traditional order, wherein colonies were distinct, independent dominions. The Albany Plan would have implemented a layer of authority between the crown and the colonies, making them a coherent unit with a well-defined relationship to the larger empire. As such, it would have created what many were already describing as a continental dominion instead of collection of disparate settlements.[34]

In support of their Plan of Union, the congressional representatives penned a "Representation of the Present State of the Colonies," and Franklin crafted his severed snake in "JOIN, or DIE." The image would, in the long run, become an icon of British North American culture, but the written text provides far greater insight into how the contours of a potential union looked to the delegates. It delineated existing British claims in North America and echoed fears that "the Whole Continent" might come under French control. Union would help address the immediate threat. But the document also suggested a long-range, geopolitical vision wherein "the Bounds of those Colonys which extend to the South Sea, be Contracted, and limitted by the Alleghenny or Apalachian mountains." The representatives did not call for a retreat behind these ranges because they constituted the natural boundary of the newly proposed union; rather, the representatives argued that "measures be taken for settling from time to time Colonies of His Majesty's Protestant Subjects, Westward of said Mountains in Convenient Cantons to be Assigned for that purpose." Continental expansion needed better regulation, not cessation.[35]

Successful regulation required recognized authority, something Britain's North American colonies lacked on a continental level. Factions existed before the late 1750s, and the pressures of war exacerbated them. The war also revealed cultural differences among the provincial military units, British regulars, and Indians. With suicidal results, General Edward Braddock was the first British commander to disdain potential Indian allies as he marched his forces on Fort Duquesne and headlong into an ambush in 1755.[36] Others followed suit, with results that were not much better. John Campbell, fourth Earl of Loudoun, wielded unprecedented power as commander-in-chief in North America, and he worked to implement a de facto military union the likes of which the colonial assemblies had rejected just two years earlier. Local officials and assemblies throughout the colonies refused quarters for Loudoun's troops, leading him to take them by force. Provincial leaders also resisted demands for joint operations between local troops and British regulars. Loudoun treated colonials as inferiors and resented that they did not see themselves as such. Assemblies also hesitated and sometimes refused to allocate funds for a war with France for a variety of reasons, ranging from

FIGURE 18. Johann Sebastian Müller's untitled frontispiece to the *London Magazine* (1758). Courtesy Library Company of Philadelphia

internal squabbles and fear of internal slave rebellion to simple intransigence toward anybody who encroached on their power and heavy-handedly demanded money, such as Loudoun.[37]

In 1757, recognizing the need to shift course and put into a position to do so by British military defeats and political winds, William Pitt, secretary of state for the Southern Department and the king's leading minister, made the conquest of New France Britain's central military aim in the Seven Years' War. British public opinion had been clamoring for the expulsion of the French from North America.[38] Now policymakers had concluded that control of the continent would secure the colonies and advance the empire's interests as a whole. The colonies found themselves treated more like imperial partners than subordinate dominions in the British Empire. Pitt's ministry subsidized provincial troops instead of coercing their assemblies to pay for them, and it stripped Loudoun's successors of much of their authority over civil officials in the colonies.[39]

The new military strategy bore fruit almost immediately. The British defeated the French at Fort Frontenac, on Lake Ontario, in July 1758, and at Louisbourg in the Gulf of St. Lawrence the following month. They had sandwiched the remaining French strongholds on the St. Lawrence— Montreal and Quebec—leaving them with little likelihood of reinforcement. The *London Magazine*'s frontispiece reflected the public's satisfaction with the year's events (fig. 18). A female figure representing Clio, the muse of history, stood with a scroll in hand recording the dates of British victories. Explaining events to her was Father Time, who had laid down his scythe to show her what Britain could reasonably expect. He wrapped his arms around a globe to show North America, including parts currently claimed by France and Spain. Reality now bore greater resemblance to the rhetoric of colonists who claimed that a war with France would be one for a continent.[40]

DEFENDING CONTINENTAL CLAIMS

As colonists became enmeshed in war, they increasingly employed metageographical categories to suggest the new world they hoped it would make. In all of the 7,096 imprints published in British North America between 1640 and 1754, the phrase "North America" appeared in only ten titles. (Two of these were the two volumes of William Douglass's prescient work in 1749.) In 1755 alone, however, nine titles bore the phrase "North America," and it appeared in the title of twenty-nine more publications before the end of the Seven Years' War. Similarly, the word "continent" appeared in only two titles published before 1755. The year 1755 saw four works with "continent" in the title, out of 279 total publications.[41] War led publishers to cover less provincial topics and seek a broad intercolonial readership interested in affairs from a hemispheric perspective. Magazines appeared for "Americans." The *American Magazine or Monthly Chronicle* (Philadelphia, 1757–58) and the *New American Magazine* (Woodbridge, N.J., 1758–60), though short-lived, captured a heightened and expansive spatial consciousness. There would not be as many "American"—referring both to place of publication and the inclusion of the term in the title— magazines again until the 1780s.

Almanacs paralleled this trend and became less provincial, even if they never sold beyond the local markets in which printers laid their type. Such almanacs might tout that they could "serve from Newfoundland to South Carolina," contain "tables . . . shewing the Distances of most of all the Places of Note on the Continent," or include a "curious prophecy . . . concerning Asia, Africa, Europe, and America."[42] A number of ostensibly continental almanacs, such as the *North American Almanac, The Continental Almanac,* and *The American Almanac,* undoubtedly expanded ordinary readers' conceptions of space and fueled their feeling of belonging to the continent they were fighting for. *The Universal American Almanack* for 1761 might claim to be accurate only for "all the northern provinces," but it included an appendix "shewing the exact Situation of all the CITIES, TOWNS, PORTS, FORTS, & c. in the known WORLD."[43]

Through such works, ordinary people—who, as Franklin quipped, "bought scarce any other books"—learned the same geographical taxonomies as their wealthier countrymen who purchased expensive atlases and geographies and read literary magazines. Like atlases and geographies, almanacs could be notoriously inconsistent in their taxonomies. The *Universal American Almanack* included a table that listed towns and then the "Provinces," "Countries," and "Quarters" in which they lay. Complicating matters—or, at least, suggesting confusion on the part of the compiler of the table—was that the globe seemed to include five quarters. Cuzco, Peru, could be found in the "country" of "South" in the American quarter of the globe. "Carthagena" lay in the country of "Terra Firma" in the South American quarter of the globe. The continental taxonomies apparent in the works of the most learned geographers had trickled into the hands of ordinary people, replete with their slipperiness and imperfections.[44]

A closer examination of some of the writings published in the years leading up to and including the Seven Years' War confirms the influence of prevailing continental taxonomies on geopolitical understandings and arguments. The Albany congress had already suggested, at least in part, that "His Majesties Title to the Northern Continent of America, appears to be founded on the Discovery thereof first made, and the Possession thereof first taken in 1497 under a Commission from Henry the 7th. of England to Sebastian Cabot." Charters stretching "Westward from the Atlantic Ocean, to the South Sea" further supported this claim.[45] The outbreak of war gave birth to similar arguments, and even as the war raged, books and periodicals rushed to defend it by presenting its "history" in an exceptionally broad context. The motive lay largely in proving that Britain rightfully occupied all of North America, for these works almost invariably stretched back well beyond the outbreak of hostilities to the arrival of the earliest Europeans in the Americas. As was the case with the Albany delegates, these works pointed to John Cabot or his sons, the mariners who sailed on behalf of the English crown in 1497, as the continent's discoverers. Such an argument—that making landfall constituted "discovering" a continent—hinged partly on the assumption that the continent was a unified, natural phenomenon, a single and unique geographic entity. It did not matter that the first Europeans to set foot in the Americas did not see the land this way or that it took a long process to construct America mentally as the fourth quarter of the globe, the "New World," one continent, or two. By the 1750s, prevailing metageographies and geopolitical interests gave credence to a very usable past.[46]

The publisher and former postmaster of Boston, Ellis Huske, opened his *The Present State of North-America* (1755) by summarizing the "Discoveries, Rights and Possessions of Great Britain." Typically for his time and nationality, Huske declared, with his opening sentence, that the "Cabots, with other Subjects of the Crown of *England,* did in 1496 and 1497 discover and take possession of . . . all the *Eastern* Coast of *North-America from Cape Florida to the North Polar Circle,* for, and in the Name of, the Crown of *England.*" Meanwhile, Columbus "did not discover the *Islands* in the *Gulf of Mexico* till 1498." It did not matter to Huske that the Cabots barely traveled south along the coast, much less anywhere near "Cape Florida," or that they did not know about the existence of such a cape or of a North American continent. Anachronism prevailed, for he had assumed a continental taxonomy that suited him well. To bolster English claims, Huske pointed to charters extending "due West from the *Atlantic* to the *Pacific* Ocean." The accompanying map emblazoned the names of the colonies clear across the Mississippi and included a paragraph describing French encroachments. Finally, and only to reinforce his argument without dismissing the validity of claims based on discovery, Huske defended war with France based on that nation's violations of modest treaty rights, as he understood the distribution of territory in Peaces of Utrecht and Aix-la-Chapelle.[47]

Such accounts of the war and treatments of North American history in general conveyed a political vision of the future that hinged on geographic inventions of the relatively recent past.

With only minor variations, a number of periodicals would make similar claims. In these, Columbus lacked the heroic quality later attributed to him, and writers continually qualified his status as the first European to reach America. In 1758, one "History of the War in North-America" began by conceding that Columbus "discovered Hispaniola and Cuba . . . but the Cabots first found out the continent." Based on the Cabots' having made landfall on the mainland, the "History of the War" claimed that they discovered "the main continent of America from the S. lat. 40° in Patagonia . . . up as far as the arctic circle above Hudson's Straits." In doing so, they "actually took possession" of the entire "main land of America" for the crown. Sir Francis Drake's voyage of 1579 only enhanced English claims by reaching North America's Pacific coast and cementing the right of the crown to grant charters stretching from sea to sea.[48]

When *The New American Magazine* published "A Complete History of the *Northern Continent of America*" in 1758, Columbus fared no better. The editor, Judge Samuel Nevill, who had served as speaker of the New Jersey Assembly, presented the history to defend Britain's North American presence. Early English colonists, the story went, struggled to improve lands that North America's Indians had left wild, and such improvement would even benefit native peoples. In contrast, the Spaniards encountered South American Indians, who made far better use of their land, and proceeded out of greed to massacre millions under the false guise of spreading the gospel. Columbus, representing Spain, spearheaded atrocity; John Cabot, who first discovered the mainland on behalf of the English, instigated progress.[49]

Stereotypical portrayals of the other parts of the world presented the war for North America in equally stark terms. The author of an article "on the present Posture of Affairs" asked his readers to look "over this globe, to view the deplorable state of your fellow creatures." In Eastern Europe and parts of Germany, the "countrymen are all slaves to the gentlemen." Life only got worse in this global tour when it got to "Turky and other parts of Asia" where people lived "groaning under a race of monsters that disgrace their very shape; in a condition so completely miserable, that all I have mentioned above is nothing compared to it." His readers were blessed that they were so distant from such tyranny. British colonists possessed unsurpassed prosperity and freedoms. Chief among these was their ability to worship God according to their "own understandings and his revealed will." As if possession of such "happiness" were insufficient cause for celebration, the colonists were likely "the instruments of diffusing it over this vast continent, to the nations that sit in darkness and the shadow of Death." The continent "was given to us for propagating freedom, establishing useful arts and extending the kingdom of Jesus."[50] Should British forces prevail, North America was destined for an exceptional future.

Almanac readers, too, learned of North America's brilliant prospects juxtaposed to its immediate threats. Nathaniel Ames's highly popular almanac for 1758 marveled at North America's nature, especially, the "vast Lakes or Inland Seas which occupy so much Space to the West of us." Politically, however, it would take unified action to realize the potential such nature promised. The backing of British claims to vast interior regions had mistakenly and almost solely depended on the British having a larger colonial population than the French. Yet, quoting Sir Francis Bacon, Ames noted that "The Wolf careth not how many the Sheep be." Success demanded the unity of the colonies, "For whilst divided, the strength of the Inhabitants is broken like the petty Kingdoms of Africa." What mainland colonists needed was tight, centralized, political organization to manage the continent's defense. Ames reminded readers of the stakes: "Curious have observ'd, that the Progress of Humane Literature (like the Sun) is from the East to the West; . . . So Arts and Sciences will change the Face of Nature in their Tour from Hence over the Appalachian Mountains to the Western Ocean." British victory over the French would "drive the long! long! Night of Heathenish Darkness from America."[51]

Cartographers offered corresponding visual and propagandistic prophecies of a sea-to-sea empire. Maps made in London that showed North America's western coast usually included "New Albion." As the geographer Emmanuel Bowen explained to George II in his *An Accurate Map of North America* (1755), Sir Francis Drake spent five weeks in 1579 at a harbor at 38° 30' latitude on the Pacific coast. Thus, "With remarkable Form & Ceremony on a Free Surender of the natives," Drake "took possession of the Country for Queen Elizabeth." Bowen reissued versions of this map in 1763 and 1772 with the same note and still suggesting the possibility of a Northwest Passage linking the Atlantic to New Albion. The 1763 edition would hang prominently in the front parlor of the Virginia Governor's Palace. In 1755, mapmaker Thomas Jefferys also made clear that Drake had secured that region as New Albion. An annotation on his map *North America* (1755) suggested that Drake's actions, combined with sea-to-sea charters and Cabot's initial discovery, solidified English claims to most of North America. Visual images of charters stretching west to New Albion reached a large audience when Bowen's map of the world appeared in the *Gentleman's*

Magazine in December 1755 (fig. 9). The same map also imagined the straits as part of a Northwest Passage and rendered North America a manageable entity for British control.[52]

The most accurate and, arguably, the most important eighteenth-century map of North America (and, ironically, the one that negotiators eventually would use in the peace negotiations at the end of the American Revolution) brashly asserted Britain's expansive claims to a North American empire. John Mitchell created his *A Map of the British and French Dominions in North America* in 1755 to defend Britain in its conflicting claims with France (fig. 19). Printed with eight copper plates and measuring roughly six and a half feet by four and a half feet when assembled, Mitchell's work offered the most accurate, comprehensive, and detailed map of Britain's North American colonies to date—and one that was every bit as partisan as its contemporaries.

A Virginian, Mitchell had distinguished himself as a botanist, even corresponding with Linnaeus on occasion. He sailed to Britain in 1745 and was elected into the Royal Society two years later. In 1750, he drafted, without seeing much of the newest geographical information in the records of the Board of Trade and Plantations, a map that drew the board's attention and admiration such that the board requested he produce an official map with access to the best data available. "Undertaken with the Approbation and at the request of the Lords Commissioners for Trade and Plantations," as an inscription explained, Mitchell's map both informed viewers of the scope of the French threat and provided a response to it. Colonial boundaries ran west across the Mississippi and presumably to the Pacific. Annotations defended British claims by noting British settlements, forts, trading posts, and titles acquired from Indians. Typical of most maps of the era, Mitchell's work displayed uncertainty about the geography of the West. The Mississippi and Missouri rivers angled tantalizingly toward the northwest with unknown headwaters cleverly covered by an inset detailing Hudson Bay. Though North America's precise contours remained a mystery, France certainly challenged Britain's claim to dominate the landmass; Britain must mount a vigorous defense.[53]

CLAIMING THE SPOILS

That victory over France might put an entire continent under British control did not lead all statesmen and political theorists to welcome it as an unadulterated blessing. The continent's suitability for rule by one nation raised the issues of how well such a continent would fit within a larger empire, and how the continent would remain linked to the imperial center. Some Britons even began to debate whether they should seek to control North America or, instead, pursue more immediately lucrative territories. In the end, however, the debate resolved quickly. Beliefs concerning long-term security and economic prosperity prevailed, and presumptions about the continent shaped the peace.

Since the early seventeenth century, many had speculated that the colonies might someday become independent. British views on the matter were clouded by disparate, sometimes poorly developed theories of empire. Indeed, most British statesmen understood the empire, at least in part, through the simple metaphor of the family. British colonies were children of their mother country. "As in natural parentage," William Douglass analogized, "so infant-colonies, ought to be tenderly and filially used, without any suspicion or surmise of a future obstinate disobedience, desertion, or revolt." But as Douglass also implied, children expect different treatment as they mature, and many writers argued that when the colonies reached adulthood, they would demand and deserve treatment as independent equals.[54]

Some had held that the French presence in North America solidified colonists' dependence on the mother country; removing the French would eliminate the need for a protective parent. In 1732, the merchant, botanist, and judge James Logan of Pennsylvania, though critical of some aspects of Britain's policy toward its colonies, conceded that "while Canada is so near, they cannot rebel. . . . It will Probably be the true Interest of both Britain and France to have each other's Colonies on the Continent supported as the most Effective Check that could be thought of, to retain them on both sides in a sight of their duty."[55] The naturalist Peter Kalm reported hearing from a number of colonists that, in "thirty or fifty years," Britain's North American colonies "would be able to form a state by themselves entirely independent of Old England." Being "harassed by the French, these dangerous neighbors in times of war are sufficient to prevent the connection of the colonies with their mother country from being quite broken off."[56] Should the continent no longer be shared, the colonies would not need Britain's guardianship.

Britain might retain its guardian role over its colonies if it deliberately kept them disparate and disunited—small, immature children instead of a continentally united polity. Logan, for example, thought it Britain's "Natural Policy to keep the several Colonies under distinct and independant Commands, the more effectually to Secure them from a Revolt from the Crown."[57] Kalm went so far as to speculate that the king never earnestly sought "to expel the French from their possessions there; though it might have been done with little difficulty."[58] Many other theorists, statesmen, and pamphleteers resisted proposals of colonial union in the belief that disunion

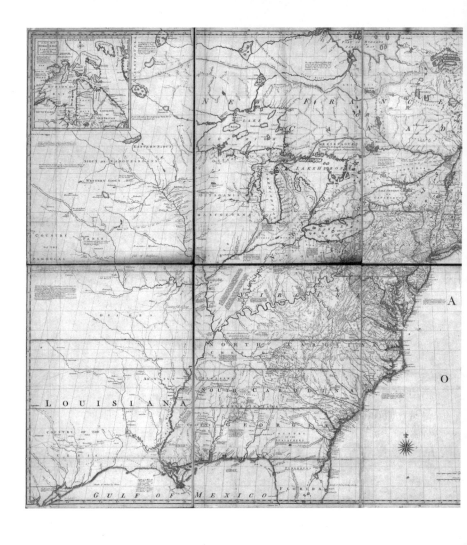

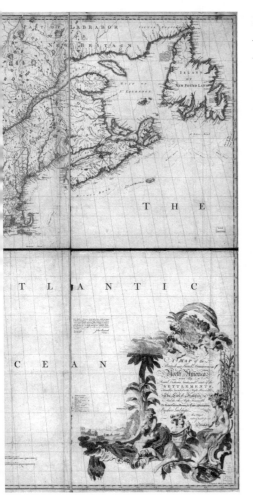

FIGURE 19. John Mitchell, *A Map of the British and French Dominions in North America* (1755). Courtesy Library of Congress, Geography and Map Division

helped maintain dependence on the mother country. The Albany Plan, for example, had prompted fears among some policymakers that it might tear the empire asunder by making the colonies virtually independent.[59]

BRITISH victories in 1759, particularly the defeat of French troops under Montcalm at Quebec and the decimation of French sea power in the Battle of Quiberon Bay off the western coast of France, made the war's end and British victory seem imminent. The battle for Quebec, in particular, became fodder for a legend seared into the memories of future generations of North Americans. Colonists had participated in attempts to take Quebec in past Anglo-French wars, but in 1759, victory finally, and improbably, came to British regulars. A sickly General James Wolfe led British forces into a siege of the city. Unable to draw the French leader into battle, Wolfe ordered a campaign of absolute terror against the countryside. As reported by a subordinate, Wolfe "reduced Operations to . . . Skirmishing Cruelty and Devastation." June 1759 saw "War of the worst Shape" when Wolfe lashed out at the rural civilian population, destroying thousands of farms. As noted by one historian, "No one ever reckoned the numbers of rapes, scalpings, thefts, and casual murders perpetrated during this month of bloody horror."[60]

When terror proved insufficient, Wolfe gambled. Under cover of night, he sent troops up the St. Lawrence, where they amazingly scaled steep bluffs and massed on the Plains of Abraham on Quebec's vulnerable west side. Thunderstruck and in a desperate panic, Montcalm ordered French troops to meet the Redcoats head-on in open battle. Wolfe, in turn, ordered his troops to stand firm until French forces were within forty yards. An inaccurate French salvo from 125 yards wounded Wolfe in the wrist and felled a handful of his men, but as the attackers drew near, the French began to wither. When the British finally let loose their first volley, French soldiers ran. Redcoats advanced and mopped up French disarray on the way to victory. As they did so, Canadians and Indians took potshots at them, mortally wounding Wolfe, who died shortly after learning of his victory. His death, along with the British triumph, gave him life as the empire's greatest martyr and hero.[61]

By 1760, with victory in the larger war imminent, the British pondered the possible spoils. Scores of pamphlets, speeches, letters, and articles outlined competing visions of the postwar world.[62] Would taking Canada or the West Indian Island of Guadeloupe prove more valuable to the empire's prosperity and security? As British opinion coalesced, it favored the retention of Canada out of fear that a French presence on the continent would lead to further hostilities, and the resulting treaty erased French claims on the North American continent.[63] Whether or not the public debate leading up to the treaty affected the outcome is debatable, but one pamphlet in particular has value to historians as a window onto how at least one very prominent and highly influential North American envisioned the empire's future. In 1760, Benjamin Franklin published anonymously *The Interest of Great Britain Considered,* commonly known as the "Canada Pamphlet." Franklin wrote as an Englishman—and, indeed, he lived in England at the time—but his sentiments were clearly those of someone who thought himself both an American and a Briton.

Britons living in North America deserved the same guarantees of their security as those living in England, Franklin argued. In England, "We are separated by the best and clearest of boundaries, the ocean, and we have people in or near every part of our territory." That England was a thoroughly settled island made it virtually impossible for foreign incursions to escape notice. In contrast, should the French remain in North America, they would share with the English colonies a porous 1,500-mile border, and they would undoubtedly manipulate Indians to "fall upon and massacre our planters, even in times of full peace." Vast expanses and the presence of "barbarous tribes of savages that delight in war and take pride in murder" meant that North America had unique security considerations. Policymakers must think about any settlement there differently from one involving the European continent.[64] Should Britain retain Canada, Indians would not be in a position to attack British colonists, because they would need colonists for "the necessaries of life to them, guns, powder, hatchets, knives, and cloathing."[65]

Franklin then tied the issue of security to the familial metaphor of the metropolis-colony relationship. He mocked the argument that the French presence on the North American continent would hold the colonies in "check" and guarantee their dependence on the mother country: " 'Tis a modest word, this *check,* for massacring men, women, and children" and "will not Britain be guilty of all the blood to be shed . . . in order to check this dreaded growth of our own people?" Rather than maintaining colonists' dependence, such a policy would signify the failure of the metropolis to uphold its parental duties, and the colonists would no longer "have reason to consider themselves as subjects and children."[66]

Franklin also marshaled economic theory to demonstrate the importance of Canada to Britain. Traditional mercantilists argued that the ideal colony had a climate that was dramatically different from that of the metropolis, that it had the ability to produce an exceptionally valuable product that otherwise was unavailable. Guadeloupe, with its rich sugar-growing potential, seemed preferable to Canada from this perspective. To counter such claims, Franklin drew on more recent arguments by economists that highlighted the value of colonies as markets for English manufactured goods. Guadeloupe could never match an expanding North America in this respect. Retaining Canada, Franklin argued, would ensure the inland growth of the British colonies. He envisioned a truly continental society, but "even suppose" that expansion were limited by the Mississippi and St. Lawrence rivers, after centuries there would be "a hundred millions of souls" living in a "sparse manner." Following the conventional wisdom, such inhabitants would naturally subsist off their own agriculture, for manufacturing was the province of people in more densely populated countries. Great Britain would thus save money on security and have a growing market for its manufactured goods if it retained Canada instead of a measly island that could produce only a finite amount of sugar.[67]

Even so, would not the mainland colonies naturally seek their independence, should, by chance, their commercial power or population grow to exceed that of the British Isles? Franklin reminded his readers that, although the colonies occupied a continent, they were still not a continental society. Franklin knew from his experience with the Albany Plan that, even when the colonies saw an urgent need to unite, they could fail. They had "different governors . . . different forms of government, different laws, different interests, and some of them different religious persuasions and different manners." If uniting to resist the French proved difficult, doing so to revolt against "their own nation . . . which 'tis well known they all love much more than they love one another," would prove impossible.[68]

Returning to the family metaphor, Franklin reminded his readers that it was not perfect, for "the human body and the political" differ. Humans had finite growth potential; nations, if properly governed, did not. A nation thought to have reached maturity might suddenly grow and "add tenfold to the dimensions it had for ages been confined to." Where the growth of a human child makes it approach the stature of its mother, the growth of colonies, in contrast, "tends to encrease the growth of the mother, and so the difference and superiority is longer preserv'd."[69] Great Britain and her colonies could grow symbiotically.

WHILE Franklin justified acquiring vast tracts of land with profit potential instead of current streams of riches, events transpired to complicate matters further. In August 1759, Charles III learned of the fall of

Quebec while en route to Madrid to assume the Spanish throne left vacant by the death of his half-brother. It was disturbing news. Spain had rebuffed British overtures of alliance and remained neutral in the war thus far. With the French defeat in North America, Britain no longer needed a Spanish alliance. Worse, throughout the eighteenth century Britain had coveted the riches of Spain's New World empire. Mexican silver, Honduran logwood, East Indian silk and spices, vast markets for British manufactured goods, and droves of Indian labor all beckoned Britain to expand its imperial orb into Florida, Cuba, Mexico, the Philippines, and Central and South America. Shuddering at the prospects, Charles quickly renewed the Family Compact, an alliance between the Bourbon dynasties of Spain and France. In a desperate attempt to prevent unchecked British power in North America, Spain promised to enter the war as a French ally if hostilities continued beyond May 1, 1762. Aware of this arrangement, and unable to persuade Madrid to withdraw its pledge, Britain declared war on Spain on January 4, 1762. Two weeks later, Spain returned the gesture.[70]

Havana, Cuba, a city of thirty-five thousand, had fortifications commensurate with its strategic importance to Spain's transatlantic trade. With the best harbor in the Caribbean and home to large stores of Mexican bullion, it was the hub of Spanish naval activity in the region. Warships needing repairs found the men and equipment necessary to carry them out, and a cache of arms kept the ships battle-ready. Merchants and planters, too, valued Havana, as vessels filled with sugar and tobacco regularly sailed in and out of its port. Little wonder that Spain designed Havana to be more impregnable than the French had Louisbourg. A permanent garrison, a bastioned wall, two forts, and a climate insalubrious to unseasoned European armies made Havana the most secure fortification in the hemisphere. It was Spain's "llave del Nuevo Mundo," its key to the New World.[71]

The leadership of the British Army and Navy began eyeing Havana well before formal declarations of war. Their preparations allowed them, once declarations were made, to mount a quick campaign against a Spanish garrison that had not yet shifted to a wartime posture. By June 1762, the British Navy and Redcoats had trapped Spain's warships in the harbor and laid siege to the city. Yellow fever, malaria, gastric disorders, and combat casualties scythed the first investment of British troops at Cuba by a third. Reinforcements, most from North America, arrived at the end of July, just in time to allow the storming of one of Havana's forts. Meanwhile, disease sapped the British, eventually killing half of their fifteen-thousand-man force. Nonetheless, on August 14, the Spanish commander surrendered, giving the British control of Havana, most of Spain's Caribbean fleet, and 3 million pounds in gold and silver. More disturbing to Madrid was that Spain lacked the means to defend the Floridas and Mexico.[72]

What Havana was to the Spanish Empire in the Atlantic, Manila was to that in the Pacific. Yet in the Philippines, the Spanish relied more on the six-month voyage from Europe than heavy fortifications as their principal means of defense. In September 1762, while negotiators in Europe sought an end to the war, a small British flotilla with only about one thousand troops, including sepoys from India, sailed into Manila Bay unopposed and commenced siege operations. Despite the meagerness of the British force, Manila quickly agreed to terms, and, by the end of October, Spanish authorities throughout the Philippines had surrendered. Spain's overseas prizes seemed to be collapsing like a house of cards.[73]

Britain's dominance on the battlefield led to a redrawing of the geopolitical map in ways that at first seem curious. For decades, British policymakers and merchants had longingly eyed the wealth of the Spanish Empire in the Americas and the Pacific. The rash search for a Northwest Passage and the Anglo-Spanish War (1739–44) displayed the wishful thinking and greed begot by the lure of Spanish Pacific riches. With the strongholds at Havana and Manila defeated, Britain seemed positioned to demand at the negotiating table, or seize on the battlefield, additional Spanish jewels such as Darien, Veracruz, Buenos Aires, and Panama City. Similarly, the British now occupied France's most lucrative New World possessions and might even have demanded concessions on the European continent. Yet when European powers reached a final settlement in early 1763, they returned the map of Europe virtually to the *status quo ante bellum* and redrew the map of North America.

On November 3, 1762, before it had committed to a peace with Britain, France secretly ceded the Louisiana territory west of the Mississippi, including New Orleans, to Spain. French diplomatic memoirs and correspondence show that officials remained woefully uninformed about the mountain and Pacific West. French explorers still had not found inland waterways leading to the Pacific, but they could not rule out their existence. Unlike in the heady decades before the Seven Years' War, however, uncertainty now translated into greater skepticism. Mention of a passage to the Pacific faded from French Foreign Office documents. France's leading minister and man behind the cession of trans-Mississippi Louisiana, the Duke of Choiseul, apparently so disregarded the possibility of a lucrative Louisiana-Pacific water route that he briefly entertained offering Louisiana to Britain. It was not that Choiseul and the French foreign ministry had discounted these western regions entirely. Instead, the French began to suspect that their expanses offered more future promise than immediate profits. The vast plains of Louisiana seemed to offer mainly agricultural riches requiring a sizeable colonial population—larger even than that of the British colonies—to reap them. If giving up the region amounted to a great future loss, at least time remained to remedy it. Changing attitudes, military defeats, and depleted finances meant that France's efforts of more than two centuries to establish an empire in western North America came to an end.[74]

Spain's acceptance of trans-Mississippi Louisiana presented that nation with problems. Spain's claims in North America were already extensive, and its ability to defend them was poor. Indian resistance in the early eighteenth century had rendered the Spanish presence in Florida hollow and settlement in Texas thin. Defeats around the globe in the Seven Years' War had further proved Spain militarily overextended. From the perspective of Spanish diplomats, having relatively friendly French colonies bordering New Mexico would help create a balance of power in North America and lessen the vulnerability of Mexico's riches. But with the French considering delivering Louisiana to the British, Spain had to find another way to check Britain's growing imperial might. Spanish diplomats also fretted over British designs in the Pacific. In 1761, Charles III received reports of Russian exploration of North America's western coast and feared that collaboration between Russia and Britain might unveil easy routes to Spain's South Sea possessions. With the possibility of a tri-imperial balance of power in North America gone, Charles accepted Louisiana to enlarge Mexico's territorial buffer and to prevent Britain from extending to the Pacific.[75]

Britain's actions during the negotiations of 1763 require the greatest explanation. Instead of demanding Spanish maritime prizes, British ministers returned Havana and Manila and settled for Florida, the "site of the most famous swamp in North America."[76] Instead of keeping France's economic powerhouse—the island of Guadeloupe produced more sugar than all of the British West Indies combined, and its annual revenue of £6 million dwarfed Canada's £14,000—the British ousted France from Canada and regions east of the Mississippi. After committing massive expenditures and suffering horrendous bloodshed to win an epochal victory, Britain left the Spanish Empire intact and allowed France to retain its most profitable possessions. Britain claimed most of its spoils in a relatively unknown region where few Britons had so much as set foot.[77] Mainland colonists who from the outset of hostilities had touted the war as one first and foremost for North America saw the British ministry and Parliament concur.

Though puzzling today, at least on the surface, the peace terms received a warm reception in a war-weary Parliament, which voted 319–65 to accept them. A fundamental policy shift made the peace palatable. In past settlements, Britain had sought to enhance immediately its revenue from maritime commerce and avoid distant territorial entanglements. At the end of the last war in 1748, for example, the British had returned Louisbourg to the French in exchange for more lucrative commercial outposts in India. Canada, the Great Lakes, and the trans-Allegheny West would for the foreseeable future cost money to administer, garrison, and defend, whereas Spanish American possessions had long enchanted Britons with promises of quick wealth. As the historian Paul W. Mapp has suggested, however, by the early 1760s the Spanish Empire no longer captured the British imagination as it had earlier in the century.[78] By 1762 and 1763, only a handful of stalwarts, including William Pitt and Henry Ellis, still harbored aggressive schemes to despoil Spanish America. But these men had either fallen from political favor—in Pitt's case, he had resigned and been replaced with the more pacific Lord Bute—or had their voices drowned out by those sobered by the high cost of British imperialism.

Politically drained but not dead, Pitt fought the settlement the best he could. The usually thunderous Pitt delivered a speech before the House of Commons that, according to the session's records, "lasted three hours and twenty-five minutes, and was uttered in so low and faint a voice that it was almost impossible to hear him." At times, he would "speak sitting . . . supporting himself with cordials." The thrust of his subdued harangue and comments made later in the day: "The peace was insecure, because it restored the enemy to her former greatness. The peace was inadequate, because the places gained were no equivalent for the places surrendered." Florida, it followed, was no compensation for Havana. Pitt wanted French sugar islands and fisheries in addition to Canada. Moreover, he pleaded, "All the Spanish treasures and riches in America, lay at our mercy."

Yet Pitt had become marginalized as others adopted a strategy of "lauding grandeur while nurturing serenity." British statesmen began emphasizing the security of contiguous mainland assets over the acquisition of scattered and immediate commercial gems. Powerful British West Indian interests in Parliament also realized that acquiring rich sugar islands, such as Guadeloupe, would sap their profits by introducing more domestic competition. Influential East India Company directors worried that directing British efforts to Manila might drain troop strength in India, where British power and revenues had grown mightily. In countering Pitt and his supporters' calls for more aggressive terms, supporters of the peace extolled the less immediate and less pecuniary benefits of the mainland. Now, the desire for territorial extent, future prospects, and, above all, security reigned. "The original object of the war was the security of our colonies upon the continent," one speaker reminded the House of Commons. The settlement's proponents "expatiated on the great variety of climates" in North America, and the corresponding array of resources available for future commerce. "The value of our conquests thereby ought not to be estimated by the present produce," they argued, "but by their probable increase." Moreover, "Extent of territory and a number of subjects are matters of as much consideration to a state attentive to the sources of real grandeur." In the long run, Britain's mainland possessions would make her the master of the entire continent. A House member concluded the debate, quoting "a Spanish proverb on the importance of North America, that whoever possessed *cold* America were masters of *hot* America."[79] The geopolitical vision that North America was ideally suited for control by one power seemed closer to becoming reality.

Benjamin Franklin had made arguments similar to those of parliamentarians in his Canada pamphlet. Now the ministry and Parliament's vision had seemingly converged with that of colonists who had argued in the mid-1750s that France and Britain could not share North America. British policy had shifted between the Treaty of Aix-la-Chapelle (1748) and the Treaty of Paris (1763) to place greater weight, in relative terms, on secure control of territory than commercial and maritime activities.[80] With the acceptance of Canada, the insularity and security of the mainland colonies took precedence over immediate riches. The Seven Years' War settlement also boosted the continental outlook of many colonists. Prophecies of growth and grandeur seemed more realistic than ever. With the benefit of more than a decade's hindsight, Massachusetts Governor Thomas Hutchinson, who lived through these events and the beginning of the Revolution, recognized the seismic shift in the colonists' outlook that resulted from the French defeat. He wrote:

> Speculative men had figured in their minds an American empire . . . but in such distant ages that nobody then living could expect to see it. . . . But as soon as [the French] were removed, a new scene opened. . . . The prospect was greatly enlarged. There was nothing to obstruct a gradual progress of settlements, through a vast continent, from the Atlantic to the Pacific Ocean. . . . Men whose minds were turned to calculations found that the colonies increased so rapidly, as to double the number of inhabitants in a much shorter space of time than had been imagined. . . . These considerations produced a higher sense of the grandeur and importance of the colonies. Advantages in any respect, enjoyed by the subjects in England,

which were not enjoyed by the subjects in the colonies, began to be considered in an invidious light, and men were led to inquire with greater attention than formerly, into the relation in which the colonies stood to the state from which they sprang.[81]

In Hutchinson's assessment, the Seven Years' War inflated the colonists' sense of self and helped precipitate subsequent conflict with Britain. Britain's decision to take what Pitt and a handful of others thought were overly modest spoils created haughty arrogance among the peace's greatest beneficiaries, British mainland colonists, and paved the way for Revolution.

DISPOSSESSING A CONTINENT

Grandiose expectations of continental expansion at the end of the Seven Years' War hinged not only on the assumption of Spanish impotence, but also on the assumption that Indians must inevitably wane as British settlements waxed. The British could perceive the continent as fully theirs only if they continued to separate it intellectually from its Indian inhabitants. The era of the Seven Years' War boosted this process. British perceptions continued to cast Indians as poorly suited for the continent. Indians might have adapted to its environment and known how to survive on it, but they had failed to improve it and thus prevented North America from reaching its full potential.

Such a view had deep historical roots. Indeed, since the founding of New England, colonists had used the stereotype of Indians as hunters who did little to "improve" or cultivate land to rationalize their dispossession. North America was a *vacuum domicilium* where Indians lacked property rights to its land. From this perspective, Indians appeared a part of the wilderness that the colonists had been fighting, and the colonists' replacement of Indians constituted progress. Civilization must inevitably trump savagery. Later generations of colonists retained and reiterated the dichotomy between their civilized selves and savage Indian others. At the same time, however, colonists increasingly and paradoxically equated themselves with Indians. Famously, the Virginia planter Robert Beverley was among the first individuals to do this explicitly, claiming, "I am an Indian."[82]

But the colonists' corporate identity would not transform wholesale until the mid-eighteenth century. A shift in print iconography demonstrates the trend. As previously discussed, artists and mapmakers from a variety of European countries since the sixteenth century had allegorically referred to the four parts of the world with differently endowed human figures, typically women. Most often, these artists used an Indian woman to personify the Americas. This practice persisted in prints through the eighteenth century, but it took a turn when the image of the Indian became equated with the English colonies. Transitively—and ironically, given that colonists used the stereotype of Indians as primitives to justify native dispossession—the colonies became the continent writ large. This shift first appeared in a print entitled "BRITAIN'S RIGHTS Maintaind; or FRENCH AMBITION Dismantled" designed by Louis Peter Boitard (fig. 20).[83] In the foreground, a small Indian personifying the colonies held a map of North America. The year of its publication, 1755, tellingly coincided with the Seven Years' War, a war for the continent.

Use of the Indian as an emblem of the colonies exploded after the war and persisted strongly through the Revolution. The Indian appeared more frequently than the snake, child, or any other symbol. Its success stemmed partly from its ability to express an expansive vision of the colonies. In print, the Indian image almost always appeared as a stereotypical Indian woman, rather than a specific individual or member of a geographically confined tribe. As such, the Indian female retained her reference to an expansive space and to a political community—an American continent and the British colonies—distant and distinct from Europe.[84]

The Indian symbol also resonated partly because whites viewed Native Americans and the continent in similarly disparate and contradictory ways. As the historian Philip J. Deloria has argued, "Americans wanted to feel a natural affinity with the continent, and it was Indians who could teach them such aboriginal closeness." But to seize the continent, "They had to destroy the original inhabitants." British colonists' views of Indians thus usually fell along an axis between positive and negative, with noble savage and ruthless savage at the extremes. Such dichotomies persisted throughout the eighteenth century and beyond. Indians fell into the category of ruthless savage who hindered the English improvement of the land or, at best, simple but noble savages doomed to extinction when confronted with the inevitable progress of the colonists' civilization. Between these two extremes, Britons emphasized the noble aspect of Indians more as their security fears diminished. Similarly, their views of the landscape usually fell into the category of idyllic paradise or howling wilderness, with the former becoming more common as settlers spread over more land.[85]

Regardless of whether they thought of Indians as noble savages or as savages, as innocent versions of themselves or as less than human, Britons' stereotypes about the Indians' relationship with the land remained remarkably constant in the eighteenth century. Though most Indians in eastern North America subsisted primarily on agriculture, most Britons on both

FIGURE 20. *BRITAIN'S RIGHTS Maintain'd; or FRENCH AMBITION Dismantled* (1755). © Trustees of the British Museum

sides of the Atlantic viewed Indians as hunters who did not alter their environment rather than as farmers. Urging the maintenance of alliances with Indians on the eve of the Seven Years' War, the influential pamphleteer Archibald Kennedy cautioned, "Every Indian is a hunter; and . . . their manner of making war, viz. by skulking, surprising and killing particular persons and families, is just the same as their hunting, only changing the object." Edmund Burke wrote of Indians, "Their only occupations are hunting and war." Two years later, in 1765, Thomas Pownall assumed that Indians were "all hunters, all the laws of nations they know or acknowledge, are the laws of sporting, and the chief idea which they have of landed possessions, is that of a *hunt.*"[86]

Stereotyping of Indians had made it easy to see them as malleable. Indeed, an imperative for fighting the French was the view that they had been manipulating Indians. "The policy of the French is so subtle," wrote George Washington in 1756, "that not a friendly Indian will we have on the continent." Undoing Indian hostility toward the English might take some time. As the trader George Croghan described the situation in the Ohio River valley in his journal, the French "never fail in telling them many lies to the prejudice of his majesty's interest. . . . These Indians are a weak, foolish, and credulous people."[87]

Without the French presence, however, it was the British who eventually could leave their imprint on Indians. Croghan, who dealt personally with Indians in the Ohio River valley, recognized that it would take patience and resources to erase the biases sown by the French and that the process would take place one village at a time. Those who were more removed from native peoples spoke in more grandiose terms. North Carolina's Governor Arthur Dobbs told his Assembly that colonists should put Indians under the English constitution, "extending it thro' the Continent, by endeavouring to civilize and incorporate with them, and to lay a Foundation for their becoming Christians." William Smith used a scientific analogy to describe what he saw as the inevitable transformation of Indians. Christianity had been progressing westward "like the Sun." Admittedly, "There is yet an immense depth of this continent," but "we may be sure the time will come, when the Heathen around us shall be gathered into his fold."[88] Indians would not long continue as such in North America.

A CONTINENT WITHIN AN EMPIRE

Many mythologies would be challenged in the aftermath of the Seven Years' War. Britain's new world order ran against assumptions that the nation rested on a foundation of Protestantism, commerce, and liberty.[89]

FIGURE 21. Illustration from the *Stationers Almanack; for the Year MDCCLXVI* (c. 1765). © American Antiquarian Society

Now, thanks to the continent's attributes and war on a grand scale, Britain theoretically could rule over all of North America. But it might have to be a new kind of rule. Populated partly by French Catholics and Indians who would continue to fight the British long after the 1763 Treaty of Paris, the newly acquired territories clearly were built not on Protestantism or liberty, but on war and geography.

Nevertheless, with military operations nearing a close in North America in 1760, Benjamin Franklin expressed great optimism for the British Empire. Writing to Lord Kames "not merely as I am a Colonist, but as I am a Briton," he celebrated the "Reduction of Canada." He saw in North America "the Foundations of the future Grandeur and Stability of the British Empire." Keeping Canada would allow the British population on the mainland to grow steadily over the next century. He envisioned a union of British equals on both sides of the Atlantic, with the center of power gradually shifting westward to North America. Franklin, like so many patriotic British Americans, saw the empire benefiting as a whole, allowing Britain to extend its "Influence round the whole Globe."[90] The defeat of the French in the Seven Years' War marked a high point in Franklin's affection for the empire. It seemed as if the colonists' aspirations of continental grandeur and the interests of ministers in London had happily converged.

Like those of many colonists, Franklin's feelings of attachment to the empire saw challenges over the next fifteen years. Soon, some of his more radical fellow colonists started to see "JOIN, or DIE" as the symbol of united and independent colonies. In 1765, this was too much for Franklin, who, with his "MAGNA Britannia: Her Colonies REDUC'D," turned the empire as a whole into a living organism that could not survive dismemberment. Franklin's sentiments were in keeping with those of his fellow printers in England's Stationers' Company, which held a monopoly on the printing of almanacs. That year, the company chose an image for its one-page calendar that celebrated "NORTH AMERICA Discovered & Conquerd" (fig. 21). In a classical scene, a child bore a scroll inscribed with the commission to John Cabot. The God of the Sea and the God of War held before King George III "A Map of NORTH AMERICA as it has been lately conquered by, and ceded to the BRITISH Crown." To the far left, a female figure emptied "a Cornucopia of the valuable Produce and Trade of the British Empire in America."

Two years later, Franklin and other Britons on both sides of the Atlantic seemed more ambivalent. In 1767, he wrote somberly to Lord Kames. Franklin still longed for union, yet he saw the mother country as its biggest beneficiary and North Americans as able to thrive on their own. Though he loved Britain, the advantages of union to America were "not so apparent. She may suffer at present under the arbitrary Power of this Country; she may suffer for a while in a Separation from it; but these are temporary Evils that she will outgrow. Scotland and Ireland are differently circumstanc'd. Confined by the Sea, they can scarcely increase in Numbers, Wealth and Strength so as to overbalance England. But America, an immense Territory, favour'd by Nature with all Advantages of Climate, Soil, great navigable Rivers and Lakes, &c. must become a great Country; and will in a less time than is generally conceiv'd be able to shake off any Shackles that may be impos'd on her."[91] Intellectual trends and geopolitical events had given many British mainland colonists a continental consciousness that colored how they viewed and reacted to political change. After 1763, these Americans, believing full well that geography blessed them with a continental destiny, increasingly pondered the nature of the relationship between the North American continent and the distant British Isles. Most important, they raised the possibility that the continent might not rest entirely within the empire.

CHAPTER 3

CONTINENTAL

CRISIS, 1763–1774

For good reason, the immediate aftermath of the Seven Years' War was a euphoric time for British North Americans. Wartime rhetoric and logic had promised that the continent's natural boundaries would make the colonies safe and that its natural abundance—rich lands capable of producing goods from rice and tobacco to wheat and timber, all connected to markets by magisterial waterways—would translate inexorably into British imperial grandeur, a grandeur in which colonists would share. Such lofty hopes were soon deflated when the postwar years brought economic depression and conflict with Indians.

Confounding matters, colonists and inhabitants of the mother country also began to see one another differently. British newspapers increasingly categorized the colonial population pejoratively as "American" after 1763, and the British press minimized the contributions of North American troops in the war. Many Britons lumped longstanding British North Americans in the same category as newly subjected populations—whether French Canadians, Native Americans, or Bengalis—that Britain had to control. Policymakers, too, snubbed colonists by restricting westward expansion. These mainlanders, in turn, harked back to the war just fought and wondered whether it indeed was truly for the continent and, if so, whether they were truly continental people.[1]

Especially grating to colonists between the peace of 1763 and the outbreak of the American Revolution were taxes and regulations that raised issues of political representation and, unavoidably, geography. As the historian Edmund Morgan notes with regard to England and America, "Representation has never in fact been based on anything but geographically defined communities."[2] Colonists could not discuss representation without regard to their physical location, an ocean away from Parliament, and how geography gave them unique interests. Their resistance to imperial measures from 1763 to 1775 raised the issue not just of their rights but also of their identity as a continental people, and much of the story of the colonists' response to imperial reforms centers on their fumbling efforts to reconcile challenges to their rights with their attachment to a continent. Events of these years deepened colonists' continental identity, which functioned as a nascent nationalism and helped set the stage for the Revolution. This nationalistic surge fueled their commitment to an ideology that centered on perceived natural rights, especially popular sovereignty exercised through representatives of the community.[3]

Once colonists cast their most cherished rights as derived from nature, rather than from their status as Britons, then the definition of their community's contours and the question of who constituted "the people" underlying their popular sovereignty became unavoidable. For these patriotic Britons who just prevailed in an epochal conflict against the empire's archenemy, it was a painful question to answer. Presumptions that British mainlanders inhabited an inherently unified geographical entity, and that its colonial inhabitants logically constituted a people, suggested that British North Americans might not be Britons at all. When colonists avowed that their continent was not and could not be represented in Parliament, they, intentionally or not, proclaimed their continent to constitute a distinct political community. Yet they would never fully confront the relationship between their metageographical assumptions and their notions about political representation until they became the United States and, even then, only once they ratified the Constitution.

Until then, these British North Americans adopted a position born of a half-century's intellectual trends and geopolitical events, a position pregnant with tension: They proclaimed themselves members of a vast continental community while challenging the possibility of political representation at a distance. They declared that geography made them unique among Britons, further setting the stage for Revolution.

REFORMS AND REGIONS

Military demobilization and debt presented the most immediate challenges to the British government in the postwar years. War had nourished the army to an unprecedented size, approximately 100,000 men, with more than 30,000 in America. Prejudices against standing armies and financial realities prevented the maintenance of such a force. Yet at the same time, few contended that the military could shrink to prewar levels. Massive demobilization would have sent shock waves through the economy. Moreover, although the North American frontier no longer posed the dire threat it had when controlled by the French, some 70,000 French Canadians and an even greater number of Indians simply could not be trusted. Nor could the nation rely on provincial troops, who had acquired a reputation in Great Britain for lax discipline and professional incompetence, to guard against potential uprisings. Many even feared that removing regular troops from North America would set the colonies there on the road to eventual independence.

Thus, a significant force seemed necessary to secure a durable North American peace, and the government decided that 10,000 troops ought to remain.[4] Estimates reckoned the cost of troops at £220,000 a year. To have North Americans help pay for such a force—and it seemed a given to many that they should—colonial revenues needed to grow. Raising revenues required more than simply raising taxes and fees, for the existing bureaucracy lacked the teeth to collect them. The revenue-collection system was so feeble that, because of rampant smuggling, royal customs collectors brought in only £1,800 a year.[5]

Understandably, the war's aftermath hatched a variety of schemes to reorganize imperial administration. In keeping with Enlightenment trends, these schemes often hinged on geographical thought. In contemplating reforms, policymakers thought about how the various colonies related to one another spatially, and they often questioned the rationale of administrative structures that departed from this natural arrangement. Though these thinkers differed on specifics, none questioned that the British mainland colonies shared a continent, a notion that would have serious ramifications for the imperial relationship.

AMONG the best-known and best-versed advocates for thorough-going reform was Thomas Pownall. Few men in the second half of the eighteenth century could match Pownall's understanding of the relationship between Britain and its American colonies. Shortly after obtaining a position as a clerk for the Board of Trade, he served as the private secretary to New York's newly appointed governor, Sir Danvers Osborne. When Osborne hanged himself in 1753, it freed Pownall to travel throughout many of the colonies, learn about their geography from the Pennsylvania mapmaker Lewis Evans, meet Benjamin Franklin, and attend the Albany Congress in 1754. Then, in the midst of the Seven Years' War, he was appointed lieutenant-governor of New Jersey and secretary extraordinary to John Campbell, Earl of Loudoun, commander of British forces in the campaign against Quebec in 1756. Shortly thereafter, he served as governor of Massachusetts, where he found himself mediating between British military commanders and a colonial Assembly reluctant to meet their demands. In 1760, Pownall prepared to assume the governorship of South Carolina but at the last moment opted to accept a position as commissary for Britain's forces in Europe.

Pownall applied his intimate yet broad knowledge of the colonies' political landscape to his most famous treatise on imperial policy. *Administration of the Colonies* appeared in six increasingly large editions between 1764 and 1777, with revisions made in response to the deteriorating relationship between Britain and the colonies. In it, Pownall felt comfortable to think big when it came to imperial policy. While some of his specific policy suggestions changed over time, his guiding principles endured. As a college student, he had come under the spell of Isaac Newton's work, and Pownall forever after viewed politics through its filter. He believed that imperial policies should conform to natural laws. Just as much of Newton's work focused on gravity, Pownall pointed to the "spirit of commerce" as the "predominant power, which will form the general policy, and rule the powers of Europe."[6] Statesmen, he thought, must work with this force to shape an empire in harmony with the world's natural systems.

Accordingly, Pownall called for a "grand marine dominion" that spanned the Atlantic. Britain stood on the edge of greatness in part because it had acquired a naturally unified North America. With the Great Lakes as the lynchpin in a continental system, North America's natural commercial potential and Britain's imperial power, if properly managed, as Pownall put it, could be "united into . . . one interest," with "one center." Britain could remain the center of the empire, with the colonies "so connected in their various orbs and subordination of orders, as to be capable of receiving . . . any political motion" from London.[7]

Even after the parliamentary measures of 1764, including the Sugar Act and the proposed Stamp Act, caused a wave of protest in the colonies, Pownall maintained that the individual colonies in North America would continue as distinctive planets orbiting Great Britain. He allayed lurking fears that the colonies might one day unite and revolt, arguing that they lacked any "communion of power or interest that can unite them," such as shared laws or governmental powers. To the contrary, "various principles of repulsion," stemming from varied governments, economies, and religions, divided the colonies. Only missteps by Britain would keep them from remaining "unconnected with each other dependent on the mother country." In the grand marine dominion, then, Great Britain "must be the center of attraction," and the colonies "must be guarded against having, or forming, any principle of coherence" beyond that which attracted them to the imperial center.[8] In other words, Pownall thought policies must harmonize with nature. Once they did, Britain and its colonies would hold together in a united system like the sun and its planets.

Pownall's argument contained contradictions. His perception of natural laws suggested that the "spirit of Commerce" would flow through North America uniformly because the continent's waterways and physiography created a coherent whole. Yet the landmass was split into artificial entities— colonies—that often were at odds with one another. Natural forces did not make colonies act like independent planets; their histories, rivalries, governing traditions, and cultural and religious differences did. Pownall himself recognized this, at least when it came to the regulation of trade: "The spirit of policy"—as opposed to the natural force, "the spirit of commerce"—"by which the mother countries send out and on which they establish colonies" was to "confine the trade of their respective colonies solely to their own special intercourse." Policy rendered the various colonies "incommunicable of all other intercourse or commerce." This was the "artificial or political state of these colonies," not to be confused with "their natural state."[9]

Pownall thus did not push his thinking to its logical conclusions. He accepted the colonial divisions as fixed instead of suggesting alterations to make policy conform to natural laws. He accepted the distinct colonies as the true planets that should circle the sun of Great Britain. Moreover, colonial unity must remain limited, for there might be a "particular danger" in "furnishing them with a principle of union" through bad policy. But what if such a principle was inherent in their nature?[10]

While Pownall raised theoretical questions about colonial administration and North America's place within the empire, other administrators, travel writers, geographers, and political theorists hinted at practical yet varied solutions by defining overarching regions within British North America. The Board of Trade had already created two superintendencies of Indian affairs, northern and southern. Daniel Fenning and Joseph Collyer's *A New System of Geography* (1766) split the colonies into three regions, with the northernmost including Hudson Bay, Newfoundland, and Cape Breton. John Mitchell, too, split the colonies into three regions, so distinct, he claimed, they "may be compared to the three British isles at home." Yet when Mitchell made this division he paid attention only to the colonies south of the St. Lawrence River, ignoring territories acquired from France after the Seven Years' War. Eight years later, differences in agriculture made Mitchell qualify his claim: "A very strong distinction is always to be made between the colonies north of Maryland and those to the south, in their importance to the mother country."[11]

Where Mitchell respected existing colonial boundaries when combining provinces into regions, Pownall's successor as the governor of Massachusetts, Francis Bernard, suggested deeper reforms. He combined Massachusetts, Rhode Island, and eastern Connecticut and joined western Connecticut to New York.[12] More radically, William Doyle criticized at length what he saw as the irrational division not only of the mainland colonies but of the entire world, and he laid out a detailed plan to make political divisions mesh better with what he perceived as the globe's natural geographic divisions. He called for the renaming of the British dominions in North America as either "Sebastia," in honor of Cabot's discovery, or the Indian term "Allegenny" could be used, in which case all of North America could be rebranded Sebastia. The "Old English" provinces demanded numerous alterations. For example, New York and New England should be combined as "Neanglia," and western Maryland should be joined to Pennsylvania and New Jersey and renamed "Messia" or "Midensia, both implying the middle."[13]

Whatever regional arrangements they proposed, all observers recognized the mainland colonies as sharing a continent. True, consensus proved elusive on whether North and South America constituted one or two continents—that would have to wait until the twentieth century. Some geography texts persisted in referring to North and South America as continents separately; others, as one taken together. Atlases also split on whether the Americas constituted one or two continents.[14] Still, none saw any of the mainland colonies as belonging to different continents. From their northern to southern and eastern to western extremes, all of the mainland colonies shared a continent. Disparate regional definitions underscored an underlying geographical consensus that would become more politically potent with the passage of time.

WARS AND PROCLAMATIONS: A CONTINENT DENIED

The idea that the British colonies shared a continent had helped foster the high expectations of the Seven Years' War in the first place. The removal of the French, it was thought, would grant the mainland colonies long-sought security by endowing them with natural boundaries. The colonies would become an uncontested British realm, free to flourish from sea to sea. Reality proved far different. Even before the conflict's end, frontier violence shattered hopes of lasting peace. Indians who had appeared malleable and inevitably doomed instead refused to be incorporated into the empire on British terms. Violence first erupted in 1759 between Cherokees and South Carolinians, prompting British Commander Jeffrey Amherst to strictly regulate trade with Indians. The new restrictions cut off the supply of gifts, ammunition, and alcohol to Indians and insisted that they conduct trade at British forts. These changes, combined with an increased flow of settlers into the Ohio River valley, precipitated the pan-Indian uprising known as Pontiac's War.[15]

That conflict began in May 1763 and raged into the following year. Like the Seven Years' War before it, this war was largely over boundaries. Trade and military alliances had drawn Indians and Europeans into a web of mutual dependence before the ouster of the French. Now, with the British claiming dominion over Indians in the Ohio River valley and Great Lakes region, Britain's aims on the continent ran up against the Indians' defense of their land. The spiritual leader of the Indian resistance movement, Neolin, relayed the words told to him by the Master of Life in a dream: "This land where ye dwell I have made for you and not for others. Whence comes it that ye permit the Whites upon your lands?" Pontiac and other Indians, though not as centrally organized as the name "Pontiac's War" implies, took heed and sought to drive the British east of the Alleghenies.

They assaulted British posts and supply lines in the vast triangular region bounded by the Appalachian Mountains, Mississippi River, and Great Lakes. They attacked a dozen forts, leaving British troops clinging desperately to only Forts Pitt, Niagara, and Detroit. They left the British Army—the most powerful and professional in the world—so bewildered that it countered with unprecedented tactics, genocidal in intent, if not in effect. The British waged a war of extermination, which included the summary execution of prisoners and the distribution of small pox–infected blankets. The conflict became one of attrition, and Indian ranks suffered from disease, dissension, and lack of materiel that cut their efforts short of total success. But the British, already war-weary, had lost roughly 500 soldiers and 2,000 civilians during the course of the uprising. The Indians had dealt a staggering blow, forcing the world's most powerful empire to realize that it could not treat them simply as conquered peoples.[16]

As was so often the case in early American conflicts, backcountry settlers suffered terribly and wreaked plenty of their own havoc. Many settlers fled the region; others, filled with fear and racism, struck back indiscriminately. In one of the most horrid yet telling examples of retribution, a group of Scots-Irish settlers, who came to be known as the "Paxton Boys," tried to cleanse Pennsylvania of Indians. In December 1763, they slaughtered and mutilated twenty Christian Indians, many of whom had been promised refuge by local magistrates. Officials in Lancaster tried to protect fourteen of the victims, including three women, five boys, and three girls, by barricading them in the town jail. It took the Paxton men only fifteen minutes to overpower the Indians' protectors, then shoot, scalp, and hack to pieces the men, women, and children. One victim had his head "blown to atoms" by a musket inserted in his mouth.[17]

In February 1764, the Paxtons set out for Philadelphia to press their anti-Indian agenda on the legislature. But at the city's outskirts a group of volunteer citizen-soldiers patched together by Benjamin Franklin confronted them. The Paxton men dispersed, never to face trial or a day in jail for their atrocities that winter. Though the killings repulsed many easterners, they also confirmed what many colonists believed: Indians and whites had no future together. Worse, victory over the French had failed to fulfill one of its greatest promises—to resolve the issue of boundaries in America. The immediate aftermath of the peace between France and Britain witnessed heightened fears and war of the worst kind, if not of the largest scale. Unfulfilled promises gave way to renewed purpose: securing control of the continent by one power. Pontiac and the Paxton Boys waged, in the words of one historian, "two parallel campaigns of ethnic cleansing," giving greater credence to the idea that the two races could not share the continent.[18]

As Pontiac's War erupted, officials in London already suspected what the violence seemingly proved. Enjoying what they thought was the empire's first peaceful spring in many years, they contemplated setting boundaries between Indians and colonists. Britain's national debt had nearly doubled over the previous decade, and the treasury could ill afford more conflict. Establishing a temporary western boundary would ensure that Britain could better regulate colonial revenues and avoid costly wars with Indians. When news arrived that violence had already erupted, action became urgent. On October 7, 1763, the king issued a proclamation prohibiting the granting and settling of lands west of the crest of the Appalachians.

Though the Proclamation of 1763 established a border between Indians and Euro-Americans, its authors had no intention to surrender any of Britain's war spoils to Indians. Indeed, the text opened with reference to "the extensive and valuable acquisitions in America, secured to our crown by the late definitive treaty of Peace," and the need for British subjects to "avail themselves with all convenient speed, of the great benefits and advantages which must accrue therefrom to their commerce, manufactures, and navigation." Most of the document dealt with the establishment of new colonies, including East Florida, West Florida, and Quebec; the annexation of land to established colonies; and the distribution of land to veterans of the war. Indians, according to the proclamation, did not own their land but had it "reserved to them." Should Indians wish to formally cede or sell land, according to the proclamation, it "shall be purchased only for us, in our

Name, at some publick meeting or assembly of the said Indians to be held for that purpose by the governor or commander-in-chief of our colonies respectively, within which they shall lie." The crown aimed to stall and regulate settlement of the continent's interior to secure British legal titles and to make sure that peace prevailed. When some imperial officials suggested the following year that Indians deserved more favorable treatment, possibly even as full-fledged subjects with a long-term future in North America, objections quickly drowned their voices.[19]

Though seemingly an elegant solution, the Proclamation of 1763 proved difficult to enforce, and it failed to stem a wave of settlement. As a writer in the *Virginia Gazette* explained, "Not even a second Chinese Wall, unless guarded by a million of soldiers, could prevent the settlement of lands on Ohio and its dependencies." Nevertheless, the Proclamation of 1763 infuriated many colonists, particularly land speculators who had assumed that the acquisition of French territories would bring them riches. Without clear titles, speculators could not sell western lands. Meanwhile, settlers in the thousands squatted on them illegally.[20]

Nonetheless, many colonial land speculators maintained a covetous eye on the west, hoping that the proclamation would prove only a temporary prohibition. In 1768, the Cherokees and Iroquois gave rise to such hopes by ceding lands south of the Ohio in the Treaties of Hard Labor and Fort Stanwix. In both cases, however, the lands ceded were home not to Cherokees or Iroquois but to Shawnees, Mingos, Delawares, and other Indians who had no intention of leaving. The continued threat of war with these and other Indians prevented royal officials from revoking the Proclamation of 1763. Continued speculative land surveys and petitions for grants proved a waste of time and money.

Among speculators—whose ranks would come to include such Revolutionary notables as Benjamin Franklin, Patrick Henry, Arthur Lee, Richard Henry Lee, Thomas Jefferson, George Mason, and George Washington—it seemed a British conspiracy against North American interests was afoot. Arthur Lee surmised, "The present ministry is antiamerican" in its refusal to grant lands, and Washington saw a "Malignant disposition to American's. . . . I can see no cause why Americans . . . should be stigmatiz'd."[21] Jefferson later cited the king's land policy as a grievance in his instructions to delegates of the Continental Congress and then enshrined his views in the Declaration of Independence, accusing the king of "raising the conditions of new appropriations of lands."[22]

Though speculators in Ohio lands were numerous and hailed from a number of colonies, George Washington provides a particularly apt example of a man whose personal financial interest became inseparable from his vision of empire. He had nearly lost his life in the Seven Years' War along the road that General Braddock's doomed force cut from Virginia to Fort Duquesne on the forks of the Ohio River. After the conflict, the colonial population swelled with immigrants, and that road had become a virtual highway for settlers violating the Proclamation of 1763. Washington had anticipated that these western regions held the key to a thriving American commerce and the future preeminence of the British Empire. He also had a vested interest in them. In 1754, Virginia had offered 200,000 acres of land as a bounty to men who enlisted in that year's campaign. As a colonel, Washington stood to acquire 20,000 of these acres, and, after the fall of Canada, he purchased the rights to another 25,000 from his fellow veterans. The treaties with the Cherokees and Iroquois reinforced his conviction that the Proclamation of 1763 was only a temporary expedient to placate Indians, and, in 1769, he convinced Virginia's governor that a representative should scout out possible tracts of land on behalf of Seven Years' War veterans. Washington then happily served as that representative, and he led a party back up Braddock's road amid the fall colors, past the remains of the fort where he had surrendered to the French in 1754, to Pittsburgh, from where he canoed some 200 miles down the Ohio River with his surveyor's eye on the lookout for the best parcels.[23]

The potential of North America's waterways to unite the continent's parts into a coherent whole captivated Washington, as it had so many other men. Washington thought Virginia, in particular, could capitalize better than any other colony on these commercial highways that bound the continent together. The colony's charter drew a northern boundary that stretched from Chesapeake Bay to the northwest at least to the Great Lakes, including Pittsburgh, and stipulated no western boundary except the Pacific. With the Great Lakes, the Mississippi River, and most of the Ohio River within Virginia's charter claims, the colony was poised to profit more than others from British continental supremacy. These lakes and rivers, combined with the St. Lawrence, would render the British masters of the continent, especially once colonists controlled the lower Mississippi by settling western Florida, a prospect Washington and other Seven Years' War veterans also endeavored to make a reality. Not coincidentally, Washington's financial interests rested on these same natural attributes.[24]

Unfortunately, Pennsylvania, too, claimed many of these western regions, including Pittsburgh, and New York had long provided the most heavily traveled routes to the continent's great interior waterways. Competition compelled Washington to solidify his colony's position within a rising empire. Nestled along his beloved Mount Vernon (which faced west), the Potomac River, he thought, could become the principal route into the continent's interior. With dredging, some canals around falls, and the building of locks, the Potomac could take travelers and traders to Fort Cumberland and a quick portage to the Ohio. The Potomac stood to become "the Channel of conveyance of the extensive & valuable Trade of a rising Empire."[25]

As late as 1774, the ongoing refusal by crown officials to revoke the Proclamation of 1763 and give currency to Washington's and other Virginia speculators' schemes did not seem a permanent obstacle to most. Indeed, in 1771 Virginia's newly appointed Governor, John Murray, Lord Dunmore, invigorated interest in western lands. Ignoring the Proclamation of 1763, Dunmore began issuing patents to some veterans holding land bounties in the Ohio country. Others expressed renewed interest, including George Mason and Thomas Jefferson, who both had purchased rights to vast amounts of land that would be worthless if they could not circumvent the proclamation. Dunmore himself toured the Ohio River valley in the summer of 1773. He had arranged Washington as his guide, but Washington had to back out to console his wife, Martha, after her seventeen-year-old daughter by a previous marriage suddenly died.[26]

In early 1774, Washington explored the possibility of importing Palatine Germans to settle his Ohio lands as indentured servants. He admitted that his desire to do so rested partly on potential profits. But, as he explained in one letter, "political motives" enticed him, as well. Although he had heard reports that ships in Philadelphia's port were having trouble unloading Germans in particular, he did not care whether settlers were German, Irish, or Scottish. Nor did he care for "these People being restraind in the smallest degree either in their Civil, or Religious principles." What mattered to Washington was their future location. He sought to amass wealth, strengthen Virginia, and build the empire geographically. He sought to capitalize on the empire's success in the Seven Years' War.[27]

Devilish details played a role in thwarting Washington's importation scheme. But on the whole, it was Indian occupancy and the crown's policies that prevented most speculators from realizing their plans, and political developments exacerbated matters. On a moonlit night in December 1773, a thinly disguised band of 200 "Indians" had smashed open 342 chests of tea with their tomahawks and dumped £10,000 of the leaf into Boston Harbor instead of conceding Parliament's power to tax it.[28] Responding to the "Tea Party" in spring 1774, an enraged Parliament foisted the Coercive Acts on the colonists, stunning even those who had damned the destruction. The "Intolerable Acts," as they came to be known by many Americans, closed

Boston's port until colonists paid for the tea; annulled the Massachusetts colonial charter; allowed for the trial of local British officials in venues outside Massachusetts; and permitted the governor to use otherwise empty public buildings to house British troops.

Though technically not part of this package of punitive legislation, the Quebec Act sparked more widespread outrage than the other acts, and its measures and its timing led many to count it among the Intolerable Acts. With the Quebec Act, Parliament and royal officials tried to stabilize the North American frontier and organize the colony of Quebec. The act entrenched the Catholic church in Quebec, infuriating especially New Englanders. French civil law—which did not guarantee trial by jury—would continue under the act, and Quebec's government would lack an elected assembly. Most abrasively, the Quebec Act extended that colony's boundaries to include the area north of the Ohio River—the Old Northwest Territory —angering land speculators and anyone who had fought to free the continent from papist influences and to spread British liberties across it.[29] Taken as a whole, these Intolerable Acts represented the unrestrained power that even many moderates in North America feared. The Virginia House of Burgesses shared enough in the alarm that it showed its solidarity with Boston by declaring May 24, 1774, a fast day. Dunmore, ever the king's man, dissolved the house. In response, its representatives held a convention and decided to send delegates to meet with those from other colonies at the Continental Congress.

Dunmore saw an opportunity in the turmoil to mollify anger toward the crown and Parliament and, at the same time, deal with Indian occupancy of the Ohio country and the Proclamation of 1763. Violence between squatting settlers and Indians had punctuated the Ohio country since 1763. Capitalizing on such violence, Dunmore trumped up a war. As a proximate cause, he fastened on retaliatory raids by Shawnees and Mingos against Virginians. Starting in June 1774, a force of 2,000 Virginia militiamen began razing Mingo and Shawnee towns. On October 10, 1774, the Shawnee leader Cornstalk sued for peace after the Battle of Point Pleasant and deeded all of the lands east of the Ohio to the Virginians. All that remained now for many Virginia gentry to become exceedingly rich was the revocation of the Proclamation of 1763.[30]

Dunmore had hoped that his unsavory scheme would appease protesting colonists—including some now sitting in Philadelphia at the Continental Congress—restore their faith in him, and, by extension, renew their affection for the empire. His confidence proved ill founded. Even as he led one of the war's campaigns, a letter en route from London explained that "every attempt on the part of the King's Subjects to acquire title to and take possession of Lands beyond the Line fixed by His Majesty's authority" was nothing more than "a gross Indignity and Dishonour to the Crown."[31] Not surprisingly, the king's Privy Council sympathized with the Shawnees and Mingos and refused to recognize the land cession the militia had coerced from them. Instead, the proclamation stayed in force, and the Quebec Act formally removed lands north of the Ohio from the control of either Virginia or Pennsylvania. The historian Woody Holton has noted that "this multifaceted assault on land speculation angered Virginia gentlemen," particularly veterans of the Seven Years' War.[32] Not surprisingly, the list of Virginia's Revolutionary leaders would resemble that of its most active land speculators. For these Virginians, the continental promise of the Seven Years' War remained a dream deferred.

DOWNTURNS AND DISAPPOINTMENTS: PITTING PARLIAMENT AGAINST A CONTINENT

Speculators such as Washington looked west not simply out of greed or an expansive and patriotic vision of a secure empire, but also to cope with the new economic constraints of the postwar world. The aftermath of the Seven Years' War saw unprecedented migration both to and within Britain's mainland colonies. It was movement sparked most often by the quest for economic opportunity. Yet desires were often dashed, as by 1764 the mainland colonies suffered to varying degrees from a depression. The economy recovered in fits and spurts before the Revolution, but only after most segments of the population felt the downturn's effects at some point. Even wealthy tobacco planters could not escape the sluggish economy. Many fell victim to extravagant debt-funded lifestyles when the flow of easy British credit slowed to a trickle and they could no longer sell their crops profitably. The allure of land speculation as an easy way to escape debt proved tempting. For many a tobacco planter, the supposed fruits of war to the west presented an opportunity to preserve one's lifestyle and honor in uncertain times.[33] These hopes proved illusory; continental expectations were doused; and many colonists cast blame on Parliament. In the process, the colonists vocalized their continental identity—their uniqueness within the empire—more than ever before.

Though the effects of the depression of the 1760s were uneven, the downturn's arrival on the heels of the Seven Years' War compounded their psychological impact everywhere. In this respect, the frustrations of wealthy Virginia planters could parallel those of humble Boston shoemakers, even if the two cohorts experienced vastly different material circumstances. In Boston, the increased demand for goods and services that accompanied the wartime economy brightened the future for many in a town that had long suffered from chronic shortages, unemployment, and poverty. Not all benefited, however, forcing many to seek alternative livelihoods, including in the armed forces.

Tough knocks drove Ebenezer MacIntosh into the military. He was one of nearly 7,000 troops raised in Massachusetts in 1758. By that year, shoemaking had provided him a meager living but not enough to prevent a thirty-shilling enlistment bonus from luring him into that year's campaign against Canada. MacIntosh served in a unit linked to that of Major-General James Abercromby and a disastrous assault on Fort Ticonderoga. After a little more than seven months of service, MacIntosh returned to Boston a changed man, having participated in one of New England's deadliest and most dismal military expeditions.[34]

For MacIntosh and many others in the laboring classes of the northern ports, military service often meant something different from what it did for, say, a young, ambitious George Washington, who saw the military as a step toward securing honor and a prominent place in the Virginia gentry. The precise motives behind the service of the thousands of men from Boston, New York, and Philadelphia varied; some linked the fight to their family's security; anti-papist feelings drove others; and many simply had no other means to support themselves. That said, they shared with Washington the hope that war would provide a path to a better future.

Wartime rhetoric, combined with a brief surge in the economy, gave such men reason to be optimistic about a postwar world. With victory looming in 1759, the minister Jonathan Mayhew of Boston foresaw the colonies as a "mighty empire (I do not mean an independent one)" with "happy fields and villages . . . through a vastly extended territory; there the pastures clothed with flocks, and here the valleys covered with corn."[35] After the formal peace of 1763, the minister Thomas Barnard of Salem, Massachusetts, offered similar exuberance when preaching from Psalms 72: "In these Events, the LORD GOD hath spoken, who can but prophecy, 'In his Days shall the Righteous flourish, and Abundance of Peace so long as the Moon endureth: He shall have Dominion from Sea to Sea.'" Britain had entered a new era in which the hard earned American wilderness "shall be a perennial Source of her Strength and Riches."[36]

Postwar depression on the heels of such prophecies cut deeply. Instead of seeing happy fields and valleys of corn, Massachusetts proved unable to feed itself between the Seven Years' War and the Revolution, and the colony imported unprecedented amounts of food. New York and Philadelphia managed to export food, yet they suffered the worst economic downturn in their histories. Almshouses and prisons were among the largest structures these cities erected.[37] The material promise of the continent had seemed so obvious, and economic stagnation so confounding, that many blamed their misfortune on external policies. Hundreds of thousands from a wide swath of society would each in their own way channel some of their economic angst against an imperial master that seemed to be a source of their problems. MacIntosh, for example, led protests in Boston against parliamentary taxes, and Washington took the reigns of the Continental Army.

ALMOST immediately, Parliament appeared to be a main source of the economic misery, especially to northern colonists. Six months after the Proclamation of 1763, the next attempt to establish imperial order came in a panoply of measures usually called simply the "Sugar Act," a reference to that which most alarmed colonists: a modification to the Molasses Act of 1733. The mainland colonies routinely had traded their surplus lumber, farm produce, and fish for molasses from foreign West Indian islands. The Molasses Act had tried to reduce trade with these islands through a prohibitive tax, which, in turn, fostered a thriving illegal trade. The Sugar Act sought to reduce smuggling by lowering the duty on a gallon of foreign molasses, from sixpence to threepence, and by tightening enforcement. The Grenville ministry, which had pushed the Sugar Act through Parliament, hoped that revenues would increase once the lower duty on foreign molasses made it cheaper to import legally and pay the tax instead of paying the bribes and accepting the risks that accompanied smuggling.

Though the Sugar Act coincided with the onset of depression, the economy's problems stemmed more from a general postwar contraction. Nevertheless, ministerial machinations provided a more readily comprehensible and visible explanation to a society expecting prosperity to flow from newly won natural abundance. Today, we know that nations rich in natural resources do not automatically experience widespread prosperity. But in 1764, many colonists viewed prosperity as a natural consequence of their new conquests. Thus, when the economic downturn of 1764 coincided with the passage of the Sugar Act, the two immediately became linked without much analysis.[38] The mercantilist pie had grown and so, too, should have colonial estates.

Even the more nuanced critiques of the Sugar Act and subsequent reforms, which acknowledged that economic problems rose partly from the end of wartime spending, saw the new duties and regulations as making a slow economy worse. Pennsylvania's John Dickinson, later a leader of the

Revolutionary movement and author of the "Declaration of the Stamp Act Congress," *Letters from a Farmer in Pennsylvania* (1768), and a draft the Articles of Confederation, told an intended audience across the Atlantic that it had misunderstood American economic conditions. In *The Late Regulations Respecting the British Colonies* (1765), he explained that, during the war, colonial goods had been "in great demand, and trade flourished. Having a number of strangers among us, the people, not ungenerous or inhospitable, indulged themselves in many uncommon expenses." The spending tap had since shut, "gaiety has ceased, and all the effect remaining is that we are to be treated as a rich people when we are really poor." Though Dickinson associated the boom-and-bust cycle with the war, the weight of imperial regulations after 1764, including the Stamp Act, which required the purchase of specially embossed paper for pamphlets, newspapers, and a host of other items, salted colonists' wounds. Already, Dickinson explained, the entire empire suffered: "Trade is decaying, and all credit is expiring. . . . The debtors are ruined. The creditors get but part of their debts, and that ruins them. Thus the consumers break the shopkeepers; they break the merchants; and the shock must be felt as far as London."[39]

Should current policies persist, he warned, much of the continent itself would be lost. Through hard work, colonists had improved "boundless forests" and "passed over immense mountains." Trade linked those probing deep into the "wilderness" to the coastal areas. Imperial policies hampered this trade and, if left in place, would "gradually cut off the connection of the interior parts with the maritime [parts] and the mother country.[40] Dickinson's scenario was reminiscent of some of the geopolitical forecasts of the early 1750s, fearful that the French and Indians would sever the English colonists' links to the interior. The late war for a continent would have been for naught if policies continued to hurt trade.

The Townshend Acts of 1767 sharpened images of British policy as economically damaging. In addition to a series of taxes on goods imported into the colonies, the acts established a Board of Customs centered in Boston. To ensure the board's powers of enforcement, Whitehall stationed soldiers in Boston. By enhancing regulatory enforcement, these troops, combined with juryless Vice Admiralty Courts, represented not only encroachments on political rights but also economic hardship. Trade regulation galvanized Henry Laurens of South Carolina into a radical pamphleteer. Lauren's personal fortune as a merchant was at stake, but he also recognized that he was part of a larger community under duress: "Every British merchant is concerned," but none more than "those who reside upon this continent." Groping for analogies from the natural world, much like

Thomas Pownall when he compared commerce to gravity, Laurens compared the "mercantile part of the community" to a human body. Within this body, "navigation, the veins and arteries through which the vitals of commerce are conveyed, is clogged and oppressed," by corrupt and greedy customs officials. "America" suffered from a "fever" and needed "some skillful physician" to "assist nature and remove the cause of the disorder," under which "trade at present languishes."[41]

To the north, in Boston, the string of imperial reforms and the presence of British troops supporting customs officers pricked the continental consciousness of locals. They returned in kind the scorn dished out by Redcoats who sang songs such as "Yankee Doodle" when, beginning in February 1774, a parody of "The British Grenadiers" became popular. In the original, British troops sang of their superiority to the forces of Greece and Rome. The takeoff, "The New Massachusetts Liberty Song," saw its first public performance at Concert Hall on February 13, 1770, and quickly became so much the rage that the lyrics appeared in broadside form in April. The song mocked the British troops by reminding them that the Greek and Roman empires had fallen and that "where now are all their Glories, we scarce can find their Tomb." Britain's time of glory, too, had passed, and the time had come to celebrate "America":

> GOD bless this maiden Climate, and thro' her vast Domain,
> Let Hosts of Heroes Cluster, who scorn to wear a chain:
> And blast the venal Sycophant, who dares our Rights betray,
> Preserve, preserve, preserve, preserve my brave AMERICA.

The next verse staged a metageographical contest in which, "Should EUROPE empty all her Force," Americans "wou'd meet them in Array." Then the final verse predicted a future, truly continental empire:

> Some future Day shall crown us, the Masters of the Main,
> And giving Laws and Freedom, to subject FRANCE and SPAIN;
> When all the ISLES o'er Ocean spread, shall tremble and obey
> Their Lords, their Lords, their Lords, their Lords of brave AMERICA.[42]

The song's publication came on the heels of the icy night of March 5, 1770, when British soldiers opened fire on a taunting crowd, killing five. The day after, the town meeting demanded justice and formed a committee to investigate what had happened in the "massacre." The resulting narrative soon became widely available in pamphlet form, with editions printed in Boston, Dublin, and London. "At the end of the late war," it explained, "a happy union subsisted between Great Britain and the colonies." Taxes and the imposition of partisan commissioners transformed what should have been peace and prosperity into political turmoil and violence, and "the commerce of the town, from the embarrassments in which it has been lately involved, is greatly reduced."[43] The townsmen linked the economic downturn to imperial officials. It seemed the most logical way to explain why the naturally abundant spoils of a war for a continent tasted so sour.

British satirists, too, did their part to imply Parliamentary policies might squander a continent and, in so doing, continued the process of defining the mainland colonists geographically as a continental people. Political cartoons used maps of "North America" to depict the colonies. The frontispiece for the *London Magazine* of 1768 presented a weeping Liberty, her cap—itself a symbol of liberty in Roman times—fallen to the ground, and her foot on a map of North America (fig. 22). A caption suggested that George III, who stood behind Liberty, still might have a chance to "support the fainting Fair / Restore her peace, & shield her from Despair." Though imperiled, North America's liberty might be salvaged.

The following year, the *Political Register* published a cartoon warning of the specter of a divided North America (fig. 23). It featured five of the king's ministers pursuing petty, personal agendas, then juxtaposed this image with that of four European powers perusing maps with an eye toward "the Partition of the Dominions of G[reat] B[ritain]." The European powers were taking advantage of the British incompetence. Spain demanded Canada and Carolina, and the King of Prussia sought all of North America. Ill-conceived policies stood to undo what Britons accomplished in the last war. The cartoon implied that policies aimed at people were problematic because they put a place at risk.

In a final example, *Liberty Triumphant; or the Downfall of Oppression* (c. 1774), North America was once again imperiled (fig. 24). Figures stood on a map showing the coasts of North America and England. The colonists, symbolized by Indians, rightfully defended themselves with bows and arrows against a corrupt ministry and East India Company merchants on the other side of the Atlantic. As in other political cartoons, North America appeared a vivid and coherent emblem of what was otherwise a fairly disparate collection of colonies and peoples.

Significant changes had occurred since the beginning of the decade. Then, jealousies and rivalries among colonies could lead Thomas Pownall to see colonies as independent planets. The colonists' disputes with Parliament subtly shifted perspectives, creating an alternative gestalt. Colonists increas-

FIGURE 22. Frontispiece to the *London Magazine* (1768). © American Antiquarian Society

FIGURE 23. "What May Be Doing Abroad. What Is Doing at Home," *Political Register* (1769). Courtesy Library of Congress

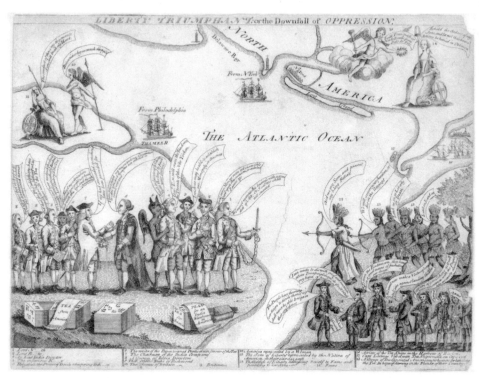

FIGURE 24. *Liberty Triumphant; or the Downfall of Oppression* (c. 1774).
© American Antiquarian Society

ingly equated themselves—and became equated—with their landmass rather than their distinct colonies, and corrupt government officials posed the continent's threat.

ISLANDERS AND MAINLANDERS

As they bemoaned their economic misery and blamed Parliament for it, mainland colonists traced an undue and corrupting influence to West Indian interests. Mainlanders, in turn, began to view islanders as strikingly different from themselves, a process that only heightened their continental consciousness. Whether or not West Indian interests cajoled Parliament into passing the Sugar Act is irrelevant. What matters is how mainlanders fulminated against Britain and the islands. The hostility moved Nathaniel Weare, the comptroller of customs in Massachusetts, to observe, "There is not a man on the continent of America, who does not consider the Sugar Act . . . as a sacrifice made of the northern Colonies, to the superior interest in Parliament of the West Indies. . . . How the apprehension of so imperious a preference, of one Colony to another, operates upon the affections of those northern people towards the mother country, may be easily imagined."[44]

Mainlanders' feelings of having been slighted at the expense of islanders percolated into the formal tracts that protested the Sugar Act. Among these, *The Rights of the British Colonies Asserted and Proved* (1764), by the lawyer James Otis of Massachusetts, drew the most attention from contemporaries. Like most pamphleteers during the imperial crisis, Otis discussed the origins of government, the English constitutional system, and the place of colonists within this system. Otis's gripe with British policy centered on more than political principles, however. The disrespect pamphleteers on the other side of the Atlantic had shown to continental colonists irked him. These writers considered the mainland colonies more as *"little insignificant conquered islands* than as a very extensive settlement on the continent. Even their law books and very dictionaries of law, in editions so late as 1750, speak of the British plantations abroad as consisting chiefly of islands." In truth, "Divers[e] of these [mainland] colonies are larger than all those [West Indian] islands together, and are well settled, not as the common people of *England* foolishly imagine, with a compound mongrel mixture of *English, Indian,* and *Negro,* but with freeborn *British white* subjects, whose loyalty has never yet been suspected."[45]

Such ignorance and disrespect, Otis thought, permeated the English government to a high level. He offered an anecdote of a man "who once was a secretary of state" yet did not know "whether *Jamaica* lay in the Mediterranean, the Baltic, or in the moon." He wrote letters "directed to the governor of the *island* of New England," who was ignorant that "New England is a part of the *continent* of North America comprehending two provinces and two colonies, . . . containing more land than there is in the three kingdoms." Upset by more than economic policy, Otis decried many Britons' blindness to North America's geographical magnificence and the favoritism shown to islanders at the expense of mainlanders.[46]

Island-versus-continent rhetoric shot through the debate over the proposed Stamp Act. The public would be better served if West Indians had smaller estates, so that fewer "*West Indian* gentlemen who now sit in the House of Commons, could obtain that frequently expensive honour," wrote John Dickinson. The power these gentlemen bought resulted in "statutes made to restrain the trade of the continent in favour of the islands." Such policy was patently absurd, for it sacrificed "the welfare of millions . . . to the magnificence of a few."[47] The *Providence Gazette* similarly fumed that Parliament had sacrificed the empire's well-being to "a few dirty specks, the sugar islands."[48]

Hostility toward islanders sometimes so angered pamphleteers that it blinded them to the implications of their own logic. They often cast "the industrious North American" against the "opulent West Indian," the mainlander living off the fruits of his own labor against the islander squeezing extravagant wealth out of his slaves. Rhode Island's Governor Stephen Hopkins recognized that the Sugar Act hurt New England more than other mainland colonies. Nevertheless, his response to the act, which appeared in a number of newspapers from Massachusetts to Pennsylvania and in pamphlet form in London, drew a sharp dichotomy between the colonies on the continent as a whole and those in the West Indies. He often referred to the "northern colonies," including "the most southern colonies on the continent, whose produce is chiefly tobacco, naval stores and rice."

Hopkins admitted that the mainland's rice and tobacco colonies had different trade patterns that made them less reliant on West Indians for their molasses and markets. Yet, notwithstanding that these tobacco and rice producers relied heavily on slavery, Hopkins singled out the West Indians for both the profits they accrued and the character degradation they suffered because of the institution. Their greedy efforts to influence Parliament and to "impoverish the poorer northern colonies" demonstrated that "these people are used to an arbitrary and cruel government over slaves." These "overbearing planters" could not resist "esteeming two millions of free and loyal British subjects, inhabitants of the northern colonies, in the same light" as their profit-generating slaves.[49]

James Otis, too, singled out the sugar islanders' depraved character as a byproduct of holding slaves. "Those who every day barter away other men's liberty will soon care little for their own," he explained. As a result, "Ferocity, cruelty, and brutal barbarity . . . has long marked the general character of the sugar islanders." These "creoles" had partnered with the devil in implementing their institution. By "creole," he meant only "the islanders and others of such extract, under the Torrid Zone."[50]

Hopkins and Otis wrote as if ignorant of the similar effects slavery might have on Britons in the mainland colonies. To be fair to these authors, the sugar islanders' slavery produced far more concentrated fortunes. Per capita assets held, including slaves, for free European colonists in the northern and southern colonies were worth £38.2 and £92.7, respectively, far below Jamaica's £1,200.[51] Still, like Thomas Jefferson who later would not recognize the hypocrisy of declaring all men created equal while owning slaves, Hopkins and Otis had so demonized the islanders that they could not see the totality of their continental selves.

Once Parliament imposed the Stamp Act, diverging reactions to it further divided the mainland colonies and the British West Indies. While the mainland colonists widely resisted the measure, they saw relative obedience among their Caribbean counterparts. The Leeward Islands offered the only radical resistance to the Stamp Act in the Caribbean. These islands relied most heavily on the mainland for food and were most vulnerable to the mainland's economic sanctions. Meanwhile, the largest and most populous islands—Jamaica and Barbados—submitted to the tax, and the British West Indies as a whole ended up paying 78 percent of total stamp revenues. They did so even though the Stamp Act contained duties that treated the islands more severely, and its revenues were earmarked for the defense of the mainland.[52]

The acquiescence of the West Indian planters spurred mockery from the mainland, prompting the Barbados Committee of Correspondence to write to its agent in London about the growing gulf dividing the mainland and island colonies. After charging the mainlanders with rebelliousness, the committee argued that their "violent spirit" had translated into a dangerous "resentment at the people of this island, for having so tamely submitted to the act."[53] On learning of this letter, John Dickinson responded by defending mainland resistance. He opened by declaring, "I am a North-American," and then lamented that they had "attacked" his "country."[54] From Barbados, prominent writers ridiculed Dickinson's "zeal for natural rights." Sir John Gay Alleyne, who would soon become the speaker of the Barbados Assembly, sarcastically commented on the natural-rights arguments of the colonists, claiming that he could not relate to them because he lived "in such a well cleared and little spot." The Barbados Assembly could not formulate similar arguments with "no woods, no Back-Settlements to retreat to."[55]

These barbs opened wounds that festered well beyond the Stamp Act crisis. The British West Indies quietly conformed to the Townshend and Tea acts. As they did so, it is little wonder that Richard Cumberland's *The West Indian* (1771) quickly became one of the most popular plays produced from New England to Virginia. Its main character was a profligate West Indian planter who had traveled to London, a caricature that fit the colonists' perceptions: "Hot as the soil, the clime which gave him birth," and with "rum and sugar enough belonging to him to / make all the water in the Thames into punch."[56] Here was the perfect libertine spendthrift to contrast with the virtuous, frugal North American.

By the time of the Intolerable Acts, the fissure between islanders and mainlanders was greater than ever. In June 1774, the *Pennsylvania Gazette* complained, "Improper Restraints have been laid on the Continent in Favour of the Islands." The following year, on the verge of armed conflict, John

Adams confidently asserted that West India planters "had been consulted in the duties on foreign molasses."[57] And when it came time for the mainland colonies to respond to the Coercive Acts, they did not even bother to invite West Indian delegates to the "Continental Congress."

SACRIFICES AND MEMORIES

Though political issues such as taxation, representation, and sovereignty weighed most heavily in debates over imperial legislation from 1763 to 1775, the protagonists often drew in the specters of the Seven Years' War: its purpose, how it was fought, and who had benefited. They thus repeatedly raised the questions of whether the war was indeed for the continent and whether mainland colonists constituted a distinct continental society.

In one extended polemic, Jonathan Mayhew, fearing the eventual establishment of an Anglican episcopate, maintained that neither Parliament nor the king had the authority to send bishops to North America; nor could Parliament raise revenue from the colonies to support these bishops without colonists' consent. The Anglican John Aplin's caustic rebuttal called Mayhew "ungrateful" for forgetting that just a few years earlier, the French and their Indian allies had threatened to snuff out New England. New England's soil had been "watered with the precious and noble blood of *Wolfe* . . . only to prepare it for larger crops of mockery and scurrility." He conjured images of British bodies strewn before the walls of Quebec and Fort Ticonderoga and suggested that New Englanders numbered few among the dead. British regulars, he told New England, had been "slaughtered in your defense."[58]

New England's veterans, though perhaps in many cases unversed in the finer points of church-state relations or political philosophy, undoubtedly reacted viscerally to Aplin's condescension. His denigration of the relative contribution of New England, whether accurate or not, would have rung hollow among the many New Englanders, such as Ebenezer MacIntosh, who had experienced Ticonderoga's slaughter firsthand. Though casualty rates varied from unit to unit and from year to year, overall mortality had an indelible effect on Massachusetts, especially Boston. One historian estimates that 10 percent of Bostonians who served perished, and "combined with the losses in the war from 1739 [to] 1748 these casualties meant that Boston had experienced the equivalent of two twentieth-century world wars in a single generation."[59]

Though Massachusetts contributed the most to the war effort, all colonies except Maryland provided soldiers. When combined with the many colonists who served as British regulars, privateers, rangers, or in the *bateaux* corps, as many as 40 percent of adult men contributed military service during the conflict, a greater percentage of the population than that of Great Britons who served in the army or navy.[60] Colonists typically served for shorter periods and did not bleed as much as those sent to fight from Britain. Nevertheless, any semblance of criticism or ingratitude grated many, especially during tough economic times. William Hicks of New York wrote two essays that appeared in newspapers from Boston to South Carolina and exalted the colonial contribution, taking "the liberty to assert, that the colonists, in proportion to their *real ability,* did more for the general cause than could reasonably have been expected, if not more than Great Britain herself." In Pennsylvania, John Dickinson suspected that Parliament would never have imposed its odious reforms if the French were still in Canada. Hence, the colonists, "their hearts, glowing with every sentiment of duty and affection towards their mother country . . . , are pierced by a fatal discovery that the vigorous assistance which they faithfully afforded her in extending her domains has only proved the glorious but destructive cause of the calamities they now deplore and resent."[61]

Thoughts about past sacrifices were tightly roped to notions of community. The Seven Years' War added just another chapter to a long tradition of colonists' viewing themselves as a people who had suffered collectively. This self-perception was especially pronounced when colonists harked back to earlier generations' improvements of uncultivated land left wild by its native inhabitants. In New England, James Otis noted that roughly 300 years had passed since the "Cabots discovered the continent," and "ten generations have passed away through infinite toils and bloody conflicts in settling this country." Dickinson described such improvement as ongoing, where the "American Continental colonies *are* inhabited by persons of small fortunes who are so closely employed in subduing a wild country for their subsistence." To the south, in Virginia, Thomas Jefferson recalled how the early colonists' "own blood was spilt in acquiring lands for their settlement, their own fortunes expended in making that settlement effectual."[62]

Both the sharpest critics of parliamentary policies and the most conciliatory shared this collective memory. In an election sermon given in the presence of the royal governor and lieutenant-governor of Massachusetts, Daniel Shute saw the continuation of past exertions as the key to the empire's future glory. For the "happiness of the whole," British North Americans needed "to multiply settlements on the uncultivated lands, and reduce the *wilderness* to a *fruitful field,* by emigration from our older towns." Two months later, the dedication of a liberty tree by Son of Liberty Silas Downer recalled that early English settlers "had fierce and dreadful wars with savages, who often poured their whole force on the infant plantations." Nevertheless, they prevailed "without any assistance from England." Their sacrifices had bestowed on the current generation a "promised land . . . no part of the habitable world can boast of so many natural advantages" as North America.[63]

In a more direct newspaper exchange, John Adams and Daniel Leonard sparred pseudonymously as Novanglus and Massachusettensis, respectively. In their exchange, the loyalist Leonard praised the sacrifices of New Englanders in the late war. New Englanders were roused "by the reverence due to the sacred memory of their ancestors, and all their toils and sufferings in this once inhospitable wilderness, and by their affections for unborn millions." Great Britain now labored under debt, yet she knew that the colonies benefited more than any other part of the empire: "Their continental foes were subdued, and they might now extend their settlements not only to Canada, but even to the western ocean." To such claims, Adams rejoined that Americans had borne their share of sacrifices in the war, and "their ancestors fled to this wilderness" to avoid some of the tyrannical schemes that had been raised. He added, "There are few of the present generation, who have not been warned of the danger of them by their fathers or grandfathers, and injoined to oppose them."[64]

Adams, like many, used this history to highlight the injustices of the present, an approach that grew common in responses to the Stamp Act. When James Otis recalled the past generations' toils, he added that none of the Anglo-American forebears had "dreamed but that they were entitled at least to equal privileges with those of the same rank born within the realm." Thomas Fitch found it shocking that those in established colonies "should now be compelled to contribute towards settling others under much better advantages in that regard than they were." In Virginia, Richard Bland, a lawyer and member of the House of Burgesses, published a tract that later appeared in the *Virginia Gazette* in which he argued that North America became linked to England only through the labors of "Englishmen at their own expense, under particular Stipulations with the Crown." Parliament could not violate these stipulations, for they constituted "the sacred Band of Union between England and her Colonies."[65] Paul Revere delivered the Continental Congress's resolves from Suffolk County, which explained:

Whereas the power but not the justice, the vengeance but not the wisdom of Great-Britain, which of old persecuted, scourged, and exiled our fugitive parents from their native shores, now pursues us, their guiltless children, with unrelenting severity: And whereas, this, then savage and uncultivated desart, was purchased by the toil and treasure, or acquired by the blood and valor of those our venerable progenitors; to us they bequeathed the dearbought inheritance, to our care and protection they consigned it, and the most sacred obligations are upon us to transmit the glorious purchase, unfettered by power, unclogged with shackles, to our innocent and beloved offspring. On the fortitude, on the wisdom and on the exertions of this important day, is suspended the fate of this new world, and of unborn millions. If a boundless extent of continent, swarming with millions, will tamely submit to live, move and have their being at the arbitrary will of a licentious minister, they basely yield to voluntary slavery, and future generations shall load their memories with incessant execrations.[66]

The message could not have been more clear, or the language more shrill.

Some across the Atlantic concurred that North Americans shared a merited inheritance based on long occupancy and ancestral improvements. As Richard Price explained, the mainland colonies were not England's: "If sailing along a coast can give a right to a country then might the people of Japan become, as soon as they please, the proprietors of Britain." Colonists, he claimed, bought most of their land from Indians. "They have since cleared and cultivated it" and, without England's assistance, "converted a wilderness into fruitful and pleasant fields. It is therefore, now on a double account their property and no power on earth can have any right to disturb them in the possession of it or to take from them, without their consent, any part of its produce." From Vienna, a Dutch physician and botanist, Jan Ingenhousz, asked Benjamin Franklin, after independence and worried that the Revolution might fail, "Will all the industrious labour of your ancestors employed in changing those wildernesses in the happiest abode for civilized men, at once been rendered useless, and their so newly erected cities converted again into uninhabited deserts?"[67]

Amid all of this reverence of ancestors, one individual who fell in relative esteem was John Cabot, the putative discoverer of North America. Although commentators still exalted his voyages as anchoring English claims to North America, Columbus, who during the Seven Years' War had been reduced to secondary status and derided for atrocities, entered the pantheon of revered forebears. In the late 1760s, he appeared in poems as an avuncular, if ghostly, guardian of the colonists' rights. "Rusticus" dedicated a poem to the author of the *Letters from a Farmer in Pennsylvania*. In it, Columbus surfaced from "the gloomy Confines of the Grave" to encourage the colonists as their "Founder," their "Chief and Friend," to remain stalwarts of liberty. In Alexander Martin's poem *America*, the goddess America laments the Stamp and Townshend acts and wonders, "Was it for this [that she] taught the bold Columbus where to steer?" and "Was it for this [that she counseled Britons to] plant this new spacious earth from sea to sea?" Columbus's name soon came into use as one for both the continent and the British colonies on it, as if the distinction were irrelevant. The *Boston Gazette* published a piece describing the authors of the Stamp and Townshend acts as attempting to "seize Columba's Money,' while France and Spain sought to divide "Britain and Columba fair." In elevating Columbus, these North Americans asserted rights to the continent that went beyond those of Englishmen, the heirs to Cabot's exploits, to rights deserved by people who had taken part in the continent's improvement.[68]

A shared memory of a struggle stretching from Columbus's voyages to the founding of the first English settlements on the continent and through the Seven Years' War did more than punctuate or provide fodder for debates over imperial reforms. By rehashing this version of the past, North Americans reinforced perceptions of the mainland as a coherent place that was distinct from the West Indies and British Isles. Mainlanders constituted more than a jumble of different and unique colonies. Though their diversity divided them, the colonists shared the place that only recently had been a distant land, improved through ancestral toils and the wartime sacrifices of the living. Shared sacrifice when they confronted a continent helped make them a people apart as they resisted Parliament's encroachments.[69]

SOVEREIGNTY, REPRESENTATION, AND PLACE

Though it is hard to imagine the Revolution taking on its contours without the lingering memory of the Seven Years' War, the core dispute revolved around colonists' rights more than their recollections. Even so, the colonists' memories of the Seven Years' War and their arguments over rights and sovereignty shared a concern with place, and thus it is not a simple matter to separate the two. In the war, colonists had fought for a continent, one to which they had become increasingly attached; in their political disputations, they proclaimed it necessary for their political representatives to have intimate physical ties—particularly property ownership—in the place they represented. With time, a tension developed in their arguments that remained unresolved until after the Revolution: Colonists embraced and emphasized a spatially expansive vision of themselves as continental people, and they proclaimed any representation they might have in Parliament absurd because that legislative body sat thousands of miles away.[70]

Before the 1760s and 1770s, Britons on both sides of the Atlantic espoused the idea of popular sovereignty. Usually, however, they did so without closely examining some of its logical pitfalls or extending its tenets to radical ends. For instance, colonial assemblies, the presumed embodiment of popular sovereignty, kept a watchful eye on royal governors, jealously guarding the power of the purse and fearing any expansion of the executive's powers. Yet the assemblies rarely challenged the very existence of such authority. Even in the face of periodicals, pamphlets, and sermons affirming the popular origins of government, the perennial contests between colonial assemblies and royal governors remained narrowly contained. Popular sovereignty, proclaims one historian, had become the "prevailing fiction in a society where government was traditionally the province of a relatively small elite."[71]

By the 1760s, Parliament, more than royal governors, appeared the most imminent threat to colonists' popular sovereignty. Given the general failure up to that point to define explicitly the meaning and limits of the people's power, the first arguments against the power of Parliament to tax colonists predictably lacked coherence. The early pamphleteers who challenged Parliament's actions could not escape their emotional attachment to the empire and conceded that Parliament's authority must somehow reach North America. James Otis, for example, believed that "an original supreme, sovereign, absolute, and uncontrollable *earthly* power *must* exist in and preside over every society. I say this supreme absolute power is originally and ultimately in the people."

Representation, according to Otis, had originally grown out of the "inconveniences, not to say impossibility, attending the consultations and operations of a large body of people." Yet the capacity of a representative government had limits. Representatives must mirror their constituents. They must share their conditions and their interests, and they must represent these interests, not those of the nation as a whole. Only through intimate connections could an individual represent the locality from which he had been chosen. But Otis's attachment to the empire also led him to believe that "the Parliament of Great Britain has an undoubted power and lawful authority to make acts for the general good" that bound colonists. Parliament, he conceded reluctantly, even had the power to modify or eliminate colonial legislatures.[72]

Otis shared his opponents' belief in the supremacy of Parliament, but he rejected arguments that colonists were represented in that institution. They could not be because they lacked mutual interests and intimate connections with Parliament's members. How, then, could one reconcile the principle of popular sovereignty with the absolute authority of Parliament over colonies an ocean away? As the crisis evolved, defenders of new imperial measures usually insisted on Parliament's sovereignty, no matter the distances involved, or they tried to argue that the colonists had "virtual" representation in Parliament. Most opponents countered, first, that Parliament's authority was limited and, second, that colonists were not represented in Parliament, nor could they be. This two-pronged rebuttal relied on assumptions about the colonists' geographical circumstances and reinforced the growing importance of place in how they thought about themselves.

The first responses to the Sugar Act foretold how spatial consciousness would help draw lines in the imperial struggle. Many writers hastily adopted the stilted dichotomy between "internal" and "external" powers. At various points from 1764 until nearly the end of the decade, men such as Richard Bland, Stephen Hopkins, Thomas Fitch, Daniel Dulany, and Benjamin Franklin insisted that Parliament could not levy taxes on the colonists for the purpose of raising revenue; they could do so only to regulate trade. Revenue-raising taxation was the purview of the colonial assemblies, the bodies responsible for the "internal" government of the colonies; regulatory taxation, since it was "external" and affected the whole empire, lay in Parliament's hands. Though this simple formulation would not last, its contours persisted in the ongoing question of *where* Parliament had jurisdiction.[73]

It did not take long either for colonists to see pitfalls in the internal-external formulation or for their opponents to shoot holes through it. Written in light of the Townshend duties—ostensibly "external" taxes that obviously had revenue generation as their goal—John Dickinson's *Letters from a Farmer in Pennsylvania* (1768) dismissed the distinction between internal and external, since all taxes produced revenue, even those intended to regulate trade. Dickinson still suggested that Parliament had regulatory authority, but he assumed, as Bernard Bailyn has noted, "An empire to be basically different from a unitary nation . . . that its sovereign body need not be supreme everywhere and in all matters in the territory it controlled."[74]

The following year, William Knox, who soon became the undersecretary of state for the colonies, mocked the distinction between internal and external taxes and set a precedent followed by future critics of the American resistance. If Parliament lacked the same power over the colonies that it had over England, Knox wondered, then how could the colonies be "of the same community with the people of England. All distinctions destroy this union. . . . There is no alternative: either the colonies are a part of the community of Great Britain or they are in a state of nature with respect to her, and in no case can be subject to the jurisdiction of that legislative power which represents her community, which is the British Parliament."[75]

Opponents of parliamentary encroachments argued, at least implicitly, just what Knox claimed absurd—that colonists belonged to a different community. They insisted that they could not have "virtual" representatives in Parliament because their alleged virtual representatives were not of the same physical community. The doctrine of virtual representation allowed members of the House of Commons to claim they represented all the people of the realm. It also explained how women, children, and the property-less in England could be bound by parliamentary power. Although such individuals could not elect representatives, the doctrine went, they did not lack representation; they simply had others elect representatives on their behalf.

During the Stamp Act crisis, Otis pointed out that those without the vote in England had representation by virtue of living in the same place as their representatives and having "fathers, brothers, friends, or neighbors" in the House of Commons. Physical proximity gave them "endearing ties" that made it possible to represent non-electors from their region. North American colonists, by contrast, could not have representation through anyone currently sitting in Parliament, since the colonists were as "perfect strangers to most of them as the savages in California." Though it would not solve the current crisis, Otis thought the colonies eventually should have representation in Parliament, not only for their own benefit, but also for that of Great Britain as a whole. It would not do to have "a continent of 3000 miles in length" and with "more inhabitants than there are at this day in Great Britain, France, and Ireland, perhaps in all Europe" to have to submit to laws made "3000 miles beyond sea."[76]

Most objections to the virtual representation of the colonies were more defiant than Otis's. They opposed both the concept of virtual representation and the possibility of actual North American representation in Parliament. Virtual representation, they acknowledged, was valid within limits. Women in England could be represented without voting by virtue of their "strict connection with the other sex," admitted a "plain yeoman" in the *Providence Gazette,* but one might as well have claimed that "ideots, madmen, and cattle" had representation in inferring that the colonists were virtually represented. They simply lacked the intimate connections and shared interests essential to representation. Indeed, it was "magic, that such a vast extent of an inhabited country as this, should be represented in parliament, and that yet the people here should never have found it out."[77]

At the problem's root, colonists occupied "a vast dominion at three thousand miles distance." To suggest that "a country, detached from *Britain,* by an ocean of immense breadth, and which is so extensive and populous, should be represented by the *British* members" was simply "a piece of mockery." The *Constitutional Courant* proclaimed members of Parliament to have powers that were "purely local." Members of Parliament could not represent inhabitants of North America, because they had no property there, and they would not suffer the burdens of American taxes. Reflecting the widespread belief in such notions, the Stamp Act Congress baldly declared "that the People of these Colonies are not, and from their local Circumstances cannot be, Represented in the House of Commons in *Great-Britain,*" a claim that was echoed until the Declaration of Independence.[78]

Opponents of virtual representation often claimed a coherent North American identity or interest to distinguish their political interests from those of other Britons. Consider the case of the lawyer Daniel Dulany of Maryland, who published the most popular objection to the Stamp Act. His *Considerations on the Propriety of Imposing Taxes in the British Colonies* (1765) went through five American editions in its first three months. His objection to the claim of virtual representation trod through familiar political theory, yet it also fulminated against the tendency on the other side of the Atlantic to see North Americans only through the negative cast of Buffonian formulations. The North American must appear "a strange animal" to English readers who "have never had an opportunity to admire that he may be neither black nor tawny, may speak the English language, and in other respects seem, for all the world, like one of them!" North Americans were physically similar to the English; what distinguished from their transatlantic brethren, Dulany insisted, was not their status, or even their character, but their distinct political interests, which, nonetheless, derived largely from their place in the world.[79]

This presumption of a mainland North American interest appeared regularly in the American press in the mid-1760s. It might be subtle and indirect, such as an advertisement for collections of English songs "agreeable to the North-American taste." Or it could be more formally elaborated. In a tract published in newspapers from Boston to South Carolina, William Hicks compared the mainland colonies to "so many different counties of the same kingdom," analogous to Scotland, but whose distance from Great Britain demanded "partial policy," instead of the same representation that Scotland had.[80]

An anonymously written letter to the *Pennsylvania Journal* in May 1766 offered further specifics when objecting to any American representation in Parliament. Beyond the usual considerations of distance and cost, the author challenged the utility of such representation and the impact it might have on the empire as a whole. Initially, the colonies likely would not have the numbers in Parliament to influence matters. But should the colonies ever seat enough members in the House of Commons to "carry points against the mother country," it would damage the "independency" of that institution. If American representatives "took care to be united," they could "render a ministry secure against the attacks of their enemies, or overthrow them by joining in the opposition." Such American power would increase over time, as "vast tracts of land remain to be settled," with "ample room" for many new colonies with "claim to representation in the house." American power in the house would inevitably exceed "that of the Britons as distinguished from it." As a natural consequence, the house would vote to move the seat of government to North America, rendering Great Britain an "American province."

The letter's author thought this future turn of events so transparently obvious that Parliament would never offer the North American colonies enough representation to have significant influence, thus making the pursuit or even acceptance of any representation in Parliament pointless. At the same time, it made perfect sense to establish a "general legislature" for the "whole British empire in America" comprising delegates from each colony and superior to the colonial assemblies. Doing so would differ from seating an American presence in Parliament or accepting parliamentary supremacy over the colonial legislatures. It would be "subjecting each part regularly to the whole; not subjecting the whole to *one part*." In a general American legislature, all provinces would have their "due share of influence," and "no collision of interests between the members of such general and provincial legislatures is supposable."[81]

Such commentators' views seem oblivious to the contradiction of opposing distant representation in and rule by Parliament while condoning a legislature for all of British America. They also seem simplistic with the benefit of hindsight, the knowledge of how difficult it would be for the United States to establish a federal system that balanced the interests of the states with those of the nation as a whole and the ongoing contested nature of such a system. They even seem to forget the failed effort to establish a form of colonial union at the Albany Congress in 1754. At the time they were written in 1766, however, such difficulty could easily be forgotten, given the trends in science and geography that suggested the viability of a continental polity. These developments also coincided with the success of widespread mobilization against the Stamp Act, which boosted confidence in the future of a geographically expansive polity.

IN Boston on August 14, 1765, two-and-a-half months before the Stamp Act was to take effect, the Seven Years' War veteran Ebenezer Mac-Intosh led the first of several popular uprisings. A crowd congregated at a liberty tree on the narrow strip of land connecting the town to the mainland

and hung effigies of Andrew Oliver, the distributor of stamps, and of other imperial officials. The crowd spent the day mockingly stamping goods coming into town, then they cut down the effigies, and MacIntosh led a farcical funeral procession through town to the office from which Oliver was to have distributed the stamps. The charade quickly turned violent as the demonstrators summarily destroyed the building and carried its timbers to Oliver's residence, where they built a massive bonfire and beheaded the effigies. They ransacked Oliver's property for several hours, destroying his carriage, breaking windows, smashing fine furniture, and emptying bottles of expensive wine. Oliver resigned his commission as stamp distributor the next day. Even so, violence targeting stamp distributors spread to towns in other colonies. By November 1, the day the Stamp Act's provisions were to become law, none of the mainland colonies had a stamp distributor.[82]

If widespread crowd violence were not enough to convince North Americans that they could act in concert, merchants in Boston, Philadelphia, and New York signed agreements to stop importing British goods until the Stamp Act was repealed, while those in other colonies simply stopped placing orders. The most formal collective action came when twenty-seven delegates from nine colonies met in October at a congress in New York to formulate a joint petition to king and Parliament. Any role that the Stamp Act Congress, as historians have subsequently labeled the meeting, had in the repeal of the Stamp Act is debatable. Nevertheless, it proved that the colonies could meet and act in unison. It "secured the desirable union of the colonies," something that "ought forever to be remembered and initiated as often as our common safety shall make it necessary," as newspapers reported. The congress, together with boycotts and crowd actions, awoke mainland colonists to their shared interests. The congress, like the shared memory of a history of environmental improvement and wartime sacrifice, made it increasingly possible to conceive of the mainland colonies as a coherent whole. Christopher Gadsden, a merchant from South Carolina and delegate to the Stamp Act Congress, expressed a common opinion well: "Nothing will save us but acting together. . . . There ought to be no New England men, no New Yorker, &c., known on the Continent, but all of us Americans."[83]

Public commemorations of the repeal touted the liberation of an entire part of the world. On Boston Common, the Sons of Liberty erected a large, translucent obelisk formed with oiled paper and lit from within by 280 candles. Images on its sides depicted colonists with the female Indian figure of "America in distress" who is saved by the king. Houses displayed paintings of the king, who signed the repeal, and William Pitt, who lobbied for it in

FIGURE 25. From *Wo des Verächters Netz uns Weg und Pfad bestrickte . . .* (1766).
Courtesy Library Company of Philadelphia

Parliament, both hailed by the Roman goddess of liberty: "How round the Globe exapand your Patriot Rays! / And the NEW WORLD is brighten'd with the Blaze." In Philadelphia, a broadside in German depicted the repeal as the resurrection of liberty and the return of spring, the sun shining through dark clouds on a globe marked "AMERICA" (fig. 25).[84]

All discussions of natural rights, sovereignty, and representation hinge on notions, whether examined or not, of community. In rejecting "internal" taxes, denying their virtual representation in Parliament, and refusing the possibility of actual representation overseas, colonists asserted, wittingly or not, as the historian Edmund S. Morgan has argued, "that the American colonies were different national communities from the one that was represented in Parliament."[85] By the mid-1770s, many colonists embraced this conclusion and denied any parliamentary authority over mainland subjects.

Benjamin Franklin, under the name "A New-England man," explained in one newspaper that British mainland colonists were no more subject to parliamentary taxation than Great Britons were subject to German taxation. "Britain," he wrote, "was formerly the America of the Germans." Saxons came in ships and found the best part of the island "possessed by a Parcel of Welsh Caribbs," whom they pushed onto marginal lands and "sat down in their Places." They believed they had secured the land through their own efforts; Germany never "pretended to tax them; nor is it likely, if she had, that they would have paid it."[86]

Unable to attend the Continental Congress, Thomas Jefferson made the same argument when he put to paper his thoughts for Virginia's delegates, a document that would circulate widely in the congress. He compared the founding of American colonies to the Saxon settlement of the "island of Great Britain" (a phrase he would use several times). Like their Saxon forebears, Anglo-American colonists exercised "a right which nature has given to all men, of departing from the country in which chance, not choice, has placed them, of going in quest of new habitations, and of there establishing new societies under such laws and regulations as to them shall seem most likely to promote public happiness." Migrants to North America thus constituted a people distinct from the inhabitants of the mother country. It was thanks to emigrants whose "own blood was spilt" that "America was conquered and her settlements made." Their tie to Britain came voluntarily when they decided "to continue their union with her by submitting themselves to the same common sovereign, who was thereby made the central link connecting the several parts of the empire thus newly multiplied." Hence, Parliament had no jurisdiction over America: "Can any one reason be assigned why 160,000 electors in the island of Great Britain should give law to four millions in the states of America?" Jefferson asked rhetorically and with an exaggerated figure for the colonies' population. The Continental Congress officially agreed with a set of resolutions on October 14, 1774.[87] The only formal political connection left between American colonists and their English brethren was their shared king.

It would take until January 1776 for Thomas Paine's ringing denouncement of royal authority in *Common Sense* to shred, in the minds of many, this link to the king. In destroying the existing political order, Paine, as will soon be described, called for the reconstruction of a political system on a more natural firmament. He talked of the continent as having a "true interest" and believed that continental institutions should replace those artificially contrived by the empire. He sought a legislature for the entire continent, bound by a "Continental Charter." Representation in a distant legislature was possible as long as the representatives were adequate in number, shared a continent, and did not assemble on the other side of an ocean.[88]

NEW QUESTIONS AND NATURAL LAWS

The rejection of Parliament's sovereignty over the mainland American colonies raised a vexing problem that would nag these Americans for many years: Where, exactly, did popular sovereignty lay? Or, put another way, who were "the people"? British mainlanders saw themselves as sharing interests that transcended colonial boundaries. They had convened congresses on two occasions to defend these interests, and they argued that they were acting on natural rights. At the same time, they had a tradition of legislative autonomy in their colonial assemblies. Were the colonial divisions on which these assemblies had been drawn in accordance with the natural laws the colonists had so often cited in their objections to parliamentary rule?

When Christopher Gadsden wrote, "There ought to be no New England men, no New Yorker, &c, now on the Continent, but all of us Americans," he feared that the delegates at the Stamp Act Congress would fasten on their colonial charters as the basis of their rights, not the "natural and inherent rights that we all feel and know, as men." That the charters varied from colony to colony created a "political trap" that could divide the colonies and prevent them from seeing their "common cause."[89]

John Adams, for example, seemed to have fallen temporarily into such a trap. He claimed, "Massachusetts is a realm, New York is a realm, Pennsylvania another realm. . . . The King of Great Britain is the sovereign in all these realms." The colonial charters demonstrated the contractual nature of government in the colonies, or, in those colonies without charters, the governors' commissions did, as they guaranteed to the colonists the rights of Englishmen.[90] Gadsden might have asked Adams, and Edmund Morgan has raised the question: "If the authority of colonial governments was thought to derive from an original grant by the people, what people could be supposed to have made the grant? The people of England? Or the peoples of particular colonies? Both together?"[91] And if the king violated the charters, thereby breaking a contract with colonists, to what state of nature would colonists then revert? It was the charters themselves that had defined the various colonies, but these would no longer be valid.

When the imperial crisis first broke, Britain's famed theoretician of empire, Thomas Pownall, now a member of Parliament, had predicted that the strong provincial identities of colonists would prevent them from uniting, barring a significant imperial misstep, because they had no tendency to unite. These fragmented identities had grown out of imperial policies, and, as Pownall admitted, represented an "artificial or political state" instead of their "natural state." Though Pownall favored such disunity, he implicitly undercut its appropriateness with his portrayal of America as a unified natural system. He also failed to realize that taxation, by virtue of its relationship to representation in English political thought, would prompt Americans to think about their geographical relationship both to Great Britain and to one another.

From the mid-1760s to the American Revolution, colonists repeatedly couched their resistance in the language of natural rights.[92] They also saw parallels between what we would today describe as "natural science" and "political science." James Otis saw a properly constructed government as reflecting "the *unchangeable will of* GOD, the author of nature, whose laws never vary." In language that echoed Pownall and foreshadowed metaphors in Paine's *Common Sense,* he declared the impulse for individuals to combine into larger communities as irresistible as gravity. Consequently, government is "most evidently founded *on the necessities of our nature. It is by no means an arbitrary* thing depending merely on *compact* or *human will* for its existence." Because he also believed in popular sovereignty, Otis thought that the task of crafting a government fell to the people. Yet just as he was unable to concede that Parliament lacked authority in the colonies because colonists lacked representation in that body, he was unwilling to examine critically his assumptions about who constituted "the people."[93]

Others diverged with Otis on the possibility of colonists' representation in Parliament and, at the same time, developed new ideas about the implications of colonial migrations for political rights. When Richard Bland of Virginia rejected virtual representation, he anticipated Jefferson's *Summary View* and argued that individuals "have a right to retire from the Society, to renounce the Benefits of it, to enter into another Society, and to settle in another Country." He conceded that Parliament had limited authority over the colonies but not the power to tax. After Virginia's governor prevented the Assembly from selecting a delegate to the Stamp Act Congress, Bland mocked the governor's claim that the colonies were part of the same community as Britons and thus virtually represented. To the contrary, imperial officials themselves had worked to perpetuate differences among the colonies, suggesting their defenses of virtual representation were two-faced. Men such as the governor "will allow Divisions to be fomented between [colonies] about inconsiderable Things" out of their own interest. Their central imperative was to "*Divide et impera* [divide and rule] . . . lest 'an Alliance should be formed dangerous to the Mother Country.'" Bland found the governor transparent, insulting, and threatening.

In the next paragraph, Bland shifted his attack from the governor to Thomas Pownall, accusing him of similar hypocrisy. Pownall's desire to have policies resting on natural principles could not be reconciled with the need to prevent any "Principle of Coherence" between the colonies: "The Colonies upon the Continent of North America lie united to each other in one Tract of Country, and are equally concerned to maintain their common Liberty. If he [Pownall] will attend then to the Laws of Attraction in natural as well as political Philosophy, he will find that Bodies in Contact, and cemented by mutual Interests, cohere more strongly than those which are at a Distance and have no common Interests to preserve. But this natural Law is to be destroyed; and the Colonies . . . are to be disjoined, and all intercommunication between them prevented."[94] Given that the mainland colonies constituted shared geographical space and political interests, any efforts by authorities to disunite the colonies reeked of a Machiavellian attempt at *divide et impera,* contrary to nature. Still unclear, however, was how these colonies ought to represent themselves to Britain. What, if anything, defined them as a people?

THAT question became urgent in 1774, when the Intolerable Acts grated like a bone in the throat. Until that point, tensions between Parliament and colonists repeatedly arose only to be defused. But the process of resistance was not benign; it refined and reinforced a burgeoning continental identity and coaxed colonists into seeing themselves as a distinct community apart from that represented in Parliament. Although most of the Intolerable Acts targeted Massachusetts, inhabitants of other colonies had come to see themselves as connected to the Bay Colony. It was not simply as if Virginians, Pennsylvanians, and others had theorized that they enjoyed the same rights as Bostonians and that if these rights could be stripped in Massachusetts, they were in peril everywhere; rather, the Bay Colony and the other mainland colonies made up the same, geographically defined people. Encroachments on the rights of Bay colonists were injustices against members of one's own community.

The Quebec Act, more than any other, challenged this ascending continental identity by directly impinging on a wide swath of mainland colonists. Quebec appeared as the key not just to Canada, but to the entire continent. Under the Quebec Act, the St. Lawrence River and access to the interior would be lost. Quebec's jurisdiction over the Ohio country further cut off British colonists from western lands. The act thus had an unparalleled ability to mobilize masses of people. Speculators felt the sting viscerally, and so, too, did countless veterans of the Seven Years' War who saw the Ohio country and Canada as their hard-earned spoils. Yet Parliament, nevertheless, had rendered the king's power in these regions "as absolute, as that of an asiatic DESPOT."[95]

In response, delegates from twelve mainland colonies convened in Philadelphia in September. There they found the tensions among provincial, imperial, and continental identities laid as bare as ever. They had to confront, at least implicitly, the issue of representation and distance. Standing objections to the possibility of American representation in Parliament claimed that that body could not act in the interest of subjects 3,000 miles away. Now delegates at the Congress claimed to act on behalf of a vast continent. It was an inconsistency that would remain unresolved until the ratification of the Constitution.

Thomas Pownall, for his part, managed to redress some of his own inconsistencies once American independence seemed a foregone conclusion. Much had transpired in his life since he had first proposed the colonies be held in Britain's orbit like separate planets. After writing the third edition of *Administration of the Colonies,* which he dedicated to George Grenville, the ministerial author of the Sugar and Stamp acts, he began a thirteen-year stint in the House of Commons. There he worked tirelessly to strengthen the ties between Britain and the colonies. Outspokenly pro-American, he hoped to mediate the crisis in such a way that Britain retained centralized power but the colonies gained representation in Parliament. But when the United States sat on the cusp of winning independence, he enthusiastically welcomed it as if it were foreordained by nature. Events had led Pownall to alter his stance, to push his earlier calls for reform to their logical conclusion.

In 1780, Pownall observed that "North-America is *de facto* AN INDEPEN-DENT POWER *which has taken its equal station with other powers,* and must be so *de jure.* " Many of Pownall's guiding principles remained firm. North America was a "primary planet in the system of the world" because it had natural attributes that drew it together into a single mass. Navigable rivers through its interior facilitated the flow of commerce, like a "vital principle of life," in "one organized being." Equally important, North America's "large-ness of territory" meant that it had a "variety of climates," that it could produce "everything that nature requires, that luxury loves to abound in; or that power can use, as an instrument of its activity." Any nation that con-trolled the continent had at its disposal all of the goods that European nations traded for among themselves and with the rest of the world. Europe, in contrast, had "difficulties of intercourse both over land, and through the seas" and had been artificially chopped into nations, restricting the flow of commerce on that continent. North America, then, had a "natural great-ness" arising from its "greatness of dominions which hath a natural *ca-pability* of systematic connection."[96]

Pownall's ultimate reconciliation of politics with geography in the face of American independence was laden with irony. His pro-American stance through the years made him one of the colonists' greatest friends in a position of power in Great Britain. Though he staunchly believed in cen-tralized control over the colonies and Parliament's power to tax them, he had called for colonial representation in Parliament. But in 1764, he had proposed modest reforms, similar to the Sugar Act, the Currency Act, the Stamp Act, and the Townshend Acts. These acts' implementation transformed him into a sparring partner for American pamphleteers who opposed new taxes. Most forgot his calls for greater freedom of trade, a colonial bill of rights, and regulated paper currency. They failed to recognize that if any British politician was positioned, and inclined, to stave off Revolution, it was Pownall.[97]

Yet one North American, perhaps more than any other, remembered and concurred with aspects of Pownall's thinking. John Adams looked fondly on the job Pownall had done as the governor of Massachusetts. He later studied the various editions of *Administration of the Colonies*. Then, in the summer of 1776 and at the behest of the Continental Congress, Adams drafted a document that guided U.S. diplomacy for many years to come. It was a blueprint for potential U.S. treaties with other nations commonly known as the "Model Treaty" or the "Plan of Treaties," and it bore the influence of both Thomas Paine and Thomas Pownall. As will soon be described, it assumed that the United States could pursue an isolationist tack and that the nation was, as Pownall might have explained, its own planet or natural system. The Model Treaty envisioned the United States as a great commercial prize for which other European nations would have to compete. The United States should avoid entangling political alliances, it suggested, for commerce alone should bind it to other nations.

Four years later, while Adams was in Paris, Pownall's influence on him remained strong. Pownall had recently presented Adams with the final edition of *Administration of the Colonies* "as a Testimony of his Esteem & Respects." While serving as the minister plenipotentiary to negotiate treaties of peace and commerce with Great Britain, Adams stumbled across the anonymously written pamphlet *Memorial to the Sovereigns of Europe*. He found it filled with "so much Knowledge of America, and So many good Thoughts" that he had no doubt Thomas Pownall had written it. Adams painstakingly presented an extensive summary of the *Memorial* to the Continental Congress; then, over the course of a week that July, Adams translated the *Memorial* into more intelligible English.[98] That month he also drew on Pownall's argument to write a series of "Letters from a Distinguished American," which later appeared in a London newspaper. After the Revolution, Adams explained that the letters contained arguments that he "repeated & extended . . . to the British Ministers in the Course of the Negotiations."[99] To these British ministers, the Pownall-inspired arguments must have sounded familiar, because the trade adviser to the leading minister, the Earl of Shelburne, was none other than Thomas's brother John.[100]

As Gregg Lint, a diplomatic historian and an editor of John Adams's papers, has noted, scholars have paid scant attention to Pownall's *Memorial* and Adams's translation of it. This is unfortunate, according to Lint, for "it is not an overstatement to say that the *Memorial* had more influence on John Adams' views of foreign policy than any other single published work."[101] Moreover, colonists outside the world of diplomats took a central thread of Pownall's and other reformers' arguments to heart: North America's place in the world—literally—must in part shape its fate. The importance of geography emerged regularly in debates on issues of regulation, rights, and representation.

Today, however, it is Thomas Paine, not Thomas Pownall, who is familiar to most Americans. Even John Adams would later concede the tumultuous years of the American and French Revolutions as "the Age of Paine."[102] It was he, more than anyone else, who would take the views of Pownall and others on geography and politics to their logical end and communicate to British North Americans a new vision of the future. Of course, Paine did not do so single-handedly. Nationalism can subsist largely on aspirations and imaginations, but nations cannot; they require institutions. It took the formation of the Continental Congress and the waging of a war to help many Americans more fully embrace their continental selves.

PART II

CREATING A
CONTINENTAL
EMPIRE

CHAPTER 4

NATIONALISM'S NATURE

CONGRESS'S CONTINENTAL

ASPECT

Although notions that geography bound mainland colonists together had gained credence by 1774 and 1775, many observers still held that these same colonists could never muster enough solidarity to resist the Intolerable Acts. Even after the First Continental Congress had convened, Governor Thomas Hutchinson of Massachusetts dismissed its ability to accomplish anything. He assured ministers in London that "a union of the Colonies was utterly impracticable," because "the people were greatly divided among themselves in every colony." Delegates themselves could be equally pessimistic. Joseph Galloway of Pennsylvania saw "such a Diversity of Interests, Inclinations, and Decisions" that would inevitably block colonists' attempts to unite, "even for their own Protection."[1]

The growing pains following victory in the Seven Years' War, to be sure, had promoted a measure of colonial union. The Stamp Act Congress and Committees of Correspondence exceeded the kind of cooperation only recently dreamed of when colonial assemblies rejected the Albany Plan. But the colonies still resisted ceding significant power to any centralized authority, much less separating from Great Britain entirely. Having rhetorically asked what the colonies would be like without Great Britain, Galloway could only answer, "They are weak in themselves, and many of them hold an Enemy within their own Bowels ready to destroy them." They lacked any "Supreme Authority" to "decide their Disputes, or to compel them to act in Concert for their Common Safety." Galloway's naysayer musings may have been tied to his loyalist leanings, but more radical delegates shared his doubts. Years later, John Adams famously compared the Revolution to the improbability of thirteen clocks striking at once.[2]

Notwithstanding such misgivings, the Continental Congress proved essential in the colonies' resistance and independence movement. The Congress may have been a weak institution when compared with the government later established under the Constitution, but hindsight should not blind us from seeing the institution's strengths. After all, the Continental Congress oversaw a Revolution against the world's greatest power, and, after the war, it implemented the blueprint for some of the new nation's subsequent expansion with the Land Ordinance of 1785 and the Northwest Ordinance of 1787.[3]

Among the Continental Congress's strengths was its ability to appeal to Americans' growing consciousness as a continental people. Until 1774, the monarchy provided political cement, joining Britons across vast distances. When the king's support of the Coercive Acts eroded his authority, colonists groped for a source of unity. They latched onto a powerful one when they began to label their collection of colonies "the continent" and their congress "continental."

That these colonists regularly referred to their collective self as "the continent" should not be taken for granted, for through this practice they enacted themselves as a people. Language is action, a reflection of a decision, albeit sometimes one made viscerally, without much conscious thought or deliberation. Colonists could have spoke more often—as they sometimes did—of defending the rights of any number of collectivities: "Protestants," "mankind," "the virtuous," "the free," "the confederation," "the united colonies," or "the association." Instead, geography most captured their imagination when they chose how to describe their aggregate self. Scientific trends and geopolitical visions had made this geographic turn possible by making the continent appear as an inherently unified entity. Once colonists defined themselves by referring to an imagined natural space, Britain became an opponent not only by virtue of its policies but also by virtue of its geography, a measly island trying to impose tyranny over a magnificent continent.

As with most actions, when colonists spoke of themselves in these terms it had consequences. Expansionism became more deeply wound into the DNA of the young United States. So, too, did racism—even amid talk of self-evident truths and the rights of mankind. Some humans were simply better suited for the North American environment than others. White Americans became the true Americans. With independence secured, continental presumptions greased the wheels to establish a geographically extensive republic. With a history of defining "the people" continentally, proponents of the Constitution had more ammunition to counter arguments that republics were suitable only for small areas.

This chapter reveals how the "continental" nature of the Continental Congress emerged to galvanize delegates and other colonists during the transitional period from 1774 to 1776. This "continental" aspect became a nationalizing force as it meshed well with prevailing natural-rights political ideology and percolated into everyday discourse. It fostered unity partly because it did not appear to be artificially produced but emerged spontaneously and almost instantly. Metageographical assumptions had made the patriot community like a liquid cooled below its freezing point: set to flash freeze around the appropriate dust particle. The congress assumed the "continental" label without debate or dissension. The term embodied colonists' natural, political, and proto-national identity simultaneously. Severing ties with Britain might have reduced the colonies to a political state of nature, but the state of nature had an inherent order. Nature conferred on North American colonists a measure of unity and future grandeur. Their institutions, boundaries, racial composition, and foreign relations, in turn, should reflect this unity and promise. The United States should have an international role that reflected North America's promise and place on the globe. The Continental Congress sought to implement such a vision, for Americans were, as nature dictated, a people, not just a collection of aggrieved Britons or fledgling states.

A CONTINENTAL EMPIRE, BRITISH OR NOT

It bears notice that, notwithstanding the contest over Parliament's attempts to raise revenue and to regulate the colonies, the metageographical notions of the 1750s and 1760s persisted into the intellectual milieu in which the Continental Congress arose. Writers on both sides of the Atlantic still forecast British imperial grandeur in North America commensurate with their assumptions about the continent's features well into the 1770s. The popular geographies and travel writings of the decade continued to invoke florid and sweeping generalizations about the different continents. Asia and Africa continued as foils for Europe and the Americas. North America's future seemed clear.

In William Guthrie's popular geography text, North America remained "that part of the globe which is best watered . . . for the convenience of trade, and the intercourse of each part with the others." Others echoed Guthrie and added that Britain's superior commercial spirit contributed to North America's promising future. The twelfth edition of Thomas Salmon's *New Geographical and Historical Grammar* (1772), for example, still sounded as optimistic as ever. In the American colonies, trade would subject "the original inhabitants [Indians] to the rule of their guests." Salmon even ventured the possibility that "British ships shall be navigated, within the next century, from their own ports on the coasts of the Pacific ocean." To generalize about the British mainland colonies in Salmon's and other geographers' works meant to generalize about North America, or even the Americas, as a whole.[4]

Little prevented the British colonies from expanding to the Pacific, especially if one conveniently ignored powerful Indian nations. Moreover, some geographers portrayed Mexico as merely an isthmus—distinct from but connecting the northern and southern continents of the Americas—making it easy to dismiss Spanish North America as an obstacle to British expansion.[5] Others simply dismissed the Spanish as too feeble to rival Britain, a claim bolstered by frequent projections of rapid growth in the British colonial population. The mainland colonies might not yet have been coterminous with North America or all of the Americas, but that did not prevent anticipating them as such. In a speech excerpted in the *Pennsylvania Gazette,* the provost of the College and Academy of Philadelphia, William Smith, told an audience in Charleston:

> It is impossible for an attentive observer not to behold an EMPIRE already planted, which, with careful culture, promises to enlarge itself to vast dimensions, and to give law as well as happiness to every other part of AMERICA. We have the staff of life, BREAD in abundance for ourselves, and to supply the necessities of others. . . . The climate too is, in general, favourable to all the powers of body and mind, nursing up a race of bold and hardy men, with whom our feebler neighbours [Spaniards and Portuguese of South America], on the southern part of this Continent, would wage but ineffectual war; should war, in ages hence, continue to be the Unchristian mode of arbitrating the differences of Christian nations! A FRIEND to humanity, therefore, cannot but adore that Providence, which, when the New world was to be portioned out among the kingdoms of the Old, called Great Britain (a nation enjoying liberty, religion and science, in their purest and most improved state) to the possession of that part of America, which seems thus ordained to empire and preeminence over the rest![6]

When he spoke, parliamentary measures were a canker to some, but the dominant voices in geography still celebrated the colonies as the sprouting bud of the empire's continental branch.

YET many could not escape the fear that tyrannical rulers might thwart the British Empire's rise and prevent the continent from fulfilling its natural potential. Liberty and power, it was widely thought, had battled one another throughout history. There were winners and losers, and the players in some quarters of the globe fared much worse than those in others. Immensely popular in the 1770s was *Cato's Letters* (1720–23), John Trenchard and Thomas Gordon's critique of the Walpole administration. It bolstered fears of an imminent tyrannical threat by looking to Asia, which appeared to be the wellspring of "almost universally absolute tyrants"; Africa, which provided "scenes of tyranny, barbarity, confusion, and every form of violence"; and even Europe, which, despite all of its advances, offered few examples of "a well constituted government or a well governed people." William Pitt feared political tyranny like a contagious disease. Extensive trade with India meant that the "riches of Asia have been poured in upon us, and have brought with them not only Asiatic luxury but, I fear, Asiatic principles of government."[7]

When parliamentary actions created fears that power threatened the liberties of Americans, many colonists embraced their continental identity more fully. Facing a shared external threat from a distant Parliament, the continent had a geographically insular and unified nature that provided a defense against tyranny's spread and a basis for an expansive circle of trust in defending rights. The North American landmass appeared as an asylum of liberty, its natural features a bulwark against the tyranny plaguing other continents.

Samuel Williams of Boston, for example, gave a sermon that partook of geography texts almost as much as it did of the Bible. His *A Discourse on the Love of Our Country* (1775) echoed *Cato's Letters* and gave a quick global tour that relied on continental taxonomies to convey the terrifying spread of tyranny. Williams took his listeners and readers around the world, continent by continent: "All Asia is over-run with this plague"; Africa, where "scarce any human beings are to be found but barbarians, tyrants, and slaves," was in equally bad shape; and "nor is Europe free from the curse." Britain clung to political liberty, but "her senators and historians are repeatedly predicting, that the time will come, when continued corruption and standing armies will prove mortal distempers in her constitution." Similarly, John Zubly, a delegate to the Continental Congress, preached on the cause of liberty before Georgia's Provincial Congress. In his widely reprinted sermon, he examined liberty's state around the world. His disturbing "survey of the globe" showed the rarity of the precious "birthright of man": "All Asia and Africa are out of the question; in the southern hemisphere of America, it is unknown, and astonishing pains are now taking, to drive it out of this northern continent."[8]

Yet Zubly and Williams remained hopeful. Zubly declared that the "bulk of the inhabitants of a continent extending eighteen hundred miles in front on the atlantic, and permitting an extension in breadth as far as the south sea [the Pacific]" knew that their liberties were under threat and were willing to defend them. If they failed to stand up for their rights, it would be an "error imbibed by millions" in the "present and future generations." Williams told his audience that it was "to our own country then we must look for the biggest part of that liberty and freedom that yet remains." Their future was bright: Americans possessed liberty, and their numbers doubled at least every twenty-five years. They were aided by North America's natural attributes: "That vigour and industry which is the natural growth of our own climate, applied to the soil, never fails to give the labourer what neither Europe nor Asia will afford him." But Williams cautioned his audience that "if we love our country" and "if you are Americans any more than by name," everyone must "reform every kind of extravagance, superfluity, and unnecessary expence."[9] Asiatic luxury threatened to engulf liberty; frugality and virtue, applied in the American environment, would protect colonists from British depredations and the fate of Asians.

As mainland colonists felt more alienated by Parliament, their rhetoric describing North America became increasingly radical. Whereas commentators such as William Smith had thanked providence that Great Britain had acquired that part of the Americas "ordained to empire" or even projected North America as the future seat of the British Empire, by the mid-1770s more writers focused on North America's distinctive and separate nature. In doing so, they pointed to a natural independence that presaged political independence. One periodical celebrating the continent's future asked Americans to "look eastward, and westward, northward and southward," where they would see that the "friendly ocean flows round you." Liberty was spreading "and flashes like lightning through the distant reaches of your vast continent. The time is coming, when the knee of empires and splendid kingdoms will bow to your greatness." A year later, in February 1775, after the First Continental Congress had convened to respond to the Coercive Acts, the same periodical prefaced an article on Indians west of the Great Lakes by noting that it would "assist the geographer in a further description of an inland part of this vast continent, which seems to be marked out by providence for the grandest empire upon the globe, and whose greatness the wickedness and folly of Great-Britain (though they mean otherwise) are hastening at a great rate." America, it hoped, would be "an assylum to the distressed and persecuted of all nations, as it was to our renowned forefathers."[10]

After independence, the logical extension of such rhetoric was to recognize North America as a continental empire instead of a continent within an empire. When the Continental Congress declared a fast day, the *United States Magazine* supported it because "our present struggle involves in the happiness not of thirteen but perhaps of an hundred states, that shall yet be added to the rising and confederate empire. The safety of the far-extended settlements that lie along the coast of the Atlantic, is not the only subject of the controversy. If you would obtain an adequate idea of the empire yet in embrio, you must extend your apprehension from the bay of Hudson to the gulph of California."[11]

Once it was clear that the British would not easily defeat the rebellious Americans, the Dutch scientist Jan Ingenhousz surmised, in a letter to Benjamin Franklin, that Britain would seek European support by casting the conflict in similarly epochal terms. Britain, he wrote, will try to convince European nations that, if the American revolutionaries succeed,

> they will soon set up as conquerors of the new world. They will subject not only to their own empire the Neibouring Empire of Mexico, the back settlements of the Spaniards. . . . They will depopulate half Europe from its inhabitants who will crowd to that happy shore where true liberty and a new wealth unknown in Europe will attend them. . . . In short America will soon become the most powerfull nation which ever existed upon the face of the earth and will as a second Rome extend their dominion far out of their own country and become arbiters of Europe itself making it dependent of its will.[12]

Not simply hyperbole, such predictions rested on plausible assumptions, given the geopolitical framework that had governed policymakers' decisions for the previous quarter-century. Nature had helped position Britain's colonies as the precarious first domino, which, if it fell, would cause other European nations to lose their colonies in the Americas. The conflict between Britain and her colonies had global ramifications to those accustomed to viewing the world through a continental template. The mainland colonies' geographic situation made them an essential part of a growing empire, whether a part of Britain or not.

KING AND CONGRESS

To transform North America from a continent within an empire into a continental empire, colonists had to sever their relationship with the king.[13] Before 1774, colonists directed their ire over taxes and reform toward Parliament. At the same time that they opposed Parliament, they maintained that they were part of the British constitutional system by virtue of the charters granted to them by the king. By 1774, many viewed the monarchy as the sole political institution formally linking the colonies to Britain. Over the next two years, however, a two-part shift in the political outlook of many colonists turned what had been a resistance movement against parliamentary rule into a revolution. First, they came to see all British authority, particularly that of the king, as illegitimate. Second, they largely acquiesced to a new authority: the Continental Congress.

Traditionally, the king had strong and legitimate powers, even within mainstream Whig thought. These powers joined a continent to an island 3,000 miles away and helped colonists see North America, even though it would eventually become the strongest part of the British Empire, as part of a unified kingdom. The king helped provide a proper balance in the ongoing battle between political authority and liberty; his authority checked liberty, which, if left unrestrained, would degenerate into anarchy. The monarch also had a number of positive roles. He protected his people, preserved order, granted governing authority through devices such as charters, and maintained unity among subjects and dominions.[14]

In the pamphlet wars leading up to independence, authors carefully distinguished between the powers of Parliament and those of the king. The Pennsylvania jurist James Wilson, in a pamphlet initially written in response to the Townshend duties but not published until 1774, argued, "Allegiance to the king and obedience to the Parliament are founded on very different principles. The former is founded on protection: the latter, on representation." The colonies continued in their allegiance to the king because he reciprocated with protection. This relationship had underpinned the founding of the colonies and their charters. According to Wilson, they "held the lands under *his* grants, and paid *him* the rents reserved upon them: They established governments under the sanction of his prerogative, or by virtue of his charters. No application for those purposes was made to the Parliament." As Arthur Lee of Virginia explained, "All territory taken possession in any manner whatsoever, by the king's subjects, rests absolutely in him." The only political tie among the colonies, and between the colonies and other parts of the British Empire, rested in the sovereignty of the king, which, in turn, hinged on a reciprocal relationship of obedience and protection.[15]

The king's reign rested on a political culture that deemed hierarchy a part of the natural social order. The king was society's metaphorical father, protecting his subjects, the children. Colonial assemblies, conventions, and committees of correspondence often referred to their "sister colonies," reflecting their equality within the British system. The colonies' charters, granted by the fatherly king, bestowed British mainlanders with their legal status within the British Empire, and outside the jurisdiction of Parliament.

Before 1776, most colonists accepted their subordinate relationship to the king even as they rejected their subjection to Parliament, which, without representation, made them inferior subjects.[16]

At the same time that British political culture situated the king atop society, it also metaphorically placed him at society's center. Within this view, the king was the heart and soul of an organic "body politic," or he could sometimes be a part of a more mechanical union, a "vast and complicated machine of government." Mixing these metaphors, "America Solon" explained in the *Boston Gazette,* "The King is the centre of union. . . . [T]he various parts of the great body politic will be united in him; he will be the spring and soul of the union, to guide and regulate the grand political machine."[17] Benjamin Franklin viewed the king's authority over the colonies as "a Means of preserving Peace among them with each other, and a Center in which their Common Force might be united."[18] Likewise, the king's relationship to the parts of the empire, according to Alexander Hamilton, was one in which he "conjoins all these individual societies into one great body politic." He must, "like a central force, attract them all to the same point."[19] These descriptions of the king as a central force analogous to gravity presented a monarchy in terms as spatial as they were hierarchical. As the unifier, the king prevented dominions from becoming too distant; he neutralized centrifugal forces.

The king performed this function well, and the colonists' loyalty to him persisted into the 1760s and early 1770s.[20] When the king assented to the Intolerable Acts, however, the relationship deteriorated. The Quebec Act cast a particularly dark shadow over the monarch. In agreeing to the normalization of Catholicism in a Quebec that now extended deep into regions claimed by older British colonies, he became a source of danger rather than protection. In late 1774, many newspapers even began to argue that the king had violated his coronation oath by sanctioning "popery, slavery and arbitrary power" in his dominions.[21] The assaults on the King's authority intensified in January 1776, when word spread that the king had taken a hard line toward the colonies in a speech to Parliament on October 26, 1775. In response to the Continental Congress's "Olive Branch Petition," which declared loyalty to the king and expressed the hope that he would seek reconciliation with the colonies after the horrendous bloodshed at Breed's (Bunker) Hill, the king declared the colonies in rebellion and desirous of "establishing an independent empire." Finding this intolerable, he would increase British forces in North America and bolster them with foreign mercenaries.[22] Except to diehard loyalists, the king appeared not as a source of unity, but as a fomenter of war.

For Thomas Paine, the time had come to push colonists over a threshold. Just as word of the king's hard-line speech reached the colonies, Paine published his popular pamphlet. In *Common Sense* (1776), George III was only symptomatic of the more deeply rooted and "exceedingly ridiculous" idea of monarchy itself. "Small islands," incapable of self-defense, "are the proper objects for kingdoms," Paine proclaimed. Far from providing protection, loyalty to the king endangered Americans. The king's foes were America's: "France and Spain never were, nor perhaps ever will be our enemies as *Americans,* but as our being the subjects of *Great Britain.*" Paine rejected the notion that the only relationship the colonies had to one another was as "sisters" under the parenthood of England. Americans' true loyalty lay with their continent, not with a supposedly strong king or united British Empire: "This continent would never suffer itself to be drained of inhabitants to support the British arms in either Asia, Africa, or Europe." The pamphlet has a well-deserved reputation for having galvanized a movement not just for resistance, but for independence. Most simply, *Common Sense* argued, "There is something very absurd, in supposing a continent to be perpetually governed by an island." And most important, it helped turn metageographical presumptions into powerful arguments favoring continental union and a new continental authority.[23]

THE CONGRESSIONAL QUEST FOR UNITY

When colonists rejected their king and severed their institutional attachment to the British Empire, they required a new source of cohesion lest they risk falling into anarchy or civil war. As the historian Jerrilyn Marston has argued, "The Congress had become both the symbol of that unity and the institution responsible for coordinating and directing a common resistance policy."[24] But when delegates converged in Philadelphia in the fall of 1774 to develop a response to the Coercive Acts, they had no expectation that their assembly would transform into a government.[25] Indeed, many of the provincial resolutions calling for a congress also professed loyalty to the king.[26] The calling of a congress was itself a conciliatory gesture. Boston, bearing the brunt of the Coercive Acts, had called on ports in other colonies to cease trade with Britain in protest. Many were unwilling to take such a radical step, and convening a congress seemed a more modest and tentative approach and a way to for colonies to defer judgment on an embargo. As such, the initial calls for a congress can be seen in part as a sign of disunion, the unwillingness of many colonies to jump headlong behind the most radical impulses emanating from those suffering the most. To many, the Continental Congress had credibility as a pragmatic and measured alternative.[27]

Understandably, suspicion among the delegates ran high, and their diversity worsened matters. John Adams noted that the delegates differed from one another as if they came from "several distinct Nations." In another letter he termed it a "Miracle" if the mixture of "such heterogenous Ingredients did not at first produce violent Fermentations."[28] If delegates remembered past failures at colonial union, they had reason to doubt that they could form a strong confederation. Moreover, radicals and conservatives divided over whether even to forge a confederation. Conservatives feared it as a preliminary step toward independence, and radicals wanted it for that very reason.

Nevertheless, the Continental Congress managed to wield enough authority to unify the colonies and declare a new nation. It was able to do so partly because delegates had common ideological ground and imperial policies severely limited their options and because it assumed only those powers traditionally reserved for the king.[29] Equally important, however, was the perception of unity conferred on the Continental Congress by nature. Even without the formal political union under the Articles of Confederation, many understood the Continental Congress, the colonies, and eventually the nation to be confederated by virtue of sharing a continent. When the delegates came together, they represented unique political entities, but they also knew—metageographical presumptions had told them—that they shared a destiny. Confronting in one another an assembly of strangers, congressional delegates realized that they had to mount a resistance movement and, later, construct a new society on a sure footing. Nothing could provide as sound a foundation as nature. On the second day of congressional deliberations, the delegate Patrick Henry argued that "by the oppression of Parliament all Government was dissolvd & that we were reduced to a State of Nature. That there were no longer any such distinctions as Colonies. That he conceiv'd himself not a Virginian but an American." Although Henry made his comments in the context of a debate over representation, his comments suggest the lurking belief in the continent as a natural geographic entity that guided his and other delegates' thinking. Two years later, and after independence, Benjamin Rush echoed the belief, again in the context of a thorny debate over representation in a federal system: "I am not plead[in]g the Cause of Pensylvania. In half a century she may be and probably will be as near the smallest as she now is the greatest states. New Hampshire & Georgia will probably receive most benefit from it if any exclusive Advantages from repres[entatio]n by numbers. No Sir—I am pleading the cause of the Continent—of mankind—of posterity."[30]

Henry and Rush invoked their continental identity in the debate over how to best represent colonies, and then states, in the Continental Congress. Their claims that their loyalty to America outweighed any provincial or state affiliation might be seen as rhetoric crafted in pursuit of their real goal—empowering Virginia or Pennsylvania, two large colonies—through representation proportional to population. Undoubtedly, their arguments partook of such ulterior motives, but proponents of allocating representatives among the states equally also put forth no less self-serving, yet equally grand, visions of a continental future.

In the summer of 1776, for instance, John Witherspoon, president of Princeton University and New Jersey delegate, argued that the delegates should strive to craft a durable confederacy that would last beyond the end of hostilities with Britain. Like many delegates, Witherspoon assumed and feared that the centrifugal forces of state loyalties would tear any confederacy to shreds once the shared British enemy had been defeated. Witherspoon tapped into such fears, arguing that small states, such as his own New Jersey, would have little incentive to stay the course in a war for independence against Britain if, as a result, it would simply make them susceptible to the tyranny of a large neighboring state, such as Pennsylvania. It would, Witherspoon maintained, "greatly diminish the glory and importance of the struggle, whether considered as for the rights of mankind in general, or for the prosperity and happiness of the continent in future times." States, in turn, would defect from the confederacy, "considering our success itself as only a prelude to a contest of a more dreadful nature." Suggesting that the bond among Americans was far stronger than any that they had had with the empire, he warned that any war between states would be "more properly a civil war than that which now often obtains the name." Witherspoon then concluded on an optimistic note. Seeing the history of societies as one of progress, he foresaw Americans keeping pace: "It is not impossible, that in future times all the states on one quarter of the globe, may see it proper by some plan of union, to perpetuate security and peace; and sure I am, a well planned confederacy among the states of America, may hand down the blessings of peace and public order to many generations."[31]

Much more lay at the heart of the comments made by Henry, Rush, and Witherspoon than the issue of equitable representation. Their words cut to the very core of what the congress was and whence it derived its authority. Did the congress represent the states or the people? Was it a body politic or more an international or multilateral response to the exigencies of war? Was it "the beginnings of national politics," as Jack Rakove and others have argued, or simply a compact among sovereign states?[32] Delegates knew that the Continental Congress's authority hinged on its representative nature, but they disagreed on what exactly it represented. At issue, then, was what kind of unity this group of people had. How would they present themselves to Britain and the world?

A "CONTINENTAL" CONGRESS

Making a case against the "nationalist" interpretation of the Continental Congress, David C. Hendrickson has argued that the "language and aspirations of later periods of American history have been imposed on an earlier epoch." Contemporaries understood the Continental Congress as a federal system. But in the 1770s and 1780s, "congress" and "federal" had different connotations from those they hold for most modern Americans. " 'Congress,' " as Hendrickson explains, "was a diplomatic term, signifying an assembly of states or nations, such as Westphalia or Utrecht, in which no state was understood in the law of nations as binding itself by its mere appearance: it would be obligated only to the extent it agreed to be obligated." Similarly, when eighteenth-century statesmen described a "federal" arrangement among states, it signified what in modern parlance might be described as "internationalism" or "multilateralism." As such, the term "federal" does not connote the strong central government it does today. It is also telling that the colonists and delegates did not construe their particular institution as a "parliament," which would have had the binding legislative powers that modern Americans associate with the U.S. Congress in its federal system. Thus, according to Hendrickson, the unity of mainland colonists in 1776 departs from the modern sense of "the nation."[33]

It is essential to avoid anachronism, and Hendrickson's approach is a fruitful one that can be carried further—but in another direction—by carefully studying contemporary labels applied to the Continental Congress. The delegates of the First Continental Congress had few precedents to draw on when they met. Perhaps the closest models for their actions were the English extralegal conventions of 1215, 1660, and 1688. These conventions sought to correct perceived illegitimate acts of government and, on doing so, disband. Some observers explicitly compared these conventions to the Continental Congress, and many delegates initially called their meeting a "convention."[34] The records of the deliberations at the First Continental Congress are notoriously thin, especially on the decision to adopt that title. But one delegate, James Duane, noted that in the first meeting, "A Question was then put what Title the Convention should assume & it was agred that it should be called *the Congress.*"[35] At first glance, this brief comment would seem to be in keeping with Hendrickson's position—and, indeed, the congress initially may have been perceived as one in a purely diplomatic sense, an assembly of representatives of sovereign powers meeting to discuss problems.

But another decision of the delegates and larger populace about nomenclature also warrants examination, even if this decision was not made consciously or after formal debate. Close examination suggests that the adjective "continental," despite its widespread use, was only an unofficial part of the institution's title. It fails to appear in the majority of the Continental Congress's broadsides, the Declaration of Independence, or even the Articles of Confederation. Instead, it was an informal label whose usage surged and to which people silently acceded.

When colonies initially called for a congress, they rarely applied the descriptor "continental." Most colonial assemblies' resolutions favoring a meeting of delegates called simply for a "congress" or a "general congress." A mere 8 percent of the references to the Continental Congress in the provincial resolutions and the delegates' credentials (documents presented by delegations that legitimized their representation) written in the summer of 1774 called for a "Continental Congress," whereas 46 percent called for a "General Congress." During the First Continental Congress, the delegates carried this practice forward. In their correspondence during the First Continental Congress, only six letters referred to their body as the "general congress," and only two referred to it as the "continental congress."[36]

Though the provincial resolutions and delegates' credentials typically avoided the term "Continental Congress," they did reveal a striking continental identity in other ways. Massachusetts called the Coercive Acts an attack on the "whole province and continent." Radicals in Massachusetts were, of course, trying to convince the other colonies to back their cause, but the resolutions of these colonies echoed Massachusetts's portrayal. South Carolina saw a threat to the liberty of all "subjects residing on the American Continent." Pennsylvania argued for the need to obtain "redress of American grievances." Virginia called for a general congress to consider the "state of the whole Continent," and its delegates' credentials noted the "alarming situation of the Continent of North America."[37] The lack of references to a "Continental Congress" suggests, then, a cautious or uncertain view of the embryonic institution, not the lack of a continental identity. Many realized that as Americans they shared a "common cause," but they doubted the ability of a congress to develop a common, continental solution.

Something changed quickly in late 1774 and persisted through 1776. Usage of the term "Continental Congress" surged dramatically. Delegates' letters referred to the "Continental Congress" sixty-five times in 1775 and 1776. Equally striking, use of the term transcended what historians have variously described as "factions," "voting blocs," or "parties." A number of historians have categorized delegates as "radical," "moderate," or "conservative." Yet there is no strong correlation between membership in these camps and the tendency to describe the congress as "continental."[38] Both the radical Son of Liberty Samuel Adams and the conservative seeker of reconciliation John Dickinson used the term. The term was settled on not through formal or published debate but through everyday practice. Thus, and perhaps because people did not dwell on whether or not to apply the term, its usage gives us a profound indicator of sincere thoughts about a communal self.

Evidence from beyond the delegates' letters demonstrates the generality of the trend, as the colonial press followed the same pattern. Readers of the *Pennsylvania Gazette,* a representative newspaper with data now readily accessible to historians, saw the term "Continental Congress" ascend in usage during the late fall of 1774 and remain popular through 1776. In a mere fourteen months the term appeared in the newspaper's pages 169 times. Then its usage plummeted dramatically, and it made it into print only forty-four more times over the next twelve years.[39] Suddenly, the delegates and the press had come to see the congress as less "continental." Why?

CONTINENTAL FAILURES

Congressional delegates may have first met in the modest Carpenter's Hall, a small building on a neck of land sandwiched between the Delaware and Schuylkill rivers, but their ambitions were grand. They were soon styling themselves a "Continental Congress," and they shouldered the label's connotations. They immediately set about creating a truly continental confederation. Yet as in all actions and decision-making processes, word choice operates within constraints. In this instance, it took time for the constraints to become apparent, but once they did, doubts surfaced about just how successful the Continental Congress would be in implementing its vision. In a kind of linguistic *Realpolitik* carried out by a large aggregate of individuals, the congress became less "continental," and the label's usage dwindled.

Congressional delegates expressed elements of their ambitious geopolitical vision early in overtures to Quebec. One of the delegates' handful of references to a "Continental Congress" in 1774 appeared in a letter to that colony. On October 21, Congress resolved to approach Quebec and established a committee including Thomas Cushing, Richard Henry Lee, and

John Dickinson to draft a letter. Following its presentation to the Continental Congress at large, it received only minor changes, suggesting a broad consensus and acceptance of the letter's geopolitical assumptions.

The letter to Quebec explained that "the crown and its ministers shall be as absolute throughout your extended province, as the despots of Asia or Africa." Then it asked the region's Catholics to look beyond their religious differences with the Protestants to their south. After all, the Swiss cantons had a union "composed of Roman Catholic and Protestant States, living in the utmost concord and peace with one another, and thereby enabled . . . to defy and defeat every tyrant that has invaded them." All inhabitants of the British Empire on the North American mainland shared threats to their rights and liberties as British subjects. But they shared more, as Dickinson wrote: "A moment's reflection should convince you which will be most for your interest and happiness, to have all the rest of North-America your unalterable friends, or your inveterate enemies. The injuries of Boston have roused and associated every colony, from Nova-Scotia to Georgia. Your province is the only link wanting, to compleat the bright and strong chain of union. Nature has joined your country to theirs." The letter then invited Quebec to send delegates to the next meeting of the "Continental Congress" the following May.[40]

This peaceful overture failed, foreshadowing the congress's inability to unite the continent politically. Undeterred, the congress followed its diplomatic overture with a military campaign modeled after those of the Seven Years' War that assumed the St. Lawrence River to be critical to control of the continent. Even as the army made its northward thrust, however, General Washington made an appeal to Canadians echoing that of the Continental Congress in 1774. "The cause of America and of liberty is the cause of every virtuous American Citizen Whatever may be his Religion or his descent," he wrote. "Come then, my Brethern, Unite with us in an indissoluble Union." Colonel Benedict Arnold and his men, who had been ordered to follow rivers through Maine to Quebec while Major General Philip Schuyler's forces traveled through western New York to Montreal, were to consider themselves "as marching, not through an Enemy's Country; but that of our Friends and Brethren." Should they disobey their orders they might bring "Shame, Disgrace and Ruin to themselves and Country." But success would help foster a "lasting Union and Affection" between the thirteen colonies and Canadians.[41] Even accounting for ulterior motives in treating the inhabitants of Canada well—a gentle campaign would surely lessen the possibility of creating more enemies—Washington's tone departed dramatically from the anti-Catholic rhetoric—and the actual ethnic cleansing of Acadians—aimed at Britain's age-old enemy during the Seven Years' War.

Equally telling is how much differently Washington approached Bermudans than Canadians. About a week before he wrote to the Canadians, Washington prepared a letter to accompany Captain Abraham Whipple, who was to embark for Bermuda in a scheme to import the gunpowder there for the Continental Army. In soliciting the islanders' support, Washington referred to them as "Brother Colonists" with whom mainlanders were "firmly united in Sentiment," for the "Cause of Virtue & Liberty is confined to no Continent or Climate." Yet these shared values were not enough to invite them to join a union as fellow citizens. Bermudans and mainlanders remained "divided by our Situation" and "separated in Space or Distance." Hence, Washington approached them more as a potential military ally than as a member of the same community. In return for the gunpowder, he offered only "provisions" and "every other Mark of Affection & Friendship which the grateful Citizens of a free Country can bestow on its Brethren & Benefactors." He did so even though large swaths of the southern mainland were technically closer to Bermuda than Quebec. Bermuda was a distinct island, not part of a shared continent.[42]

DESPITE the warm, welcoming tone adopted toward Canada, the northern campaign of 1775–76 delivered the first major military setback for the Americans' cause. When Schuyler's and Arnold's forces assaulted Quebec on December 31, 1775, British troops withstood the attack and forced the Continental Army's eventual retreat. Quebec—the city that throughout the eighteenth century had guarded access to the St. Lawrence and thus the continent—remained in British hands. The congress and the army had failed in their attempt to fashion militarily a reality that matched their continental aspirations. For the rest of the war, these Americans would, as they understood it, lack "the only link wanting" to ensure their eventual control of the continent.

But the territorial ambitions did not cease after this first, failed northern foray. Revolutionaries dreamed—"assumed" might be a better word—that the conflict would resolve the issue of boundaries in their favor. Secure borders, they thought, constituted as much a natural right as popular sovereignty. Unfazed by the failure at Quebec, John Adams wrote to James Warren in February 1776: "The Unanimous Voice of the Continent is Canada must be ours; Quebec must be taken." In 1778, his tone remained the same. "As long as Great Britain shall have Canada, Nova Scotia, and the Floridas, or any of them," he wrote, "so long will Great Britain be the enemy of the United States." Regarding these same disputed regions, Samuel Adams predicted, "We shall never be upon a solid Footing till Britain cedes to us what Nature designs we should have, or till we wrest it from her." Regarding western lands, John Witherspoon gave a speech to the congress slighting the relevance of charters in determining the nation's rights to these territories. Instead, in a passage that could just as easily have been delivered in the run-up to the colonists' war with France twenty years earlier, he suggested that the continent was obviously big enough for only one power: "This nation was known to be settled along the Coasts to a certain extent; if any European country was admitted to establish colonies or settlements behind them, what security could they have for the enjoyment of peace."[43]

Failure at Quebec could not quench the "attitude of expectant heirship," as one historian has described it, that persisted in congressional maneuvers through 1776.[44] By the middle of that year, the congress had already established a Committee of Secret Correspondence and sent Silas Deane to France to investigate the possibility of foreign aid. Many in the Continental Congress thought that securing significant aid required a declaration of independence and that maintaining independence would, in turn, hinge on obtaining more extensive aid than France had already covertly supplied. Accordingly, on June 10–11, Congress resolved to appoint committees to draft a declaration of independence and a "plan of treaties to be proposed to foreign powers."[45] The declaration committee delegated most of its work to Thomas Jefferson, and the treaty-plan committee entrusted most of its task to John Adams.

Before Adams began writing, Thomas Paine had already laid out a vision for American foreign relations in *Common Sense*. There he argued that commerce, not politics, should bind the United States to Europe. Commerce could "secure [to the United States] the peace and friendship of all of Europe." Because North America produced so many of the "necessaries of life," an independent United States would have a market to sell its goods as long as "eating is the custom of Europe." Americans should thus simply allow Europeans to compete for American trade instead of privileging or establishing a "partial connection" with any European power.[46]

Paine's ideas on international relations have aptly been described as "idealistic internationalism." In short, he foresaw a new world order that relied largely on presumptions of continental grandeur. He offered a blueprint for American diplomacy predicated on the marriage of two seemingly countervailing tendencies—insularity and expansionism—made compatible by metageographical assumptions. The United States could avoid entangling European alliances as long as it assumed its natural state and became a continental society whose trade constituted a prize for which Europeans competed. Paine envisioned the continent as a self-ordering society, following geographical precepts more than those of governmental power. Hence, the interests of the king or any particular European power could never be fully reconciled with those of Americans, and Paine distrusted traditional European diplomacy for its pursuit of parochial state concerns instead of true, North American—indeed global—interests. *Common Sense* helped turn metageographical presumptions into guiding principles for U.S. diplomacy that endured well beyond the Revolutionary era.[47]

Although Adams undoubtedly drew inspiration from a number of sources, his work echoed many of the principles spelled out by Paine. The "Model Treaty" or "Plan of Treaties" voiced the same striking assumptions, even arrogance, as *Common Sense* when it came to the bargaining position of the fledgling United States. As he told his fellow committee members, "We should avoid all Alliance, which might embarrass Us in after times and might involve us in future European Wars." Instead, "A Treaty of commerce which would . . . Admit France into an equal participation of the benefits of our commerce . . . would be an ample compensation to France for Acknowledging our Independence."[48] The lure of North American markets and products would suffice to gain the support necessary to secure American independence. Correspondingly, the Model Treaty envisioned only ties of commercial equality with European allies. The United States would not encumber itself with political or military alliances; nor would European troops step foot on American soil to support the United States. Instead, the French—at whom the Model Treaty was initially aimed—would pay no higher duties on American imports than Americans would on French imports, thus opening American trade with France, exposing that nation's shipping to British depredations and drawing Louis XVI into the war.[49]

Among its more notable terms, the first draft of the Model Treaty required, in case of war between France and Great Britain, that France "shall never invade, nor under any pretence attempt to possess" any part of "the Continent of North America." Rather, the United States "shall have the sole, exclusive, undivided and perpetual Possession of all the Countries, Cities, and Towns, on the said Continent, and of all Islands near to it, which now are, or lately were under the Jurisdiction of or Subject to the King or Crown of Great Britain, whenever the [same can be invaded, and conquered by the said united States, or shall in any manner submit to or be] shall be united or confederated with the said united States."[50] The drafters of the proposed treaty thought it worth reserving for the United States only those islands in intimate proximity to the mainland that had strategic value in relationship to the St. Lawrence River: Newfoundland, Cape Breton, St. John's, and Anticosti. When it came to the West Indies, they wanted to stipulate that, should France conquer any islands under British control, the United States was only to be guaranteed "Rights, Liberties, Priviledges, Immunities and Exemptions in Trade, Commerce and Navigation to and from the said Islands."[51]

The congress approved an only slightly modified draft of the Model Treaty in September 1776, and it sent Benjamin Franklin and Arthur Lee to join Silas Deane in Paris to negotiate it into reality. Franklin had already lent the congress his diplomatic skills that spring with an arduous journey to Canada to try to bring that colony into the resistance movement. There the spectacle dismayed the man who had so eloquently argued for the necessity of acquiring Canada after the Seven Years' War. On the heels of Montgomery and Arnold's failed assault, and lacking adequate supplies, the continental troops "must starve, plunder, or surrender," wrote Franklin. They were alienating, not liberating, the populace. Yet Franklin's desire for Canada remained steadfast, and as he traveled to France he had congressional support. The final version of the Model Treaty, similar to its predecessor, restricted France from "Labradore, New Britain, Nova Scotia, Acadia, Canada, Florida," or any other part of the continent. Any lands on or in very close proximity to the continent that had been under British rule eventually were to be "united or confederated with the said United States." The goal had been the same since the Seven Years' War: Mainlanders wanted contiguous settlements with clear natural boundaries.[52]

During Franklin's voyage, the American war effort deteriorated. While Franklin was at sea, New York, proclaimed by John Adams a "key to the whole Continent, as it is a Passage to Canada, to the Great Lakes, and to all the Indian Nations," fell to the British, and Washington's army steadily retreated across New Jersey to Pennsylvania.[53] Not surprisingly, a congress that had fled Philadelphia also felt its sense of expectant heirship to the continent wither. Desperate for alliances with Europeans, it revised its diplomatic instructions. Now, the congress would allow Franklin and his compatriots to use half of Newfoundland and half of the neighboring fishery as bargaining chips to lure France to the American cause. Spain, too, could be enticed with territory. If that nation entered the war, the United States could promise assistance in securing to it "the town and harbour of Pensacola." The United States would demand in return only use of the harbor and free navigation of the Mississippi River.[54]

Congress had become less "continental" in its expansionist pursuits, and it soon became less insular politically. French diplomats saw intervention in the American Revolution as a way to reshape the European balance of power in their favor. Yet the pace of French naval armament left them unwilling to enter the war until the 1778 campaign season. The slow pace of the French softened the negotiating position of the Americans, even after the Continental Army won a resounding victory at Saratoga in October 1777.[55] When the French and Americans finally came to terms, their agreement included a commercial treaty similar to the Model Treaty in that it established trade on a most-favored-nation basis. At the same time, however, it included an entangling military alliance binding the two states together. In addition to requiring mutual military assistance should France enter a war with Great Britain, the "Treaty of Alliance" prevented the United States from concluding a peace with Great Britain without the consent of the French. This encumbrance became even worse than it initially appeared when France, in order to lure Spain into the conflict, secretly promised to fight until Spain had recovered Gibraltar. Unbeknownst to the United States, the struggle for a continent was now tied to the fate of a rock in the Mediterranean. Paine's and Adams's visions of a continental power immune from political wrangling and interest-based European diplomacy had faded. Franklin, Lee, and Deane had conceded, as one historian has put it, to "an entangling alliance made at the behest of a superior power."[56]

AGAINST the backdrop of these events, usage of "Continental Congress" waned just as quickly as it had waxed. The term appeared in delegates' letters only nine times from 1777 to 1789, and five of these were in 1777.[57] By the end of 1776, the continental aspirations of the congress had suffered severe blows, and, as is apparent in delegates' correspondence, the institution's "continental" aspect had faded.

Yet this happened only after ideas about continents gave patriots something to latch on to—a view of themselves that helped check some of the potent forces working against a functioning union from 1774 to 1776—and only after the Continental Congress had built a resistance movement capable of defeating the British. In this respect, the decision of colonists to describe themselves as "continental," to choose and to use a metageographical conception of themselves, was a collective action that, although perhaps less dramatic, was no less important than, say, Washington's crossing the Delaware, or France's declaration of war on Britain, in determining the outcome of the Revolution.

One of the functions of nationalism is to create a common identity or ambition among a large group of people who do not know one another and likely never will. The idea that the continent had an inherent unity, expressed and reinforced through linguistic practice, did just that; it made Americans a "people" in the minds of many. Although the congress failed to draw Quebec into the union and to keep Americans politically insulated from European commitments, the idea of British mainland colonists as a continental people provided a foundation for the institution to assume some of the powers of a rejected king and to declare and defend independence.[58] In this respect, the idea of the continent functioned much like a shared language or ethnicity did in some of the nationalist movements of nineteenth- and twentieth-century Europe. There, ideas about a common bond—whether linguistic or ethnic—drove people who did not know one another personally to struggle and fight together to establish nation-states, such as Germany and Italy. In the case of the mainland North American colonies, the idea of the continent led many colonists to presume that they shared something with other North Americans—even French Catholics—beyond threats to their liberty.

To be effective, the Continental Congress had to overcome the colonists' fear of centralized power, the lack of historical examples of successful large republics, the absence of a strong national consciousness, and the long history that the states had as distinct corporate entities.[59] All of these obstacles permeated the paramount issue dividing radicals and moderates, revolutionaries and loyalists, from 1774 to 1776: independence. Conservatives sought to preserve, as much as possible, the sovereignty of existing colonial governments and worried that independence would force a reordering within newly created states. They feared independence because they viewed domestic turmoil—even revolution—as a possible corollary.[60] The idea that the congress was continental alleviated these worries. The metageographical assumption that states or nations—or, as was the case from 1774 to 1776, colonies—constituted the building blocks of continents, like pieces of a jigsaw puzzle, allowed for their continued sovereignty, even as the idea of the continent imparted unity to the whole.[61] As Martin Lewis and Kären Wigen note in a modern context, "Political maps that also highlight continents encourage us to imagine that nation-states are the building blocks of these higher-order entities, and therefore must nest neatly within them. States, in a word, are seen as constituent units of continents."[62] Conservatives could see colonies, with their sovereign legislatures, as constituent units of the continent, something that radicals would have readily acceded to even if they implicitly saw in the idea of the continent hints of potential independence from the British Isles.

At the same time that conservatives feared independence and democratic impulses because they would relentlessly lead to disruption, radicals feared strong, centralized authority. Here the idea of continental unity worked to conservatives' advantage, for the unity of the continent stemmed from its being a part of a natural system—not from political machinations or human beings' quest for power. The continent might not present an example of a successful, large republic, but it did reveal an inherent natural order. Indeed, the idea of a "continental congress" appealed to many because it was something other than a "national congress." As use of "continental congress" surged and faded, delegates consistently avoided the term "national congress." Although the word "national" appears 182 times in the *Journals of the Continental Congress* and 496 times in *Letters of Delegates to Congress,* demonstrating that it was part of the lexicon, "national congress" does not appear once in either of these vast collections of documents.

In the debates over declaring independence, the idea of the continent provided common ground that was more than rhetorical. The "Continental Congress" represented a compromise between what could have been even more starkly divided factions of radicals and conservatives. It helped colonists dodge the issue of whether their collection of colonies exceeded the size of a manageable republic, for it did not establish one. At the same time, the label offered the comfort of a unity rooted in nature that helped allow a legislative body to assume executive powers and replace the discredited king. And unlike a carefully crafted seal, emblem, or motto, the provenance of which can readily be traced and which takes time and money to produce, the idea that the colonies were "continental" was readily available, emerged spontaneously, and did not appear as the product of a particular individual or interest group. It thus worked well within a group of mutually suspicious people and provided a symbol of stability—something new governments desperately need.[63]

ALTHOUGH modern Americans most admire and emphasize the second paragraph of the Declaration of Independence, with its ringing phrases about self-evident truths and the equality of all mankind, contemporaries thought the opening paragraph more important. Though today it seems relatively mundane, this portion of the Declaration of Independence was breathtaking in its arguments and assumptions. It created a union, implied a government, and asserted the equal status of the United States among the sovereign "Powers of the Earth." The declaration presumed the existence of "one People" distinct by virtue of location from that of Great Britain. It proclaimed this people's reasons for dissolving the "Political Bands which have connected them with another." And it presumed that the people had a right to "the separate and equal Station to which the Laws of Nature and Nature's God entitle them." Left unspecified was the people's territory, the limits of the United States.[64]

But the spontaneous emergence of a "Continental" Congress, Paine's arguments for independence, and congressional debates over its declaration make apparent the metageographical assumption that the people's territory was continental. Six months before the declaration, Paine had argued that, as long as the colonists insisted on calling themselves British subjects, foreign nations would see them as nothing more than "rebels" and refuse mediation. Nor would foreign nations such as France or Spain assist the colonists as long as they professed a desire to reconcile with Britain. A declaration of independence, as an expression of state sovereignty, would allow for the kind of equal commercial relations with other Europeans that only a continent could expect. That is why the congress resolved to draft the Model Treaty at the same time as the declaration. They were interconnected steps: The Declaration of Independence would establish state sovereignty; the Model Treaty would implement it.[65]

When congressional delegates divided in June 1776 over whether to declare independence, they disagreed partly over whether it was the right means to advance a geopolitical vision they otherwise shared. A declaration, opponents warned, might prevent the establishment of a continental society insulated from European political and military disputes. Although these men doubted whether "we should ever again be united with Gr. Britain," they thought that formally declaring this independence would threaten the very union they sought. Hopes for a foreign alliance, they argued, were equally misguided. Instead of backing the United States, "France & Spain had reason to be jealous of that rising power which would one day certainly strip them of their American possessions." European statesmen recognized the United States as a continental empire in embryo, one surely to become more powerful than any European state, and European nations might prefer to partition the United States rather than fuel its independence movement. Even Britain, fearing it could not reconcile with its rebellious colonies, might ally with other European powers and "agree to a partition of the territories restoring Canada to France, & the Floridas to Spain," thus reversing the gains colonists had made toward insularity and security during the Seven Years' War. Instead of fulfilling their metageographical ambitions, a declaration might transform North America into another Europe, with competing nations jockeying for power within it.[66]

These admonitions butted up against arguments that the threat of partition already existed and that a declaration would counter it. John Adams wrote to his fellow Massachusetts patriot James Warren on April 16, 1776, that America needed independence and a commercial treaty with France so that "France and Britain will not part the Continent between them." Four days later, Richard Henry Lee, who eventually introduced the resolution calling for a declaration, asked Patrick Henry whether he could believe that "whilst we are hesitating about forming alliances, Great Britain may not, and probably will not, seal our ruin by signing a Treaty of partition with two or three ambitious powers that may aid in conquering us—Upon principles of interest and revenge they surely will. When G[reat] B[ritain] finds she cannot conquer us alone, and that the whole must be lost, will she not rather choose a part than have none?" Apparently, Henry agreed, for he wrote to Adams a month later explaining the necessity of a declaration to avoid the "half of our Continent offered to France." Nearly a year later, having just been appointed as the secretary of the congress's Committee on Foreign Affairs, Thomas Paine explained that the Continental Congress had declared independence because "the continent ran the risk of being ruined every day that she delayed it. There was reason to believe that Britain would endeavor to make a European matter of it, and, rather than lose the whole, would dismember it."[67]

Whether congressional delegates opposed or favored a declaration, most shared a goal: to preserve the unity of the mainland colonies. Proponents saw a declaration as a means of using diplomacy to secure that end; opponents feared that a declaration would undercut it. Both saw the declaration as an act of foreign relations that proclaimed the existence of people and created a state commensurate with the natural unity integral to North America. It was the first public document to use the name "the United States of America."[68] The states were to be an independent union as continental as their congress.

DEFENDING independence eventually required diplomatic concessions greater than the delegates had hoped. The deterioration of the war effort in 1776 and 1777 forced diplomats to seek and accept a political and military alliance with France. Yet although it entangled the United States and departed from the remarkable vision of 1776, the alliance did not mark the complete demise of Americans' metageographical aspirations; rather, it allowed the survival of a continental empire in embryo. The congress might have lost some of its credibility as a "continental" institution, but the French alliance proved essential to the Revolution's success. News of the alliance came just in time for the United States to rebuff a British peace commission eager for reconciliation. French money and supplies sustained the American war effort. The French helped bring the Spanish and the Dutch into the war, turning the Revolution into a global conflict that spread British forces thin. And French troops and the French Navy made possible the final siege at Yorktown.

The alliance's benefits to the expansionist ambitions of the United States outweighed its entangling costs, especially given that France renounced any claims to territory it had held before the Seven Years' War. To be sure, some contemporaries—probably because they envied or carried grudges against their principal diplomat, Benjamin Franklin—criticized the French alliance for conceding too much, even territorially. Ralph Izard, for example, was in Paris but excluded from meetings with French ministers by Franklin. After the treaty, he complained that Franklin and Deane should have called for precise descriptions of the regions reserved for American conquest. Izard's grousing grew as much out of a personality conflict with Franklin as it did out of any real sense that Franklin had compromised America's continental promise, for Franklin held a vision for the continent as expansive as any.[69]

Although diplomatic and military hurdles weakened the congress's continental nature, the idea of a continental union remained. Indeed, the Continental Congress itself managed to nurse the idea along after 1778 in several ways. It placed men with strong metageographical visions—such as Benjamin Franklin, John Adams, John Jay, and Thomas Jefferson—in diplomatic positions at a time when the vagaries of transatlantic communication often left them making considerable decisions without consulting the congress. It kept American expansionism alive with the Land Ordinance of 1785 and the Northwest Ordinance of 1787, which allowed for the incorporation of large tracts of territory into the confederation. It oversaw the ratification of the Articles of Confederation in 1781, which allowed Canada to join the union despite obvious cultural and religious differences. Most important, however, was the congress's ability—tenuous and reliant on international aid though it may have been—to keep a military force in the field, because few things nurtured patriots' continental character more than war.

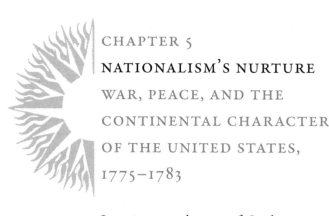

CHAPTER 5

NATIONALISM'S NURTURE

WAR, PEACE, AND THE

CONTINENTAL CHARACTER

OF THE UNITED STATES,

1775–1783

Location put the city of Quebec among the most highly prized pieces of real estate in North America. Situated at the juncture of the mighty St. Lawrence River and its St. Charles tributary, Quebec's garrison and its guns commanded the main artery through which most of Canada's commerce flowed. Contemporaries recognized the city as the "Key of Canada," the gateway to Montreal, to the upper reaches of the St. Lawrence, to the Great Lakes, to the headwaters of the Mississippi, and to regions beyond. As British North Americans strove to make their territorial dreams into territorial realities, they recognized that if they could win Quebec, they could secure much of the continent.[1]

Location also favored Quebec and vexed the calculations of those who coveted the city by making it one of the most defensible places in the world. Steep cliffs guarded it against assault from the St. Lawrence; mudflats threatened to swallow forces approaching from north; and a bastioned, thirty-foot wall shielded the city from troops that might mass to the west, on the relatively flat Plains of Abraham. When Continental forces led by Philip Schuyler's second in command, Richard Montgomery, and Benedict Arnold converged on the city in November 1775, with nearly 1,000 soldiers, they also faced the pressure of time. Enlistments were set to expire at the end of the year, and the men would be eager to return home. Arnold had already lost nearly a third of his force as he struggled northward in what had been one of the most audacious and trying military marches of the century: a damp, cold journey up the Kennebec River, a thirty-mile portage, and a float down the Chaudière River, which flowed into the St. Lawrence opposite Quebec. For the 600 who survived the journey, provisions had run so low that some survived with "nothing to eat but dogs."[2] Montgomery's 300 men who had sailed down the St. Lawrence after victories at St. Jean, Montreal, and Three Rivers joined them. Meanwhile, 1,800 troops sat inside the city ready for an assault. If they could defend the city until the spring thaw, they would surely see relief from British forces sailing upriver.

December 31, 1775, saw the only serious attempt by Continental forces during the Revolution to take Quebec. It proved disastrous. Within a couple of hours of launching a two-pronged assault, while it "snowed and blowed very plenty," the attacking troops realized that the city's defenses would hold. Montgomery took a shot in the head, and, as his corpse reddened the snow, his troops fell into chaos. Arnold's forces managed an organized retreat, carrying their leader as he bled heavily from a leg wound. At day's end, sixty Continentals had been killed or wounded, and as many as four hundred and fifty were in British hands.[3] It was all that the remaining Continental forces could do to maintain a desultory siege until British reinforcements ousted them in the spring.

Patriots' desires to incorporate Canada into the union did not die with Montgomery. The Continental Congress began planning a second Canadian incursion in January 1778. Washington, however, feared that such an expedition would either lack resources or need to rely too heavily on French assistance, opening the possibility that France, despite assurances to the contrary, might try to reclaim the region. In January 1779, the congress formally laid aside plans to assault Canada, but many delegates continued to harbor a strong urge for another expedition. After the climactic battle at Yorktown, Washington began drawing up plans to launch a major operation in September 1782. Peace talks prevented their implementation, but at the negotiating table American Commissioners pressed hard for Canada.[4] Though the United States came away from the talks with sizeable holdings, Canada was not a part of them. The concession disappointed even southerners, such as Charles Carroll, who could not help but "wish that the Canadians were confederated with us: but perhaps this must be the work of some future day."[5] Americans would have to wait until the War of 1812 for their next significant, but ill-fated, opportunity to incorporate Canada.

These attempts to promote union with Canada make sense within a broader context. The roots of the Revolution predated 1763, the year Parliament began implementing legislation that antagonized many Americans. What made the acts commencing in 1763 so irritating, so offensive, was, in part, the Seven Years' War. Masses of Americans had forged their continental identity with blood in that conflict. It bequeathed Americans a continent, and they fought the Revolution, in no small measure, to defend the war's legacy. The men whose bones strewed the battlefields of the Seven Years' War could not be allowed to have died in vain.

The Revolutionary War fostered, in turn, its own common, public memory of shared sacrifice among Americans and gave the incipient nation stories that could be told and heroes who could be venerated in all of the states. Revolutionary War memories were not created in a vacuum. Rather, they added another layer, albeit a substantial one, to those accumulated during the Seven Years' and earlier wars. This collective memory often countered Americans' strong provincialism and localism. The death of Montgomery and the failure of the Canadian expedition reinforced that a continent was at stake.[6]

To wage this war for a continent, many patriots aspired to have a truly continental army. They also realized that their hopes, not just of union with Canada, but of an independent American continent, rested more on military force than on any political institution. Still, support for the army in men and materiel from the states was sometimes thin at best, absent at worst, and the army's continental aspects proved limited. Long-standing suspicions of standing armies and growing war-weariness strained relations between the army and the broader population. Equally important in tempering widespread material support for the army was the view that it—and the war effort in general—had abundant *natural* support, soothing the consciences of armchair soldiers and reluctant state assemblies who skirted enlistment and funding calls. The continent's expanse and plentiful resources appeared not only as one of the army's greatest goals, but also as one of its most profound military assets.

Paradoxically, then, the apparent wealth of the continent heightened many patriots' optimism and kept them committed to the revolutionary cause, even as they eyed the army warily and witnessed its defeats. Notions about the continent helped many to assume that their independence movement could survive with a poor man's army, or at least it prevented them from fully grasping that the Revolution was doing just that. Moreover, when they saw their war become one against Indians, it reinforced their racial identity as white Americans, the true North Americans. Thus, a broad willingness to wage war—even if only nominally instead of through direct material support—drew sustenance from and nurtured Americans' continental character at the same time that the Continental Congress foundered. The Revolutionary War, like the Seven Years' War before it, revealed, rested on, and reinforced Americans' continental aspirations.

MEMORIES

Just as Americans at the beginning of the twenty-first century recalled Munich appeasement, Pearl Harbor surprise, and Vietnam quagmire as they entered yet another war, the Revolutionary generation bore the weight of their own past. Only sixteen years had passed since Wolfe captured the same city that Montgomery and Arnold sought. That said, Revolutionary efforts to have Canada represented in the Continental Congress and to soothe Catholic's fears of Protestant tyranny differed dramatically from the approach toward the region in the Seven Years' War. Wolfe invaded the heart of a longtime enemy's territory, and hence his assault on Quebec differed fundamentally from Montgomery and Arnold's. His campaign hinged on ruthless terror against the region's population. The resulting victory, as perceived by most colonists, gave Britain the key to the continent. Later, soldiers in the Continental Army, including those of the Canadian campaign, remembered that the gains of 1763 came at a tremendous cost. Theirs was a fight, in part, to preserve what others had struggled so hard to obtain.

The skeletons in the colonists' closet could be literal. Continental soldiers might trod over the same ground as their predecessors, sometimes stepping on their bones. Thirty-six-year-old Chaplain Ammi Robbins riddled his journal with observations of grounds consecrated by the previous conflict. On one occasion, he "visited the graves of those who died in the French war in this place; found my dear uncle Foot's, dropped a tear over it."[7] In 1776 Colonel Anthony Wayne commanded a sickly, depleted force at Fort Ticonderoga in New York. Ticonderoga had been the site of horrendous violence in 1758, when British General James Abercromby's forces suffered two thousand casualties, including hundreds of New Englanders, in a failed frontal assault against the fort's French and Indian occupants. Wayne and his Revolutionary forces could not escape Ticonderoga's haunted past. He described the site as an "ancient Golgotha or place of skulls—they are so plenty here that our people for want of other vessels drink out of them whilst the soldiers make tent pins out of the shin and thigh bones of Abercrumbies men." Chaplain Robbins, too, "viewed the place of Abercrombie's defeat in 1758. Saw many holes where the dead were flung in, and numbers of human bones, thigh, arms &c., above ground.... I never so much longed for the day to approach when men shall learn war no more, and the lion and lamb lie down together."[8]

Wayne's troops faced grim reminders of a recent past. But one did not have to drink out of a skull or drive a tibia tent stake to revisit the Seven Years' War. Many colonists knew firsthand the suffering and sacrifices of that epochal struggle. This was especially true in the colonies that had contributed the most to the fighting of the Seven Years' War—Virginia, Massachusetts, and New York—the same colonies that took the lead in resisting imperial reforms.[9] Many Revolutionary generals, including Philip Schuyler, Horatio Gates, Charles Lee, Israel Putnam, and George Washington, cut their military teeth during their service in the Seven Years' War. Washington never forgot that he twice narrowly escaped with his life in 1754 and 1755. Weeks after the Declaration of Independence and a full year after he had assumed control of the Continental Army, he still paid solemn remembrance to the anniversaries of his surrender at Fort Necessity and the slaughter of Braddock's troops and camp followers.[10]

Younger, ordinary soldiers, many of whom were mere toddlers during the Seven Years' War, could no more avoid recollections of the war than they could escape their genes or their commanding officers. They often viewed the possibility of combat through the filter of stories they had heard from their elders or their military superiors. Joseph Plumb Martin recalled his childhood: "I used . . . to inquire a deal about the French War, as it was called, which had not been long ended; my grandsire would talk with me about it while working in the fields. . . . I thought then, nothing should induce me to get caught in the toils of an army." Although he had forgotten the name, shoemaker Sylvanus Wood could still remember sixty-five years later that his first commander in the Revolution "was in the fight on Abrahams Plains with the brave General Wolfe."[11]

Consider, also, the case of Benjamin West. Although born in 1738 and raised in Pennsylvania, West had no more combat experience in the Seven Years' War than Joseph Plumb Martin or Sylvanus Wood. Instead, one of ten children of an innkeeper, he spent the war studying the classics and wielding a paintbrush instead of a musket. Still, he associated closely with those involved in the conflict. In 1756, he took up residence at the home of William Henry and his new wife Ann to compose their portrait. Henry was the primary gunsmith for the Pennsylvania forces attached to General Braddock's fatal expedition on Fort Duquesne and General Forbes's successful campaign three years later. West's elder brother served in that Forbes campaign. A few years after hostilities drew to a close, Benjamin West traveled to London, where he had the good fortune to earn the patronage of the King's Royal Academy, an institution just beginning to support some of the nation's finest painters. West cemented his reputation in 1771 when he unveiled his *The Death of General Wolfe,* a work that prompted both accolades and controversy (fig. 26).[12]

Critics complained that West had departed from artistic convention by depicting his subjects in modern dress rather than garbing his heroes in Roman togas and carrying the weapons of antiquity. When told that he should depict his subjects in classical trappings, even though they participated in a recent battle, West sharply rejoined that the death of Wolfe "took place on the thirteenth of September 1759, in a region of the world unknown to the Greeks and Romans. . . . The same truth that guides the pen of

FIGURE 26. Benjamin West, *The Death of General Wolfe* (1771). National Gallery of Canada, Ottawa

the historian should govern the pencil of the artist. . . . I want to mark the date, the place, and the parties engaged in the event."[13] Help mark the date he did. Many already recognized the British victory at Quebec as a pivotal moment in the war and Wolfe as a martyr in the cause. As West's painting drew more acclaim, such perceptions deepened. West garnered three orders to paint copies, and William Woollett made an engraving of the painting, the basis for what became the most widely circulated print of the century. It made both the painter and the engraver rich, and it reinforced and popularized the view of Wolfe as the singular martyr who helped unify the empire.[14]

Yet West's Wolfe was largely a product of the artist's imagination. Wolfe did not spend his last moments stretched out like a man just taken off a cross, with light beaming on him while a messenger hastily approached to announce the defeat of Montcalm. Nor was he surrounded by a contingent that included a variety of ranks and nationalities—from a British general to a grenadier private, an American Ranger to a Mohawk warrior—united in their sacrifice for the empire. In spite of such inaccuracy, or, better yet, because of it, West produced an icon exalting the empire. While the painting's style was innovative and controversial, its purpose was conservative.[15] Confronted with the inaccuracies of his painting, West cast aside his past rhetoric about the artist as historian: "Wolfe must not die like a common soldier under a Bush," but appear according to "the highest idea conceived of the Hero." Wolfe, as West presented him, apotheosized the empire against the backdrop of misgivings over the war's cost and colonial protests against Parliament's imposition of taxes to help pay it. One of West's students later hailed the painting for capturing the import of a victory that "annihilated the power of France on this continent, and established reformed religion, English language arts and literature, and more than English liberty from Mexico to the North pole, and from the Atlantic to the Pacific."[16]

From 1763 through the American Revolution, Britons, especially colonists, struggled to come to grips with the legacy of the Seven Years' War. West's painting was just one part of a broader phenomenon of celebrating Wolfe in the face of lingering doubts about whether his sacrifice was worth it. Just as the geographical taxonomies in expensive, leather-bound, color atlases found ways to reach ordinary people, so too did hagiographic treatments of Wolfe's martyrdom on the Plains of Abraham reverberate among common people. Prints from Woollett's engraving of *The Death of General Wolfe* may not have been a mainstay in the average mainlander's home, but they flooded European and colonial markets. Men and women who might never see West's painting, or own the print, could still read in the *Pennsylvania Gazette* about West's "most excellent Piece of Painting," which captured Wolfe's "Delicacy" and the "Purity of his Genius."[17] Or they might have seen the ten- by fourteen-inch print hanging in a shopkeeper's window or on a tavern's wall.

Even before the appearance of Woollett's print, future patriot general Israel Putnam had named his Connecticut tavern the "Genl Wolfe"; a New Haven printer had published *A Poem to the Sacred Memory of James Wolfe* (1761); and Boston engraver Nathaniel Hurd had advertised his print of the general. Further south, printers in Baltimore, Philadelphia, and Albany ran copies of George Cocking's play celebrating Wolfe, *The Conquest of Canada; Or, the Siege of Quebec*, in 1772 and 1773, and theatergoers in Philadelphia could have seen the play in February 1773. A month earlier, the *Virginia Gazette* paid tribute to Wolfe with two columns of prose and verse.[18]

Colonial commencement poems of the 1770s found Wolfe inspirational. Among the most popular, and one that would be republished in pamphlet form into the nineteenth century, Philip Freneau and Hugh Henry Brackenridge's address at Princeton lamented Wolfe's death, but offered hope that

"Britain's sons shall spread . . . Far from th' Atlantic to Pacific shores." Likely in the audience was Philip Vickers Fithian, who, two years later in Virginia, entered into his journal how "remarkably pleased" he was to see yet another "Monument erected to the memory of General Wolfe" in the *Universal Magazine*. In spring 1775, Thomas Paine published a musical homage to the general. It was a song Paine had composed to be sung at meetings of the Headstrong Club, an informal debating society that met regularly at an inn in Lewes, England. Once in America, Paine found that the tumultuous political broil made conditions ripe to print it in the *Pennsylvania Magazine*. It is easy to imagine men sitting in taverns shortly thereafter singing it.[19]

This song was Paine's second published tribute to Wolfe of that year. Three months earlier—still before there was a Continental Army and a year before he published *Common Sense*—Paine published an imaginary dialogue, as it might have occurred in 1775, between General Wolfe and General Thomas Gage, the last royally appointed Governor of Massachusetts. Wolfe's ghost came from the Elysian fields at the urging of a "group of British heroes," because the "Quebec Bill in a particular manner has roused their resentment." At their urging he came to "remonstrate with you [Gage] upon your errand to this place. You are come upon a business unworthy a British soldier, and a freeman. You have come here to deprive your fellow subjects of their liberty." Contrasting himself with Gage, Wolfe noted that, in a more virtuous past, Englishmen used force only to defend their "liberty and the Protestant religion, or to extend the blessings of both to their unhappy neighbors." Paine's Wolfe explained that he freed Frenchmen from the despotic rule of a pope and a king. He rejoiced at "having communicated to an inslaved people the glorious privileges of an English constitution." More than a conqueror, Wolfe was a "DELIVERER."[20] Now, the British occupied a place that the colonists could remember having liberated, even if French Canadians saw it otherwise. When the Continental Army thrust northward at the end of 1775, it did so partly to preserve the legacy of Wolfe and of all those colonists who had bravely served in that war for the continent.

COMMON SENSE AND A CONTINENTAL COMMUNITY

Paine did not cement his reputation with these early celebrations of Wolfe, of course, but instead with that ornery seventy-seven-page pamphlet that made him the most popular author of eighteenth-century British North America.[21] Paine put his finishing touches on *Common Sense* while Montgomery and Arnold made their final preparations for the assault on Quebec, and the pamphlet entered the mainstream just as news spread of Montgomery's death. Through a process of mutual reinforcement, Paine's work and the memory of Montgomery's sacrifice helped galvanize a national identity and an independence movement. Both cast the British as the French had been in the past war—as one power more than the continent could sustain.

Paine's personal history and interests bore directly on his views of North America and his ability to communicate them. His father, in England, made whalebone stays for corsets. Paine followed in his father's footsteps, rising from apprentice to master staymaker. He then worked as an excise collector, before sailing to America in 1774 at the age of thirty-seven. He must have immediately felt that in America he had found his true home. While staymaking and revenue collecting had provided a livelihood—often meager—Paine's passion was science. He was an intellectual, inspired by the Enlightenment quest to apply scientific principles to the ordering of human societies. On his arrival in Philadelphia, he, like so many, must have been enamored by the city's religious tolerance and the rational grid system of its streets. He attended lectures at the American Philosophical Society, and he found good company in his fellow scientists such as Benjamin Franklin.[22]

Paine sat comfortably at the nexus between a relatively fluid American learned class and the laborers, craftsmen, and farmers who constituted the bulk of the colonial population. He befriended Virginia planters such as Washington and Jefferson, as well as radical Philadelphia artisans.[23] A genius at transforming Enlightenment principles into popular parlance, his works swayed a broad cross-section of colonists. He was also able, perhaps because he was a newcomer and had no strong local attachments, to see a nation where longtime residents might have seen separate colonies.

Much of the popularity of *Common Sense* stemmed from Paine's use of readily understood language instead of turgid, academic prose. His writing, as John Adams later opined, was "suitable for an Emigrant from New Gate [the English Jail]."[24] But Paine's novelty can be overstated, as some of his rhetorical devices were tried and true. Prophetically, Robert Livingston had supposedly mentioned to Montgomery, three years before the general perished at the walls of Quebec, that "It is intolerable that a continent like America should be governed by a little island." Even if this incident were apocryphal, ever since the Sugar Act of 1763 mainland pamphleteers had profitably cast the mainland colonies as a continent and used anti-island rhetoric. Paine's claim that "'tis repugnant to reason . . . to suppose that this continent can long remain subject to any external power," and that the "continent" should not "be perpetually governed by an island" drew on time-tested scientific and geographic analogies.[25]

Several months before *Common Sense* appeared, the *Pennsylvania Gazette* published excerpts from a Londoner's letter explaining that he had heard people "50 years ago predict" the current imperial crisis, because "It is in the Nature of Things, that the Greater will not longer obey the Lesser, than when an Opportunity presents to exert itself." Similarly, pamphleteer Richard Wells called for political reforms using arguments and even language that anticipated Paine's. "If America was contiguous to Great-Britain," Wells reasoned, the two "should undoubtedly have been connected in legislation." Given North America's soaring population, however, it would only be a matter of time before "the present high claiming islanders would be but as a trifling county in the mighty senate." He then asked how it was "that distance of situation, can so totally reverse the system of equity and natural right, as to persuade the people of England, that because we sprang from their loins, they are to have eternal sway?" Paine tapped such existing arguments and analogies and polished and pushed them to the point that an island's rule over a continent was contrary to nature itself: "In no instance has nature made the satellite larger than its primary planet; and as England and America, with respect to each other, reverse the common order of nature, it is evident that they belong to different systems. England to Europe: America to itself."[26]

Paine had company aplenty in equating the British colonies with an entire continent, and even his most vocal critics tacitly accepted the equation. The most noted rebuttals to *Common Sense* challenged virtually every premise in the work except the continental metaphor. James Chalmers and Charles Inglis published two of the most extensive works refuting Paine's various arguments, but neither objected to the notion of British North America as a continental society. Far from it, they embraced the idea to challenge another hallmark of Paine's pamphlet—the call for a republican form of government. Inglis and Chalmers cited Montesquieu's argument on the limits of republics, which "may do well enough for a single city, or small territory; but would be utterly improper for such a continent as this." Self-described Tory Francis Hopkinson could make only an exasperated counterargument, "The King of Great-Britain hath, in my humble opinion, authority, jure divino, to govern absolutely not only that small island with its appendages, but the East and West Indies; not only the East and West Indies, but the continent of North-America; not only the continent of North-America, but the whole of this insignificant planet—if he can."[27] The American Revolution really was, then, a war to determine the fate of a continent, a continuation of the metageographical struggle begun in the Seven Years' War. *Common Sense* had cast the patriots' struggle in common, familiar terms.

On January 17, 1776, exactly a week after *Common Sense*'s first printing, the delegates at the Continental Congress in Philadelphia learned of General Montgomery's death. They immediately moved to eulogize him as a fallen hero, allocating funds for a stone monument from France. They also staged an elaborate funeral for Montgomery, whose body still lay in Quebec. Anticipating that newspapers throughout the colonies would cover the funeral, the congress drew on the services of Dr. William Smith, Provost of the College of Philadelphia and, coincidentally, a former mentor of Benjamin West. On February 19, an elaborate procession of congressmen, local officials, Pennsylvania assemblymen, and Continental soldiers wound its way through the streets of Philadelphia and past throngs of curious people while musicians set the mood. To the somber tones of violins and a choir, Smith took the podium at the German Calvinist Church.[28]

Smith's eulogy proved controversial. Indeed, it would have been hard not to create a stir in such a politically charged atmosphere. Squabbles over the issue of independence, the funding of the war, and, now, a failure on the part of American troops divided delegates and the larger populace. Smith himself favored reconciliation with Britain, and it showed in his oration. He emphasized Montgomery's loyalist leanings and justified his attack on Quebec as a defensive measure. It was not the speech that most delegates wanted to hear. When some congressmen made a motion to thank Smith, radical delegates blocked it. The congress would not even publish Smith's oration, leaving him to do so himself.[29]

Smith's remarks irked independence-minded colonists, who must have winced when he urged "praying for a restoration" with Britain. Though Smith's cautiousness reflected the views of Montgomery and others in a pre–*Common Sense* world, he was athwart rapidly changing times and incapable of making Montgomery the one-dimensional martyr patriots wanted as a unifying symbol for the Revolutionary cause. Smith raised patriots' hackles not mainly because he dwelt on Montgomery's desire for reconciliation with the crown. Rather, he incurred their anger because he defended the very nature of the Canadian campaign. He raised the specter that some "will now strive to misconstrue into *hostility* and *offence*" the Canada expedition. By so doing he cast a shadow over those who had planned, funded, and bled in that failed effort. To many, the rightness of the attack on Quebec was beyond discussion. A rapidly growing number of patriots knew—for common sense dictated—that American soldiers had fought to defend that for which many had already bled.[30]

By June 1776 when *Common Sense* appeared in its third edition, its arguments for independence would be firmly bound to the memory of Montgomery's death, both figuratively and literally. Now appended to the pamphlet, just as a committee of congressional delegates began drafting the Declaration of Independence, was Paine's newest work, another imaginary dialogue, this time between Wolfe's symbolic heir, General Montgomery, and a congressional delegate. Montgomery's ghost, having learned a thing or two after Montgomery died, tells the cautious delegate that the only way the American colonies will see "permanent liberty, peace and security" is by their independence. The delegate counters that perhaps the American colonies might find peace and security if they could return to their situation of 1763, the year of the Peace of Paris, but Montgomery's ghost will have none of it. "Who shall make restitution to the widows—the mothers—and the children of the men who have been slain by their arms?" he asks. Montgomery would feel he had died in vain should the colonies acknowledge British sovereignty: "For my part if I thought this continent would ever acknowledge the sovereignty of the crown of Britain again, I should forever lament the day in which I offered up my life for its salvation."[31]

The specter of the Seven Years' War haunts the discussion between the two men. Montgomery's death, in Paine's imaginary dialogue, will be more tragic than Wolfe's if the colonists failed to defend the legacy of both. Montgomery concludes the conversation with some of the same themes that appeared in Wolfe's dialogue just over a year earlier: "It was no small mortification to me when I fell upon the Plains of Abraham, to reflect that I did not expire like the brave General Wolfe, in the arms of victory. But I now no longer envy him his glory. I would rather die in *attempting* to obtain permanent freedom for a handful of people, than survive a conquest which would serve only to extend the empire of despotism."[32] Paine had earlier portrayed Wolfe as a "deliverer" of liberty, and now his Montgomery is a liberator and defender of Canadian rights. If the colonists failed to defend the liberties of Canadians from current encroachments, Wolfe will have turned out to be simply the unknowing bearer of future despotism. Both men's lives will have been wasted.

Paine's interpretation of Montgomery came to dominate as Smith's withered. Even staunch opponents of independence came to recognize Montgomery's valor and what his death meant to patriots. Thomas Anburey, a lieutenant camped with Burgoyne's army at Quebec before its campaign into New York, felt moved by the site of Wolfe's death and that of another "officer of considerable merit, though an enemy, the brave Montgomery." He wrote home that Montgomery "possessed all the fire of military ardor."

Though the general died young, he "lived long enough to establish a reputation, Quod nec Jovis ira nec ignis, nec poterit ferrum, nec edax abolere vetustas [which neither the rage of Jupiter, nor fire, nor iron, nor consuming age can destroy], as no doubt it will be handed down by the Americans to the latest ages."[33]

Poems, songs, plays, and paintings lent Montgomery martyrdom for independence and fame second only to that of George Washington. A 1776 broadside issued in Danver's Massachusetts offered "A Song on the Brave General Montgomery," comparing his death to that of Wolfe at Quebec, "That grave of heroes slain."[34] Hugh Henry Brackenridge's play, *The Death of General Montgomery* (1777), invoked the memory of Wolfe more extensively and linked Montgomery to the cause of independence directly. Starting with the frontispiece, the relationship between the men who had died in 1775 and those who had died in 1759 is apparent (fig. 27). Wolfe's ghost looms over a battlefield strewn with corpses, including that of Montgomery. The play is then shot through with Continental troops' remembrances of the earlier battle on the Plains of Abraham. Montgomery tells a subordinate with certainty that had Wolfe lived he would have been the one leading an army to Quebec, "To drive the tyrants out." British tyranny meshed with the French desire to be liberated to render the cause just. And when Montgomery lies dead, the ghost of Wolfe eulogizes him:

> From your death, shall spring the mighty thought
> O separation, from the step-dame rule
> Of moon-struck Britain . . .
> Yes, from your death shall amply vegetate,
> The grand idea of an empire new,
> Clear independence and self-ballanc'd power,
> In these fair provinces, United States.

In addition to American independence, Montgomery's death would lead American soldiers to seek revenge for their martyr. The enemy would eventually succumb. For

> In retribution, of dire loss in war,
> Awaits these murderers, yet hence compel'd
> To reimbark, ingloriously struck down
> From every hope to win the Continent."[35]

Montgomery's ill-fated assault on Quebec did much more than transform him into a martyr. His death further stirred memories of the Seven Years' War's legacy, which in turn would be refashioned to suit the Revolutionary

FIGURE 27. Frontispiece for Hugh Henry Brackenridge's *The Death of General Montgomery* (1777). Courtesy Library Company of Philadelphia

FIGURE 28. John Trumbull, *The Death of General Montgomery in the Attack on Quebec, December 31, 1775* (1786). Yale University Art Gallery, Trumbull Collection

cause. It is fitting that, after independence, one of the most celebrated paintings to commemorate the war was John Trumbull's *The Death of General Montgomery in the Attack on Quebec* (fig. 28). Completed in 1786, Trumbull's painting borrowed heavily from the work of Benjamin West. Trumbull presented Montgomery lying Wolfe-like and Christ-like in the arms of a volunteer. Though he died in defeat, Montgomery stood first rank in the pantheon of Revolutionary heroes. Lingering memories of Montgomery's martyrdom had firmly cemented the continental vision of the Seven Years' War to the Revolutionary cause.

THE "CONTINENTAL" ARMY AS ASPIRATION

Just before hostilities broke, the Connecticut minister, scientist, and soon-to-be president of Yale College, Ezra Stiles, predicted that "A continental army will soon be raised . . . and perpetuate itself till such a system of Polity shall be eventually established." A little more than a year later, with talk of independence in the air, John Adams proclaimed, "We must all be soldiers." Yet when prodded to enlist seven weeks later, Adams rebuffed: "We cannot all be soldiers."[36] Stiles's and Adams's view of the army and soldiery—and especially Adams's inconsistency—provide a suggestive glimpse into the existence of two very different Continental Armies during the Revolution: the army of aspiration and that of reality; the army that patriots wished they had and that which they actually relied on to accomplish their goals. Patriots wanted to believe that theirs was a people's war, waged by virtuous citizen-soldiers rather than regular troops. They hoped that the army necessary to win would be one commensurate with their political principles. Yet many soldiers, like Adams, were of the armchair variety. The army struggled to get men to fight far from home, and state assemblies regularly refused to fund the troops adequately.

Opposition to standing armies, and the unwillingness on the part of many individuals to serve in one for an extended period, fostered widespread ambivalence toward the Continental Army. Patriots needed it for their resistance and then independence movement to survive, but its very existence threatened their political principles. Admiration of the army was thus tempered, but when Americans did admire it, they often did so through rose-colored, "continental" glasses. Viewing the army as continental diffused it and helped mollify misgivings about the fighting force, just as viewing the congress as continental helped ease concerns about centralized political power. A sense that the army reflected the continent and that nature favored it boosted patriots' optimism; heightened their fragile will to fight in the face of repeated setbacks; and prodded them to keep troops in the field long enough to secure independence—even if these troops found their support utterly inadequate.

LIKE the Continental Congress, the army went by a variety of names. On the army's founding, the Continental Congress appointed George Washington general of "the army of the United Colonies." Washington, in turn, referred to the "Troops of the United Provinces of North America" in general orders he issued on taking command at Cambridge, Massachusetts, on July 3, 1775.[37] Gradually, however, "Continental" became the army's most common descriptor, and use of the title "Continental Army" persisted with only moderate ups and downs until the end of the war. As appearances of the term "Continental Congress" in the *Pennsylvania Gazette* fell from sixty-three in 1776 to fourteen in 1777, appearances of "Continental Army" rose from eighteen to twenty-four. Shortly thereafter, the newspaper's annual usage of "Continental Army" began consistently to exceed that of "Continental Congress," and would continue to do so until well after both institutions ceased to exist. The army, then, assumed the "continental" mantle as the congress lost it. The persistence of the term "Continental Army" also suggests that the label "Continental Congress" did not fade just because people found the term cumbersome. Nor did the people use the term "Continental Army" only to distinguish it from provincial forces. These "militias" would not have been confused with the army any more than the state "assemblies" would have been mistaken for the congress.[38]

The Continental Congress intended to build unity among the colonies when it created and oversaw the army, especially when it appointed George Washington, a Virginian, to lead what was at the time predominantly a group of New Englanders. When John Adams of Massachusetts brokered Washington's appointment, it was the first—and, arguably, the most important—sectional compromise in American history and a first step toward creating a national institution. But with more than 90 percent of the soldiers hailing from New England in 1775 and early 1776, calling the army "Continental" was more aspiration than a reflection of fact. Yet Americans began to do just that, immediately on Washington's appointment at its head. The minister Charles Chauncy of Boston offered a cocksure, exaggerated assessment: "The style of our army is, the American Army, the expence is defrayed by the Colonies in common. The cause contended for is not looked upon as the cause of Boston . . . but of the whole American continent."[39]

As the historian Fred Anderson aptly argues, Washington himself "knew that the New England Army was not only an ephemeral force but a regional one."[40] Washington understood that, for the army to succeed, it had to become a national institution. It could not continue as a New England militia or the "people's army" he first encountered in July 1775. Instead of relying on the largely volunteer, democratically run body of New Englanders with short enlistments, he would have to forge an army on the hierarchical, highly disciplined, and professional British model. The men he encountered needed to be "properly Officered," and he "hoped that all Distinctions of Colonies [would] be laid aside, so that one and the same Spirit [might] animate the whole."[41] Washington's realization that New England forces were inadequate and that an army of men loyal to the common cause rather than to individual colonies needed to be created was, as Anderson puts it, "the hinge of the Revolution." By the end of 1776, Congress and the states had made significant strides toward the creation of a truly continental institution. Washington's force would have officers commissioned by the congress and soldiers recruited from all of the states. It would be in service by the spring of 1777, and it would continue to be viewed as "continental."[42] It by no means assured American success, but it saved the struggle from sure defeat.

The desire to create a truly continental fighting force to represent a truly Continental Congress was part and parcel of the embryonic nationalism that transformed resistance into a movement for independence. Metageographical assumptions had rendered the congress a proto-national institution and sustained the institution and its resistance movement long enough to establish the army and declare independence. Although the idea of a Continental Army often reflected more the hopes of many colonists for broad, geographical unity than a reality, the creation of the army was nevertheless fortuitous, because, as the inability of the congress to unite the continent revealed itself, it fell to the army to sustain and nurture Americans' continental attachment and thereby secure their independence.

But much as the congress foundered as a continental institution, the army struggled in the field and had limited success at melding the states together. With the exception of the British withdrawal from Boston, most of the news to the end of 1776 was bad. After British forces abandoned Boston, they quickly took New York, a city of much greater strategic importance. A major port, it also offered them a waterway inland, which they could use to sever New England from the rest of the continent. The situation deteriorated before it improved. And as the war dragged on, problems of recruitment and supply, worsened by a deep aversion to standing armies, meant that the army's "continental" aspect still rested as much on aspirations and rhetoric as reality. The best example of a master rhetorician using propaganda to sustain the "continental" army, and American nationalism, was none other than Thomas Paine.

WHILE *Common Sense* rolled off the presses—eventually in twenty-seven editions, which appeared in thirteen American cities and towns and constituted possibly hundreds of thousands of copies—and as memorials to Montgomery continued, Paine witnessed the battering that the Continental forces took in the fall and early winter of 1776.[43] It must have devastated him. He knew that the American cause hinged on a strong army. *Common Sense* had exalted the army, albeit with some exaggeration. Undeterred by his readers' fears of standing armies, Paine described the Continental Army of late 1775 and early 1776 as the "largest body of armed and disciplined men of any power under heaven." Once the royalties from *Common Sense* began rolling in, Paine donated them to the army.[44]

By the fall of 1776, Paine was serving as an aide-de-camp to General Nathanael Greene, commander of New York's Fort Washington, all the while writing pieces for the *Pennsylvania Journal*. As a member of the army and, as one historian has noted, one of the first war correspondents in American history, Paine became the army's most recognized voice.[45] From the vantage point of Fort Lee, across the Hudson River from Manhattan, he,

General Greene, and General Washington watched the last Continental Army stronghold on the island fall on November 16, 1776. In the process, the British force led by General Cornwallis had captured nearly 3,000 men—one-fifth of the American army. Cornwallis's troops then marched on Fort Lee, sending Continental forces scurrying across New Jersey to Pennsylvania.

After this disaster, Paine walked to Philadelphia, only to find that many residents had fled and that the congress had moved to Baltimore. The Revolutionary movement needed a jolt, and Paine set out to provide it, publishing his most famous dispatch from the front, the first in what would eventually be the series of sixteen numbered essays entitled *American Crisis.* The essay debuted in the *Pennsylvania Journal* on December 19, 1776. Four days later, Philadelphia printers flooded the streets with 18,000 inexpensive copies, because, as with *Common Sense,* Paine prized circulation over profits. That evening, Washington ordered Paine's words read to his weary, frost-bitten men. Finally, like all of the *American Crisis* essays, the first installment would be pirated by a number of printers and make its way into many newspapers. Soon it circulated widely through the colonies.[46]

Paine's work appeared at, and contributed to, a turning point. Beginning in 1777, and in response to earlier failures, the congress tried various measures to reform its supply system. It had already taken the desperate step of granting Washington "virtually dictatorial powers over military affairs," as one historian has put it, for six months.[47] These included the power to reorganize and rebuild the army. The army still included a disproportionate number of New Englanders and men with terms of enlistment due to expire at the end of the year. With the authorization of the congress, Washington changed this, recruiting heavily throughout the colonies and getting men to serve until the war's end or for three years. "It was to be a new army," as one historian has recently explained, "a genuinely continental army, the first truly national institution after Congress itself." Now residents from every state would eventually serve under its command.[48]

American Crisis reflected, with some exaggeration, this expansion of the army's roots. It also contributed to it by bolstering the morale of men to continue serving after the end of their terms and by making other Americans see their fate as linked with that of the Continental Army. "Not a place upon earth might be so happy as America," but not until it gained its independence, Paine explained. Until then, "Wars, without ceasing, will break out," but "the continent must in the end be the conqueror." In the "times that try men's souls," Paine reassured Americans, "our new army at both ends of the continent is recruiting fast." The day after Continental soldiers read or heard Paine's exhortation, they counterattacked and defeated the enemy first at Trenton and then at Princeton, providing victories that were invaluable to American morale. Convinced of the power of Paine's pen, Washington and other patriots arranged to fund his writing.[49]

THE Continental Army, Jefferson said, "is all that the States have to depend upon for their political existence."[50] Yet as vital as that role was, the army was far more than a shield and a sword. It quickly became a focal point of national attention, an engine of national action, a creator of national unity. "Seldom if ever," the historian Don Higginbotham has noted, "had a civilian population lavished such attention upon its military forces." Skirmishes, battles, and campaigns often local in scope and episodic in nature took on wider significance as patriots spun from them the thread they used to stitch the nation together. The army gave continental-minded patriots a spacious canvas on which they could show ordinary Americans that the war was vast in scope, a great geographical adventure. Battles and campaigns that covered a relatively small part of the emerging country captured wide attention and familiarized Americans with distant places.[51]

Victories at Trenton, Saratoga, and Yorktown, and defeats at Quebec, New York, and Charleston filled newspaper columns in Williamsburg, Philadelphia, and Boston. From north to south, preachers and publishers, poets and pundits trumpeted the army's trials and triumphs in sermons, pamphlets, editorials, plays, and songs. Newspapers told wives why they must, at least for a period, sacrifice their husbands. Editors urged women to take up collections to send to Martha Washington in Virginia so she could pool the money to buy blankets for the troops in distant campaigns. When Hugh Henry Brackenridge of Pennsylvania eulogized fallen heroes in 1781, he gave his audience a geography lesson—a map of the continent for which those heroes died: "The angel of America shall write . . . the names of those who have fought at Lexington, at Bunker's Hill, on the lakes of Canada, at Three Rivers, and before Quebec; the names of those who have fought at Danbury, at Fort Stanwix, Fort Montgomery, Fort Washington; at the German Flats at Bennington, and on the heights of Saratoga: The names of those who have fought at Trenton, at Princeton, at Ash-swamp."[52]

Among those heroes, Washington eventually surpassed all others. "Alexander, Pompey, and Hannibal were but pigmy Generals, in comparison with the magnanimous Washington," wrote the bitter, sarcastic loyalist Nicholas Cresswell in his journal. People put Washington's picture in their parlors and named their children after him. He was feted in feasts, parades, and toasts. Although initially he was little more than a compromise as the

commander of the army, he proved to be an able leader, an effective pro-
pagandist, an adroit politician. As a result, he, like the army he led, became a
symbol for and a creator of the nation. At the war's end, Henry Knox
proudly summarized the army's role: "It is a favorite toast in the army, 'A
hoop to the barrel,' or 'Cement to the Union.' " The same was said of Washington. "The continent of North-America," observed a traveling Frenchman, the Marquis de Chastellux, "is a great volume, every page of which
presents his eulogium."[53]

THE ARMY IN REALITY

With residents from every state and Canada serving in the Continental Army at some point during the war, the institution seemingly stood
to advance a strong national identity among its soldiers, not just the larger
population. Yet the "continental" aspects of the army had severe limits.
Indeed, if "continental" implies an army that was representative of people
who thought of themselves as the continent, one whose members traveled
widely over the continent, or one well funded by the rest of the continent,
then the army hardly deserves the term. The disjuncture between the army
of rhetoric and the army of reality at times paralleled that between metageographical presumptions and underlying geographical realities. Just as
many presumed their continent to be porous and manageable enough for
control by one people and themselves that ideal people, they also preferred
to think of their fighting force as continental and filled with citizen-soldiers.

The ordinary soldier who spent the duration of the war in the Continental Army bore little resemblance to Washington or the other heroes
who appeared in paintings or published sermons, essays, and newspaper
accounts. Just as the arrangement of the figures in Benjamin West's and John
Trumbull's paintings veered from actual events, the legend of the citizen-
soldier defending his home and farm is largely myth. The broad brush-
strokes of historians who have ably analyzed the army's composition make
clear that waging war was a far messier, less romantic affair than any bit of
propaganda might suggest. Actual and extended military service in itself had
limited power as a nationalizing force compared to more widespread armchair aspirations.

During the war's first year, to be sure, a popular enthusiasm for the
conflict, a *rage militaire,* prevailed, at least in those parts of New England
thoroughly researched by historians. In areas of Massachusetts and New
Hampshire, citizen-soldiers bore arms in significant numbers, and a large,
representative cross section of the white, male population served in either a
militia or the army for a short period of time.[54] As the war dragged on

and shifted to regions beyond New England, however, only a small percentage of eligible white males served for an extended period, and few fought far from home.

Take, for instance, the most populous state, Virginia. One historian has noted "most middling and upper-class Virginians expected that only lower-class Virginians should serve in the Continental Army." The result, even on Virginia soil at Yorktown, was "an indifferent contribution from Virginians."[55] Despite objections from southerners, Washington had to accept African Americans into the army out of desperation for manpower. Some of these men served in a regiment created when not enough white Rhode Islanders would join the Continental Army. One-fourth of Rhode Island's male slaves of military age served in the army. Masters who freed their slaves for service received compensation and avoided service themselves. Pennsylvanians and Jersey men did only slightly better in moving south to fight. As a whole, property owners, including those of modest means, may have cared deeply about the fate of the army and recognized that the Revolution depended on it, but they generally proved unwilling to make the sacrifices that the army ostensibly needed to succeed.[56] Instead, they passed the burden on to others. The longer the war lasted, the more likely it became that ordinary and elite whites would serve only from the sidelines.

As a result, the army had to rely increasingly on poor, dependent, and foreign-born whites to fill its ranks. For example, in the late 1770s Concord, Massachusetts—a place that helped make the "minutemen" famous—struggled to fill enlistments. When not even enough landless poor volunteered, citizens hired slaves to fill quotas. By 1780, Concord ran out of its own poor, servants, and slaves who could serve and had to rely on transients to fill its quotas. Of its enlistees that year, only eight of sixteen "had any known connection to the town."[57] In Pennsylvania, a similar story played out, with the average army recruit being born outside the United States.[58] One regiment in the Continental Army came to be known as "Congress's Own," because so many of its members claimed no state as their home. Many of its members were refugees, including hundreds of Canadians, immigrants, deserters, and prisoners of war. "It truly was," as one historian has written, "a regiment of others."[59] Understandably, other historians have similarly described the typical Continental soldier as "less well anchored in the society," as having "shallow roots in *any* community," and as "not normally engaged in the defense of home and family because they rarely had either." Writing privately, angry loyalists were less charitable, calling the Continental soldiery "a contemptible band of vagrants, deserters and thieves," for example, and "a Banditti of undisciplined people, the scum and refuse of all nations on earth."[60]

In this respect, the reality within the army might have theoretically made for a membership with a continental identity greater than that in the larger society. Continental soldiers shared much with their most famous spokesman, Thomas Paine. Though they might not be students of the Enlightenment, or even able to read, much less write, they lacked strong local attachments. Like Paine, they would have been more likely to see British North America as a nation, where other colonists saw separate colonies. And those exceptional soldiers who did have community ties often had them undermined.

The most detailed memoir of the war by a common soldier came from Connecticut's Joseph Plumb Martin. Raised by his freehold farmer grandparents, Martin served in the army from the time he was fourteen until he was twenty-two. Throughout his memoir he is self-consciously a Yankee and aware of the differences between himself and those from other regions. He might as well have been "incorporated with a tribe of western Indians as with any of the southern troops, especially of those which consisted mostly, as the Pennsylvanians did, of foreigners." Service in a mixed unit made Martin homesick, but, at the same time, shared hardships and hatred of the enemy bonded him with his comrades in arms.[61] When finally relieved from duty in 1783, all of the men went their separate ways, and Martin wistfully admitted that "the soldiers, each in his particular circle of acquaintance, were as strict a band of brotherhood as Masons and, I believe, as faithful to each other."[62] As Washington later recalled, "A century in the ordinary intercourse, would not have accomplished what the Seven years association in Arms did" in breaking down fierce localism.[63]

This *espirit de corps* did little to change the larger society's ambivalent views toward the army, and the state assemblies—on which a Congress without the power to tax had to rely for funds—treated the troops such that they became a small, organic community threatened by outsiders, instead of a microcosm of the nation at large. As a member of Washington's army, marching at the end of 1777 toward what became its infamous encampment at Valley Forge, Private Martin remembered just how harsh state neglect had made life for the troops. Congress had ordered a "Continental thanksgiving," but "We had nothing to eat for two or three days previous, except what the trees of the fields and forests afforded us." Nevertheless, and in keeping with the congressional order, the troops celebrated, in Martin's sarcastic words, "a sumptuous Thanksgiving to close the year of high living we had now nearly seen brought to a close." The soldiers each received as a reward from their country on this special occasion a "*half* a *gill* of rice and a *tablespoonful* of vinegar!!"[64] Conditions only got worse over the winter, and subsequent years saw little improvement. The winter encampment at Morristown, New Jersey, in 1779–80, proved more miserable than that at Valley Forge. There, tree bark, boiled shoes, and pet dogs were all that kept some of the men alive.[65]

Under such a feeble provisioning system, desertions skyrocketed, and, by the spring and summer of 1780, mutinous rumblings reverberated through the army. By December, Washington showed a dark sense of humor when he suggested that it would be nice if the troops, "like Chameleons . . . could live upon Air, or like the Bear, suck their paws for sustenance during the rigour of the approaching season." Unable to live on air or suck nourishment out of their paws, enlisted men in the Pennsylvania and New Jersey Lines revolted in January 1781. The Pennsylvania soldiers appropriated artillery pieces and killed one of their officers and wounded several more in an ugly melee before parleying through a state appointed committee and receiving amnesty, timely discharges, and promises of back pay. The New Jersey men fared worse. Washington dispatched troops from New England with heavy cannon to suppress the mutiny. Under orders, a firing squad comprised of some of the mutineers reluctantly and tearfully executed two of their ringleaders.[66]

With mutinies in the ranks suppressed, officers soon sang their own chorus of discontent. In January 1783—after Yorktown and with a peace treaty and demobilization looming—many officers began grumbling because Congress had no way to pay its officers the pensions it had promised. Continental Army officers threatened mutiny from their winter quarters in Newburgh, New York. Washington deftly defused the crisis with a theatrical address to congregated representatives from each regiment. As he prepared to read a letter from a member of congress promising that the officers would not be forgotten, he pulled out his glasses and reminded the men that he had not only grown gray but almost blind in service to his country. Having suffered for so long, the man who more than any other symbolized the patriotic sacrifices of the army was not about to abandon the ideal of civilian supremacy over the military. Designed to build unity in the confederation, the Continental Army had teetered on the brink of destroying it. Only Washington's singular leadership kept the ill-treated army in line.[67]

Though disaster was averted, a history of lackluster recruiting, starving soldiers, and angry officers meant that the Continental Army—the army of the camp, of reality—fell far short of aspirations. Instead of comprising simply citizen-soldiers who represented the continent and who served self-lessly, the army's ranks contained many men who might have been dispro-portionately nationalistic but ended up feeling betrayed by their country. Washington expressed amazement that the Revolution had succeeded at all, given the inadequate size and poor treatment of the army. "If Historiogra-phers should be hardy enough to fill the page of history with the advantages that have been gained with unequal numbers (on the part of America) in the course of this contest, . . . it is more than probable that Posterity will bestow on their labors the epithet and marks of fiction," he wrote to General Nathanael Greene in 1783. No one would believe "that such a force as Great Britain has employed for eight years in Country could be baffled in their plan of Subjugating it by numbers infinitely less, composed of Men often-times half-starved; always in Rags, without pay, and experiencing, at times every species of distress which human nature is capable of undergoing."[68]

THE CONTINENT AS ALLY IN
RHETORIC AND REALITY

Undeterred by Washington's admonition that their work might be labeled as "fiction," historians have, of course, tried to explain how the Continental Army prevailed against long odds. It has been estimated that patriots had to resist the world's most powerful military with the support of no more than half of the white populace, and Native Americans and African Americans aligned heavily with the British.[69] Financial disarray, the loss of major cities, and mutinies dampened enthusiasm among patriots; allegiances were fluid and surrender tempted many. Yet enough patriots sustained enough will to fight to keep an army in the field long enough to secure independence, even if just barely.

Another puzzle historians have grappled with is how the American popu-lace could have treated the army so callously. Some scholars have suggested that, although individuals avoided long enlistments and rarely fought far from home, military mobilization was widespread enough to rival that of the Civil War or World War II. Or, as the Marquis de Chastellux observed about American men of fighting age: "I have not found two who have not borne arms, heard the whistling of balls, and even received some wounds." Thus, many men likely felt that their sacrifices were adequate, even as others contributed much more. Other scholars have argued that the same ideology that prompted resistance to imperial reforms in the first place—a wariness of political power and an almost paranoid fear of its conspiratorial tendency to encroach on a peoples' liberty—translated into suspicion of the army.[70]

Yet ideology and the diffusion of military service only partially explain the disjuncture between the Continental Army of aspiration and that of reality, and, even then, only in certain situations. As important in shaping attitudes toward the Continental Army was the prevailing belief that the British army faced not only the Continental Army and the various militias, or even an array of patriot forces and their French allies, but also the continent itself. Reluctance to support the Continental Army—a powerful, man-made institution, but not nearly as formidable as that of the enemy— gained traction from the optimistic belief that the army already had a powerful ally in nature, that it drew sustenance from the grandeur and resources of the North American continent. Ironically, this optimism, although it sometimes left the army starving, also sustained a will to fight in the face of repeated military setbacks. With the patriots' facing little room for error, the notion of the continent as an ally made a difference, it helped give rise to the United States.

THE continent appeared as ally in two fundamental ways. First, its vastness created a logistical nightmare and made British military conquest difficult. Speaking before the House of Lords on the eve of hostilities, the Earl of Camden challenged the very possibility of a military solution in America, given the number of rebels (albeit exaggerated), their unity, and the spaces involved: "To conquer a great continent of 1,800 miles, containing three millions of people, all indissolubly United . . . seems an undertaking not to be rashly engaged in. . . . It is obvious, my lords, that you cannot furnish armies, or treasure, competent to the mighty purpose of subduing America."[71] Other Britons' anxieties about conquering expansive American spaces swirled through the American press. The *Boston Gazette* reprinted a British pamphlet cataloging the difficulties of waging war "at more than 3000 miles distance . . . in country where fastness grows against fastness, and labyrinth on labyrinth; where a check is defeat, and a defeat ruin. It is a war of absurdity and madness." When Scotswoman and foe of independence Janet Schaw traveled in North Carolina at the Revolution's outset, she found the local militia ragtag but still worried, for in the rough, wild terrain of North America, "the worst figure . . . can shoot from behind a bush and kill even a General Wolfe." After the Continental Army's stupendous victory at Saratoga, one of the British lieutenants blamed British leaders "who, sitting in their closets, with a map before them, ridiculously expect the movements of an army to keep pace with their rapid ideas . . . carried on through a country in interior desarts, and at a distance of three thousand miles."[72]

American military leaders took advantage of the continent's size. During the winter of 1776–77, they placed their hopes in an essentially defensive strategy. It would be foolhardy, they realized, to engage in risky operations to defeat the British when American forces' greatest asset was a spacious and, as some saw it, virtually unconquerable continent. To conquer the Americans, Britain could not simply take a locale and move on to the next conquest; instead, its forces must keep moving "*and secure* their conquests at the same time," as General Greene explained to Washington.[73] To conquer the Americans, Britain must control space. The continent could prove the deciding factor by making it difficult for an army from overseas to spread across it and be everywhere simultaneously.

The personal correspondence of that quintessential sideline soldier, John Adams, reveals how he confronted news of the war with the continent in mind, taking consolation in the army's defeats by remembering that the revolutionary cause had a whole continent on its side. In Philadelphia in 1777, he and the rest of the Congress nervously monitored British troop movements. When General Howe's army departed New York and headed south to take Philadelphia, it vanished over the horizon, then it sailed south past the mouth of the Delaware and into Chesapeake Bay. Having lost track of the British, yet sensing that Howe must still have Philadelphia in his crosshairs, Adams described to his wife, Abigail, how rampant speculation had racked the city: People "might as well imagine" Howe's troops "gone round Cape horn into the South Seas to land at California, and march across the Continent to attack our back settlements." About a month later, with Howe's army spotted approaching Philadelphia from the southwest, Adams, who would soon be reduced to flight, took comfort in the thought that it might be in the Patriots' best interest for redcoats to occupy the United States' largest city and the home of the Continental Congress, "because it would employ nearly the whole of his Force to keep Possession of this Town, and the rest of the Continent would be more at Liberty."[74] Three years later, the Continental Army suffered its worst defeat when General Benjamin Lincoln surrendered three thousand men to the British at Charleston, South Carolina. Adams conceded it a "disaster." Yet he took heart that "the English will hold it no longer than they did Boston or Philadelphia." And even "if they had and were to hold quiet Possession of all the Great Seaport Towns upon the Continent, it would be no Conquest of America." In fact, the war was going better than initially expected, for in 1774 he and other congressional delegates had pondered the possibility that they might "lose all our Seaport Towns and laid our Account accordingly."[75] They knew that if they did, they would still control the bulk of the continent.

Where it was thought that the vast and contiguous nature of the thirteen continental colonies made patriots nearly invincible, able to withstand sustained losses, the same conditions rendered the world's most powerful army thinly spread, vulnerable to a single mighty blow. Adams reminded the Marquis de Lafayette that, on top of needing supplies from Europe, the scattered "British Possessions in America depend upon each other for reciprocal support." Depots in Canada and Nova Scotia provisioned red coats in the United States; the West Indies relied on British posts in Florida for supplies; and the West Indies provided the army with rum, sugar, and molasses. Should the British lose control of just one of these regions, their entire presence in North America could collapse. It was a "Chain" where "the Links mutually support each other, in such a Manner that if one or two were taken away the whole, or at least the greatest Part must fall."[76] No army, even one as powerful as Britain's, could establish indomitable control over a distant continent.

Space made the continent an ally in a second way: it translated into population growth. Demographers since at least Benjamin Franklin's publication of *Observations on the Increase of Mankind* (1755) had tied the colonies' population growth to the expansiveness of North America. During war, this became an asset, for as population grew, so did the number of men eligible for military service. In the first year of the Continental Army's existence, assumptions about a burgeoning population begot a naïve confidence in victory and an enthusiasm for the conflict. Part of this *rage militaire* stemmed from visions of future American grandeur. An early rallying cry from "A SOLDIER" reminded his fellows in arms of projections that, by 1800, the colonies would have six million inhabitants, and, by 2000, they would have "one thousand five hundred and thirty six millions." Lest the number seem exaggerated, he reminded readers of the "almost unbounded desarts which extend from our most western settlements to the pacific ocean."[77] Surely, given these projections, any prospective soldier would be joining the winning side.

As prolonged war brought fatigue, debt, and doubt, space and demographics continued as a source of solace, resources, and optimism. Debts might spiral and dollars depreciate, yet abundant land lent the nation a bright future. In a circular letter from Congress, President John Jay answered the question of "whether the natural wealth, value and resources of the country" would suffice to pay the debt. He reminded readers that it "is well known that the inhabitants of this country increased almost in the ratio of compound interest." This growth came only through natural increase; add to it immigration and it became obvious that "every person's share of the debt will be constantly diminishing by others coming in to pay a proportion of it." North America's uniqueness as a "young" country allowed this advantage, while Europe's population would remain the same. The nation's population growth rested on the notion that "Extensive wildernesses, now scarcely known or explored, remain to be cultivated, and vast lakes and rivers, whose waters have for ages rolled in silence and obscurity to the ocean, are yet to hear the din of industry, become subservient to commerce, and boast delightful villas, gilded spires, and spacious cities rising on their banks."[78]

YET insofar as the continent's size seemed an ally, it could also befuddle the American war effort. The Continental Army simply could not fight everywhere at once. And no one could ignore British military victories, the loss of outposts and cities, or the suffering and death that patriots suffered. But metageographical propaganda could mollify bedevilment. It could amplify the positive, and present as unwavering the optimism that men such as John Adams felt only cautiously when they mulled over matters in private.

In spite of repeated military defeats, Thomas Paine's United States became a fortress of invulnerability because of its continental resources. The theme appeared in his second *American Crisis* and he returned to it throughout the war. "This continent," he wrote, "is too extensive to sleep all at once." Taunting the British from Philadelphia in the aftermath of American victories at Trenton and Princeton, he had "no other idea of conquering countries than by subduing the armies which defend them: have you done this, or can you do it?" Taking cities, as the British had New York and soon would Philadelphia, simply added the burden of occupation to that of defeating the army. Paine could "laugh" at the British "notion of conquering America." Their delusion stemmed from their having "lived in a little country, where an army might run over the whole in a few days." Should British forces "garrison the places you might march over" in America, "your army would be like a stream of water running to nothing. By the time you extended from New York to Virginia, you would be reduced to a string of drops not capable of hanging together."[79] The Americans could also outspend the British because "the country is young and capable of infinite improvement, and has an almost boundless tract of new lands in store; whereas England has got to her extent of age and growth."[80]

Even after the Continental Army surrendered Charleston, South Carolina, Paine still sang optimistic: "It is not the conquest of towns, nor the accidental capture of garrisons, that can reduce a country so extensive as this." Instead, "there is no situation the enemy can be placed in that does not afford to us the same advantages which he seeks himself." In dividing their forces, the British had created more positions that Americans could attack. Far from a resounding victory, the British occupation of Charleston "carries with it a confession of weakness, and goes on the principle of distress rather than conquest."[81]

Given his optimism in the face of one of the Continental Army's worst setbacks, Paine's ebullience after its greatest victory comes as no surprise. The defeat of British troops under General Cornwallis at Yorktown, October 19, 1781, hinged partly on delicate timing and luck. It required moving large numbers of troops from New York to Virginia, in coordination with a French naval victory against British ships approaching the Chesapeake. Rather than portray the victory as a stroke of good fortune or military genius, however, Paine declared events inevitable. He ridiculed a speech by the king calling on Parliament to continue the war in America. "The final superiority of America over every attempt that an island might make to conquer her," he preached in the tenth *American Crisis*, "was as naturally marked in the constitution of things, as the future ability of a giant over a dwarf is delineated in his features while an infant."[82] All of the desperate straits faced by the army could be glossed over, the heroics of individuals ignored, and the contingent nature of war in general neglected; North America's geography was its destiny.

North America's continental status trumped any possibility that it would succumb to an island. The reason was at times as metaphysical as it was strategic or tactical. By the fifth *American Crisis*, written during the Continental Army's darkest hours at Valley Forge, Paine took a providential view of American geography: "The vast extension of America makes her of too much value in the scale of Providence, to be cast like a pearl before swine, at the feet of an European island; and of much less consequence would it be that Britain were sunk in the sea than that America should miscarry." Americans need look no farther than their own past, the "discovery" and "peopling" of America, the "rearing and nursing it to its present state," and the "protection of it through the present war," to realize that "Providence has some nobler end" than to please "the ignorant and insignificant king of Britain."[83]

Later issues of the *American Crisis* elaborated on the relationship between geography and American character without invoking a higher power. Sounding more like a missionary of the Enlightenment than a New England preacher, Paine could tell British commissioners that "We [Americans] live in a large world, and have extended our ideas beyond the limits and prejudices of an island." Or, ostensibly addressing the people of England, he could propose:

There is something in the extent of countries, which, among the generality of people, insensibly communicates extension of the mind. The soul of an islander, in its native state, seems bounded by the foggy confines of the water's edge, and all beyond affords to him matters only for profit or curiosity, not for friendship. His island is to him his world, and fixed to that, his everything centers in it; while those who are inhabitants of a continent, by casting their eye over a larger field, take in likewise a larger intellectual circuit, and thus approaching nearer to an acquaintance with the universe, their atmosphere of thought is extended, and their liberality fills a wider space. In short, our minds seem to be measured by countries when we are men, as they are by places when we are children, and until something happens to disentangle us from the prejudice, we serve under it without perceiving it.

An exception to this theory of the geographical determination of men's character would have been Paine's hero, Isaac Newton. All Paine could suggest was that "the heavens had liberated him from the prejudices of an island, and science had expanded his soul as boundless as his studies."[84] On the whole, however, the expansive mindset and superior character of continent dwellers virtually guaranteed their victory over any islanders.

THROUGHOUT the Revolution, satirical prints continued the tradition of representing both the continent and the mainland British colonies as an Indian. For instance, in *The Present State of Great Britain* (c. 1779), Great Britain appeared as the dozing figure of John Bull while an Indian princess lifted a liberty cap off a pole he held. In another print, *The English Lion Dismember'd* (1780), an Indian held a pole with a liberty cap in one hand and an axe in the other. He had just hacked away the paw of the lion—emblematic of Britain—while it was chained to Lord North, who carried a heavy sack representing the budget.[85]

So it was nothing new when patriots attributed human characteristics to their continent. What was new was how they adapted this tradition to their everyday discourse when they identified themselves collectively. It is hard to exaggerate how heavily larded the letters of congressional delegates, military leaders, and diplomats were with the cause—"the continent"—acting or being acted on. Just leafing through the papers of Washington, Adams, or virtually any other patriot who left behind a body of correspondence, makes apparent that "the continent" could be enslaved, distressed, and burdened. It could have expenses and debts, patience and courage. It could suffer, sacrifice, and bleed. Such anthropomorphism reinforced communal ties among disparate peoples. It took diversity and turned it into a cohesive living organism, an asset greater than the sum of its parts.

American newspapers and pamphlets, too, relied on rhetoric that anthropomorphized the continent in contradistinction to human enemies such as the king or Parliament. Richard Wells, seeking reconciliation between the United States and Britain, warned that the continent was a "formidable figure" that could stand equal to English officials: "Let English Statesmen clamor for power, let a British parliament boast of unlimitted supremacy, yet the continent of America will contend with equal fervency." As mentioned earlier, Wells's rhetoric anticipated that of Thomas Paine, who argued in *Common Sense* that "until an independence is declared, the Continent will feel itself like a man who continues putting off some unpleasant business from day to day." The choice, according to Paine, had to be made between the king and "Continental authority."[86]

In a sermon appropriately titled *The Love of our Country* (1777), army chaplain John Hurt combined the anthropomorphism of the continent with a familial metaphor. He told Virginia troops in New Jersey during the desperate times of 1777 that mainlanders were "all children of one common mother, *America,* our country; she gives us all our birth, nursed our tender years, and supports our manhood. In this light, therefore, our regards for her seem as natural as the implanted affection betwixt parents and children."[87] The people of America were not the continent's only children. In a whimsical piece published in the *United States Magazine,* the Continental Dollar told his (her?!) life story in which he was the offspring of father Liberty and mother America, who "for youth and beauty, far exceeded all the terrestrial painted beauties of Europe, the tawney beauties of Asia, and the charcoal beauties of Africa." In telling his story, the Continental Dollar slipped back and forth between having America as his mother and his home. In either case, he was thankful for not being born in England, "a petty island, a cage for slaves, and a nursery for banditti and cutthroats," and he praised "the vast continent of North-America, whose boundless and unexplored regions are fit to be inhabited only by such free and uncontrouled souls as mine."[88]

An anthropomorphized continent remembered the men who had perished in its defense. Two-and-a-half years after William Smith gave his poorly received memorial of General Montgomery, Hugh Henry Brackenridge stood at the same pulpit in the German Calvinist Church in Philadelphia and eulogized all of the men who had fallen in the fight for independence. Britain's onslaught, "like the ocean whence it came, rolled its angry waves, and beat upon our coasts . . . filling every bay and every river." America's war "like the bold and steady winds that pass his mountains, met and tempested the ocean, whose waves were seen to roll, and break, and dash upon the shore." Brackenridge emphasized the geographic totality of the war, fought from "Canada to Georgia . . . from the ocean to the mountain." The enemy "fought the land." The American land, in turn, aided American soldiers, witnessing, in the process, tremendous feats of heroism. Many of these heroes lay buried along the banks of the Kennebec, St. Lawrence, Hudson, and Delaware rivers. The land could not speak to the feats of these men in a literal sense, of course, but its future glory would testify plenty to the brave soldiers who had fallen.

The soldiers' "birth-place shall be immortal," Brackenridge predicted. He urged his listeners not to shed tears, but to look "to fairer prospects, the woods, and the plains, and the rivers of America. Smile, O Woods! exult O plains! and be not insensible, O rivers! of the fame to which you are advanced."[89] The eulogy was as much a celebration of the land as the soldiers who had advanced its cause. Together, North America and the sacrifices of its military forces would prevail. Patriots such as Brackenridge knew they had a metageographical homeland. Watching the war unfold allowed them to experience that land in ways they never had before. They followed the army as it trod the continent's roads, crossed its rivers, and ate its produce. They looked on as the continent that they knew they had gave rise to the country they had created, the United States of America.

ERADICATING INDIANS, UNIFYING PATRIOTS

The Revolutionary War reinforced patriots' continental identity not only when they faced an external, island enemy, but also when they turned inland and unleashed their Revolutionary terror against Indians. Figuratively, images of Indians might symbolize the continent or the United States, but, since the seventeenth century, English colonists had seen real Indians as lacking a future. Revolutionaries acted to bring this perception to fruition, to prove themselves the true Americans.

The overwhelming majority of Indians sided with the British when forced to choose between that power and the Revolutionaries, or they fought against the United States independently to prevent encroachments on their land. By summer 1776, Cherokees attacked dozens of American settlements in the southern backcountry. In the second half of 1778, Iroquois and loyalist forces struck the northern parts of Pennsylvania and western New York. Meanwhile, Ohio Indians spread fear in settlements such as Boonesborough in Kentucky and posts in the Illinois country. American retaliation and the ongoing war over the next several years would lead to thousands of dead, and violence would not subside for another two decades in many regions.

Whether fighting in New York against Iroquois, in Ohio against Shaw-nees, or in Kentucky against Cherokees, patriots, as expressed by historians Fred Anderson and Andrew Cayton, "were learning to practice what we now call ethnic cleansing, a way of making war that (then, as now) built a sense of political and ethnic solidarity within the group that perpetrated it." Soldiers, militia, and civilians from different states and of different ethnic and religious backgrounds saw their differences fade in the face of their shared and growing hatred of Indians. The anvil of war helped further forge them into the continent's true people, into white Americans.[90]

TWO examples suffice to demonstrate the brutality of war against Indians; how its perpetrators dehumanized the Indians they sought to eradi-cate; and how they often rationalized their violence as a quest to purify the continent. One of the most ruthless campaigns by Continental troops against Indians came in 1779, when General John Sullivan, General James Clinton, and Colonel Daniel Brodhead led expeditionary forces into the Iroquois homeland. Theirs were not actions borne out of the renegade justice of backcountry settlers, but campaigns driven by orders directly from the top commander of the Continental Army. Washington instructed Con-tinental soldiers not to treat Indians the same as they had been ordered to treat Quebecois. Rather than treading lightly through the country of "Friends and Brethren," they were to "lay waste all the settlements around... that the country may not be merely overrun but destroyed."[91] A Fourth of July toast in the officers' tent promised "civilization or death to all American Savages."[92] A Hessian surgeon who wrote a narrative of his travels in Amer-ica described the campaign as, "nothing less than an entire extirpation," based on the widespread belief that "these Indians must be forced quite to relinquish their haunts if the numerous but helpless settlers of the frontier were to be given any hope of lasting peace and security."[93] Though initially encountering strong resistance, the soldiers eventually destroyed dozens of villages and thousands of acres of crops at harvest time.

On their return, Chaplain Israel Evans delivered a popular sermon, subse-quently published at the request of the army's officers and distributed among the soldiers. Evans cast the army's actions in a defensive light, for it was the king who had "sent his emissaries to raise the savages of the wilderness to war . . . then our defenceless frontiers became the seat of savage fury." He also reminded the soldiers who took war to the heart of Iroquois country of their actions' continental implications. He explained that, where Braddock had failed, they had "opened a passage into the wilderness." Soon they and their brethren would be settling all around the Great Lakes and the gospel would spread, "for it cannot be supposed, that so large a part of this continent shall forever continue the haunt of savages, and the dreary abodes of superstition and idolatry." Future generations would look even more thankfully and reverently on their deeds. Because of them, the gospel would eventually travel to the "western extremities of this continent," and the persecuted of other parts of the world could continue to find asylum in America. Posterity would remember these men in the army for giving "liberty and religion . . . wide dominion from the Atlantic through the great continent to the western ocean."[94]

Less formal, but uglier, military action sprang up elsewhere, proving even pacifist Indians were not immune from some white Americans' wrath. At Gnadenhütten, in what is now eastern Ohio, a "loose simulacrum of a militia" acted as "latter-day Paxton Boys," in historians' words, and attacked Christian Indians from Moravian missions who had been foraging for food. Indian prisoners, who put up no resistance, met their demise in a gruesome, ritual massacre. Their captors restrained them and led them to the mission buildings, "which they called the Slaughter Houses," according to a contemporary account. There they first stunned their prisoners with blows from cooper's mallets to their heads. Then they fatally scalped them. One of the murderers boasted of having personally beaten fourteen Indians with one of the wooden mallets before his arm got so tired that he had to turn his weapon over to another to continue the work at hand. The two-step method of murder eerily resembled the killing of cattle in an abattoir, and probably intentionally so, for the victims, in the perpetrators' eyes, deserved to die like animals. In the end, more than ninety-four Indians died, including more than thirty children. The peaceful nature of the victims, the scale of the killing, and the process adopted all suggest systematic ethnic cleansing. The Pennsylvania legislature later condemned the massacre, but took no further action against the murderers.[95]

THE army's incursion into Iroquois country and the Gnadenhütten massacre may have represented extreme cases of United States brutality toward Indians. But such actions were in keeping with widespread sentiments, and portrayals of Indians in propaganda justified such violence. To travelers from Europe the animosity was striking. Johann Schoepf found "consuming hate," particularly in western areas. Indians appeared in popular and prominent tracts as subhuman pawns of the British, as peoples to be driven from lands to which they had no legitimate claims. *Common Sense* appealed to neutrals and loyalists by declaring that there were already "thousands and tens of thousands, who would think it glorious to expel from the continent, that barbarous and hellish power [Britain], which hath stirred up the Indians and the Negroes to destroy us." Paine's ghost of General Montgomery called on Congress to declare independence because the British had prodded "savages and Negroes to assist them in burning your towns— desolating your country—and in butchering your wives and children." The fear mongering found amplification in the Declaration of Independence. There, Jefferson accused King George of attempting to "bring on the inhabitants of our frontiers, the merciless Indian savages, whose known rule of warfare is an undistinguished destruction of all ages, sexes, and conditions."[96]

In fanning the fears of frontier violence, Paine, Jefferson, and countless others relied on stereotypes, even duplicity, to jog deep-seated memories, however inaccurate, of the Seven Years' War and innumerable other wars that involved frontier violence with Indians. The parallels between these wars and the Revolution would have been inescapable to American patriots. History's lesson was clear: the Revolution would have to be more than a war for independence; it would have to be a war of expansion to render frontiers safe, and to render the continent "civilized." The popular hymn "America" called for Americans to "sing unto the Lord . . . From East to West his Praise proclaim. From Pole to Pole extol his Fame."[97]

To many colonists the British threat bore comparison not only to that of the French, but also to a seventeenth-century Indian menace. New Englanders, in particular, could look back on King Philip's War—at least as they remembered it, through the victor's histories written by their ancestors—for inspiration. On December 31, 1775, the Reverend Nathan Fiske preached in Brookfield, Massachusetts, not far from where fellow New Englanders and redcoats had first shed blood. Thankfully, he reminisced, the Indian threat was gone and the wilderness had been improved: "Instead of a desolate uncultivated wilderness . . . Instead of the smoky huts and wigwams of naked, swarthy barbarians, we now behold thick settlements of a civilized people, and convenient and elegant buildings." Now New Englanders confronted a new enemy, a challenge similar to that faced by their pioneering ancestors. Fiske asked, "are not the dangers and distresses, the cruelties and sufferings which our forefathers underwent, renewed in part in our day and practiced upon some of their posterity?" Never would their forefathers have thought that their descendants "would be disturbed in their possessions by *Britons,* more than themselves were by savage Indians."[98]

Colonists, of course, fought in many wars besides King Philip's. But these wars—Bacon's Rebellion, the Yamasee War, and Queen Anne's War, to name a few—did not result in the publication of nearly as many printed histories.

For this reason, New Englanders contributed disproportionately to the historical memory that the patriots drew on in their resistance to the British. One of the most read books to come out of King Philip's War, Mary Rowlandson's *The Sovereignty and Goodness of God,* went through four editions in 1682, when New Englanders craved stories of their recent tribulations. In it, Rowlandson loses her freedom when Indians attack her hometown of Lancaster, Massachusetts and steal her away. Her captivity tests her faith, but in the end she rejects Indian culture and all of the savagery it represents, and divine providence guides her to freedom. As memories of King Philip's War faded, however, the story lost its poignancy, and Rowlandson's narrative, with the exception of a single republication in 1720, fell out of print until 1770. That year it was published three times, then once the following year, and twice more in 1773. All editions came out of New England, hotbed of patriot resistance, site of the Boston Massacre and Tea Party. The revived interest in the Puritan captivity narrative stemmed from the colonists' sense that they were themselves captives of the British. Stories of how their ancestors had survived Indian threats resonated as they faced British threats to their own freedom.[99]

Among the gravest perils British tyranny seemed to present was the manipulation of Indians and their "savage" form of war. The Revolution saw new stories of alleged Indian threats that capitalized on the Indians' savage image. Hugh Henry Brackenridge's play memorializing General Montgomery cast the British as goading hostile Indians in Canada. Brackenridge embellished on a December 1775 letter, printed in American newspapers at Congress's urging, that purported to prove that the British had actively recruited Indian allies. Canadian Indians who agreed to ally with the British "were invited to FEAST ON A BOSTONIAN AND DRINK HIS BLOOD. An ox being roasted for the purpose, and a pipe of wine given to drink." Brackenridge worked cannibalism into his play, having the British general at Quebec call "the Savages, to taste of blood . . . / Of a Bostonian." Later in the play, after Montgomery's death, the same general taunted Americans outside the city with the display of Montgomery's corpse while encouraging Indians to torture and eat American prisoners. Though Indians did not kill Montgomery, Brackenridge presented them as a lurking menace subject to British machinations.[100]

An epic poem dedicated to General Horatio Gates and published in 1779 by "an OFFICER of Rank in the CONTINENTAL ARMY" told a similar story. In the opening scene of the second book, General Washington speaks to his officers:

Let us be firm, not rash nor impotent,
To guard the rights of this vast Continent.
Our armed legions well secure the coasts,
And terror awes the western Pagan hosts;
But in the north th' unpolish'd race reside,
Who basely yield to *Britain's* lawless pride:
Led blindly on to interrupt our weal
By threats of tyrants, and by priestly zeal,
The tawny Savage, and the *Gallic* band,
May pass the lakes and penetrate our land:
Wisdom invites this Senate to prepare,
And make *Canadia's* land the seat of war.[101]

As if the allusion to French and Indian attacks on frontier settlements in the 1750s were not enough, the author attached "A concise HISTORY of the Former WARS in AMERICA."

The author dedicated this poem to a General who knew the value of propaganda during wartime. General Gates took command of troops in the Hudson Valley on August 19, 1777. Charged with blocking the advance from the north of British troops under General John Burgoyne, Gates arrived at Albany, New York, with the region in uproar over the death on July 27 of a young woman named Jane McCrea. McCrea lived in the area near Fort Edward and was engaged to an officer in Burgoyne's army. Though the exact circumstances of McCrea's death have long been disputed, she likely fell at the hands of Indians perhaps only loosely allied with the British. New York and New England newspapers immediately began publishing accounts of her death with gruesome details, even before they knew her name. In Hartford, the *Connecticut Courant* of August 3 described a girl shot and scalped, "a sweet heart to an officer in the enemy's service, and a great tory—Hear, O Heavens! and give ear, Oh, America!" Gates was less circumspect. Rather than plea to the heavens, he published a letter accusing Burgoyne of urging Indians to terrorize the population and blaming him for resulting death of McCrea, "a young lady lovely to the sight, of virtuous character, and amiable disposition." Gates pinned Indian savagery to British duplicity, and McCrea's death foreshadowed life under British rule where even loyalist women were not safe.[102]

Gates attempted to turn word of McCrea's murder into Revolutionary fervor, and, by some historians' estimates, he succeeded, turning neutrals into patriots and drawing New England militiamen away from their farms to join Continental forces. Continental troops outnumbered and surrounded

Burgoyne's forces at Saratoga, forcing the surrender of nearly six thousand men on October 17. It would be the Americans' most decisive victory until Yorktown. Whether or not it affected the outcome of the battle, McCrea's death became one of the most talked-about of the entire Revolution. Yet it offered just one of many portrayals of British collusion with Indian savagery that helped to unite otherwise diverse white patriots and to justify native dispossession.[103]

White Americans also spoke more about how Indian claims to the land lacked substance. "It is beginning to be extensively and learnedly posited," observed traveler Johann Schoepf, that "none of the Indian tribes . . . have the remotest right to the land wherein they and their forefathers for unthinkable ages have lived."[104] Schoepf was likely responding, in part, to a tract from the pen of Hugh Henry Brackenridge. After he memorialized General Montgomery, Brackenridge eventually moved west to Pittsburgh to set up his legal practice and help establish the *Pittsburgh Gazette*. Pittsburgh's residents knew all to well about frontier violence. They lived a morning's stroll from the site where many of the corpses from Braddock's disastrous expedition, ambushed by French and Indian forces in 1755, still lay. And the region had seen more carnage since, on which Brackenridge elaborated in *Narratives of a Late Expedition Against the Indians* (1783).

The claim of "the animals, vulgarly called Indians," to "the extensive countries of America, is wild and inadmissible," Brackenridge asserted. Indians' title to land rested on "occupancy":

A wild Indian with his skin painted red, and feather through his nose, has set his foot on the broad continent of North and South America: a second wild Indian with his ears cut in ringlets, or his nose slit like a swine or a malefactor, also sets his foot on the same extensive tract of soil: Let the first Indian make a talk to his brother, and bid him take his foot off the continent, for he being first upon it, had occupied the whole, to kill buffaloes, and tall elks with long horns. This claim, in a reasoning of some men would be just, and the second savage ought to depart in his canoe, and seek a continent where no prior occupant claimed the soil.

Brackenridge traced this logic to the policies of European monarchs who contrived the right of discovery to make their claims to lands in the New World. But, like many an apologist for colonization before him, Brackenridge invoked the doctrine of use and the stereotype of Indians as nomadic hunters. So long as Indians did not till the soil, and thus support a large population on the land, rights of discovery did not apply. Moreover, episodes of Indian violence in the Revolution and earlier wars had implicated the entire race as having the "character of Devils." Indian treatment of prisoners, particularly torture, justified "extermination." The argument served patriotic interests well. Neither Indians nor the Kings of Europe had a right to the Americas. War to expand American frontiers was entirely justified. The true heirs of the continent were those who "improved" it. War with Indians made this seem truer than ever.[105]

WAXING AND WANING DIPLOMATIC ASPIRATIONS

Although Indians would continue to defend their lands for decades to come, the Revolutionary struggle with Britain shifted primarily to the diplomatic arena after Cornwallis's defeat at Yorktown in 1781. Then, in a twist on Clausewitz's famous adage, American diplomats continued to pursue the war's aims, just by different means. These men overseas now assumed the continental mantle that the army had borne for so long. They took to positioning the United States as the dominant power of North America; to codifying an expansive yet insular state; to making European powers recognize explicitly that which the United States had already made implicit by declaring itself a people—"of America"—and its Congress "continental." Like the army, diplomacy existed in two realms, that of aspiration and that of reality. And the 1783 Peace of Paris would leave U.S. diplomats, and the Americans they represented, wanting to believe that their metageographical vision was finally within reach. Yet time would show that work remained.

In fall 1776, when a seventy-year-old Benjamin Franklin braved an Atlantic crossing in search of an alliance with France, he literally carried evidence of the patriots' expansive territorial quest: orders and funds from Congress to commission King Louis's official sculptor to craft a monument for General Montgomery's tomb.[106] Yet only after France had declared war against Britain did Congress formally articulate its territorial objectives. On February 23, 1779, a congressional committee drafted its desired peace terms, and the Congress modified them slightly before relaying them to its diplomats that fall. Once Britain acknowledged independence, negotiators could seek lands that, given the young nation's fledgling state, would astonish the British and, especially, the French and Spanish ministers.

The United States, though proclaiming itself independent, had not forgotten its colonial charters. On the basis of these and the outcome of the Seven Years' War, it sought to extend west to the Mississippi River. The lands in question included the Illinois and Ohio countries—the Old Northwest, as the region has come to be called—and lands as far south as the thirty-first parallel, the southern border of Georgia. In addition to its longstanding hopes to someday conquer Quebec, Congress also wanted to acquire a portion of present-day southern Ontario—if not all of Canada—delineated by the Proclamation of 1763. In that year, the crown had separated from the rest of its mainland colonies a vast tract of land north of the Great Lakes and south of the "Nipissing line." The land comprised an area bounded by Lakes Huron, Erie, and Ontario, and south of a line that stretched west from the St. Lawrence through Lake Nipissing and beyond to the source of the Mississippi River (which, at the time, was presumed to lie further north than it actually is). Colonists, especially in Virginia and New York, saw the creation of this imperial holding as a curtailment of their charters, heightening their opposition to the Proclamation. Now, Congress sought these lands at the negotiating table.[107]

The claims were audacious. Save for the victories of a few hundred troops under George Rogers Clark at Vincennes and Kaskaskia in the Illinois country, the United States had by no means conquered or occupied the Old Northwest. Instead, Indians and French still constituted the bulk of the region's settlers. Even feebler, the United States' claims to lands north of the Great Lakes to the Nipissing line rested only on tenuous legal arguments and dreams. Making the territorial aims of 1779 all the more brazen, Britain at the time controlled New York City, Rhode Island, and Savannah.

That is not to say that the congressional aims were not logical, given the metageographical assumptions held by congressional delegates and diplomats. Long-term security and peace would result only if the continent came under the control of one power, an outcome that appeared within the realm of possibility. In June 1778, Virginia delegate Richard Henry Lee wrote George Washington that, should France enter the war, the United States would find itself in a position to push Britain "quite off this Northern Continent, which will secure to us peace for a Century, instead of War in 7 years, which the British possession of Canada, N[ova] Sco[tia] & the Floridas will inevitably produce." After France entered the war, John Adams sensed from his post in Europe that British "Spirits . . . are terribly sunk." As he explained to Patrick Henry, some in Parliament were "not expecting ever to get America back." And "so great a Body of People . . . are terrified at the Foresight of the Consequences of American Liberty—the Loss of the West India Islands of Canada Nova Scotia and the Floridas." Momentum and metageographical destiny seemed to be on the United States' side.[108]

Beyond the sheer vastness of its aims, Congress reached greatest in 1779 when it sought the free navigation of the Mississippi and a port at the Gulf of Mexico. Although the Spanish had entered the war first and foremost to recover Gibraltar, they also had strategic aims in North America that had changed little since the Seven Years' War. The Spanish crown had little interest in fueling the United States' expansionist colonial independence movement so close to its own colonies. Instead, King Charles III zealously guarded the navigation of the Mississippi River, and, soon after entering the war in June 1779, his troops seized Natchez and Baton Rouge to assure control of the river's mouth. The larger aim was to protect shipping in the Gulf, the lifeline of Spain's empire in Mexico. The Spanish held objectives in North America logical for an empire already richer in land than the resources and population needed to colonize it. Spain could not allow the United States unbridled access to the Mississippi or the Gulf, or let the fledgling nation grow to the point that it might easily conquer these regions in the future.[109]

In 1780, Congress sent its former President, John Jay, on what was thus an unrealistic diplomatic mission to Spain. French and Spanish diplomats had already told Congress that it had no legal or practical right to a border extending to the Mississippi, but Congress nevertheless dispatched Jay to seek such a border, including the river's navigation, topped off by a Spanish alliance and financial aid.[110] The rationale for American passage on the Mississippi, as Jay explained shortly after arriving in Spain, was that "Americans, almost to a man, believed that God Almighty had made that river a highway for the people of the upper country to go to the sea by." More than a trading route, the Mississippi bordered a country that was "extensive and fertile," and many prominent Americans, including George Washington, wished "that it would rapidly settle."[111] Persistent though he was, Jay had little negotiating power and found the Spanish aloofly refusing to recognize the United States. To be sure, Spanish military actions advanced the United States' war effort by supplementing French naval power and forcing Britain to wage war on additional fronts.[112] But Spain's unwillingness to formally recognize the United States or to allow it free passage on the Mississippi greatly distressed American diplomats. On learning that negotiations with Spain had sputtered, a "mortified" Benjamin Franklin wrote Jay from Paris, "I would rather agree with [Spain] to buy at great Price the whole of their Right on the Missisipi than sell a Drop of its Waters.—A Neighbor might as well ask me to sell my Street Door."[113] Keep in mind that this preacher of frugality in *Poor Richard's Almanack* (1732–58) was representing a United States that had virtually no money.

Many Americans thought, as one French observer noted, that the territorial demands of 1779 represented "an act of moderation." After all, the original colonial charters had specified lands stretching to the Pacific, and colonists had bled in the Seven Years' War to win the continent.[114] But to the French and Spanish foreign ministers, the U.S. territorial quest appeared extravagant, imprudent, and impudent. France may have renounced its claims to Canada, but it could not afford to jeopardize the war effort by letting the United States overextend itself. France's foreign minster, Charles Gravier, Comte de Vergennes, warned that the "United States should not concern themselves with a distant expedition until they become the masters of their own house." He hoped to "cure the United States of the mania for conquering foreign provinces before having conquered and secured their own territory." Likewise, Spain's unofficial representative to the United States, Juan de Miralles, tried to convince members of congress of the "absurdity of their ideas." The United States demanded lands west of the Appalachians already "conquered by Spain from the enemy, while they have not the means to liberate their own territory."[115]

The French and the Spanish also had ulterior motives. They did not, as Vergennes explained to his envoy in Spain, wish to see "the new republic mistress of the entire continent."[116] American independence served French and Spanish interests best with Canada in British hands and the Floridas under Spanish control. Dividing the continent accordingly would keep the United States dependent on France and prevent the new nation from growing too powerful. The idealism of the United States' diplomacy—Thomas Paine's vision of an expansive, insular nation with only commercial ties to Europe—ran headstrong into the realism of European-style, balance-of-power diplomacy.

With little to offer but his own resolve, Jay gained neither the navigation of the Mississippi nor a formal alliance with Spain, despite spending twenty-nine frustrating months in Madrid. Jay's failure, combined with a deteriorating war effort and the fear of tightening French purse strings, prompted Congress to send a more realistic, even desperate, set instructions to its peace commissioners in June 1781. Independence remained the *sine qua non*. Now, however, Congress thought it unwise "at this distance to tye you up by absolute and peremptory directions." Congress's "desires" regarding boundaries remained the same, but the commissioners could, if they saw fit, compromise on both them and the navigation of the Mississippi. Highlighting just how desperate Congress had become, it also ordered its commissioners to cede ultimate judgment on these matters to the French, to "undertake nothing in the negotiations for peace or truce without their [French] knowledge and concurrence and ultimately to govern yourselves by their advice and opinion."[117] Diplomacy that had initially espoused Paine's vision of insularity and expansion now ostensibly depended on European aims and affairs.

Sitting in Philadelphia, Congress experienced the souring war effort close at hand, and the peace ultimatums of 1781 reflected a compromise borne of necessity, urgency, and immediacy. But peace negotiations took place an ocean away, distanced from the war effort by three thousand miles and irregular ship sailings. The United States' commissioners in Paris typically had to wait five to six months for replies to letters they sent home. In contrast, correspondence between London and its representatives took less than two weeks. Slow communication left the American plenipotentiaries acting less as agents of Congress—an institution whose "continental" aspect had waned significantly—than as an "independent privy council," wrote Robert Livingston, Congress's frustrated Secretary of Foreign Affairs. On top of that, Congress itself, as a legislative body, sometimes worked at a snail's pace. It took until August 1782, ten months after Yorktown, for example, for Congress to consider modifying its diplomatic instructions that it had made when the war was going poorly the previous June. The debate was passionate but went nowhere. All Congress could do, while events transpired quickly in Paris, was establish a committee to consider "the most adviseable means of securing to the United States the several objects claimed by them and not included in their ultimatum of the 15 day of June, 1781."[118] American diplomacy had thus bifurcated between that in Philadelphia and that in Paris. And once peace talks with Britain began in earnest in April 1782, the skills, personalities, and idealistic aims of the main American diplomats came to matter more than Congressional declarations and debates.[119]

Few men had more potent and durable notions of the United States' potential as a continental society than the three who did the bulk of the work in Paris: John Adams, an admirer of Thomas Pownall's ideas and drafter of the Model Treaty; Benjamin Franklin, the author of *Observations on the Increase of Mankind* (1755) and the "Canada Pamphlet" (1760); and John Jay, a former President of the Congress. Congress may have directed these commissioners to "govern" themselves according to the "advice and opinion" of the French ministry, but they were also to remember Congress's territorially ambitious instructions of 1779.[120] The two stipulations soon became incompatible. The realization that the French did not share their territorial vision caused the American diplomats to negotiate directly with a British ministry that, ironically, had developed aims more commensurate with those of the United States than France or Spain.

Although Congress sent four envoys to negotiate the peace, Benjamin

Franklin initially served as the sole American commissioner in Paris in the spring of 1782. Jay did not arrive until late June, only to spend much of July bedridden with the flu. Then Adams arrived in October and Henry Laurens in November, barely in time to sign his name to the preliminary peace. Franklin thus set the early tenor of the talks with Britain, a role that concerned some. Franklin had become a Francophile during his years in France, and John Adams had already accused him of displaying gratitude bordering on subservience toward the French. To be sure, Franklin basked in Parisians' adulation, and he savored their city's pleasures. He strolled through the Louvre where could see his own bust on display near the freshly sculpted monument to Montgomery that he had commissioned; he operated a small printing press; he played chess and flirted with glamorous women; he aided savants with their scientific experiments; he witnessed the world's first hot air balloon flights; and he indulged heavily in fine food and wine.[121]

Yet for all the pleasures he found in Paris, Franklin remained at his core proudly, defiantly, American. At a dinner with more than a dozen people, the consummate diplomat Franklin could not resist a pointed demonstration. Half of the guests were American and the other half French—including the Abbé Raynal—and the two groups sat across the table from one another. When one of the Frenchmen asked Franklin to comment on a popular Buffonian tract, the five-foot, ten-inch Franklin surveyed the room and asked everybody to rise. As it happened, Raynal, whose writings had taken Buffon's theories about degeneracy in the Americas to provocative extremes, was particularly short, and "there was not one American present who could not have tost out of the windows any one or perhaps two of the rest of the company," recalled one of the Americans present. The subject did not arise the rest of the evening.[122]

Franklin may have savored France's offerings, but he was still proudly an outsider, the man who displayed his roots by choosing a fur cap over a powdered wig. To the extent he was more compliant in dealing with the French than Adams or others may have liked, it grew not out of a fondness for things French but the United States' beggarly status and its need for French aid. Franklin never compromised his vision of a thriving continental empire in North America. He could no more hold back his expansive hopes for the United States in the peace negotiations than he could resist exposing facts embarrassing to Buffon's adherents.

Ironically, as British diplomats became more amenable to American independence, their vision of North America also became more commensurate with Franklin's. At the outset of negotiations, British politics were in transition. Two men, Charles James Fox and the Earl of Shelburne, vied to direct policy. Fox believed in recognizing American independence so that Britain could focus on fighting the French. Shelburne, in contrast, worried as late as March 1782 that North America's resources were too great, and the United States' future too bright, for Britain to relinquish all thirteen mainland colonies. Shelburne, like Franklin before the Revolution, thought the future of the British Empire lay in America, so reconciliation, even if it left British control of the colonies weakened, seemed the more prudent path than independence.

The king backed Shelburne and, following the death of Lord Rockingham in July 1782, made Shelburne effectively the Prime Minister, prompting Fox's resignation. Shelburne's rise proved fortuitous to the United States, for although he initially opposed independence, Shelburne and his principal envoy in France, Richard Oswald, held underlying beliefs akin to those of Franklin. The views of Adam Smith and Thomas Pownall bore heavily on Shelburne and Oswald's thinking. Indeed, Smith had introduced the two men, and Pownall's brother John now served as a trade advisor to Shelburne. In the course of the diplomatic proceedings, Shelburne and Oswald concluded that if the United States were independent, Britain could still profit commercially from the continent's resources. Peace and trade, not dominion, must link Britain to the United States. As Oswald wrote in his journal that spring, "the more these states extend themselves in population and cultivation, the better it will be for England." Echoing Franklin's *Observations,* Oswald mused that while the United States "have such immense expansion of vacant lands behind them to be taken into appropriation at almost no expense, they will never become manufacturers," and a nation with "free and safe access" to the United States' ports "will never fail to profit." By July, Shelburne shared Oswald's perspective. Although he expressed concern over separating countries "united" by "every tie short of territorial proximity," the task seemed necessary, and "it should be done *decidedly,* so as to avoid all future risque of enmity, and lay the foundation of a new connection better adapted to the present temper and the interest of both countries." Although it had thin support in Parliament, Shelburne's government had become more amenable to the Americans' territorial aims than administrations previous or subsequent.[123]

With a sympathetic ear at the helm of British politics, the American commissioners needed to seize their opportunity. Franklin first broached the possibility that Britain might cede Canada to the United States in a conversation with Oswald in April 1782. His argument resembled that which he had developed to keep Canada at the end of the Seven Years' War.

Now Britain, not France, was the hostile neighbor, and Americans living near the border with Canada could never forget the violence they suffered during the Revolution. "The resentment of those injuries will remain, & break out again in vengeance," hence any peace that included a "long extended frontier . . . will never be secure." If Britain voluntarily delivered Canada to the United States, however, the gesture would foster reconciliation and potentially gain Britain access to American markets. It was a position John Adams had backed just two days earlier, in a letter he had sent to Franklin from Amsterdam.[124]

Oswald, for his part, expressed openness to Franklin's suggestion before returning to England, and an entry in his journal a few weeks later makes clear that he understood Franklin's perspective. If he were an American, Oswald wrote, he could foresee no lasting peace unless all of the British dominions on the mainland were "brought under the cover of one and the same political constitution."[125] Yet despite the common ground, negotiations sputtered for the next six weeks. Still, Franklin's desire for Canada endured. In July, Franklin presented to Oswald a list of "necessary" and "adviseable" articles. The necessary terms included restoring Canada's boundaries to those under the Proclamation of 1763, thus giving the United States land as far north as the Nipissing line. This demand was a minimum; fuller reconciliation, Franklin argued, would result if Britain agreed to his adviseable terms and surrendered "every part of Canada."[126] In July and August, a war-weary British cabinet twice endorsed Franklin's necessary articles, including a boundary at the Nipissing line.[127] But in Paris, Franklin and Jay never learned of these maneuvers across the channel.

Misfortune, and perhaps even poor judgment, partially derailed the United States' envoys in August and September and prevented them from taking advantage of British eagerness for a settlement. Franklin fell victim to a fierce bout of kidney stones, forcing Jay, who had just recovered from the flu, to assume a more prominent role in the negotiations. In one of his first acts, Jay refused to treat with Oswald because Oswald's written commission authorized him to treat with the American "colonies" rather than an independent United States. Franklin was willing to overlook the wording as a technicality, but Jay interpreted it as bad faith on the part of Shelburne. Recognition of independence would not be a treaty term but a precursor to negotiation, Jay insisted. Oswald had to procure a new commission from England before Jay would parley.[128]

Having thus rebuffed the enemy, Jay soon grew suspicious of his supposed ally, the Comte de Vergennes. At a meeting with Jay and Franklin on August 10, 1782, Vergennes, perhaps to mollify his Spanish ally, opined on the outlandishness of American boundary claims. France simply did not share in the American principles rooted in metageographical visions. Instead, the Bourbon power saw the Revolution principally as a way to deal a blow to Britain, and France valued Spain's war aims at least as much as those of the United States. Jay recognized that Vergennes preferred to seek compromise, to chop up the North American map, just as statesmen had created equilibriums on maps of Europe after past conflicts.[129] Jay now lurched back toward negotiations with a British administration he had recently spurned and violated his instructions from Congress by excluding the French. Franklin and Adams backed Jay, and the negotiations continued.

Jay's erratic maneuvers caused delays, during which Shelburne's position hardened. And Jay's newfound conciliatory posture toward the British left the Americans pressing for much less than they might have gotten just a month earlier. Jay drafted provisional peace terms in early October. By then, Shelburne learned that British forces had repelled Franco-Spanish attacks on Gibraltar, making peace less urgent. Meanwhile, loyalist interests in Parliament pressured Shelburne to seek the Old Northwest. Granted, some of Shelburne's close advisors continued to argue that these lands were not worth the trouble, since Indians there would continue to trade with Britain while resisting American expansion. Indeed these same Indians would slow United States settlement in the Old Northwest for many years to come.[130] Still, Shelburne stood to benefit politically by demonstrating greater firmness with the United States.

Anxious and committed to extending the boundary of the United States west to the Mississippi, Jay drafted provisional terms that retreated from Franklin and Adams's longstanding quest for all of Canada, even as a bargaining chip. Instead, Jay's provisional terms settled for the Nipissing line as a boundary. Jay also encouraged the British, out of vindictiveness fostered by his past diplomatic failure in Spain, to seize West Florida. Presumably, he thought a powerful former enemy turned trading partner would make a neighbor preferable to the steadfast Spanish, who, as Franklin put it, were trying "to coop us up within the Allegheny Mountains." The commissioners also subsequently defended this proposition, which made its way into the preliminary treaty, as a way to make the British more pliable on the issue of the Old Northwest.[131]

When negotiations resumed in late October, the British rejected Jay's provisional draft, and their envoys pressed for a border at the Ohio River. Instead of demanding the Nipissing line or all of Canada, the Americans responded with a quick compromise, the line running through the Great Lakes that forms the boundary of the United States today. After sorting out some sticky issues regarding access to fisheries, treatment of loyalists, and payment of debts, the commissioners signed a preliminary treaty at the end of November 1782, and a definitive treaty nine months later.

The American diplomats came away with less than the Shelburne administration had earlier been prepared to offer, prompting some historians to argue forcefully that the commissioners bungled the peace.[132] These historians have a point. Jay's delays improved Shelburne's bargaining position, and they led the Americans to miss a narrow window of opportunity when Shelburne was more amenable to generous terms. Furthermore, had the Americans pressed harder they still might have acquired the Nipissing boundary. But historians work with hindsight and access to British diplomatic correspondence. None of the American commissioners knew in August that events of the following month on a rock in the Mediterranean would threaten their vision for a continent.

The American diplomats' suspicion of their allies also seems reasonable, given the United States' commitment to westward expansion and how strongly the French and Spanish opposed it. In September 1782, Vergennes's deputy in London, Joseph-Matthais Gérard de Rayneval, proposed a western boundary for the United States closer to the Appalachians than the Mississippi.[133] Vergennes himself made clear in an October 14 letter to his representative in Philadelphia, Anne-César, Chevalier de la Luzerne, that he had no interest in backing the Americans' Canadian or western aims: "I do not see on what grounds the Americans would form claims to the lands that border Lake Ontario. . . . But I know . . . all the extravagance of the Americans' claims and views. According to Congress the charters that emanated from the British crown extend the domains of America from the ocean to the South Sea. Such is the system proposed by Mr. Jay as the basis for his negotiations with Spain. A parallel delirium does not merit being seriously refuted." Ever the guarded diplomat, Vergennes reminded Luzerne that "this fashion of thinking ought to be an impenetrable secret from the Americans." If they found out, "it would be a crime for which they would never pardon us." He instructed Luzerne to "leave them in the illusion, to make all the demonstrations necessary for them to think we share" their views.[134] Thus if Jay is to be criticized, he also deserves credit for circumventing a cagey French ministry that would have preferred imperial balance to U.S. dominance in North America.

Perhaps the strongest evidence of the commissioners' success was the international response. Vergennes remarked that the "English are purchasing the peace rather than making it," their concessions "exceed all that I had thought possible." In Britain, war-weariness could not mollify the perception that the terms were humiliating. Domestic politics had already weakened Shelburne, and calls for his impeachment arose immediately. Just months after the preliminary peace had been signed, Shelburne resigned. Meanwhile, Spain and many Native American tribes simply refused to recognize the terms of a treaty to which they were not a party and that directly impinged on their claims.[135]

Within the United States, celebrations of the peace were tempered by annoyance in Congress that the commissioners had acted independently and that they had opened the possibility that Britain might control part of Florida. Much of this grumbling grew out of longstanding personality conflicts and factionalism, and it surprised and pained the commissioners.[136] Yet although generally taken aback by the sullen reaction in Congress, the same commissioners also anticipated that the delineation of the Canadian border would rile some. When they sent the preliminary treaty to Congress, they defended the article on boundaries: "We knew this Court [France] and Spain to be against our claims to the western country, and having no reason to think that lines more favourable could ever have been obtained, we finally agreed to those described in this article: indeed they appear to leave us little to complain of, and not much to desire."[137] It was perhaps not the most resounding defense. Still, they stood proud. When asked to defend themselves against congressional criticisms for having acted independently, they responded with words that could have been written by Thomas Paine or Thomas Pownall: "since we have assumed a place in the political system of the world let us move like a primary & not like a secondary planet."[138]

THE United States' ability to operate as an independent planet would be severely tested in coming years. The defeat of the British at Yorktown and the subsequent peace of 1783 had made many think that the United States would finally realize its potential as a continental empire. It did not matter that, technically, the United States only claimed lands east of the Mississippi River, south of Canada, and north of Florida, or that Indians continued to occupy and defend many of these lands. Just as in 1763, fine distinctions seemed trivial. Peace ostensibly should have fulfilled longstanding predictions of grandeur. The natural abundance of the continent that had supported the military effort could be plumbed for prosperity.

Instead, of course, the years after 1783 presented surprising obstacles, just as the years after 1763 had. Debt, the difficulties of demobilization, economic depression, Spanish obstruction of the Mississippi, British troops lingering in northwestern forts, and Indians left out at the negotiating table all thwarted the United States' ambitions. Most problematic, the tension between Americans' declaration of themselves as a continental people and their rejection of the possibility of representative government over vast distances remained unresolved.

But before delving into how Americans tackled this issue, the years after the Peace of Paris provide an opportunity to return to the dispute over Buffonian formulations and the most celebrated contribution from the United States. Thomas Jefferson's only book, and the social and cultural context in which he wrote it, help to explain further the contingent and piecemeal fashion by which the United States became more committed to appropriating a continent than colonists in other parts of the Americas.

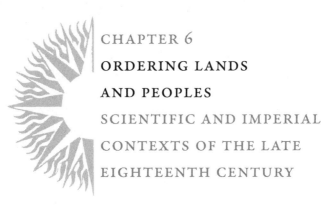

CHAPTER 6

ORDERING LANDS
AND PEOPLES

SCIENTIFIC AND IMPERIAL
CONTEXTS OF THE LATE
EIGHTEENTH CENTURY

What kindled the distinctive sense of geographic destiny among the European Americans in the former British mainland colonies? Why did they, more than others, feel such a strong attachment to an immense metageographical abstraction and think of themselves as the rightful occupants of their entire continent, as the true Americans? Returning to the debate over Buffonian formulations and placing the most cogent contribution from the United States—Thomas Jefferson's *Notes on the State of Virginia* (1785)—in a transnational, comparative context helps to explain how these mainlanders, unlike other European colonists, mentally appropriated as their rightful domain the lands they settled and, beyond these areas, the continent they imagined.

Britons living in other parts of the world recognized emerging continental taxonomies. Yet geographical compartments alone did not make a people. Neither Britons in India nor those in the West Indies came to see themselves collectively as the true Indians or West Indians to the same extent that British mainlanders saw themselves as the true Americans. And British colonists in Newfoundland and Nova Scotia emerged as the most British of all colonists, even as their compatriots to the south embraced their American identity. North American Spaniards, likewise, recognized emerging continental taxonomies while still differing from Britain's revolutionary mainlanders. To a greater degree, Spanish Americans recognized the limitations of their North American presence, and acknowledged and accepted, sometimes grudgingly, the existence of multiple Americans.

Among European Americans, then, those in the rebellious thirteen British colonies and the subsequent United States most emphatically merged their metageographical and political identity to create a vision of the future.[1] Their past experiences and their interpretation of them facilitated this appropriation of the continent. Their understanding of their history allowed them to see their future as *America,* and the social and economic context in which they lived provided rich soil for this intellectual construct.

SCIENCE AND GEOPOLITICS IN THE REVOLUTIONARY ERA

In January 1786, the U.S. minister to France, Thomas Jefferson, made plans to secure a stuffed elk to give to his new acquaintance, George Louis Leclerc, Comte de Buffon. "Perhaps your situation may enable you to aid me in this," Jefferson wrote to Archibald Stuart, his friend in Virginia. If convenient, he thought Stuart might send the horns, skeleton, and skin, the belly stuffed and sewn so that "it would present the form of the animal." In 1785, Jefferson had published his only book, *Notes on the State of Virginia,* which disputed Buffon's arguments. Parts of a dead elk would further support Jefferson's contention that species did not degenerate in North America.

In pursuing his longstanding argument with Buffon, Jefferson demonstrated that the relationship between science and imperial politics remained as important as ever. It is telling that Jefferson sandwiched scientific pursuits, including that of an elk, into a schedule filled with matters that affected the fate of the nation. He wrote *Notes on the State of Virginia* while governor of Virginia, a state struggling to muster soldiers while British troops marched within its bounds. He sought his elk while serving as the U.S. minister to France, a time when much of his other correspondence dealt with his fledgling nation's domestic tumult and precarious position in the international arena. Jefferson made time for science because he and others in the founding generation viewed the scientific, military, and political defense of the United States as part and parcel of the same battle.

Jefferson's letter to Stuart captured this outlook in microcosm. In it, Jefferson shifted seamlessly between elk stuffing to musings about geopolitics. Disturbing news from home made Jefferson fret about whether the United States would attain its continental potential. Kentuckians seemed to be on the verge of splitting from Virginia and the national confederacy, and Spain claimed sole right to the navigation of the Mississippi. He believed the United States must retain both Kentucky and free passage on the Mississippi. Indeed, the "confederacy must be viewed as the nest from which all America, North and South is to be peopled."[2]

The elk and the geopolitical vision: scientific observations had political implications. As a principal source of natural history information, even seemingly innocuous travel literature had become valuable currency in the struggle to discern and define the character of North America. At the most basic level, settlers on the ground liked to know which plants were edible, which snakes poisonous. From an imperial perspective, policymakers needed to know what realms had potential, what places had strategic value. Travel writers, in turn, interjected occasional political commentary amid their observations of "natural curiosities."

The line between naturalists' observations and their political implications blurred, sometimes appearing on the same page. Amid his catalog of flora and fauna, for example, Peter Kalm had predicted the eventual independence of Britain's colonies following the ouster of the French from North America. Likewise, a British officer in the Revolution editorialized on the prematurity of American independence, claiming that Americans would regret it, and then he suddenly shifted to discuss "a little animal that was brought me lately, called a flying squirrel." After the Revolution, one of George Rogers Clark's traveling companions in the Ohio country wrote in his journal about Indians assaulting settlers and, without pause, mentioned petrified shells and hornets' nests. And John Filson's tract promoting the settlement of Kentucky happily announced that "serpents are not numerous," compared the "bones of the old and new continents," and discussed the possibility that some species may have gone extinct. It also advised seizing New Orleans and the Floridas from Spain.[3]

One commentator lamented the heavy reliance of natural history on what were often flawed observations. Like voices in an echo chamber, these authors'

> blunders assume different shapes, and come recommended to us under various authorities. You see them mustered and embodied in a gazetteer or a geographical grammar, marching in the splendid retinue of all the sciences in the Encyclopedia; you find them by regiments pressed into the service of De Paw, tortured into discipline and taught to move to the music of Raynal, and then mounted among the heavy armed cavalry of Robertson.

Speaking of those who perpetuated Buffon's degeneration theory, he complained that "a few light superficial travelers . . . are the men whose errors have been uniformly copied by succeeding writers, systematized by philosophers, and acted out by politicians." Jefferson, although brilliant and ambitious in his attempt to set the record straight, was not that unusual for juggling scientific observations with politics.[4]

Just as individuals mixed their scientific and political observations, Europeans powers intertwined their scientific exploration with their geopolitical aims. The British and French monarchies intervened in scientific study and exploration in the aftermath of the Seven Years' War. Their study of nature did not seek knowledge solely for knowledge's sake; it proceeded from the belief that government must rest on natural foundations. Knowledge of nature allowed them to extend imperial control. Since 1763, France had promoted unprecedented cooperation between its botanists and its navy and colonial administrators. Ships shuttled botanists around the globe in a vigorous search for plants with medicinal or commercial potential. Foods, dyes, and drugs that could transform distant lands into profitable colonies stood to enhance France's power. Thus, the crown patronized some of the best naturalists in the world, including Buffon, who directed the Jardin du Roi from 1740–88, making it Europe's premier collection of plant, animal, and mineral specimens.

Britain's scientific globetrotting rivaled that of France. In August 1768, the Royal Navy's *Endeavour* sailed from Plymouth, England, bound for the Pacific. On board, Captain James Cook hosted a scientific party to make astronomical observations, collect specimens, and chart new lands. When the *Endeavour* returned to England, it brought thousands of fish, bird, and plant specimens; 1,300 sketches and paintings; and a plentitude of Polynesian artifacts. In subsequent voyages in 1772–75 and 1776–79, Cook's parties mapped the Australian coastline (and thus paved the way for British colonization there in 1788), became the first Europeans to land in Hawaii, and searched for a Northwest Passage, charting much of the Alaskan coastline as they proceeded. After the voyageurs returned (without Cook, who died in a violent skirmish in Hawaii), some of them published accounts that expanded British territorial claims to the explored regions and stimulated European rivals to chart more of their own global expeditions.[5]

Jefferson grasped the geopolitical ramifications of scientific exploration. He glimpsed ulterior motives behind other nations' scientific ventures, particularly Britain's, seeing in them a threat to the continental destiny of the United States. Though Spain claimed the trans-Mississippi West and obstructed the United States' passage on the Mississippi River, it remained comparatively weak. Britain stood as the nation best situated to thwart the United States' interests in the West. Given news of Cook's explorations and British activity in the Pacific, the danger seemed palpable: "I find they have subscribed a large sum of money in England for exploring the country from the Missisipi to California. They pretend it is only to promote knolege. I am afraid they have thoughts of colonising in that quarter."[6]

In response, Jefferson sought to hasten the United States' own explorations. In 1783, he unsuccessfully urged the American Philosophical Society to fund an overland expedition to the Pacific to be led by George Rogers

Clark. Five years later, in Paris, Jefferson solicited the services of John Ledyard, a veteran of Cook's final voyage, to traverse North America from west to east. When Ledyard tried to cross Russia to sail across the Bering Strait, Russian authorities arrested him. He returned to Paris, where Jefferson suggested that he journey from Kentucky westward to the Pacific. Unsuccessful in these schemes, Jefferson had to wait another sixteen years to see U.S. explorers blaze routes to the Pacific.[7]

THE DEFENSES OF JEFFERSON AND CLAVIGERO

Although Jefferson stands as the most famous defender of the Americas against scientific assaults, his was one voice among many. Indeed, Spaniards and Spanish Americans spilled far more ink than any other Americans in critiquing the arguments and methodologies of Buffon, Raynal, de Pauw, and others. Notable among them, the Mexican Jesuit Francisco Clavigero wrote from exile in Italy after the Spanish monarchy expelled the Jesuits from Spanish colonies in 1767. Comparing Jefferson's and Clavigero's works illuminates the particular assumptions each had about the unity of the American landmass and the relationship between it and the character of its inhabitants. The differences in their science grew out of the distinctive histories and experiences of their communities and, in turn, contributed to incipient provincial proto-nationalism in Mexico and a more robust, expansive, and continental nationalism in the United States.[8]

Jefferson's *Notes on the State of Virginia* originated as a response to a request for information about each state by the secretary of the French legation, François Marbois. Jefferson took on the task with respect to Virginia and completed a manuscript response in December 1781, and he continued to revise the work thereafter in response to suggestions from friends. He brought the manuscript to Paris after taking his ministerial post there in 1784. The first edition appeared in 1785—in French—as part of a small print run of 200 copies. Two years later, a French publisher issued the first English edition, translated from the French, to Jefferson's dissatisfaction. In response, and at the urging of James Madison, Jefferson employed an English publisher and, in the summer of 1787, printed 1,000 copies of *Notes,* which, for the first time, bore his name.[9]

Jefferson's countrymen lauded the book for both its scientific and its political value. During the 1780s, portions of *Notes* were reprinted in dozens of newspapers in the United States. In Britain, John Adams, serving as the U.S. minister, commissioned one of Benjamin West's students, Mather Brown, to paint his portrait (fig. 29). Though known more for his legal and political mind, Adams opted to be painted with a quill pen, some paper in

FIGURE 29. Mather Brown's portrait of John Adams (1788). Boston Athenæum.

hand, and a volume that read "Jefferson's Hist. of Virginia" on its spine. Partly this was a tribute to his good friend, who had also arranged for the portrait. But it was also as if Jefferson's book contained the evidence Adams needed to defend the United States politically. And, in fact, at times it did. He prefaced his *A Defence of the Constitutions of the Government of the United States of America* (1787) with a paean to a litany of American geniuses in the arts and sciences. The U.S. constitutions "were contrived merely by the use of reason and the senses." Just as West painted Wolfe, and Franklin "practiced" electricity, so, too, did Paine reveal "the mistakes of Raynal, and Jefferson those of Buffon, so unphilosophically borrowed from the despicable dreams of De Pau."[10]

When Jefferson began his work on Virginia, Clavigero in Italy was finishing his opus on Mexico. Though both men refuted Buffonian formulations, their choices of titles manifested key differences between their works. Clavigero's four-volume *Historia antigua de México* (1780–81) was a "history," whereas Jefferson compiled "notes on the state." Clavigero spent more than half of his *Historia* on the Indians before the arrival of Europeans, focusing on the people of central Mexico. Jefferson spent most of his discussion of Indians speaking in what almost sounds to the modern ear as the ethnographic present.

Jefferson's discussion of differences among Europeans, Asians, Africans, and Americans revealed his belief that the four-part division of the world was of fundamental importance and that it provided a blueprint for the future. Like many scientists of his day, he believed his effort to systematize nature would illuminate an underlying and fundamental order. The four parts of the world—often granted continental status at the time—may not yet have revealed their precise boundaries, but they were a part of nature's plan. So, too, were the variations among their human inhabitants, and it was possible to generalize about all Native Americans, since they shared a continent. Even though all of Jefferson's examples of Native Americans came from "those within and circumjacent to the United States," he equated North America's eastern Indians with Native North Americans as a whole.[11] What he had read about South American Indians he would not "honor with the appellation of knowledge." He had concluded, based on what he had "seen of man, white, red, and black, and what has been written of him by authors, enlightened themselves," that these materials on South American Indians were "fables." In short, the descriptions of South Americans veered too much from what Jefferson knew of North Americans to seem plausible, betraying his belief that one should be able to generalize about the whole of the Americas.[12]

Conversely, when Jefferson saw superficial similarities between two groups of humans, such as the "red men of America" and those of Asia, his belief in the distinctiveness of continents prompted him to ferret out differences between peoples. Jefferson took tremendous interest in figuring out "from whence came those aboriginal inhabitants of America."[13] In his time, the limits of the Americas were just dimly emerging. But he could be confident that, "if the two continents of Asia and America be separated at all, it is only by a narrow streight."[14] This led him to posit a shared origin for East Asians and Native Americans. Nevertheless, he highlighted a deep temporal fissure rather than any cultural continuum between them. Looking at the number of radically different languages spoken by the "red men" within Asia and the Americas, Jefferson found "there will be found probably twenty in America for one in Asia." Assuming that it took "an immense course of time" for one language to become two, Jefferson reasoned that Americans must be of far "greater antiquity" than Asians.[15] The Americas, a fairly recent geographical invention in Jefferson's time, thus had aboriginal inhabitants fundamentally different from Asians by virtue of the Americans' ancient roots.

The notion of ancient roots served Jefferson's concept of the Americas' continental distinctiveness, but he did not linger on the dead past. Instead, he focused on his real concerns: the present and, especially, the future. Though he defended Native Americans against Buffonian attacks, he ultimately believed Indians would either assimilate into U.S. society or disappear entirely. They would not be the Americans of the future. Indians equaled Europeans in their intelligence, but they lagged in their development. For this reason, Jefferson thought it unfair to compare Indians' mental capacity to that of Europeans. He noted that when the Romans first crossed the Alps, Europe had a dense population but no signs of advanced letters. Indeed, "It was sixteen centuries after this before a Newton could be formed." Jefferson implied that, given time, Native America, too, might have produced a Newton. Instead, those already at a higher level of cultural evolution would engulf Native America, dooming its peoples to extinction.[16]

It would have been difficult for inhabitants of central Mexico in the late eighteenth century to see their future in Jeffersonian terms or to produce science that followed Jefferson's continental template. Having conquered the dense, sedentary populations of central Mexico, the Spanish colonists immediately noticed the stark contrast between these Indians and the no-madic Chichimecs to the north. In many respects, the Spanish and the Aztecs saw themselves as having more in common with each other than either group did with most of the other native peoples of the hemisphere. Events throughout Spanish America in the seventeenth and eighteenth centuries only compounded this sense of difference. The success of the Pueblo Revolt in late-seventeenth-century New Mexico, the rise of the Comanches on the southern plains, and the Túpac Amaru Rebellion in eighteenth-century Peru, for example, tempered the Spanish ability to see the Americas as a blank slate, as New Englanders essentially did in the aftermath of their victories in King Philip's War and the Seven Years' War.[17]

Moreover, central Mexico during the era of the American Revolution had an Indian majority—occupying an inferior status and often subject to tribute obligations—as well as sizeable populations of black slaves, mulattoes, mestizos, and other peoples of mixed descent. The nominally white population made up roughly 18 percent of the society's total. Within this small group existed further shadings and divisions. In contrast to British North America, race mixture between Europeans and native peoples was common in New Spain; most American-born Spaniards (creoles, as they came to be known) had some Indian ancestry, though they did not always acknowledge it.[18] These creoles often found themselves in power struggles with the small population of *peninsulares* (Spanish colonists of European birth). Creole consciousness heightened under imperial reforms that limited the group's power after 1765. Even though creoles had a long history of self-rule and outnumbered the newcomers, they found themselves shunned as they sought patronage appointments and *peninsulares* gained majority control over the *audiencias* (high courts).[19]

This tumult meant that Spanish Americans, like their British American counterparts, confronted Buffonian formulations amid an imperial crisis. But because relations between Europeans and Indians had taken a different course in central Mexico, colonists there mounted ideological defenses against scientific slanders and Spanish imperial encroachments that differed dramatically from those of British North American colonists. The creation of a Mexican national consciousness largely involved forming a mythological bond among the region's Indians, mestizos, and creoles. The crown inadvertently spurred the formation of such a bond when it tried to limit the power of Jesuits and expelled them from Spanish dominions in 1767. Among the 680 Jesuits expelled from Mexico, Francisco Clavigero, himself a creole, used his time in exile to defend Mexico against Buffonian formulations and, in the process, became a forefather of Mexican nationalism.

In his *Historia antigua de México,* Clavigero told his readers to discount Buffon's claim that "America is an entirely new country."[20] Crediting Indian traditions, Clavigero celebrated a Mexico with an epic heroic past, comparable to the histories of ancient Greece and Rome. In contrast, Jefferson's truncated history of North American natives focused largely on two questions: How did these first Americans arrive on the continent, and what happened to local Indians in the period after English colonization? Jefferson's cursory treatment of the past did not deal with the specifics of a region or any particular Indians, as did Clavigero's. His Indians belonged as much to the continent as to the state of Virginia. That Jefferson could jump from the first settlement of the continent to the colonial period also suggested a denial that local Indians had a history before the arrival of the colonists.

Jefferson had trouble comprehending that local Indians might have had complex civilizations. "I know of no such thing existing as an Indian monument," he wrote, only to concede later in the same paragraph the existence of a mound "in my neighborhood." Any perceived Indian shortcomings stemmed not from innate inferiority or environmentally induced degeneration, but from a relative lack of exposure to arts and letters or time to develop them. "Before we condemn the Indians of this continent as wanting genius," he wrote, "we must consider that letters have not yet been introduced among them."[21]

To be sure, Jefferson offered examples of Indian talents. But these came from his contemporaries, and he used them to present a vision of the future. Most notably, he praised the oratorical skills of the Mingo Chief Logan, comparing them to those of Demosthenes and Cicero. But this example came from a speech given in 1774 by a man lamenting the murder of his family and the end of his race. In the Mingo chief's alleged words, "Who is there to mourn for Logan?—Not one." Jefferson concealed some of the details surrounding the murder of Logan's family and some of the whites' provocations of violence. The death of Indians thus appeared at once tragic and natural. Though Indians were not innately inferior, confronting a more advanced Euro-American society they were doomed. White settlers would inevitably acquire their land.[22]

Clavigero, too, saw the decline of Indian societies as tragic, but he did not associate it with progress. Clavigero identified with the Indians more than Jefferson. They were part of his community; they belonged to Mexico every bit as much as the creoles.[23] Asserting the Mexican identity of the creoles, Clavigero traced his society's history back to the glories of ancient Mexico rather than Europe. By adopting the pre-Conquest Aztec world as his people's classical antiquity, Clavigero expressed the desire of many creoles to have a deep past in the New World. Where Jefferson's work offered a history with shallow roots and sweeping generalizations that presented more a vision of the future than the past, Clavigero's traced his people as far back and as specifically as possible. Clavigero's work implicitly supported Mexican independence based on the premise that the Mexican people's problems stemmed from the injustice of the Conquest and subsequent imperial policy. He made Indians a vital part of his community and cast the conquistadors as violent intruders.

The two men differed in their portrayals of space as well as time, with Jefferson emphasizing a continental framework that echoed the traditional four-part division of the world and Clavigero dwelling on the uniqueness of the valley of Mexico. Clavigero placed little importance on the four parts of the world when analyzing "the Physical and Moral Constitution of the Mexicans." To be sure, he saw "four classes of men" in Mexico. But these did not mirror global geography. Instead, he could not ignore Mexico's history and demographic development. The four types of people inhabiting Mexico that he enumerated were not simply Indians, Europeans, Africans, and Asians. Rather, they included, first, "the proper Americans, commonly called Indians"; second, "the Europeans, Asiatics and Africans" living in America; third, "the sons or descendants of them . . . that is Creoles"; and, finally, "the mixed breeds called by the Spaniards castas."[24]

In analyzing Indians alone, Clavigero saw variation where Jefferson homogenized. Clavigero accused the Americas' critics of "forming arguments against the whole of the new world, from what has been observed in some particular people," and that "not to distinguish between the Mexicans and Peruvians, and the Caribs and Iroquese . . . is obstinate persistence in an endeavour to revile the new world . . . instead of pursuing . . . the investigation of truth."[25] Regarding aspersions against the Americas, nothing held true with respect to Mexico. Mexico was a productive, populous region, unlike some other parts of the continent. Mexicans, for example, would have "nothing to do with California, nor could they expect any advantage from the conquest of a country so distant, so unpeopled, and so miserable."[26] The land was diverse, as were the histories of its peoples. For example, Clavigero believed, based on indigenous claims of an ancient migration from the north, that Mexico's Indians may have descended from Asian migrants, whereas for the "other nations of America as there is no tradition . . . we can say nothing." He speculated, however, that ancestors of Indians between Florida and "the most northern part of America" came from the "north of Europe."[27] For Clavigero, the Americas might have been one of the four parts of the world, even a continent, but this did not lend unity to the inhabitants, even the natives; nor did it provide a template for the future.

By tracing Mexico's history into a distant past and celebrating the specific virtues of its people, Clavigero's work foreshadowed the thinking of subsequent Mexican nationalists. Servando Teresa de Mier and Carlos María de Bustamante, for example, equated the conquistadors' brutal campaign in central Mexico in 1519–21 with imperial assaults on Mexican nationals in 1810. Mexican nationalism fed on the construction of a long and local history. Creoles created a societal family tree that placed their roots in the valley of Mexico. By incorporating natives into their family tree, they made Mexico their *patria,* their inclusive fatherland. Clavigero led the way in his proto-national *Historia antigua de México,* which he described in the dedication as "A history of Mexico written by a Mexican." The whole work was a "testimony of my most sincere love for my *patria.*"[28]

British American colonists, in contrast, frequently referred to England as the mother country, but rarely if ever did one call his North American province or the continent as a whole the fatherland. If anything, the English on both sides of the Atlantic tended to view North America as in an infant state that they would raise and bring into accordance with nature's plan. They stared antiquity in the face when they viewed their Indian neighbors. Looking at North America was like looking into the past. Edmund Burke proclaimed, "We possess at this time very great advantages towards the knowledge of human Nature. We need no longer go to History to trace it in all its stages and periods." The eighteenth-century historian William Russell claimed that the chronicler of North America could follow the Indian "in his progress, as he gradually advances from this infant state of civil life to its maturity." John Adams explained to Benjamin Franklin that it would be absurd for Euro-Americans to withdraw from the New World, "leaving America to grow up again with Trees and Bushes, and become again the Habitations of Bears and Indians."[29]

Coveting a continent dotted with native communities in a seemingly infant state, many British colonists in the Revolutionary era looked more to the future than their Mexican counterparts. They foresaw future generations bringing civilization to the land, and, because the land was so vast, this progress could continue for an unprecedented length of time. They came to believe, as historians have noted, that the political and social decay that beleaguered aging empires could be forestalled. By expanding across space, the American economy would remain dominated by politically virtuous, independent yeomen. The United States could thus avoid the corruption that arose in European commercial economies when the means for the masses to support themselves off the land diminished.[30] British newcomers declared themselves the nursemaids of North America's expansive, durable future. Washington, Jefferson, Hamilton, Adams, Madison, and Franklin donned the mantle of founding fathers, sweeping native fathers, such as the Mingo Chief Logan, into the dustbin of history.

Creole Mexicans in the late eighteenth century thought in nearly opposite terms, forging their identity out of an Indian past and seeing their future as one that embraced Indians. Many of these Mexican thinkers lamented that Indian-Spanish miscegenation had not occurred more completely. Clavigero wished that the early Spaniards had "married the Indians so that the result of this fusion would have been a single and integrated nation."[31] Anglo-American patriots such as Jefferson, by contrast, saw no virtue in marrying Indians and proudly proclaimed that British North American colonists sprang from British roots. Indeed, because British tyranny bore down on members of the British family, it seemed especially odious.[32] Opposition to British policy and colonial ties to a land distinguished men such as Jefferson from other Britons. Being American, then, was largely about conforming to a geographically determined future. A perceived tie to an expansively defined continent, in accordance with nature's plan, helped unite white patriots as citizens of the United States.

BRITONS, SPANIARDS, AND INDIANS

Jefferson's and Clavigero's differences grew out of the different material conditions that they faced and the historical trajectories that their societies had taken. By the late eighteenth century, creole Mexicans and British Americans were worlds apart in how they related to Indians and, hence, the land. This is not surprising; English and Spanish colonists saw their relations with the Americas' lands and peoples in markedly different ways. These groups brought to the Americas cultural preconceptions that would cause them to act differently. They carried with them different assumptions about how to justify seizing lands and riches from indigenous peoples.

More than other Europeans, the Spanish asserted their rights to the Americas through conquest and its associated rituals. An ethos born of centuries spent expelling the Moors from the Iberian Peninsula and Canary Islands, along with Caribbean conquests in the fifteenth and early sixteenth centuries, shaped the Spanish legal rationale supporting overseas expansion. In their signature ritual, conquistadors read a formal proclamation demanding that Indians convert to Christianity and accept Spanish rule or suffer a "just war" against them. With this *requerimiento,* the Spanish ritually pinned blame for the horrors of the Conquest on supposedly defiant Indians who often could not understand a word of the rigmarole.

The English shunned formal proclamations. Instead, they justified their land grabs by asserting that they were better stewards of the land and, hence, had more right to it than did scattered "primitive" Indians. Houses, gardens, and fences, instead of formal proclamations, provided the foundation of English authority in America. Seventeenth-century English usually referred to their colonial settlements as "plantations." In doing so, they metaphorically asserted their rightful possession of the land. Fences and natural boundaries, which helped give shape to plantations and farms, were important markers of English power. They constituted core English "ceremonies of possession" in the seventeenth century.[33] This early English preoccupation with clearly bounded and "improved" land also helps explain the appeal of geographical taxonomies, which appeared to rely on natural boundaries, in the eighteenth century.

New World conditions, even more than Old World baggage, determined the relationships between Britons and natives and Spaniards and natives. Mexico presented dense, urban, sedentary, sharply hierarchical, indigenous societies that a relatively small number of privileged Europeans exploited by exacting tribute from Indians. To encourage settlement, the crown granted and recognized titles to Indians' labor, known as *encomiendas*. Should the Indians abandon the land, the owner of the *encomienda* would have no title to it. The Spanish conquest of central Mexico was, then, principally one of Indian labor. To the extent Spaniards seized land, it was a means to the end of acquiring labor. After all, land without labor presented little more than dirt or, worse, rock-strewn dirt overgrown with brush and trees that needed clearing before it could yield crops and profits. Conquistadors sought honor and riches, not menial work, and the easiest route to wealth lay in securing the labor of indigenous peoples and exacting the tribute that their leaders once claimed.[34]

In the early seventeenth century, nearly a hundred years after Hernán Cortés had ventured into Mexico, the English planted their first permanent New World colony at Jamestown. Along the eastern coast of North America, the largest Indian groups the English encountered numbered in the low tens of thousands, a trifle compared with the roughly 25 million the Spaniards conquered in central Mexico.[35] The Indians of North America's Eastern Woodlands, compared with those of Mexico, proved of little use as laborers for local European colonists. These Indians were not just fewer in number; they also relied on seasonal mobility to feed themselves, and their ability to extract tribute was rudimentary compared with that of the Indians of Mexico or Peru. Although a profitable fur trade appeared in places while the supply allowed, the English colonists usually made the North American mainland habitable and profitable by shunning and dispossessing indigenous inhabitants. Even in the areas where Indian labor figured most heavily in the economy, such as South Carolina, it was only for a relatively short period and it consisted mostly of the sale and export of the laborers into distant slavery, not the regular exaction of tribute from them. Charles Town, South Carolina, functioned as a macabre Ellis Island for African slaves headed to destinations throughout the British mainland, but only in the early eighteenth century and only after thousands of native slaves had been exported from its docks, mostly to plantations scattered throughout the British West

Indies.[36] Farther north, in Virginia and New England, wars genocidal in effect, if not intent, led to the demographic collapse of native peoples, precluding the possibility of economies resting primarily on Indian labor.

Instead of relying on Indians' labor to make colonies profitable, English mainland colonists focused much more on the taking of Indian land. To encourage settlement, for example, Chesapeake colonies implemented a system starkly different from the *encomienda*. Instead of awarding rights to Indians' labor, they granted titles to land. Individuals who came to Virginia or Maryland or paid for someone's transportation there received a "headright" of fifty or one hundred acres.[37] As long as Europeans steadily migrated to the Anglo-American colonies, and as long as Anglo-Americans knew little of how the West differed from the East, expansion to acquire more Indian land seemed desirable, if not inevitable. Spaniards, by contrast, may not have known of many of North America's geographic particulars, but they had seen enough of the continent as early as the mid-sixteenth century, with the wide-ranging, northward probes of Francisco Vásquez de Coronado and Hernando de Soto, to know that it did not contain any civilizations analogous to those of central Mexico or Peru. Subsequent Spanish explorers saw to the north "the rather poor lands of the Californias," and comparatively few individuals wanted to live in what is now Arizona, New Mexico, Texas, or Florida. The historian J. H. Elliott has appropriately deemed these northern borders of New Spain "the orphans of Spain's empire in America. . . . They represented a constant and unwelcome drain on resources, and they were also unattractive to emigrants, who preferred to make for the more settled regions of New Spain and Peru." Spaniards in these regions needed significant Indian cooperation—usually forced and unwilling—just to maintain their meager presence.[38]

The same did not hold for Britons in many mainland colonies by the eighteenth century. War and disease had considerably reduced the Indian population in New England, for example, fostering the belief that the English were physically better suited to the North American environment than were Indians. Subsequent generations of New Englanders came away telling stories that honored their ancestors for their sacrifices and triumphs.[39] In contrast, just four years after New England's Indian population collapsed, New Spaniards confronted one of the most successful Indian rebellions in history. In a violent uprising in 1680—the "first American Revolution," in the words of one historian—Pueblos drove Spaniards from New Mexico. After colonists returned to Santa Fe more than a decade later, they recognized that New Mexico would be little more than a buffer zone between Mexico and the interior of North America, and matters only grew more complicated over the course of the eighteenth century as the Comanches rose in power.[40]

The contrasting experiences of the mainland's Britons and New Spaniards made the former far more receptive to emerging racial theories and categories. One reason settlers in the British colonies warmly received Linnaean taxonomies is that, throughout their history, these colonists had drawn a much sharper dichotomy between themselves and Indians than did other Europeans in the Americas. Indeed, the *relative* lack of sexual relations between Briton and Indian distinguished that nation's American colonists from all others. By the early eighteenth century, central Mexico had developed an extensive caste system with more than a dozen categories based on degrees of racial intermixture that acknowledged the reality of relationships between red, white, and black. As early as 1529, one could see Spaniards traveling Mexico's roads with an Indian mistress or two.[41]

In contrast, Virginia legislated against intermixture. Though such legislation might be seen as the reaction to a problem, it could not have been a rampant one. As late as 1717, the colony's governor reported he did not know of "one Englishman that has an Indian wife, or an Indian married to a white woman." The same could be said in New England at least as late as 1676. In the mid-eighteenth century, Benjamin Franklin held the ethnic and racial purity of the colonies so dear that he lamented the influx of Germans into Pennsylvania and criticized the growth of slavery in the south. On the eve of the Stamp Act, James Otis took pride in the relative lack of race mixture in the British colonies, inhabited not principally by "a compound mongrel mixture of *English, Indian,* and *Negro,* but with freeborn *British white* subjects."[42]

DIFFERENCES between Spanish and British relations with Indians affected the respective colonists' ritual forms of rebellion. Rebellion often illuminates the participants' views of their proper place in society in terms of rights held and relationships established, including those to the land. Two examples, though separated by 200 years, highlight how Spanish and British colonists related to native peoples differently. The rebels in each case related to Indians—and, in turn, the land—in ways similar to Clavigero and Jefferson, respectively.[43]

Tumult prevailed in central Mexico from 1565 to 1568. Led by Martín Cortés, son of the leader of the Aztec conquest, colonists fearful of royal threats to their *encomiendas* contemplated rebellion. When rumors circulated that the crown intended to withdraw support for the *encomienda,* conquistador elites and their heirs staged a dramatic demonstration in 1565.

Donning the garb of Mexican chieftains and Indian warriors, they paraded through the streets of Mexico City to the house of Cortés, where they gave him a crown of flowers. The demonstrators had symbolically reenacted the submission of the Indian leader Moctezuma to the Spanish. When the leaders of the incipient revolt were later put on trial, the judges saw the meaning clearly. In dressing as Indians and offering Cortés a crown, the demonstrators, in the words of one judge, indicated that Cortés "was to be king of this land."[44] His ongoing relationship to the symbolic Indians gave him that right.

More than 200 years later, on the night of December 16, 1773, another set of colonists expressed their frustration with imperial authority by assuming Indian identity. In an episode familiar to countless American schoolchildren, a crowd dressed as "Mohawks" clambered aboard the *Dartmouth,* which sat in Boston Harbor with orders from Governor Thomas Hutchinson not to move until the ship's captain paid a tax on its cargo of tea. Refusing to allow the tax or permit customs officials to confiscate the tea, the crowd illegally destroyed the private property in what has come to be known euphemistically as the Boston Tea Party. "Cutting and splitting the chests with our tomahawks," as one participant put it, the costumed men spent three hours tossing £10,000 worth of the East India Company's tea overboard while a crowd of Bostonians looked on.[45]

Just as no colonists thought themselves real Indians when they appeared figuratively as such in political cartoons, no Bostonian actually believed that Mohawks had marched all of the way from the Hudson River valley, through the heart of Boston, and to the wharf just to vandalize the East India Company's shipment. Nor did the costumes convince anyone that the perpetrators were Indians. One tea partier recalled that he transformed himself into a Mohawk by just blackening his "face and hands with coal dust in the shop of a blacksmith." Others only had a daub of paint on their face and a blanket wrapped around their shoulders. Most onlookers would have understood the purpose of the Indian garb. Reverting to a symbolic state of nature by dressing as Indians, the colonists tossing tea over the ship's rails expressed a desire for their natural rights, for their liberty as *Americans.* Their freedom became, in one historian's words, "an ancient thing linked intrinsically to the continent, its custom, and its nature."[46]

Obvious parallels link the episodes in Mexico City and Boston. In both instances, the ritual assumption of Indian identity served to assert a defense of rights and a position within society. But the different ways participants played Indian reveal how divergently they had construed their relationship to the New World. Fewer than fifty years after the Conquest, Spaniards already had ritually assumed the role of those very Indians they had conquered. They emphasized the submissive qualities of the natives. In New England, more than 150 years after the first settlement, nearly the opposite took place. Rather than adopt the persona of local Algonquians, the Bostonians either called themselves "Mohawks," an Iroquoian tribe still residing primarily in New York and Canada with a reputation for ferocity, or they represented themselves as generic Indians without a particular homeland, culture, or history. Moreover, the Bostonians assumed the role not of submissive warriors but of "savages" committing "ravages." As one participant later put it, "We surely resembled devils from the bottomless pit rather than men."[47]

It seems as if some of the savages committing ravages may have been avid readers, for many of the Indians in the Boston Tea Party resembled those of popular captivity narratives. After decades out of print, five new editions of Mary Rowlandson's captivity narrative, *The Sovereignty and Goodness of God* (1682), had appeared in New England in the three years before the Tea Party. In both the Tea Party and Rowlandson's work, the Indians were distant outsiders. As such, they were as much a symbol of the land they occupied as they were actual people. These Indians contrasted starkly with those portrayed by Spaniards when they assumed the role of Moctezuma and his warriors in Mexico. The colonists' impersonations of "savages" hurling tea overboard sprang from a society infused with memories of Indian wars. It was irrelevant who the specific Indians impersonated were as long as they displayed the stereotypical traits. These colonists wanted to maintain their perceived superiority to Indians while replacing them as the natural inhabitants of the land. Indians provided a useful tie to the land, not an essential component of the society that was to be.[48] Their role was to retreat on the other side of an expanding frontier. Creole Mexicans and white New Englanders lived in separate worlds, related to indigenous peoples in different ways, and, as a result, diverged in their ties to the land.

BRITONS ON THE SUBCONTINENT

The drive to define the contours of a land that had been improved or was amenable to improvement was an important dynamic throughout Britain's far-flung colonies in the eighteenth century, not just North America. Yet when British colonizers confronted a situation resembling Mexico more than Massachusetts, they adjusted their attitudes toward the land. India provides a good example. British colonists there never assumed an Indian (or Asian) identity in the way that mainland American colonists came to think of themselves as Americans. In India, the challenges of colonization bore similarities to those faced by the Spanish in Mexico. Exploitation of labor and gathering of tribute underpinned British colonization in India more than the acquisition and "improvement" of land. Nevertheless, from the fifteenth century through the eighteenth century, India gradually came to appear as a distinct region within what had been the ill-defined "Indies," to the east of the Indus River. Changes in geographical conceptions and the growth of empire went hand in hand, even if Britons never really became Indians.

The idea that there were at least two Indias—one to the west and one to the east of the Ganges—lingered from antiquity to at least the late eighteenth century. Geographers and mapmakers began to shift away from this conception in the sixteenth century. They focused first on India as the southern part of the modern subcontinent, where European colonizers initially concentrated their activities. Then some began to associate India primarily with the northern part of the subcontinent, excluding the southern part of the peninsula, as the realm of the Mughal Empire, including some lands west of the Indus River, such as the Punjab and part of Afghanistan that had not traditionally been seen as part of the Indies. To complicate matters, some geographers added a "South India" to their taxonomies, which included their vague understandings of New Guinea and Australia.[49]

The historian Mathew Edney ably argues that Britain's "commercial and imperial ambitions" eventually gave meaning to "an image of India that coincided with the territory of the subcontinent."[50] As was the case with North America, the British had virtually eliminated the territorial ambitions of the French in India during the Seven Years' War. In so doing, they became the only significant European colonial power there.[51] On the whole, the idea of an India coterminous with the entire modern subcontinent began to emerge over the next decade as the British East India Company became a territorial, instead of just a commercial, power in the region. Mappers and surveyors instigated the shift with a "massive intellectual campaign to transform a land of incomprehensible spectacle into an empire of knowledge."[52] Maps and the perception they created of an area with natural territorial integrity were an essential component of empire building, alongside commerce, land revenues, and armies.

Even though Britons worked steadfastly to define India and increase their territorial control within it, they still did not view themselves as the true Indians to the extent that mainland American colonists thought of themselves as the true Americans. The British might have defined India's "natural" contours, but they did not settle it and improve it as in mainland North America. Instead, they had conquered its people and relied heavily on them for revenues, much as did the Spanish conquistadors in central Mexico. Indeed, beginning in the 1750s, many British commentators on both sides of the Atlantic began to criticize the actions of Englishmen in India by comparing atrocities there to those of the Spanish in the Americas. Robert Clive's profiteering with the East India Company gathered the accusation of "Crimes scarce inferior to the Conquerors of *Mexico* and *Peru.*"[53] By the 1760s, many Britons referred pejoratively to those who served in the East India Company as "nabobs"—an Indian term that originally designated high rank. The term implied corruption and the acquisition of wealth through the exploitation of natives. Pundits, playwrights, and politicians feared that the corrupt nabobs might spread their "luxury, effeminacy, and profligacy"— traits long associated with the entire Asian continent—through England. When Clive died, Thomas Paine excoriated him as an "emblem of the vanity of all earthly pomp" and later pointed to British actions in India as an example of "prodigal barbarity," a reason to wish Britain had "not a foot of land but what is circumscribed within her own island." Mainland American colonists, by contrast, demonstrated a morality and industry in which Britain could take pride.[54]

North Americans feared, however, that they might backslide into East Indian-style corruption. Henry Laurens, president of the Continental Congress, lambasted profiteers in fancy clothing while the army and militias scrambled to find uniforms. When the congress could not come up with "the suit of cloaths" promised to men who reenlisted in the army, Laurens sent a circular letter to the legislatures of the states calling on them to implement measures to prevent profiteering. The budding nation's "bright prospect" had become "endangered by the languor of too many, & by the arts and avarice of designing individuals, who like the British Nabobs of the East, are corrupting the manners of a whole nation, & building vast fortunes on the destruction of the liberties of the Western World."[55]

Where Laurens feared the fragility of American morals in the face of easy wartime profits, the political philosopher Richard Price explicitly compared the English colonization of the New World with that of India to highlight the virtue of the American settlers and the injustice of the Revolutionary War. He argued, with some historical amnesia, that North American colonists had bought most of their land from the natives, and "they have since cleared and cultivated it, and, without any help from us, converted wilderness into fruitful and pleasant fields." The land was thus "on a double account their property and no power on earth can have any right to disturb them in the possession of it or to take from them . . . any part of its produce."

But in India, Price continued, "Englishmen, actuated by the love of plunder and the spirit of conquest, have depopulated whole kingdoms and ruined millions of innocent people by the most infamous oppression and rapacity."[56] Change the people and the location, and Price's criticism of the East India Company could just as easily have been the voice of Francisco Clavigero castigating the conquistadors, except that Price had no presumptions or aspirations of being Indian.

Shortly after Britain recognized American independence, Benjamin Vaughan, a West Indian-born man who married a woman from Boston, lived in England, and assisted the Earl of Shelburne in negotiations at Paris in 1783, reflected on the differing trajectories of Britain's colonies in Asia and those it had lost in North America. He asked, "What is the India company in all its parts but a Colony, of which the *owners* live in England? In what does it differ from the late Pennsylvania & Maryland colonies? Answer. The object of these Western colonies has been agriculture; of the Eastern, fighting, tax-gathering, and a trade made subject to monopoly. The former colonies produced a *people;* the latter only *agents* to manage a people already formed."[57] Vaughan's musings contained lingering doubts about the propriety of Britain's East Indian ventures and perhaps a need to explain why the successful revolution had erupted among relatively well-treated British Americans instead of Indians. It was Americans' relationship to the land, he concluded, that created a people.

From the late eighteenth century to the mid-nineteenth century, Britain's colonial relationship with India changed little. Insofar as the British invested in India, it was not metropolitan capital but, as the historian C. A. Bayly puts it, the reinvestment of "fortunes made during an earlier period of conquistador imperialism. Investment in internal trade and production remained as it had been since the eighteenth century—a way of laundering profits and returning them to England." Britons eschewed "improving" the land themselves, and the East India Company discouraged British citizens from directly owning the land, for fear that their ownership might disrupt the revenue system. When Britons tried to alter land-owning practices among Indians, as with the Permanent Settlement of 1793, they did so with the aim of enhancing revenues. Efforts to mimic the cotton agriculture of the antebellum southern United States failed, as Britons functioned as only "another level of appropriators living on the Indian peasantry rather than the harbingers of a true capitalist agriculture." If there was a people created during this process, it was "by hammer blows from the outside . . . the Indian peasantry."[58]

Indians revolted against this extractive colonialism in 1857, prompting the dissolution of the East India Company and the institution of crown rule through a government of India. Six years later, in 1863, the term "subcontinent" entered the English lexicon.[59] The timing was not coincidental. Defining India as a subcontinent entailed part of an effort to portray the British Empire as not just another tyrannical Asiatic state, but as the creator of an imperial structure working in accordance with natural precepts. As such, the British presented their rule as scientific, rational, and liberal—the virtual opposite of the long-held stereotype of Asia as a land of irrationality and despotism. Ironically, however, it would be indigenous Indians who would eventually and more fully appropriate the subcontinent, even though the British in large measure defined it. In the twentieth century, Indian nationalists seized the British conception of India as a unified and coherent geographical entity.[60] British colonization helped create a place and a people. But unlike in North America, the British colonists in India did not themselves become the people of that place.

BRITONS IN ATLANTIC CANADA AND THE WEST INDIES

The British colonists in Atlantic Canada did not share the continental vision of their mainland counterparts. Two colonies in particular, Newfoundland and Nova Scotia, suggest why. In the case of Newfoundland, the explanation is relatively straightforward. Although the colony had readily apparent natural perimeters not conducive to the same spatial imaginings on the mainland or in India, its proximity to the mainland might have led its inhabitants to see their island as a natural appendage to the continent and to partake in some of the presumptions that flourished there. But Newfoundland's economy, demography, and governing structure minimized the possibility. The fishing industry dominated Newfoundland's economy. Year-round residents numbered approximately 10,000, most of whom lived in port areas and made their livelihood in fishing-related enterprises. Every summer, the island's population doubled with the influx of English ships carrying fishermen. The migratory, heavily male population precluded Newfoundland from seeing any significant natural increase. Yet the island's inhabitants assumed importance beyond their numbers to an empire whose power rested on maritime commerce and a powerful navy. Newfoundland had powerful ties to English merchants and interests in Parliament. Policymakers viewed the colony as a valuable source of seamen and a training ground for the navy. Its governor was the naval officer who saw to the safety of the fishing fleet that sailed in and out each summer, a man who was away all winter. In his absence, and without an elective assembly, governance was left to a few justices of the peace. Some even contended that Newfoundland was not a colony in the conventional sense but "a great fishing ship anchored off North America."[61]

Nova Scotia, too, had strong fishing interests, but it differed fundamentally from Newfoundland. It was physically connected to the mainland; it also had an elected assembly by 1758 and a sizeable population of "planters," as they came to be known, half of whom had recently migrated from New England. On the surface, these traits should have made the colony ripe for resistance, revolution, and a growing American identity. Yet although Nova Scotians offered minor resistance to the Stamp Act, the colony remained strongly loyal to the empire.

On the eve of the American Revolution, Anglo-Americans had just concluded a fifty years' war in Nova Scotia with Acadians, Indians, and French. More than any other British colonists on the mainland, those in Nova Scotia confronted war or the threat of war in their daily lives.[62] The British first seized the colony from the French in 1710, but British authority in the colony remained weak until the Seven Years' War. British leaders tried to force the Acadian population (that is, American-born French colonists) to take loyalty oaths. The Acadians resisted, and the British began recognizing the Acadians as "the French Neutrals." British Nova Scotia by the mid-1740s was thus as much the product of accommodation and negotiation as it was conquest. When they were not waging wars against the region's Indians, the British governors—such as Paul Mascarene, a descendent of French Huguenots—ruled the overwhelmingly Acadian population with a light hand.

After 1744, relations between Acadians and Anglo-Americans deteriorated, as Nova Scotia became a front in King George's War between France and Britain. In the conflict, New Englanders coveted the region's lands. Indeed, New Englanders fought hard to capture the nearby Fort Louisbourg, only to see the crown subsequently return it. The peace of Aix-la-Chapelle may officially have brought peace between the European powers, but brutal war ensued in Nova Scotia as the various groups there had become more suspicious of one another than ever. Anglo-Americans and Acadians, with the help of indigenous Mi'kmaqs and Maliseets, sought to decide to whom the colony belonged. The conflict degenerated into a protracted guerrilla conflict and a brutal counterinsurgency. Beginning in 1755, British and Anglo-American forces began systematically deporting Acadians in what modern Americans might refer to as a program of ethnic cleansing.

More than 10,000 Acadians had been removed from the colony by 1763, with thousands dying as a result.[63]

In October 1758, the governor announced the availability of the removed Acadians' lands. The next year, New England "planters" began settling the region, and their numbers reached 14,000 by the late 1760s.[64] Before they could reap the land's profits, they had to rebuild the destroyed Acadian infrastructure. The rotting carcasses of livestock and burned-out remains of barns were replaced easily enough. But the New Englanders did not know how to repair the elaborate and ingenious dikes with which the Acadians had reclaimed much of their farmland from the sea. Somewhat grudgingly, planters brought back some 1,700 Acadians to repair and maintain the dikes and to work as laborers. Laws prohibited the Acadians from again owning the land, and the planters often consigned them to menial tasks such as drawing water and hewing wood.

Although the planters vastly outnumbered Acadians, they feared the Acadians as much as they depended on them. Nova Scotia planters lacked the memories of having "improved" their land, since they still relied on a despised people to do so. The planters realized they had a bitter labor force working lands it once possessed, and memories of recent wars with Acadians and Indians haunted them. The fear of uprisings made many planters welcome the ongoing presence of the British military. Throughout the 1760s and 1770s, Britain faced virtually none of the turmoil in Nova Scotia that it did in New England. When Britain's War Office transferred troops from Nova Scotia to Boston to address unrest there, the Nova Scotia planters feared their vulnerability to an Indian and Acadian revolt. The governor pleaded that the crown remember his "infant struggling province." Nova Scotia remained a far-removed and more violent place than much of British North America. Because of this, and despite how much members of the Continental Congress might have wanted to add the colony to the union, Nova Scotia remained, in the words of the historian John Grenier, "the most British of the British colonies in North America."[65]

BEFORE 1763, British colonies in the Caribbean had close ties to those on the North American mainland, but after the Seven Years' War, events drove a wedge between mainlanders and their West Indian counterparts. Mainlanders thought that West Indian interests in Parliament had influenced the passage of the Sugar Act to the detriment of mainland colonies. The relative quiescence of West Indians in the face of the Stamp, Townshend, and Tea acts expanded the breach to the point that mainland colonists did not invite West Indian delegates to the Continental Congress.

Beneath this falling out, fundamental differences in the economic and social structures of the island and mainland colonies had prompted these colonists' diverging reactions to imperial political developments.

The perception of geographic space in the island colonies presented a relatively straightforward process. The small size of the Caribbean colonies —Britain's most populous, Barbados, encompassed only 166 square miles— and the readily perceived natural perimeters of the islands simplified matters compared with the mainlanders' imagination of a coherent, unified continent or Britons' creation of a "subcontinent." Geography also meant that islanders lived their lives in relative isolation from one another. In the Caribbean, distances could be vast, winds and currents strong, and storms deadly. A thousand miles separated Jamaica from Barbados, an especially treacherous distance during hurricane season. Communication among the islands was slow and intermittent; it was often easier to communicate with England than with another Caribbean island. Consequently, the islanders thought locally more than regionally and had strongly provincial attitudes toward one another.[66]

The islands also shared an economic structure far different from that of the British mainland, India, or central Mexico. Unlike India and the North American mainland, they had climates and soil well suited to sugar and coffee production, and they lacked indigenous populations suited to institutionalized labor and tribute. These two traits, along with sugar's high value, presented tremendous incentives for the English to reap the economies of scale of large plantations worked by African slaves. By the early eighteenth century, the Caribbean colonies had become "amazingly effective sugar-production machines, manned by armies of black slaves."[67] Barbados, Jamaica, and other sugar-producing islands developed populations with slave majorities, small numbers of poor whites, maroons (runaway slaves holding out in autonomous communities, particularly in the mountainous parts of Jamaica), and an exceptionally powerful and wealthy planter elite. The per-capita wealth of free colonists in Jamaica, including that in slaves, amounted to nearly thirteen times that of those in the southern mainland colonies and thirty-one times that of those in the northern colonies.[68]

Their close identification with the land also distinguished the mainland colonists from those on the islands. Mainlanders were a people bound together by ties to the land. A French observer at the beginning of the American Revolution noted that the colonists were "permanent, born in the country and attached to it; they have no motherland save the one they live in." The islands presented virtually the opposite. There, "Far from settling," the West Indian colonists regarded the islands "as a land of exile, never as a place where they plan to live, prosper and die." The Scotswoman Janet Schaw saw no "cure" to "the longing they have to return to Britain." Echoing such sentiments a year later, in 1778, John Drummond wrote to Lord George Germain, secretary of state for America, that the islanders hoped "only to get Fortunes & return to their native Land." Drummond contrasted island and continental colonies: "Every Subject, My Lord, you engage to Inhabit our Sugar Colonies, you acquire a valuable object to the State; every Subject that settles upon Continental America is eventually lost to the Mother-Country."[69]

Building on such contemporary observations, the historian Andrew Jackson O'Shaughnessy has demonstrated that Britons in the West Indies maintained much closer cultural and social ties to the home country than did inhabitants of the continental colonies. The islanders were far more likely to belong to the Anglican church, possess minor titles, or serve in Parliament than their continental counterparts, indicating a fuller membership in the society of the British Isles. Unlike mainlanders, West Indian Britons contributed little to the establishment of schools, colleges, and roads in their colonies. The islanders' ties to the mother country, O'Shaughnessy notes, "restrained the development of a nationalistic creole consciousness among whites and was a contributory factor in the failure of the British Caribbean to support the American Revolution."[70] Not only did British West Indians by and large fail to back American Revolutionaries, but their society increasingly anglicized over time—so much so that, by the early nineteenth century, Barbadians had begun to refer to their colony as "Little England." They were still English living abroad as much as, if not more than, they were West Indians.[71]

GEOGRAPHIC MOBILITY AND
CONTINENTAL APPROPRIATION

One thing that the white populations of the mainland and the West Indies did share in the second half of the eighteenth century was a high degree of transience. Beneath this commonality, however, deep differences of degree and substance fostered a greater feeling of attachment to the land among mainlanders than islanders. Both the British Caribbean and British mainland received approximately a half-million European immigrants before 1780. Yet at the end of this unprecedented movement of people, the British Caribbean included only about 50,000 whites compared with North America's 2 million. A corollary to this disparity was that places such as Jamaica never had a native-born majority among whites in the eighteenth century, while all mainland colonies did. Immigrants in the mainland constituted less than 10 percent of the mainland colonies' population as a whole.[72]

The mainland's immigrants differed from those of the Caribbean in ethnic composition, as well. England remained the source of most Caribbean migrants, while voyagers to the mainland increasingly hailed from other regions. Between 1760 and 1775, English immigrants amounted to only 30,000 of the 137,000 European immigrants to North America. The French traveler Hector St. John de Crèvecoeur, observing the migrants from Connecticut into Pennsylvania's Wyoming Valley in 1774 and 1776, could only describe them as coming from a variety of "sects and nations" and reassembling in "a strange heterogeneous reunion of people . . . without law or government, without any kind of social bond to unite them all." Thomas Paine would have described them simply as Americans: "In this extensive quarter of the globe, we forget the narrow limits of three hundred and sixty miles (the extent of England) and carry our friendship on a larger scale; we claim brotherhood with every European Christian, and triumph in the generosity of the sentiment."[73] The West Indies presented a different picture. There, most whites had recently arrived from England and maintained ties to their native country. Migration to Jamaica, the island for which the best data are available, remained predominantly English at 86 percent, among whom many were affluent individuals with strong connections to London merchants.[74]

Where the migration of whites to the British West Indies contributed to demographic stability, in the mainland it led to territorial expansion and political tension. Tropical diseases scythed the Caribbean's white population, and many who lived returned to England, so even with substantial immigration, the white population increased slowly. For example, Jamaica's white population grew merely 20 percent between 1752 and 1774. In contrast, migration to the mainland in the aftermath of the Seven Years' War, combined with natural increase, led to unprecedented growth that created both alarm and optimism. Every year, 15,000 people, a number around which Boston's total population hovered during this period, arrived in the mainland, most initially in crowded seaports. From there, both immigrants and natives fanned out to the north, south, and west to take advantage of abundant land. As the historian Bernard Bailyn has noted, perhaps with a bit of exaggeration, "Nowhere in this thinly settled land did stable communities approach Malthusian limits to population growth; yet people moved continuously as if there were such pressure."[75] Benjamin Franklin estimated that 10,000 families had moved to North Carolina from Pennsylvania in just three years.[76] Networks of roads began to reach hundreds of miles inland. Northern New England and New York saw their white populations swell. Georgia's population tripled between 1760 and 1763. Sizeable populations of Scots-Irish and Germans appeared in almost every colony. Back-country settlements sparked conflicts with Indians, sometimes deadly, as in the case of the Paxton massacre in Pennsylvania or the Cherokee War in South Carolina. The population growth and corresponding territorial expansion presented problems to both provincial and imperial officials. Again in the words of Bailyn: "This surge of innumerable farming families from all over North America and from western Europe, could not be contained within the margins of the existing colonies, or even within the newly extended boundaries of permissible white settlement outside the established provinces. Settlers defied all legal constraints."[77] Eighteenth-century British North America was a world on the move.

Mobile newcomers, from Thomas Paine to the countless ordinary men and women who served in the army or as its camp followers, lacked the deep community ties that bound many Americans to their particular colony or locale. Like blank slates, such "new" Americans were highly receptive to the nationalizing effects of war. Addressing the puzzle as to how an outsider such as Paine could have written one of the seminal texts of the Revolution, the historian Trish Loughran explains that only someone "uninitiated and unassimilated to the fierce local attachments of late eighteenth-century provincial politics" could have written *Common Sense*. Paine's recent arrival meant that "he was not a Virginian or a New Yorker, a Bostonian or even a Pennsylvanian."[78] To Paine and most Englishmen, the vast ocean separating them from North America could blur the distinction among colonies to the point that together they constituted a single entity.

Westerners forging new settlements far from eastern centers of power held similarly weak loyalties to provincial or state governments, and they had greater reason to think of themselves as Americans.[79] In particular, Revolutionary War veterans and widowed and orphaned families led much of the expansion with a sense of righteousness, as though the continent were the spoils the nation owed them. George Washington saw this sense of entitlement as justified. "Let the widow, the Orphan and the suffering Soldier, who are crying to you for their dues, receive *that* which can very well be rendered to them," he pleaded with the congressional delegate William Grayson. Washington waxed optimistic that, over time, and as long as commercial ties were maintained, the migrants' westward push would strengthen the nation and "disarm localities of their power."[80]

THE enhanced ability of migrants to see America as a continental society cross-fertilized with many native-born colonists' memories of ancestral "improvement" of the land. Men such as Thomas Jefferson began to articulate a future for the United States that combined elements of the two strains of thought. Jefferson thought territorial expansion and agricultural improvement would allow Americans to maintain the values of early colonists and their society to develop without acquiring some of the defects of Europe. Western lands would allow the United States to avoid the dangers of urbanization and commercialization. The United States could maintain the political virtue of an infant society, avoiding Asian- and European-style corruption. He envisioned a society composed mostly of yeoman farmers with the wisdom and independence of mind necessary to act virtuously in the political realm, a society where public good trumped private interests. Expansion across the continent would allow the United States to avoid the moral corruption that, over time, plagued other societies in other quarters of the globe. As the French traveler Jacques Pierre Brissot de Warville projected, "Americans are and will be for a long time free; it is because nine tenths of them live by agriculture; and when there shall be five hundred millions of men in America, all may be proprietors."[81]

Jefferson made clear his views on the links between North America's politics and geography in *Notes on the State of Virginia.* A work of political science as much as of natural science, it touted the "improvement" of land through agriculture as the brightest prospect for North America. Jefferson disputed the common contention among European political theorists that "every state should endeavour to manufacture for itself." Lacking any more land to cultivate, Jefferson argued, Europeans had turned to manufacturing by necessity "to support the surplus of their people." Jefferson noted the decline inherent in dependence on manufacturing:

Those who labour in the earth are the chosen people of God. . . . Corruption of morals in the mass of cultivators is a phænomenon of which no age nor nation has furnished an example. It is the mark set on those, who not looking up to heaven, to their own soil and industry, as does the husbandman, for their subsistence, depend for it on the casualties and caprice of customers. Dependance begets subservience and venality, suffocates the germ of virtue, and prepares fit tools for the designs of ambition. This, the natural progress and consequence of the arts, has sometimes perhaps been retarded by accidental circumstances: but, generally speaking, the proportion which the aggregate of the other classes of citizens bears in any state to that of its husbandmen, is the proportion of its unsound to its healthy parts, and is a good-enough barometer whereby to measure its degree of corruption. . . . It is the manners and spirit of a people which preserve a republic in vigour. A degeneracy in these is a canker which soon eats to the heart of its laws and constitution.[82]

The United States would benefit if it let its "work-shops remain in Europe." To do so, U.S. citizens required access to plentiful land. The first step the United States must take was to consolidate its control over the North American continent.

In 1783, the founders of the United States looked forward to enjoying lands and fruits they thought had been secured by their triumph over Britain. Within four years, however, it seemed to most of them that their confederation government was unable to help them realize those hopes. Once again, they were stirred to defend their continental vision. In 1787, they turned to "the people," politics, and, yet again, metageographical presumptions to win their struggle for a continent.

CHAPTER 7

SEIZING NATURE'S ADVANTAGES

THE CONSTITUTION AND THE

CONTINENT, 1783–1789

As with the aftermath of the Seven Years' War, the years following the Revolution transformed the exuberance of victory into trepidation about the future. Peace had initially heightened Americans' optimistic visions of continental grandeur. Then military demobilization, backcountry violence, constricted economic opportunity, and diplomatic obstructions gave credence to fears that the United States might fumble its potential.

To address the nation's problems, delegates to what became known as the Constitutional Convention trickled into Philadelphia in May 1787 for meetings scheduled to begin on the fourteenth. Their secret discussions through that summer have become legendary, and, today, few historic sites in the United States receive as much attention as their meeting place, Independence Hall. Arguably, only the National Archives' rotunda—where the "Charters of Freedom" rest, including the Constitution itself—garners more reverence. By modern standards, Independence Hall's two-story brick structure with a bell tower seems small and quaint. Its modesty might be seen to suggest, like the National Archives exhibit, that the nation's founders sought timeless, enlightened principles more than imperial grandeur. Yet since the delegates gathered partly out of fear that the United States stood on the precipice of failing to realize a continental destiny, metageographical concepts had a central role in the debates over the Constitution. In fact, they figured so prominently that it is hard to imagine the Constitution's ratification occurring at all had the document's backers not been able to invoke these concepts, which were already deeply lodged in people's minds, to win its approval.

The Constitution's proponents, the Federalists, saw a strong but limited national government over a vast region as a solution to some of the problems the nation faced. Their calls for a new government drew on familiar geographic ideas, but they also challenged traditional political assumptions, including the notion that republics were suitable only for small, homogeneous regions. Perhaps even more daunting was that many opponents of the Constitution—Anti-Federalists, as they came to be known—thought that because the Constitution proposed a small number of representatives, seated in a distant central government, the document provided for representation more virtual than actual.

Despite Anti-Federalists' objections, those accustomed to thinking in metageographical terms and identifying with the continent found consolation in the document's familiar aspects. In a refrain of rhetoric derived from the scientific debates and geopolitical developments of the previous half-century, proponents of the Constitution hammered away at the idea of the continent as a discrete entity that was well suited to, and destined for, political unity. Failure to realize this destiny, they argued, was itself a grave betrayal of the Revolutionary legacy.

By extending the federal government's sphere, the Federalists sought not only to secure the nation from external threats, prevent domestic insurrections, and improve the quality of the nation's leaders; they also pursued longstanding continental ambitions. Federalist tracts in periodicals and newspapers—including the most famous, the Federalist Papers—hailed the Constitution's ability to right the nation on its continental trajectory, and they highlighted the nature of the continent to allay Anti-Federalists' fears of centralized power. Geography, they argued, allowed Americans to form a secure state while keeping the national government inconspicuous and light.[1] Predictably, opponents argued that the Constitution betrayed the Revolution's aims and that such a republican form of government was ill suited for a large nation.

In the end, principles concerning actual representation, which had long been in tension with presumptions of continental identity, fell secondary to prevalent metageographical concerns. Many realized that if the United States seized nature's advantages, if they made the nation truly continental, it would solidify rule by propertied elites and weaken the voice of ordinary men. Yet a governing structure facilitating a continental nation would also keep alive some of the visions of metageographic grandeur that had sustained struggles before, during, and after the Revolution. Elaborating on the historian Carl Becker's aphorism that the Revolution was as much a struggle over who shall rule at home as it was over home rule, visions of the continent and assumptions about its nature—in short, ideas about "home"—bore directly on the argument over who shall rule. They facilitated the Constitution's ratification.

In 1783, relief, pride, and optimism reigned, coupled with the realization that work lay ahead. Territorial growth and expansion—hallmarks of the United States and girders in the geopolitical vision of a generation—presented challenges to political unity. Yet confidence born of the Enlightenment also fostered the conviction that, with reason and the application of scientific principles, Americans could construct institutions that maintained unity and accommodated growth. When George Washington stepped down as commander of the Continental Army, he bid his troops farewell with a reminder that, thanks to them, the "Citizens of America" reigned "as the sole Lords and Proprietors of a vast Tract of Continent." Americans, because of the army's efforts, could draw on "all the various soils and climates of the World." They were "Actors on a most conspicuous Theatre, which seems to be particularly designated by Providence for the display of human greatness and felicity."[2]

Granted, Washington's vision of national, continental grandeur contained a Virginian's regional quirks. The possibility of improving the Potomac to make it and the Chesapeake the main arteries from the Atlantic to the Ohio, and on to the Mississippi, infatuated Washington. Yet ironically, given the eventual location of the nation's capital that now bears his name, he argued, in 1785, against establishing the capital in such an eastward location. The Potomac was merely the gateway to the future "Seat of Empire" to the west, and Washington suggested that a riparian network extending off the Potomac could lead migrants even as far as California.[3]

Notwithstanding his regional biases, Washington believed the only guarantee that Americans had against falling into anarchy or succumbing to tyranny lay in their "united Character as an Empire."[4] From the day he assumed command of the Continental Army and realized the need for a national force, Washington called on Americans to cast aside their provincial loyalties and personal interests. What stands out is how, as he faced peace, Washington tempered his optimism with a caveat about the challenges ahead. He feared for Americans' future if they failed to embrace their continental selves. Patriots had waged war not against imperialism, just the British form of it.[5] The Revolution left Americans the heirs of the British Empire in North America. With peace, it remained to secure western lands and prevent the dissolution of a new North American empire.

Fortunately, the United States was blessed with more than the continent's natural abundance: Its citizens had the knowledge to craft a society suited to it. Politics had progressed like science, Washington maintained. The United

States arose not "in the gloomy age of Ignorance and Superstition" but in "an Epocha when the rights of mankind were better understood and more clearly defined, than at any former period." The United States could use this "collected wisdom" in the "establishment of our forms of Government." Though not the most learned American, astute political theorist, or distinguished scientist, Washington sensed the general shape of a government best suited to North America: "Without an entire conformity to the Spirit of Union, we cannot exist as an Independent Power."[6]

Optimism similar to Washington's reverberated widely. Thomas Jefferson boasted of the capacity of the United States to produce geniuses: With only a fraction of the population of France or the British Isles, "we produce a Washington, a Franklin, a Rittenhouse." Newspapers, too, touted the character and capabilities of Americans. "We boast a *Washington,* as the great master of the art of war," bragged the *Massachusetts Centinel,* "a *Franklin* the chief of *Philosophers*—an *Adams,* and an infinitude of others, as statesmen and politicians whose abilities have been acknowledged throughout the civilized world."[7] Clearly, the United States had already proved degeneracy theorists such as Buffon, Raynal, de Pauw, and Robertson wrong. With such genius already demonstrated in its infancy, the United States stood positioned to craft a durable, expansive union.

Americans showed a remarkable predilection to downplay or ignore Britons to the north and Spaniards to the south and west of the United States. The visiting Marquis de Chastellux observed "an opinion which I found generally diffused throughout the state" of New York. There, inhabitants believed "no expedition more useful, nor more easy than the conquest of Canada." He thought it "impossible to conceive the ardour" with which New Yorkers desired the region. Another traveler found Americans pushing west with astonishing speed to the Mississippi, where the "posterity of the new western states must and will seek to make the mouth of the Mississippi free." Promotional tracts touted Kentucky as the "best tract of land in North America, and probably the world," and predicted the "time is not far distant when New Orleans will be a great trading city." Since it would be "absurd" for Americans to rely on a treaty with Spain to guarantee free passage of the Mississippi, the United States should secure New Orleans "as our own."[8]

In Boston, Benjamin Hirchborn saw the United States benefitting geopolitically from the hand dealt it by nature. At an Independence Day celebration, he minimized foreign threats. "America has no enemy to fear but from herself," he explained, for no nation had such a "lust of dominion" that it would "carry war into a civilized country beyond the vast oceans which divide the habitable parts of the globe." Only "political suicide" stood between Americans and grandeur—hence, the "importance to form some great continental arrangements." A year later, an Independence Day audience in Boston heard a similarly ebullient John Gardiner remind them of the "vastness of our country, the variety of her soil and climate, the immense extent of her sea-coast, and of the inland navigation by the lakes and rivers." Taken together, the continent's assets made the United States "a *world within ourselves.*" At an Independence Day oration in Providence, Rhode Island, in 1786, Enos Hitchcock saw a strong federal union as the key to the United States' settling its "vast tract of uncultivated lands" and extending is commerce "from pole to pole."[9]

The language in such celebrations resembled that of political theorists who continued to link geography to politics. In a passage that appeared in many U.S. newspapers, the Englishman Richard Price described the United States as "spread over a great continent . . . a world within themselves." Appended to Price's pamphlet, and distributed widely in newspapers, a letter from the French political economist Turgot insisted that Americans must not "neglect the immense deserts which extend all the way to the western sea." He saw unity as the key to the new nation's promising future, for should North America imitate Europe, it would become "a mass of divided powers contending for territory and commerce and continually cementing the slavery of the people with their own blood."[10]

Published maps and geographies encouraged U.S. citizens to see their empire's future beyond the horizon and deep into the continent's interior. John Wallis's 1783 map of the United States—the first based on the treaty of that year—depicted the Mississippi as a substantial spine with tributaries connecting to it from both sides like ribs (fig. 30). The source of the Mississippi and Missouri remained obscure, but little blocked their exploration. Tributaries that flowed into the Mississippi from the west dominated the Louisiana Territory, and one had to look closely to see evidence of any Indians, much less Spaniards.

The following year, William McMurray produced *The United States According to the Definitive Treaty of Peace Signed at Paris* (1784). The sixty-seven- by ninety-six-centimeter map included another highly suggestive map as an inset (fig. 31). In the smaller map, the United States appeared as blank space, eliminating the nagging reality that Native Americans controlled most western regions. It left open the political boundary that defined the northwestern corner of the United States, an area with promising topographical features. McMurray borrowed heavily from the map that accompanied Jonathan Carver's bestselling travel narrative, which had touted a

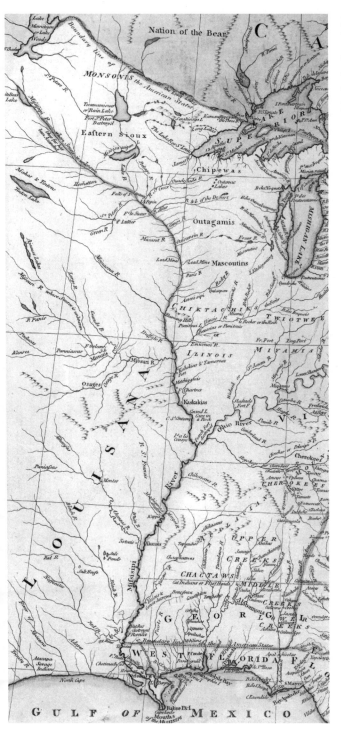

FIGURE 30. From John Wallis, *The United States of America* (1783). Courtesy Library of Congress, Geography and Map Division

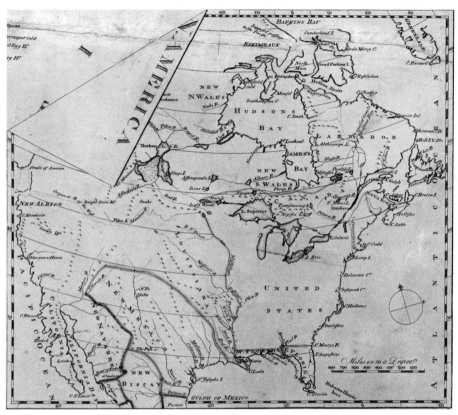

FIGURE 31. Inset from William McMurray, *The United States According to the Definitive Treaty of Peace Signed at Paris* (1784). Courtesy Library of Congress, Geography and Map Division

passage to the Pacific. He posited waterways just south of the Lake of the Woods that stretched westward to the "Origan [Oregon] or R. of the West," which, in turn, flowed into the fabled Straits of Annian. As if to remind viewers of the geographic potential of the United States, the corner of the inset map appeared folded over to reveal the words "N. America."

Two years later, an equally optimistic portrayal of the West appeared. Most Americans would have been able to afford the map of the United States "Engraved by H. D. Pursell for F. Bailey's Pocket Almanac" (1786) (fig. 32). On it, the political boundaries were unintelligible; the topographic features, conspicuous. The Mississippi predominated, but the land to its west remained entirely empty, save for rivers flowing from the west and the mention of the "Head of the Oregon which runs W. to the Pacific Ocean."

FIGURE 32. *A Map of the United States of N. America,* "Engraved by H. D. Pursell for F. Bailey's Pocket Almanac" (1786). Courtesy Library Company of Philadelphia

The United States might very well already control the headwaters of a route to the Pacific Ocean.

Geographers' prose, too, cloaked uncertainty with optimism. Thomas Hutchins offered one of the most influential descriptions of the Louisiana Territory. Hutchins had served as an officer in the Seven Years' War, and, during the Revolution the Continental Congress named him "Geographer to the United States." The Mississippi figured prominently in his work "as the great passage made by the hand of nature . . . principally to promote the happiness and benefit of mankind." Beyond the Mississippi, he knew, French traders had traveled some "thirteen hundred miles" up the Missouri, and "it appeared to be navigable many miles further." These rivers, taken together with the vastness of the continent, meant that the "empire" of "North America" would surpass all those of the past. It could easily include the portion of the continent not yet a part of the United States: "If we want it, I warrant it will soon be ours."[11]

The bestselling geography textbook in the war's aftermath, *Geography Made Easy* (1784), also made a slippery and implicit equation between all of

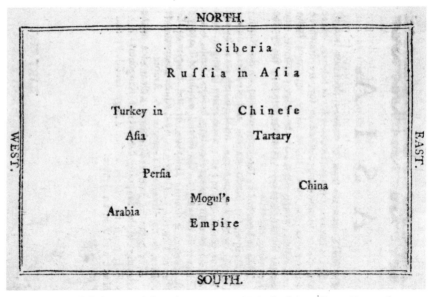

Siberia

Ruffia in Afia

Turkey in   Chinefe

Afia   Tartary

WEST.

EAST.

Perfia

China

Arabia   Mogul's

Empire

SOUTH.

FIGURE 33. Jedidiah Morse's "newly constructed Map" of Asia, from *Geography Made Easy* (1784). Courtesy Library Company of Philadelphia

North America and the United States. The author, the Congregationalist minister Jedidiah Morse, allocated separate sections to South America, Europe, Asia, and Africa.[12] Within these sections, pupils studied "newly constructed Maps" that Morse had adapted to the "Capacities and Understanding of Children" (fig. 33). Each map presented its part of the world as a simple rectangle with the names of the respective countries arranged within it. The rectangular depictions made no attempt to convey the shape of the regions in question or the nation-states they represented. Morse treated North America differently, however. Rather than showcase in this section one of his innovative rectangular maps that included all of the countries within North America, he provided a traditional map, *A Map of the United States of America* (1784), by Amos Doolittle (fig. 34). Morse's presentation minimized the divided political nature of North America and implicitly suggested that to talk about North America was simply to talk about the United States. To be sure, students who examined the text more closely would find that Morse did not entirely ignore either the Spanish or British holdings in North America, but reading this work and his others, students would also learn that North America was primed for rule by just one empire.[13]

This readiness hinged partially on lingering ignorance of the trans-

FIGURE 34. Amos Doolittle, *A Map of the United States of America* (1784). EducT
247.84 (A), Houghton Library, Harvard University

Mississippi West and a sense that the continent's interior features united
North America. "In North America," Morse explained, "there are no very
considerable mountains, excepting those towards the Poles, and that long
ridge, extending from Lake Erie to the Gulf of Mexico, called the Apalachian
or Alegany Mountains." Morse downplayed the Appalachians as a barrier, as
authors had for at least thirty years, and highlighted the system of waterways
that glued North America together: "Such is the wisdom and goodness of
the Creator, that those vast tracts of country . . . are watered by the extensive
Lakes of Canada, and several of the finest Rivers in the world."[14] Morse's

Seizing Nature's Advantages (269

audience was just the latest generation to imagine itself as a continental people. The terms of the peace; the presence of the Spanish and their denial of the U.S. right to navigate the Mississippi; the continued British fur-trade activity near the Great Lakes; and the numerous Indian nations resisting U.S. expansion did not cloud this vision. Acknowledgments of these constraints on the nation's continental status often minimized or depicted them as temporary obstructions.

Washington knew better. Just a year after his resignation, when he waxed optimistic about Americans and their "vast Tract of Continent," the specter of disunity that haunted him appeared more imminent, and his confidence waned. In his diary, Washington fretted over the presence of the Spanish and British on the Mississippi and the Great Lakes and the ease with which the country's western inhabitants might trade with them:

> No well informed Mind need be told, that the flanks and rear of the United territory are possessed by other powers, and formidable ones too—nor how necessary it is to apply the cement of interest to bind all parts of it together, by one indissolvable band—particularly the Middle States with the Country immediately back of them. For what ties let me ask, should we have upon those people; and how entirely shod. we be with them if the Spaniards on their right, or Great Britain on their left, instead of throwing stumbling blocks in their way as they now do, should envite their trade and seek alliances with them. . . . The Western Settlers—from my own observation—stand as it were on a pivet—the touch of a feather would almost incline them any way.[15]

More than ever, the United States required a delicate yet deliberate hand to maintain unity. The nation's leaders had plenty of reason to doubt that the United States would become a truly unified continental nation, especially as both foreign nations and disaffected Americans became a source of disorder.

TROUBLE BEYOND THE PALE:
FOREIGN NATIONS AND ILL-GOVERNED REGIONS

Instead of establishing the United States in the international order as a primary planet, the Peace of Paris only partially fulfilled the diplomatic vision of 1776, and the remaining imperfections helped precipitate the Constitutional Convention.[16] Following the ouster of the Earl of Shelburne, Parliament implemented severe trade restrictions on the United States, including the exclusion of American ships from the West Indies. Independence also cost the United States the protection of the British Navy in the Mediterranean, where Barbary pirates preyed on commerce. Assumptions that U.S. trade was a prize so important that they could demand its free flow proved false; individual states could not counter foreign-trade restrictions; and the congress failed to formulate a coherent trade policy.

Worse than gummed-up trade, sticking points over boundaries with Britain, Spain, and Native Americans plunged the United States into further diplomatic disputes, frontier wars, and internal divisiveness. Although the terms of the peace did not grant the United States lands as far north as the Nipissing line, much less all of Canada, Americans hoped that the treaty had at least established a functioning international boundary. But the treaty line derived from Mitchell's map represented little more than an imaginary line, and it bore no relation to the social geography of the Great Lakes region. The Revolution had led many Indians near the Great Lakes and in the Ohio country to strengthen their ties with the British. Absent from the negotiations, many Iroquois, for example, worked to maintain a borderland between the British and the Americans as their home rather than recognize the creation of a fixed border line that ignored their existence. Some Iroquois threatened violence to pressure British leaders into remaining at Fort Niagara. The British also remained at forts Michilimackinac, Detroit, and Oswego.

American leaders tried reduce this complex borderland to a crisp international border by extorting land cessions from captive Indian leaders. The resulting Treaty of Fort Stanwix (1784) created a boundary that, like the Peace of Paris, ignored the complex reality on the ground. "The price of the Americans' geographic fantasy," in the historian Alan Taylor's words, "was the alienation of—rather than reconciliation with—the great majority of the Iroquois." Subsequent years saw similar treaties, but the British troops remained, arming Indians who occupied a buffer between British Canada and the United States.[17]

The year after the Treaty of Fort Stanwix, the United States sought by similarly dubious means to expel Indians from the most lucrative regions of southern and eastern Ohio. The resulting treaties of Fort McIntosh (1785) and Great Miami (1786) coerced a minority of Delawares, Wyandots, Ottawas, Ojibwas, and Shawnees to relinquish most of their lands. Most Indians in the Ohio country ignored the treaties, which would have confined them to a corner of northwestern Ohio. Meanwhile, thousands of people had migrated into the Ohio country and settled lands without formal title. Violence escalated between Indians and American settlers, and the United States found itself unable to control the actions of either. The settlers were strong individualists who showed little deference to traditional social or political authority, and eastern elites feared they might tear the fledgling nation's social fabric asunder. George Washington worried as early as 1783 that, instead of coming under congressional authority, the Ohio country would be overrun by "a parcel of banditti, who will bid defiance to all authority."[18] Treaties did little to allay such fears.

Farther south, the Creek leader Alexander McGillivray entered into a treaty at Pensacola wherein the Spanish recognized the Creeks' independence and funneled them arms.[19] Among European powers, the Spanish, with vast colonial holdings in the Americas, felt most threatened by the United States. A wave of American settlement in the very regions that Spain and the Creeks wished to deny the United States worsened matters. Kentucky's settler population exploded from 150 at the beginning of the Revolution to 73,000 by 1790; Tennessee's from 7,700 to 35,691; and the backcountry valleys of the Carolinas and Georgia saw comparable increases.[20] Creeks attempted to thwart this expansion, killing roughly 200 Virginians in October 1786 alone and threatening Savannah the same year. Meanwhile, the total number of Anglo-American dead in Kentucky between 1783 and 1790 approached 1,500.[21] Extorted land cessions from north to south only heightened the violence and amplified the complaints from U.S. citizens of national ineptitude.

The apparent incompetence of the United States in securing the West spawned burgeoning separatist movements. Men of questionable character, such as the self-promoting and corrupt Continental Army veteran James Wilkinson, treasonously turned to the Spanish to secure special trading privileges or land titles. So, too, did more reputable individuals, such as the "Geographer of the United States" Thomas Hutchins. It is little wonder that eastern elites, particularly southerners such as Washington, Jefferson, and Madison, fretted that the southwestern parts of the United States might cleave from the rest.

Tensions over the Mississippi prompted renewed negotiations in 1785 between John Jay, who now served as secretary of foreign affairs, and Spain's Diego Maria de Gardoqui. Gardoqui had orders to maintain Spain's "exclusive right" to navigate the Mississippi and to exclude the United States from most of the region to the west of present-day Georgia. In return, he could offer the United States a commercial treaty and an alliance of mutual protection within North America. Gardoqui's agenda ran up against Jay's instructions from the congress that he demand the navigation of the Mississippi and seek the boundaries of the 1783 peace with Britain. The congress expressed openness to minor compromises on the boundaries, but the general sense was that Britain had every right to cede all of the lands it did by virtue of the treaty that ended the Seven Years' War. Beyond that, claimed James Madison, "the use of the Mississippi is given by nature to our western country." Spanish diplomats found such claims absurd, because Spanish forces had seized many of the western regions from the "common enemy" during the recent war.[22]

Negotiations lasted more than a year and culminated with Jay's reluctantly agreeing to a treaty under which the United States would refrain from navigation of the Mississippi for twenty-five years. In exchange, Spain would grant the United States lucrative trading privileges and an alliance. As soon as Jay presented the treaty to the congress for ratification, southern delegates opposed it.

Charles Pinckney of South Carolina argued in a lengthy and impassioned speech that Jay's concessions sacrificed U.S. "national honor." Spain, he argued, watched guardedly the "emancipation of these states" so close to "her rich and extensive, tho' feeble colonies of South America." The contagion of revolution threatened Spain; "hence we find she holds the deserts of Florida as a barrier, and wishes to deprive our citizens of the use of the Mississippi, hoping to postpone an event which she dreads." But, according to Pinckney, in its absolutism the "Spanish Monarchy carries in its bosom the seeds of its dissolution." To refrain from navigation of the Mississippi would, at best, postpone the inevitable expansion of the United States and stall the dissolution of Spain's American empire. At worst, thought Pinckney and plenty of like-minded individuals, the treaty would lead to "uneasiness" among the states. Southerners and westerners would see the congress as favoring the interests of maritime regions at the expense of the south and west, fostering disunity and sacrificing the welfare of the union.[23]

James Madison forged a coalition among middle and southern states that opposed the treaty while northern delegates offered more sanguine assessments. Rufus King of Massachusetts, for instance, agreed that "popular opinion throughout the U.S. is in favor of the free navigation of the Mississippi" and that it would someday come.[24] The United States need not rush, given the state of its finances and its inability to assert its rights in western regions. Northerners, such as Jay and King, feared that opening the Mississippi would skew representation in the congress in favor of a southern and western faction with interests counter to those of northerners. They envisioned an expanding United States, but they also stressed that governmental authority in the West needed to keep pace with the rapid rate of settlement. Postponing secure navigation of the Mississippi would slow expansion, prevent anarchy in the West, strengthen the economy of maritime regions, solidify the union, and thus render the nation better prepared for expansion in the future.[25]

By the spring of 1787, factionalism in the congress had killed the Jay-

Gardoqui agreement, but only after severely damaging the congress's credibility and shattering, for many, the hopes that the United States might maintain a continental union in the near future. An article in the February 15, 1787, issue of the *Boston Independent Chronicle* called for the five New England states to form the nation of "New-England, and leave the rest of the Continent to pursue their own imbecile and disjointed plans," at least until they "acquired magnanimity and wisdom sufficient to join a confederation that may rescue them from destruction." Nineteen newspapers in ten states reprinted the piece before the Constitutional Convention.[26]

Yet despite the shrillness in the press, differences of degree, not substance, divided the congress.[27] The factions shared the conviction that the future of the United States lay in the West and that the congress must take some action to ensure that expansion proceeded. On this common ground, the congress crafted one of its greatest successes, the Northwest Ordinance of 1787, even as men down the street at the Constitutional Convention found the congress so ineffective that they contemplated replacing the body entirely.

The ordinance established an institutional framework whereby the Northwest Territory could be incorporated into the union. It allowed for a strong dose of government control over these lands, control aimed at making the new states interdependent with the old. Instead of allowing individuals simply to go out and purchase, seize, or squat on land, the ordinance prescribed a series of progressive stages designed to restrain individualist excesses and establish a strong social order. To begin, responsibility for acquiring lands from native peoples lay with the national government, not the states or private interests. The congress then sold the lands, following rectilinear survey patterns, which made the oversight of land claims easier from a distance than the more haphazard surveys that were traditionally used and that relied on surveyors' interpretations of the lay of the land. The ordinance encouraged the establishment of schools and churches; provided for the extradition of convicted criminals; implemented property requirements for voting and office holding; and made inhabitants liable for their share of the national government's debts and expenses. In short, the ordinance sought to establish territories and new states inhabited by individuals whom nationalist members of the congress thought were civically virtuous— men like themselves—and then tie them to the nation as a whole.

As the historian Peter Onuf has suggested, an important result of the Northwest Ordinance was "to encourage expansionist sentiment in the North and to commit the United States as a whole to the creation of new States."[28] It renewed faith among strong nationalists in New England and coastal and urban areas that expansion might continue with sufficient governmental authority to maintain an ordered, civil society of loyal, virtuous citizens. In coming months, supporters of a new Constitution relished the ordinance even as they sought to replace the congress that wrote it. Indeed, the ordinance is best seen as part of larger package, including the Constitution, Bill of Rights, federal assumption of state debts, and the location of the capital on the Potomac, all of which contributed to a stable federal government. The first congress to convene under the new Constitution moved swiftly—before submitting to the state legislatures the first twelve amendments to the Constitution—to reenact the Northwest Ordinance in August 1789, and it soon legislated a similar institutional framework for expansion in the southwest. Taken together, the Constitution and the territorial ordinances made the expansion of the American empire possible by allowing new states to enter the union voluntarily while maintaining centralized authority over the whole.[29]

Politically, however, 1789 was still a world away from 1787. From Canada to Florida, on the seas and in international ports, evidence appeared that the emergence of the United States had not created a new world order. The idealistic internationalism resting on natural principles and prophesied by Thomas Paine had failed to materialize. Instead, messy borderlands, anarchic squatters, wars with Indians, obstructed navigation, trade restrictions, and British forts challenged the United States diplomatically. Few Americans wondered whether these issues needed righting. Instead, the question became how deeply political reforms needed to cut to foster the insular, cohesive union that nature had made possible. For some, the answer became clear after trouble arose within firmly established states. Worse, the trouble seemed to emanate disproportionately from the remnants of what had formerly been a symbol of continental unity: the army.

TROUBLE WITHIN:
DEMOBILIZATION, BETRAYAL, AND DIVISION

Patriots' continental attachment had drawn some of its sustenance from war, so peace attenuated their continental sense of self. For many, the army of aspiration faded into nostalgia, and demobilization meant that the Continental Army of reality had ceased to exist by December 1783. Yet the hopes and sense of entitlement of men who fought in the army could not be dismantled so easily, and the states and the nation faced repercussions for their poor treatment of soldiers. In extreme cases, former soldiers channeled their disappointment into local rebellions. The cacophonous calls and seemingly anarchic actions of veterans and others who struggled in the postwar world became the most proximate cause for the Constitutional Convention.

Confronting the disillusioned remnants of the army, elites pushed for a representative form of government over an "extended sphere." They embraced the continent not just out of lingering habit but to keep power out of the hands of men whom they believed were ill suited to govern. They could do so, even though Revolutionary principles called for actual representation, because it seemed to conform to nature.

For many Continental soldiers, hopes for the postwar world included a tangible connection to the continent itself. Many would have remembered, or recently learned, that the Proclamation of 1763 promised land to soldiers who served in the Seven Years' War and resided in North America. It only seemed reasonable that the United States ought to treat its soldiers at least as well as Britain had, especially since many enlistees had been drawn into service by land bounties in the first place. In August 1776, the congress tried, albeit without much success, to lure Hessians and other foreigners serving with the British into deserting with promises of land. Later that year, and in 1780, Congress promised land mostly in what became the northwest and southwest territories to soldiers who enlisted for the duration of the war. Pressures after the war to make good on these land bounties mounted to an extent that, in 1787, Secretary of War Henry Knox wrote to the congress about the "incessant enquiries respecting the lands due to the late army."[30]

The calls went unheeded, and most veterans never received land. Congress, whatever goodwill it may have harbored toward veterans, simply lacked the financial and political means to allocate significant tracts.[31] Nor in the wars' aftermath could it provide soldiers their back pay adjusted for inflation, or officers their promised pensions. (Many would have to wait until the passage of pension acts in 1818 and 1820 to see compensation, and among those who lived that long, some were not even that lucky.) As a result, many veterans fell into destitution. Depreciated certificates for back wages proved nearly useless after mustering out of the army, and soldiers sometimes sold them to speculators for just enough to return home. A sad, bitter Private Joseph Plumb Martin later recalled how many soldiers "got their final settlement certificates, which they sold to procure decent clothing and money sufficient to enable them to pass with decency through the country."[32] On the whole, veterans, in a typical recollection, "returned to the bosom of their country, objects of jealousy, and victims of neglect."[33] Any heightened expectations they might have held quickly disintegrated into disgust and distrust.

At war's end, few recruits remained in, or returned to, the area that had recruited them. They could not go to a home like Mount Vernon. In the case of Joseph Martin, feelings of betrayal over land festered. Like so many enlistees, he had been promised bounty land. But "when the country had drained the last drop of service it could screw out of the poor soldiers, they were turned adrift like old worn-out horses, and nothing said about land to pasture them upon."[34] Under such circumstances, many long-term soldiers became mobile, rootless laborers. Others partook in the haphazard settlement of the West that distressed many elites.[35] Although these former soldiers forged ahead in settling the continent's interior, their country's betrayal of them undoubtedly lessened any notions they might have had that their purpose in migrating was to fulfill the nation's continental destiny. They were on their own.

When demobilization first loomed, some of the nation's leaders did take up the soldiers' cause and turned it into a rallying cry for greater centralized political authority. They became angry at the states, whose quotas the soldiers had filled but that now would not make good on the men's pay. In September 1783, John Mercer, congressional delegate from Virginia, wrote irately under the pseudonym "The North-American," reminding the congress that "this long extended continent has been stained" with the soldiers' "best blood," and asked, "to whom shall that part of the continental army apply whom no state will now acknowledge"?[36] Mercer had entered the congress as a vocal states' rights advocate just seven months earlier. But confronted with the poor treatment of the army, he developed an outrage at the states that many soldiers shared. He came to see states as having continental obligations and became a proponent of greater centralized power.

Outside the congress, a number of officers acted to make sure their countrymen remembered their contributions and, in the process, created an institution that became a nationalizing force. The Society of the Cincinnati, formed on May 10, 1783, was a fraternal order named after the Roman hero Cincinnatus, who twice led his country in war and, following each occasion, embodied the Revolutionary generation's citizen-soldier ideal by rejecting power and position to return home and work his farm. The Society of the Cincinnati comprised only officers and entailed hereditary membership that passed through elder sons. The society elected Washington as its first president-general and met regularly in subsequent years. The officers sought to maintain the strong bonds forged among them during the war; make sure that the congress and the states compensated them as promised; and perpetuate the memory of their patriotic sacrifices.

Critics initially attacked the aristocratic trappings of the society: the hereditary membership and the eagle badges on ribbons they wore.[37] Nevertheless, the society became a conduit to express the overwhelming support of former officers to restore order and establish a stronger federal union. The officers' voice thus outlived the army itself. In newspapers and magazines the society used the memory of the soldiers' sacrifices, much as the memory of the sacrifices of men in the Seven Years' War had been used during the Revolution, to support their patriotic vision of an ordered and united republic. It was a new incarnation of the army of aspiration.

The Society of the Cincinnati embraced the order-imposing Northwest Ordinance and led the settlement of the Northwest Territory by founding the Ohio Company. Six of the eleven men who founded the company, which financed and oversaw the establishment of Marietta, Ohio, were Cincinnati members, and they named the town's streets after other prominent members.[38] The society also heavily influenced the Constitutional Convention in 1787. George Washington presided over it, and it came on the heels of the society's triennial meeting in the same city. Though Washington did not attend the society's meeting, the timing and the location of the two events was intentional. Alexander Hamilton had arranged for the federal convention to coincide with the society's meeting, understanding that a number of individuals would be attending both events. Sure enough, twenty-one of the convention's fifty-five delegates, or 38 percent, were Cincinnati members, even though society members made up only 0.7 percent of the nation's population.[39]

THE unity of the Society of the Cincinnati, like the impetus for the Constitutional Convention, grew in reaction to fractures in the society at large. Calls to reform the Articles of Confederation were, to a large extent, a response to the agitations of ordinary farmers, including a large number of former soldiers, which the society found repulsive. During the war, the army had survived mutinies, and Washington's reputation and skill had staved off crisis and preserved civil rule over the military at Newburgh. Yet the former commander could do little to alleviate the resentment many officers and soldiers felt toward the states after demobilization. True, some, including many Cincinnati members, took a leadership role in efforts to unite the nation and to shift more powers to the federal government, but others joined movements with fiery, localist impulses and lashed out at their state governments. The culminating event that drove delegates to the Constitutional Convention came to be symbolized by a decorated former army officer, Daniel Shays, who was eligible for Cincinnati membership but rejected it.

Shays was just one of several ringleaders in a movement in 1786 and 1787 that subsequently took his name.[40] The uprising, just one of many that affected states besides Massachusetts, grew out of private debtors' desire for relief and the anger of men unable to pay taxes and mad at the state government that imposed them, largely to pay bondholders. For these men, peacetime taxes rubbed salt in the wounds of wartime neglect that they had suffered in the army of reality.

As rebellions go, Shays's proved tame. Men gathered at courthouses in Northampton, Springfield, Worcester, and other towns in western Massachusetts to disrupt proceedings and prevent property foreclosures. The secretary of war for the Continental Congress, General Henry Knox of Massachusetts, worried that the unrest threatened the unprotected Continental Arsenal at Springfield. Although his letters to George Washington described a situation verging on anarchy, Knox confidently dubbed Shays the leader of the amorphous rebellion and worked with Governor James Bowdoin to assemble a private army of 4,400 men, led by Benjamin Lincoln, who had infamously surrendered his 3,000 Continental soldiers to the British at Charleston seven years earlier. Shortly thereafter, on January 25, 1787, a contingent of militiamen dispersed some 1,500 Shaysites with a single burst of cannon fire that killed four and wounded several others. They then surprised and drove off rebels who were eating breakfast and tending fires at their camp at Petersham. The last major engagement, near Stockbridge, lasted six minutes and resulted in four casualties between the two sides. When it was all over, the state had hanged two of the insurgents and doled out a number of fines, whippings, prison sentences, and short disenfranchisements. Coming on the heels of a Revolution that had lasted seven years and killed 25,000, the bloodshed may have been comparatively minor, but the instability nonetheless helped convince most states to send delegates to the Constitutional Convention in Philadelphia that May.[41]

During the Revolution, Washington had longed for more soldiers like Shays. Like most Continental soldiers, Shays fought for a pittance. He served five years, suffering with the troops through the winters.[42] But in peace, Shays and his alleged followers offended Washington's and other elites' notions of hierarchy, deference, and public virtue. Shays was no Cincinnatus and thus earned the ire of many officers, even though a preponderance of veterans felt as betrayed as Shays.

In fact, the Shaysites included a far higher percentage of Revolutionary War veterans than did the army sent to quash it. In many western Massachusetts towns, veterans were ten times more likely to side with the rebels than with the state. Nor were these veterans uniformly a motley crew of ordinary soldiers or low-level, "wretched officers," as Knox had tried to convince Washington. Shays and other leaders had been recognized by their commanding officers for serving with distinction. When large numbers of veterans failed to rally to his cause, Lincoln ended up with an army that fell 1,400 men short of what he had hoped.[43]

Massachusetts and the nation were partly reaping what they had sown when they failed to reward soldiers as promised. Like the Society of the Cincinnati, the Shaysites cast themselves as fighting for the legacy of the Revolution and assumed the mantle of the Continental Army. Unlike the crowds that protested against the Stamp and Tea acts, the insurgents of 1786–87 adopted military protocol and ritual. They enlisted men with muster rolls and carried deadly weapons to the beat of drums. Many, including Shays, wore their Continental Army uniforms, and Shaysites sported evergreen sprigs in their hats, just as soldiers in the Continental Army had once done.[44]

To some degree, it made sense that rebels protesting unfair tax policies developed by moneyed men in Boston would present themselves as a reconstitution of the Continental Army, especially if they had been suffering economically. After all, it was the inequitable taxes of a distant Parliament beginning in the 1760s that originally had provoked American resistance, and it was the army that had saved the United States from tyranny. The army, too, had represented a means of securing and capitalizing on the wealth and abundance of the continent. The hostility toward the state held by the Shaysites also made sense in light of the military experience that so many of the men shared.

Yet Henry Knox, Benjamin Lincoln, Alexander Hamilton, George Washington, and other Society of the Cincinnati and Constitutional Convention delegates abhorred the Shaysites and believed exaggerated reports depicting the men as self-serving enemies of the public good. These soldiers did not represent the aspirational army. Rather than fulfilling the Revolutionary ideal of citizen-soldiers who set down their weapons when hostilities ended to return to private life, the Shaysites, especially if their spark ignited veterans in other states, threatened to destroy the fruits of the Revolution. Such fears moved George Washington to preside at the Constitutional Convention. Shays's Rebellion convinced him that, "without some alteration in our political creed, the superstructure we have been seven years raising at the expence of much blood and treasure, must fall. We are fast verging to anarchy and confusion!"[45]

REFORM AMID CONTINENTALISM

Delegates converged on Philadelphia in 1787 assuming that North America had an essential nature and, with a scientific approach, that they could devise its ideal political system. Unless this core belief was widely shared, however, attempts to create a centralized power over a continent would have been futile. The delegates swam against the current of much conventional scientific and political theory. Buffonian theorists still cast doubt on the physical and mental capabilities of humans born in the Americas, suggesting that Americans would be unable to formulate, implement, and sustain a novel, enlightened political system. And while Americans may have rejected such degeneracy theories, a large number still subscribed to Montesquieu's argument that a republic "cannot long subsist" in a large territory. "In an extensive republic the public good is sacrificed to a thousand private views," the Frenchman explained. Small republics, in contrast, contained a relative homogeneity of interests, making possible an espirit de corps that served the public good. The newspaper editor Thomas Waite of Maine translated the theory for one Federalist: The "vast Continent of America cannot be long subject to a Democracy, if consolidated into one Government—you might as well attempt to rule Hell by Prayer." Or, as a widely reprinted article in the *Philadelphia Independent Gazetteer* put it, the "continent of North-America can no more be governed by one Republic, than the fabled Atlas could support the heavens."[46]

A literary genre just becoming popular in the years surrounding the constitutional debate sheds light on the far-reaching, metageographical notions that countered such thinking and gave Federalists essential intellectual ammunition. These political and literary journals offer a catalog of readings targeted to the tastes of both the delegates and more typical urban, white households. Among the most influential were the *American Magazine,* edited in the 1780s by the prolific author, ardent nationalist, and lexicographer Noah Webster, and two periodicals edited by Mathew Carey: the *American Museum* and the *Columbian Magazine.*

The *American Museum,* for example, drew a remarkably diverse readership. One historian has traced the occupation of subscribers and found that the "bulk" were "teachers, cabinetmakers, boatbuilders, cordwainers, blacksmiths, tailors, tobacconists, innkeepers, and shopkeepers, the widest range of the middling sort." The magazine also drew the attention of the U.S. political elite; subscribers included twenty of the Constitutional Convention's fifty-five delegates, among them Alexander Hamilton and George Washington. On the day that his native Virginia became the tenth state to ratify the Constitution, Washington wrote to Carey, telling him that his magazine had "met with extensive, . . . universal approbation from competent Judges." He hoped that such "Magazines, as well as common Gazettes, might be spread through every city, town & village in America—I consider such easy vehicles of knowledge, more happily calculated than any other, to preserve the liberty, stimulate the industry and meliorate the morals of an enlightened and free people."[47]

Carey, of Irish birth, migrated to Philadelphia in 1784 and, like the immigrant Paine before him, identified more strongly with the nation than with his state. Before arriving in Philadelphia, he had worked at Benjamin Franklin's printing press in Passy, France. He began the *Columbian Magazine* and the *American Museum* in 1786 and 1787, respectively. In them, Carey aimed to print the preeminent literary, political, and economic writings of the day.[48]

Both Webster's and Carey's magazines revealed their editors' convictions, resting on much of a generation's scientific beliefs and geopolitical views, not only that the United States could become a continental people, but that it must do so to fulfill its destiny. Featured authors often dwelt on scientific themes, both to refute Buffonian formulations and to argue for the usefulness of science in fashioning a political system harmonious with nature. Authors also endowed the United States with a future of imperial grandeur and security thanks to North America's insularity, cohesiveness, and abundance. In short, these popular periodicals of the day show that the Constitutional Convention delegates, along with many whites of middling sorts, partook of a culture eager to embrace North America's continental expanse.

THE first volumes of Carey's magazines refuted Buffon's aspersions on North America by celebrating the rise of genius in the United States. "The time is come to explode the European creed, that we are infantine in our acquisitions, and savage in our manners, because we are inhabitants of a new world, lately occupied by a race of savages," wrote one author. As proof, he listed artistic and literary luminaries, including Benjamin West, whose *Death of General Wolfe* earlier symbolized the unity of a transatlantic empire; John Trumbull, who did for Richard Montgomery what West had done for Wolfe; and the poet Joel Barlow, a Revolutionary war chaplain whose epic poem *Vision of Columbus* (1787) included lines not just rejecting Buffon but, as an advertisement described it, celebrating "the Advantages of America in every Point of View; as being in many Respects the greatest Theatre for the Improvement of human Nature, in every Article in which it is capable of Improvement."[49]

An extended comparison of the arts and sciences in America and Europe appeared in the *Columbian Magazine*'s serialization of Colonel David Humphreys's *A Poem on the Happiness of America* (1786). Virtually reversing Buffon's argument, Humphreys's verse celebrated a reciprocal relationship between the North American environment and the valiant character of its men. America produced "Men of firm nerves who spurn at fear and sloth; / Men of high courage like their fires of old, / In labour patient as in danger bold!" With such men, time had come for the continent to "Awake to glory, and to greatness rise!" The magazine prefaced Humphreys's work itself as an example of North American genius "much delighted with our sylvan scenes."[50] Characteristically, Humphreys and the magazine embraced the metageographical taxonomies on which Buffon rested his case; they just turned Buffon's argument on its head.

Although authors rejected Buffon's degeneration theory, they embraced science generally and endorsed a scientific approach to solving their political problems. The time had come to analyze nature; realize that North America constituted a distinctive, cohesive entity with bountiful potential; and apply this finding to the construction of government. Before the Constitutional Convention, "Pro Republica" recognized that "the arts and sciences have arrived to a degree of improvement that justly distinguishes the present century as the era of refined genius and learning." But citing the virtual paralysis of the congress, he charged that it was "not enough that we understand civil polity, as a science; but, by a proper application of its principles to our own situation and circumstances, we must learn the art of governing well. We must reduce our theory to practice"—that is, the congress must have greater powers.[51]

Poems contrasted Europe, where wars and "all-aspiring pride" reigned, with America, where "reason shall new laws devise" or "Fair science her gates to thy sons shall unbar."[52] Predictions that North America or the Americas provided the theater for scientific advancement and the greatest political liberty the world had ever seen, and that the two were inextricably linked, filled magazines. "It is a very common and just remark that the progress of Liberty, of Science and of Empire has been with that of the sun, from east to west, since the beginning of time," reflected Timothy Dwight, and, sure enough, "this empire is commencing, at a period, when every species of knowledge, natural and moral, is arrived to a state of perfection."[53] If the United States could secure political stability—and there was no reason it could not, given that the "present is an age of philosophy, and America, the empire of reason"—then surely "the arts and sciences shall flourish," strife and tyranny would wane, and "the age of innocence shall seem to be revived."[54]

Periodicals' contributors suggested that scientific principles should underpin a political system for the continent as a whole. True, Spaniards sat to the south and west of the United States; Britons sat to the north and west; and Indians sat throughout the interior, but these writers saw themselves as heirs of Britain's North American empire. Casting themselves during the Revolution as a continent rejecting island rule, they had waged a war not just for colonial liberation; they had fought to assume their master's imperial mantle.

Seizing Nature's Advantages (283

Instead of mirroring the official treaty stipulations of 1783, their definition of U.S. boundaries often reflected a broader spatial conception. Poems urged the continent's "blessings roll, / To southern oceans and the northern pole," and celebrated how "gales of health, from Darien fan the / pole." A poem that envisioned a people "stretch'd immense from Cancer to the pole, / On either side contending oceans roll" called for a political system to rule such a "mighty land." The same work explicitly called on the "Continental Convention" to "perfect her federal system, public pow'r; / For this stupendous realm."[55]

Since continental taxonomies had not yet gelled into the form memorized by today's schoolchildren, the continent might be coterminous with what we now recognize as North America, or it might comprise both of the Americas, sometimes referred to as the new continent or the western continent. Timothy Dwight defined the theater of future American actions as "North America," extending from the Arctic Circle to the isthmus of Darien and from the "50th degree of west longitude, almost to the eastern shore of Asia." In a later song, however, he pleaded directly to the Americas, "Let the crimes of the East ne'er encrimson / thy name." Joel Barlow similarly contrasted the virtue of the "western continent" with the imperfections of the "eastern continent."[56]

Either way, the United States stood to possess an insular and internally interconnected continent, a world within itself. Some writers completely ignored the British and Spanish: North America sat "remote from the broils of the eastern world . . . and curst by no foreign dominions, which to others have often occasioned the most destructive contests." The nation had tremendous natural advantages, possessed of a land with climates that spread "from the torrid to the frozen zone" and that had "amplest scope for mutual intercourse and exchange." At the same time, it was well protected: "On the one hand rolled the wide Atlantic, a powerful barrier against the intrigues, the ambition, the avarice of the European world; On the other hand, the vast Pacific, that also might secure us from the corruption and luxuriant effeminacy of the Asiatic."[57]

Any potential enemy, Timothy Dwight noted, would stumble over many difficulties: "the immense distance between us and them, the consequential difficulty of transporting troops hither, and of furnishing them with provisions when they arrive." The geographic situation of the United States "must blast their brightest prospects, and whelm them in ignominy and ruin." When Dwight acknowledged the presence of Spaniards, he dismissed them "as vicious, luxurious, mean-spirited and contemptible a race of beings, as any that ever blackened the pages of infamy." They posed no threat and had no future. They were "generally descended from the refuse of mankind, situated in a hot, wealthy and plentiful country, and educated from their infancy under the most shocking of all governments." Dwight concluded that "the moment our interest demands it, these extensive regions will be our own," its current inhabitants "exterminated" or saved under U.S. rule. "A distinction therefore between them and ourselves, in the present consideration of the necessary, future greatness of the Western World, will be useless and impertinent."[58]

With the Spanish gone, the United States would have no trouble drawing together all of North America's regions, thanks to the continent's magisterial waterways. Without them, North America would more resemble other parts of the world, "but heaven, resolving that all circumstances of this continent should be of a piece," had bestowed it with thousands of miles of seacoast dotted with deep harbors, and, above all, rivers. Without detailed knowledge of the Rocky Mountains or the arid west, authors presumed that "the most copious streams" or "a thousand extensive intersecting rivers" provided the "amplest scope for mutual intercourse and exchange." The Mississippi alone provided "as extensive an inland navigation, as half the rivers in Europe united." Moreover, "No country in North-America, or perhaps in the universe, exceeds the neighborhood of the Mississippi in fertility of soil and temperature of climate." It seemed inevitable that the "trade, wealth, and power of America [would], at some future period depend, and perhaps center upon the Mississippi."[59]

The United States, then, was an "infant empire" just beginning to taste its greatness.[60] Webster's and Carey's magazines confirmed readers' assumptions —the assumptions of Constitutional Convention delegates—that the United States stood on the verge of becoming a truly continental empire. Its people possessed the unsurpassed genius and knowledge necessary to capitalize on its geographic insularity and interconnectedness. No country had ever been born under such fortuitous circumstances, with such natural advantages and the knowledge to capitalize on them. Since "all human knowledge is progressive," the United States would eventually make the world forget "Rome, once mistress of the world."[61]

THE FEDERALIST PAPERS: CONTEXT, RECEPTION, AND MESSAGE

Constitutional Convention delegates presented their final draft to Congress on September 17, 1787. Historians have argued that the document itself demonstrates how much geography permeated its authors' thinking. Its signatures, Robert A. Ferguson writes, "appear neither in alphabetical order, nor by presumed importance or seniority, nor in haphazard fashion. They are grouped, instead, by state with the states themselves appearing in *geographical* order from north to south." Elaborating on Ferguson, Martin Brückner argues that it was as if the Constitution itself was "innately structured by the diction and grammar of the national map."[62]

In the nine months after the delegates submitted the Constitution to the states, the nation engaged in a great ratification debate. In it, advocates of the Constitution resurrected and honed the metageographical arguments that had shaped both their own thinking and that of their forefathers over the previous half-century. They reasoned that the people of the United States had demonstrated wisdom, fortitude, and brilliance, belying Buffonians. These same people had proved themselves united by staging a successful Revolution, and they were blessed to live in a land that was large, ideally suited to their character, and amenable to an enlightened republic.

Opinions on the Constitution appeared in an array of places beyond the halls of the states' ratifying conventions: woodcuts, songs, poems, almanacs, and, especially, newspapers. Much of what was said sounded familiar. The *Boston Gazette* echoed Thomas Paine by proclaiming the Constitution "not the concern of a City, a County, or a State, but the Freedom, Independence and Safety of the Millions that now inhabit, and that will hereafter people this immense Continent." It called for unity "upon a Scale that the World hath never known," for the new federal government "will throw a Glory round this Western Hemisphere."[63] Despite the continent's vast scale, an author in the *Pennsylvania Gazette* still found it porous and yielding enough for rule under the Constitution. "The various parts of the North-American continent are formed by nature for the most intimate union," trumpeted "An American." Easy navigation via natural waterways or easily built canals made navigation between "Georgia and New-Hampshire" simpler that between most cities within Britain, France, or Spain. "The voice of nature therefore directs us to be affectionate associates in peace, and firm supporters in war. As we cannot mistake her injunctions, to disobey them would be criminal."[64]

Widely reprinted newspaper articles made metageographical contrasts between Europe and America. "The cloud which gathers in the European hemisphere," suggested the *Philadelphia Independent Gazetteer,* "serves, as a foil, to set off the lustre of the prospect that opens upon America." Across the ocean, one saw a land "rent with civil discord, and national contention." The "parent continent is stained with wild ambition and phantastic pride," while the United States "expands under the influence of reason and philosophy." As a result, according to "One of the People" in the *Massachusetts*

FIGURE 35. Frontispiece to *Bickerstaff's Boston Almanack,* 4th ed. (1788). ©
American Antiquarian Society

Centinel, "this continent will soon become," under the Constitution, "the
delight and envy of the European world."[65]

Newspapers' and almanacs' celebrations of "American genius" refuted
Buffonian aspersions and reinforced Americans' continental sense of self. At
the same time, they suggested that Constitutional Convention delegates had
the wisdom and aptitude to accomplish what many had thought impossible:
frame a republic suited to an expansive area. The *New York Journal* declared
that, in the preceding century, Americans had demonstrated "unparalleled
progress, important improvement and revolution." Surely Americans need
not worry "while we have a Franklin, a Washington, a Morris, the Adamses,
a Dickinson." There had been "so many instances of philosophic and en-
larged minds, who have appeared among us" that "we cannot doubt of our
abilities for self-government," or of our "future greatness."[66]

With the Constitution close to ratification, *Bickerstaff's Boston Almanack*
for 1788 included a frontispiece that foreshadowed not just a bright future,
but the iconic nineteenth-century painting most emblematic of manifest
destiny: John Gast's *American Progress* (1872) (figs. 35 and 36). The almanac's frontispiece showed the "heroick" Washington and the "sagacious and
philosopick" Franklin in the "Federal Chariot," drawn by thirteen men
representing the states. Franklin held a pole topped with a liberty cap, and
Washington held a copy of the Constitution, "the grand FABRICK OF
AMERICAN INDEPENDENCE," which he offered "with paternal affection"

FIGURE 36. John Gast, *American Progress* (1872). Chromolithograph published by George A. Crofutt. Courtesy Library of Congress, Prints and Photographs Division (LC-DIG-ppmsca-09855)

to the "SONS OF COLUMBIA." The Goddess of Fame flew overhead, blowing her trumpet and "spreading the glad Tidings of Union." Finally, "The SUN, entirely clear of the Horizon," shone "resplendently on the AMERICAN FEDERAL UNION, denoting that every ray of light has now burst forth, and beautifully illumes the whole UNITED CONTINENT OF AMERICA." Westward, it appeared, the course of empire would take its course.[67]

AMID the flurry of articles, pamphlets, poems, songs, and cartoons favoring ratification, those written by Alexander Hamilton, James Madison, and John Jay have come to be regarded as the most important. Hamilton organized their journalistic blitzkrieg to promote the Constitution's ratification in New York, and later, the essays originally written for newspapers were published in two hardcover volumes as *The Federalist*. The mere fact the Federalist essays were anthologized attests to how highly contemporaries regarded them. Yet much of *The Federalist*, including those parts found most persuasive at the time, simply restated metageographical themes that appeared in other newspaper pieces.

In enlisting the help of Jay and Madison, Hamilton ensured that a continental vision would shine forth in the Federalist Papers. Hamilton himself had shaken off the provincialism of his island birthplace and had ambitions for his new nation and for himself that transcended state boundaries. Jay, whose name appeared on the list of subscribers to the *American Museum*, had presided over the Continental Congress, where he fought to break down provincial habits, helped negotiate the formal end of the war with Britain, and, as the nation's secretary of foreign affairs, struggled to gain the navigation of the Mississippi. Madison is probably best known for initiating the move at the Constitutional Convention to scrap the Articles of Confederation entirely by drafting and presenting the "Virginia Plan." He then took the most detailed daily minutes of the convention's proceedings. Equally important is that Madison participated avidly in the "dispute of the New World" by collecting fauna specimens.

Added to these men's cosmopolitan, nationalist outlook was tireless commitment. Together, Hamilton, Madison, and Jay produced eighty-five essays, roughly four a week. Though it is doubtful whether *The Federalist* alone made a difference in the ratification process in New York, or in any other state where its essays could be read in periodicals and newspapers, at the very least it contributed to the whirlwind of metageographical arguments swirling around at the time. It also offers profound insights into some of the framers' visions, and especially their ideas of what might convince others of their validity.[68]

The Federalist Papers had to counter the Constitution's critics, particularly those who promulgated Montesquieu's views. Hamilton, Madison, and Jay took such ideas head on. The Federalist Papers suggested that the continent's unity and insularity made "the practicable sphere"—indeed, the desirable sphere—of the United States the continent as a whole and, in turn, gave the nation potential for grandeur on a global scale. In short, Hamilton, Madison and Jay relied on pervasive trends in thinking about North America.[69]

Americans today read the Federalist Papers differently from the way contemporaries did. Madison's Federalist No. 10 became the most praised in the twentieth and twenty-first centuries because of its intellectual rigor and path-breaking political theory. Its rebuttal of Montesquieu's stance that republics were ill suited for large areas attempted to do for political theory what North American critics of Buffonian formulations did for natural history. No. 10, like Jefferson's *Notes on the State of Virginia,* sought to

Seizing Nature's Advantages (289

destroy ideas critical of the possibility of a thriving, continental American empire. Yet the essay's innovative qualities and exalted status in recent times should not blind us from recognizing that other, less sophisticated Federalist papers sought the same end and often had greater contemporary resonance. Simply put, readers in 1788 had different priorities and saw other essays as more important than No. 10. They did not initially realize the relevance of the most sophisticated and innovative analyses. These novel ideas, as the legal scholar Larry Kramer argues, took longer to become fully considered and digested than the ratification process allowed, and the evidence is that No. 10's innovative aspects had little initial effect.[70]

During ratification, it was the Federalist Papers' more mundane and time-tested arguments about North America's geopolitical future, the kind of ideas that could be read in myriad places, that resonated most with at least one highly influential reader. Over the course of four issues, from March to June 1788, Noah Webster's *American Magazine* published the most extensive review of *The Federalist* to appear in print during ratification. The author, likely Webster himself, wrote eleven pages of praise.[71] Most of the review briefly summarized the essays in chronological order. The April issue encapsulated the arguments of No. 6 through No. 36 in just over four pages. No. 10 garnered only minimal attention; its summary appeared with that of No. 9 for a combined total of less than half a page. The same issue devoted its greatest attention by far to essay No. 11, by Hamilton, which ostensibly dealt with the effects of union on commerce and the navy.

The reviewer did not dwell on ideas specifically related to commerce or the navy in No. 11. Instead, he presented the following excerpt from No. 11—which alone was longer than the entire review for all but one of the other Federalist papers—as "some striking remarks, which deserve particular attention":

> I shall briefly observe, that our situation invites and our interests prompt us to aim at an ascendant in the system of American affairs. The world may politically, as well as geographically, be divided into four parts, each having a distinct set of interests. Unhappily for the other three, Europe, by her arms and by her negotiations, by force and by fraud, has, in different degrees, extended her dominion over them all. Africa, Asia, and America, have successively felt her domination. The superiority she has long maintained has tempted her to plume herself as the Mistress of the World, and to consider the rest of mankind as created for her benefit. Men admired as profound philosophers have, in direct terms, attributed to her inhabitants a physical superiority, and have gravely asserted that all

animals, and with them the human species, degenerate in America—that even dogs cease to bark after having breathed awhile in our atmosphere.* Facts have too long supported these arrogant pretensions of the European: It belongs to us to vindicate the honor of the human race, and to teach that assuming brother moderation. Union will enable us to do it. Disunion will add another victim to his triumphs. Let Americans disdain to be the instruments of European greatness! Let the thirteen States, bound together in a strict and indissoluble Union, concur in erecting one great American system, superior to the control of all transatlantic force or influence, and able to dictate the terms of the connection between the old and the new world.[72]

Hamilton's prophetic passage in Federalist No. 11 relied on conventional scientific, metageographic, and geopolitical concepts. It portrayed a natural order with the world divided into four distinct parts—Europe, Asia, Africa, and the Americas—and in which geography and politics meshed. The image of dogs ceasing to bark alluded to the Dutch writer Cornelius de Pauw's elaboration on Buffon's theory, which argued that the American environment led to human degeneration. Like de Pauw and Buffon, Hamilton accepted the four-part division of the globe. But like Jefferson and Madison, Hamilton took the degeneracy argument as a rallying cry to prove the Americas' superiority to Europe. Union presented an essential first step toward winning the debate. The creation of "one great American system" would make that part of the world immune to Europe's unnatural intrusion; it would allow the United States to speak on behalf of the entire New World. The polity and the place ought be considered one.

Despite the attention the *American Magazine* gave to Hamilton's comment, it has gotten scant scholarly scrutiny, perhaps because Hamilton admitted its speculative quality that could "lead us too far into the regions of futurity . . . not proper for a newspaper discussion."[73] Yet this prescient passage begs for deeper analysis. Hamilton's assertions rang true because colonists and patriots had been thinking along similar lines for more than half a century. Predictions can also become self-fulfilling prophecies, especially when clad in the armor of immutable principles. In Federalist No. 11, readers heard what they wanted to hear and took comfort, as Hamilton did, in imagining a scientifically preordained continental future they wanted to have.

The lengthy excerpt from No. 11 in the *American Magazine* exemplifies a scientific approach that pervaded much of the larger corpus of *The Federalist*. The prevalence of scientific themes made sense, if for no other reason than James Madison was passionate about them and saw a close relationship between geography and politics. The year before he attended the Constitutional Convention and began writing essays for *The Federalist,* Madison corresponded extensively with his fellow Virginian Thomas Jefferson, then the U.S. minister in Paris. Much in Madison's letters typified the correspondence of eighteenth-century Virginia gentlemen: observations on the weather, comments on tobacco prices, insights into local politics. Given that Jefferson's *Notes on the State of Virginia* had been circulating in France, it also comes as no surprise that Madison warned Jefferson to guard against errors introduced by translators. But Madison's interest in *Notes* and the dispute of the New World went beyond the casual; he himself had become a competent and devoted amateur scientist. In 1785, the American Philosophical Society elected him a member in a class that included the British chemist Joseph Priestley and Thomas Paine.

Madison pored over Buffon's work during the spring of 1786. He then offered to send Jefferson skins of "some of our animal curiosities," stuffed if so desired. Madison lamented that the "female opossum with 7 young ones, which I intended to have reared for the purpose partly of experiments myself and partly of being able to forward some of them to you . . . all died." He wrote 1,000 words describing the exterior appearance and internal anatomy of a weasel—"female and came into my hands dead"—all to bolster Jefferson's corrective to Buffonian formulations. Opossums and dead weasels made perfect ammunition in that debate. So, too, did a comparison of Native Americans and native Siberians. In March 1787, Madison wrote to George Washington, having remembered the general mentioning that the empress of Russia wanted to compare the languages of the two peoples. Madison had come on a "sample of the Cherokee & Chactaw dialects" that he thought might prove useful. Then, without missing a beat, he mentioned that preparations for the Constitutional Convention, just two months away, had been going smoothly.[74]

Madison seems to have engaged Buffon's work as much as those of any other Enlightenment figure in the year before the drafting of the Constitution, and the same metageographical assumptions that grounded Madison's scientific interests colored his political theorizing. Like Jefferson, he slipped seamlessly between scientific and political pursuits, for he and his compatriots applied similar methodologies toward understanding politics and the natural world. The construction of a political system, like science, they believed, should rest on an empirical foundation.[75] The evidence and controlled observations for politics lay in the laboratory of the past. Madison, Hamilton, and Jay looked to history for examples from which they might draw larger, universal principles, just as they looked at weasels and opossums to understand the fundamental differences between the Americas and other parts of the world. Human beings had inviolable characteristics that shaped how they behaved under different systems, and both, in turn, operated under the influence of their natural environment. Government structures needed to be commensurate with their natural environment. Not surprisingly, *The Federalist* often presented its arguments with language and metaphors from science—maybe not always good science or sophisticated science, but science nonetheless. Such a rhetorical strategy made sense to those who believed in a "parallelism between the world of nature and the world of human existence."[76]

"The science of politics, like most other sciences," argued Hamilton in Federalist No. 9, "has received great improvement." Rattling off "discoveries" made since "the ancients" that improved "popular systems of government," he cited institutions that Americans had become accustomed to, such as legislative checks and balances and elected representation. Human progress, he believed, had brought Americans to the possible realization of the next great advance in the science of political systems: "the ENLARGEMENT of the ORBIT within which such systems are to revolve."[77] Madison spoke a similar language of scientific discovery in Federalist No. 14, treating parts of the world as revealers of knowledge. He paid homage to Europe for founding "the great principle of representation," in accordance with the natural law of popular sovereignty. Though "Europe has the merit of discovering this great mechanical power in government, by the simple agency of which the will of the largest political body may be concentered, and its force directed to any object which the public good requires, America can claim the merit of making the discovery the basis of unmixed and extensive republics."[78]

The Americas would—even must—discover the extensive republic, partially because they occupied a natural environment well suited for it. The laboratory of the past confirmed this by highlighting the benefits held by an insular nation. Simply put, the United States should look to the success of Great Britain to avoid the pitfalls of life on the European continent. Though Revolutionary rhetoric had pitted the great continent of North America against the "island" of Britain, *The Federalist* found much to admire in Britain's "insular situation." As Jay explained in No. 5, "common sense" dictated "that the people of such an island should be but one nation, yet we find that they were for ages divided into three, and that those three were almost constantly embroiled in quarrels and wars with one another." North America, should it split into multiple nations, would follow a similar

Seizing Nature's Advantages (293

fate. It would resemble the Britain of yore or contemporary Europe, with "neighboring [American] nations, acting under the impulse of opposite interests and unfriendly passions." Various North American nations would pose greater threats to one another than they would ever face from any distant European power.[79]

In the next essay, Hamilton amplified Jay's logic, deducing "from long observation of the progress of society . . . a sort of axiom in politics, that vicinity or nearness of situation, constitutes nations' natural enemies." Then, in Federalist No. 8, he argued that North America, like Britain, had a "peculiar felicity of situation," bestowed by nature but dependent on political union. The United States, like Britain, would have minimal need for a standing army at home, should the continent unite, but multiple standing armies would be the inevitable consequence of the union's dissolution into numerous nations, just as armies had proliferated in Europe.[80] Madison concurred; the distance of the United States from other nations enabled it, like Great Britain, to rely on "maritime resources" for defense instead of a standing army. Dissolution of the union would mean that, "instead of deriving from our situation the precious advantage which Great Britain has derived from hers, the face of America will be but a copy of that of the continent of Europe," with liberties falling prey to "standing armies and perpetual taxes." Worse, the United States would face not only internal rivalries and animosities but also attention from "another quarter of the globe" when Europeans sought to capitalize on a divided continent. But if the continent could stay united, its geography would reduce the need for a standing army and the taxes to support it. The national government could be inconspicuous and light, mollifying, one hoped, the Anti-Federalists who feared onerous, distant, centralized power but also largely conceded that responsibility for defense belonged to the congress. Geography and security went hand in hand, a theme British North Americans had been familiar with since at least the eve of the Seven Years' War.[81]

Surrounding oceans provided only one "advantage which nature holds us," as insularity took other forms familiar to readers of *The Federalist*. The continent constituted a world unto itself by virtue of its ability to produce a wide array of products. "Providence," Jay wrote, "has in a particular manner blessed it with a variety of soils and productions." Hamilton offered a practical example of how the coordination of diverse production capabilities could further heighten the nation's insularity. Different parts of the country, he argued, "possess each some peculiar advantage" to contribute to a national navy's stores. The southern states grew the best timber; the middle states produced the best iron; and the "seamen must chiefly be drawn from the Northern hive." Hamilton rendered the diversity of North America's climates complementary. Together they could create a store of products to rival the navy of that other insular maritime power, Great Britain. The continent comprised an array of latitudes, and a strong navy needed men or materiel from them all. A strong navy thus bore analogy to the natural system North Americans inhabited; in a navy's creation, states in the different climates would become politically dependent on one another, bound together just like the geographic features of the continent itself.[82]

The Federalist built on the tradition of foreseeing geopolitical and commercial cohesiveness in North America. Indeed, the essays include passages that could have been written by Thomas Pownall at the end of the Seven Years' War, when he urged imperial administrators to organize a commercial empire in harmony with natural geographic systems. Jay first introduced the theme, expressing "pleasure" that "independent America was not composed of detached and distant territories." Instead, "one connected, fertile, wide-spreading country" sat amid "navigable waters [that] form a kind of chain round its borders, as if to bind it together." Through North America flowed "the most noble rivers in the world, running at convenient distances," usable as "highways for the easy communication of friendly aids and the mutual transportation and exchange of their various commodities." Hamilton followed suit, writing of "the number of rivers with which they [the states] are intersected, and of bays that wash their shores; the facility of communication in every direction." And Madison weighed in, with a slight twist, by emphasizing the relative ease of "new improvements" that would build on a superior natural infrastructure. The United States could improve communication between west and east, thanks to "those numerous canals with which the beneficence of nature has intersected our country, and which art finds it so little difficult to connect and complete." Only an "unnatural voice" would suggest that Americans could not have a strong continental union, given the belief that rivers ran through the continent like arteries through a human body.[83]

In refuting Anti-Federalist arguments inspired by Montesquieu, *The Federalist* did not argue that republics could be extended indefinitely. The United States needed a "well-constructed" union. For Madison, "well-constructed" meant, only in part, the proper distribution of sovereign powers between state and national governments. The extent of a "practicable sphere" for Madison and his Federalist cohort also had an inherent relationship to geographical particulars. Governments must reflect geographical knowledge, and *The Federalist* aimed to convince readers that such was the case under the proposed Constitution. Hamilton, Jay, and Madison amplified what appeared in other newspapers, and they continued the intellectual tradition of looking at the world through the filter of continental taxonomies and thinking seriously about the relationship between politics and geography. Scientifically and geopolitically, the North American continent—even though its exact shape remained slippery and elusive—constituted a natural system, and the U.S. government should somehow parallel it. It was a message contemporaries would not have missed in the great ratification debate.[84]

REPRESENTING A CONTINENT

Federalists lacked a monopoly on continental visions for the United States. Instead, most Anti-Federalists, too, celebrated the geographic isolation of the United States and viewed the world through the same metageographical lens as their opponents.[85] The playwright Mercy Otis Warren, for example, couched her Anti-Federalism in a global context: "The banners of freedom were erected in the wilds of America" with the "hope they would continue for ages to illumine a quarter of the globe, by nature kindly separated from the proud monarchies of Europe, and the infernal darkness of Asiatic slavery."[86] Like most Anti-Federalists, save those with strong populist leanings, Warren supported an expansive union; she just questioned the distribution of power in the Constitution.[87]

Anti-Federalists saw pitfalls particularly in the Constitution's representational scheme, which veered from the cherished—if somewhat unexamined—principle of actual representation. In the run-up to the Revolution, many pamphleteers had argued that elected officials needed an intimacy and familiarity with their constituents that was incompatible with distant rule or an expansive polity. The Constitution, in contrast, proposed a bicameral national legislature without popular election of senators and with a House of Representatives whose members would spring from elections in large districts. The Constitution specified that each house district have a minimum of 30,000 constituents, resulting initially in only sixty-five representatives.

Representational units defined by head count also ran counter to traditional units defined by space, such as the town, county, or parish. Indeed, no colony before the Revolution had systematically based representation on population.[88] Apportionment based on population presumed individuals equal—even if they came from vastly different parts of a large state—and their interests interchangeable instead of reflecting local circumstances. It rejected longstanding assumptions that communal sentiment grew out of physical proximity. Ignoring spatial considerations, critics argued, would make it impossible to maintain any semblance of actual representation, wherein representatives had an intimate relationship with, and similar interests to, their constituents.

Federalists found arrows in their continental quiver to address such concerns over representation, just as they had found ways to counter Buffon's theories. What seemed on the surface to Anti-Federalists an abandonment of spatial considerations in determining representation was only partially such. True, under the Constitution apportionment in the House would rely on head count rather than geographic entities such as towns, counties, or parishes. But the impetus for demographically based representation gained momentum from the ongoing embrace of what seemed a more natural and rational spatial identity. Demographic representation reflected a shift in priority, from locally oriented to metageographical conceptions of space.

Demographic representation at the national level *was* spatial representation if those represented—"the people"—thought of themselves collectively as the continent, as the true "Americans." Notions of the United States as a continental nation, and of its inhabitants as a continental people, had helped prompt a reexamination of the principles of political representation. They did so, ironically, even though U.S. independence grew partially out of a rejection of virtual representation and a vehement denial that colonists could be represented in Parliament because of distance. During the ratification era, the Constitution's backers tried to make the document's virtual representation more palatable by wrapping it in the Revolution's metageographical legacy. They offered repeated reminders that "we the people" were continental, a position Anti-Federalists found difficult to refute.

WELL before delegates convened in Philadelphia, presumptions of American grandeur led men of a variety of political stripes to propose governments that could better encompass the continent as a whole, that could provide representation to those in its farthest reaches. Consider three examples. The first came from Thomas Paine, whose *Common Sense* lambasted the British government—"a government which cannot preserve the peace is no government at all"—and called for a republican Continental Congress with "at least 390" representatives who would, in turn, elect from among themselves a president for each session. They would be bound by a "Continental Charter," for "our strength is continental, not provincial," Paine explained.[89]

Paine continued to hammer at the need for a strong continental government in *The American Crisis*. Following the defeat of Cornwallis at Yorktown, and after the ratification of the Articles of Confederation, he proclaimed that "the union of America is the foundation-stone of her independence; the rock on which it is built." Such a union needed to move efficiently: "When a multitude extended, or rather scattered, over a continent in the manner we were, mutually agree to form one common centre whereon the whole shall move to accomplish a particular purpose, all parts must act together and alike." To do so, the federal government needed supremacy: "Each state is to the United States what each individual is to the state he lives in." Peace only heightened his sense of urgency, leading him, in 1783, to proclaim, "Our citizenship in the United States is our national character. Our citizenship in any particular state is only our local distinction. By the latter we are known at home, by the former to the world. Our great title is Americans—our inferior one varies with the place."[90]

At the same time Paine wrote *The American Crisis*, Alexander Hamilton, by now a wealthy lawyer with aristocratic sympathies, produced "The Continentalist," a series of four essays in the *New-York Packet* in July and August 1781. Echoing Paine's call for unity—but not his relatively populist vision of a republican government—Hamilton warned that the United States faced dangers even in peace. "Remote as we are from Europe, in a little time, we should fancy ourselves out of the reach of attempts from abroad," he wrote. Without a strong federal government, states might test their "strength at home." The United States would limp toward civil war, for "political societies, in close neighbourhood, must either be strongly united under one government, or there will infallibly exist emulations and quarrels." Hamilton already saw this tendency emerging when states failed to comply with congressional demands to pay for the war. He hoped to convince readers that "too much [centralized] power leads to despotism, too little leads to anarchy, and both eventually to the ruin of the people."[91] Hamilton shared Paine's belief that the United States constituted a people, not just a collection of states.

A wealthy western agrarian, Herman Husband, generally opposed most of Hamilton's political leanings and thought the best way to preserve "the people" was to strengthen the voices of ordinary men. Husband had served as chief spokesman of the North Carolina Regulator Movement, which sought to "regulate" officials' conduct in that colony's backcountry in the late 1760s and early 1770s, a forerunner of sorts to Shays's Rebellion. He fled the colony after the governor placed a reward on his head. Then he resettled in western Pennsylvania, and, during the Revolution, served a year in that state's new and remarkably democratic State Assembly. After he retired, growing conservatism in that state during peace prompted him to formulate a new structure of government for the state and the nation, one he believed was superior to the Constitution because it adhered to principles of actual representation.[92]

His plan for a continental government, though unique, resembled Paine's more than Hamilton's in its goal to make representatives responsive to popular will. Husband held a millenarian view of the North American continent's place in history and a desire to empower its small freehold farmers and protect them from slaveholders, merchants, lawyers, land speculators, and others he deemed unproductive members of society. He concluded that truly representative government over such an expanse required several layers to create small legislative districts. These layers should reflect the proportions of the human body. Small townships, analogous to the bones in the hand or foot, would form the smallest election districts so that constituents could have intimate familiarity with their representatives. Then, representatives from the townships would elect one of their own to serve at the next representative level above the township, analogous to a hand or foot. Such successive and incremental levels of representation would eventually constitute the body as a whole, a confederation of four regional empires under the oversight of a supreme council, comprising twenty-four individuals, six elected by each region.[93]

On the Constitution's ratification, Husband immediately called for modification of its representational scheme. Among his rationales was the need to avert the cumbersome growth of Congress as the nation expanded. He wrote:

> The territory, now possessed by our United States, is capable of containing thirty states within the mountains, besides the thirteen or sixteen on the out-side; this territory consisting of forty or fifty states, will produce two or three hundred members of Congress; and this territory is but about one quarter of the whole continent—the whole of which will from necessity come into the union to preserve peace. Even if these other three quarters are settled under different powers of Europe—yet if we wisely lay this our foundation on these universal principles of peace and equity, and on a plan large enough to be capable of receiving them—we shall thereby make it in their interest, and consequently induce them to join us.

Spreading the existing representational system over the entire continent, Husband argued, would result in a congress with "one thousand members," far too large to legislate effectively.[94] To demonstrate how his proposed system could accommodate a continental expanse with successive layers of representatives that mimicked the proportions of the human body, he presented a diagram with legislative districts stretching far into Spanish and British territories (fig. 37).

As his authoritative biography notes, Husband's writings of the 1780s and 1790s lacked a wide readership, and no prominent Federalist felt the need to respond directly to him in print. Even his neighbors ignored him.[95] His importance here, however, is not as an individual author but as part of a wide-ranging trend to experiment with theories of government and representation in ways that incorporated large expanses. Although Husband may have disagreed with Paine or found Hamilton's views completely anathema, he shared with these men a vision of a continental union. All three, and others, sought to reconcile their continental presumptions with their views on popular sovereignty.

AT the Constitutional Convention, most delegates shared such metageographical presumptions and a desire to somehow "extend the sphere." That this desire grew out of a sense that North America was a discrete entity and that the United States was best suited to rule it should not be overstated. Beyond such considerations, delegates also wanted to enhance the quality of representatives at the national level and ensure that it was these representatives, not the state assemblies, who had sovereignty over fiscal and military matters. Many delegates believed the locally oriented state assemblies deficient, as too democratic and susceptible to pressures for popular measures such as debtor relief.[96] In short, delegates wanted to avoid schemes such as Husband's, and the document they produced ensured that he and many others with similar leanings would become Anti-Federalists.

Elections in large legislative districts, it was widely realized, favored the well known and the well-to-do. Delegates found this bias appealing, for they blamed much of the disarray of the postwar years, such as Shays's Rebellion, on an excess of democracy, on state assemblies that were overly responsive to the interests of masses of farmers upset over monetary policy and taxes. Madison, for example, complained that a "spirit of locality" endangered "the aggregate interests of the community." Delegates thus sanctioned a degree of virtual representation to ensure that the government's most important powers remained in the hands of an elite few, those with property and thus thought best able to govern in the national interest. The greater empowerment of propertied elites would simply enable those most naturally suited to rule to do so. Property signified ability and character traits that translated into public virtue: The affluent had the leisure time necessary for public office and, because they had so much property, a healthy devotion to property rights.[97]

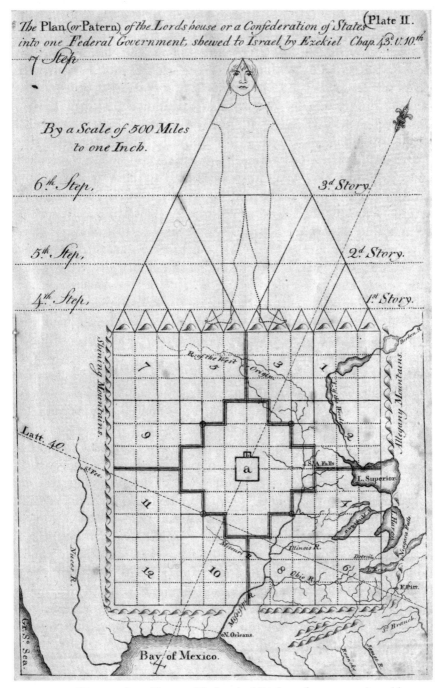

The Plan (or Patern) of the Lords house or a Confederation of States (Plate II.) into one Federal Government, shewed to Israel by Ezekiel Chap. 43. v. 10.ᵗʰ

7 Step

By a Scale of 500 Miles to one Inch.

6ᵗʰ Step,

3ᵈ Story.

5ᵗʰ Step,

2ᵈ Story.

4ᵗʰ Step,

1ˢᵗ Story.

FIGURE 37. Diagram from Herman Husband, *A Dialogue between an Assembly-man and a Convention-man* (1790). Historical Society of Pennsylvania

Partisans on both sides of the debate also agreed that enlarging the polity and its legislative districts would deprive grassroots political movements—especially those seeking debt or tax relief—of unity and power. At the same time, most expected that members of select groups—comprising individuals whom the delegates at the Constitutional Conventions happened to consider the best suited to rule, such as urban merchants, respected military officers, and bondholders—would do better at communicating among themselves and exerting pressure on public officials than the "lower sorts."

Delegates to the Constitutional Convention had evidence practically under their noses that some groups were more capable of organizing on a national scale than others. The convention met just a week after the Society of the Cincinnati had convened down the street. Since 1783, the society had been lobbying the congress and the states for measures that would give them at least some of the deferred pay the congress had promised during the Revolution. Meanwhile, insurgents in Shays's Rebellion shared grievances with men in other states, yet their agrarian resistance movements remained local affairs. Both sides in the debate over the Constitution agreed that larger legislative districts tended to elect men more capable of organizing among themselves, but the document's authors welcomed them as an opportunity to enhance the power of the proper rulers, such as the propertied or Cincinnati members, while critics bemoaned them as favoring aristocratic tendencies.[98]

Although the quest of Constitutional Convention delegates to improve the quality of representation demonstrates that they had aims beyond simply constructing a state suited to North America's nature, the two goals were complementary. Delegates believed that North America constituted a landmass best ruled by one power, and increasing the size of the polity and its legislative districts conveniently provided one of the most subtle, rhetorically plausible, and palatable ways for convention delegates and Federalist writers to favor the few. Large legislative districts thus enhanced ratification's chances more than other potential means of favoring elites, such as election of representatives by state assemblies instead of through popular elections or granting the congress a veto over state legislatures.[99] Anti-Federalists might find sympathetic ears when they objected that expanding the sphere would filter ordinary people out of the House of Representatives, but they had trouble refuting the position that the continent's people needed a collective voice or offering an alternative scheme that acknowledged the nation's continental aspects.

Much of the Anti-Federalist response to the Constitution predictably cast the Constitution as a betrayal of actual representation and, at times, of the American Revolution itself. Melancton Smith of New York, for example, argued that national legislatures ought to "resemble those they represent. They should be a true picture of the people, possess a knowledge of their circumstances and their wants, sympathize in all their distresses, and be disposed to seek their true interests." Beyond the Society of the Cincinnati, propertied elites, or bondholding merchants, the House ought to include ordinary farmers and artisans. Rawlins Lowndes of South Carolina argued that the Constitution provided representation "merely virtual, similar to what we were allowed in England." Britain had explained to colonists that they "were represented in Parliament: and this would, in the event, prove just such another."[100]

In response, Federalists sometimes conceded that the Constitution departed from strict notions of actual representation. Hamilton wrote, in Federalist No. 35, "The idea of an actual representation of all classes of the people by persons of each class is altogether visionary. Unless it were expressly provided in the Constitution that each different occupation should send one or more members [to the legislature], the thing would never take place in practice."[101] Hamilton argued for elite rule by claiming that elites would serve the interests of their constituents. Merchants could be counted on to represent the interests of "mechanics and manufacturers," for they shared a commercial interest that bound their different occupations together. Similarly, just because the "wealthiest landlord" belonged to a different class than the "poorest tenant," the two, by virtue of their ties to the land, shared a "common interest [that] may always be reckoned upon as the surest bond of sympathy." Merchants and wealthy landlords, as part of the natural aristocracy, also led a more cosmopolitan life and had more leisure time than tenants and mechanics, making them better suited to represent everyone's true interest.[102]

Hamilton and other Federalists could acknowledge that the Constitution departed from traditional notions of representation without killing their movement, partially because their Anti-Federalist opponents were in a similarly awkward position, caught on the horns of a dilemma between granting a continental people a truly collective voice in government and adhering to localist notions of actual representation. To deny that a representational scheme could incorporate the entire nation was, in a sense, to deny a potent facet of popular sovereignty, to reject the will of a "people" defined by nature or geography, and, in turn, to defend the powers of states, which were the products of human machinations and the arbitrariness of the old British imperial order.[103]

DELEGATES at the convention found their solution to the deficiencies in state governments in a national government whose authority rested on the will of a people—not the will of the people of the states, but the will of an American people. To place much of the states' sovereignty in the hands of such a people, they had to remind opponents that such a people indeed existed.[104] They had to tap into their readers' and listeners' metageographical habits of the mind. There they found a well of inspiration to undermine the spatial assumptions central to Montesquieu's theory of a small republic and, thus, the sovereignty of states.

Some of the first convincing had to occur among the delegates themselves. Gouverneur Morris of Pennsylvania reminded delegates that colonies "were originally nothing more than colonial corporations." States, in turn, had no natural basis as discrete entities, and thus they did not deserve representation as discrete communities. Alexander Hamilton summarized the views of many at the convention when he asserted that states "are a collection of individual men[.] Which ought we to respect, the rights of the people composing them, or of the artificial beings resulting from the composition[?]" In making the argument that government served the people, not states, delegates portrayed states as artifices of British rule, corporations created under British law, not natural communities.[105]

Outside the convention, similar sentiments appeared in periodicals and newspapers with Federalist leanings. Noah Webster countered Anti-Federalists' fears by claiming that the proposed congress would be one with the people; it would have "the *same interest* as the people—they are a *part* of the people—their interest is *inseparable* from that of the people; and this union of interest will eternally remain, while the right of election shall continue in the people."[106] The Federalist Papers chimed in as well, presenting U.S. citizens as much a single, united people as the continent was a unified system. Union would seem inevitable with Madison's Americans, "knit together as they are by so many cords of affection." John Jay ignored the polyglot nature of society and the internal divisions that had prompted the push for the Constitution in the first place. Instead, the people, as he imagined it, and the continent, as he presumed it, presented the perfect marriage: "Providence has been pleased to give this one connected country to one united people." Jay took great comfort in knowing that "this country and this people seem to have been made for each other, and it appears as if it was the design of Providence that an inheritance so proper and convenient for a band of brethren, united to each other by the strongest ties should never be split into a number of unsocial, jealous, and alien sovereignties."[107]

Periodicals reprinted patriotic essays from the Revolution that highlighted, even if it was largely imaginary, the unity of the people and the land they inhabited. The *American Magazine* returned to Timothy Dwight's commencement oration at Yale in 1776, wherein he told graduates to expect their future stage to extend from the Atlantic to the Pacific, from Darien to the Arctic. Providence had created a unique situation where the land and its people mirrored each other in their unity. "That a vast continent, containing near three thousand millions of acres of valuable land, should be inhabited by a people, in all respects one, is indeed a novelty on earth," Dwight said. Americans had "the same manners, the same interest, the same language." They had been "united in sentiments, customs, and language" and constituted a single people. Men should not think of themselves as "members of a small neighbourhood, town or colony only, but as being concerned in laying the foundations of American greatness."[108] It was a fitting, nostalgic reminder of the Revolution's legacy from a publisher seeking to extend the sphere in 1787.

It was also a crass appeal to wartime patriotism. Failure to strengthen the union would betray the unity and sacrifices of those who had shed blood; it would allow the Revolution's dead to have fallen in vain in a war for a continent. Americans forged their unity "fighting side by side throughout a long and bloody war." Challenges to the proposed Constitution thus became "poison," for "the kindred blood which flows in the veins of American citizens, the mingled blood which they have shed in defense of their sacred rights, consecrate their Union."[109] To squander the spoils by failing to act, by failing to render the continent a unified polity and thus preventing it from realizing its potential grandeur reeked of ingratitude and a betrayal of the Revolution's legacy.

Memory of past sacrifice thus became a call to present action: "Who, after all that has been done and suffered . . . , would basely relinquish and leave unfinished the illustrious task of rearing an empire, which, from its situation and circumstances, must surpass all that have ever existed, in magnitude, felicity, and duration?" A reprint of David Humphrey's "Address to the Armies of the States of America" of 1782 touted soldiers for having helped spread blessings to "southern oceans and northern pole." In one poem, "Curtius" pronounced it time to "render our situation worthy the ashes of our slaughtered brethren." The Continental Army may have dissolved, but America still owed its soldiers a debt. Anti-Federalists became "unworthy sons" who did not live up even to the "manlier blustrings of more daring Shays." One member of Virginia's ratification convention proclaimed, in 1775, that "it was not a Virginian, Carolinian or Pennsylvanian, but the glorious name of an American that extended from one end of the continent to the other." And since it took that spirit to "triumph over our enemies," he asked, "does not our existence as a nation depend on our Union?"[110]

Only slightly less explicit than these crass appeals to the memory of the dead were the eulogies and other commemorations celebrating military heroes. In 1787, a short newspaper announcement described the inscription that was to appear on the long-awaited monument in St. Paul's Church, in New York, "to transmit to posterity a grateful remembrance of the patriotism, conduct, enterprize, and perseverance" shown by Richard Montgomery in the attack on Quebec. Magazines published lengthy eulogies celebrating men from Wolfe and Montgomery to Nathanael Greene, who had died that year. It would have been difficult for newspaper and periodical readers to miss these solemn remembrances or the political message they carried. They assured that it was up to America's "sons to secure" what these great men had delivered.[111] These martyrs won wars to control the fate of the continent; these wars offered proof that Americans could act as a people.

FEDERALISTS' appeals to the unity of Americans carried great irony. After all, the movement for political reform grew out of concern that division threatened to destroy the nation. The imagination of a unified people echoed the belief in the army of aspiration; both were products of wishful thinking. They were also expedient—and in some cases, disingenuous—means to an end. James Madison really did not want a unified people. As he explained in a letter to Jefferson dated October 24, 1787, "Divide et impera, the reprobated axiom of tyranny, is under certain qualifications, the only policy, by which a republic can be administered on just principles."[112]

Divide and rule: how far things had come. In 1776, Madison began his first stint as a public servant after his election to the Virginia Provincial Convention, the colony's legislature in the absence of royal government. After independence, Madison served in the state legislature, entering that assembly just as one of its founding patricians, Richard Bland, died. Bland had served as one of Virginia's delegates to the Continental Congress. He had acquired a reputation as a vocal patriot during the Stamp Act crisis, when he wrote *An Inquiry into the Rights of the British Colonies* (1766). Jefferson called Bland "the most learned and logical man of those who took a prominent lead in public affairs." When Bland criticized imperial officials for invoking the doctrine of virtual representation, he also accused them of trying to foster disunion among the colonies, even though they had a natural bond as "Bodies in Contact." "*Divide et impera* is your Maxim," he lashed out at the anonymous author of a royalist tract who defended virtual representation.[113]

Twenty-one years later, Madison's vision in Federalist No. 10 of how an extended republic would multiply factions and enable the worthy to rule was not clear to many. But veterans in the mold of Ebenezer MacIntosh, Joseph Plumb Martin, Daniel Shays, and the thousands of poor men who had filled the ranks of the Continental Army and suffered disproportionately in defense of Bland's principles—not to mention slaves, camp followers, and other ordinary men and women—would essentially find their new rulers callously, or perhaps just obliviously, embracing that of which British officials had earlier been accused. Metageographical understandings —notions of North America's insularity and cohesiveness and a commensurately unified people—had helped grease the wheels for this change that had been unfathomable just a decade earlier. Madison and the Federalists had defended their vision of the continent against deeply held notions about political representation and Montequieuian theory, just as Jefferson and other naturalists had defended the continent's nature against Buffonian formulations. Virtual representation became the law of an extended republic with the ratification of the Constitution in the summer of 1788.

THE INDIAN'S DEMISE, COLUMBIA'S RISE, AND WASHINGTON'S INAUGURATION

Backcountry violence between Indians and whites had influenced the decision of many to seek a stronger national government. In the ratification debate, writers typically ignored the part backcountry whites often played in instigating this violence. Instead, Indian violence appeared as yet another reason to extend the power of the national government. The natural order was for Indians to recede before a wave of white settlers. A French traveler surmised that population growth in the United States meant that "the savages must either blend with the Americans, or a thousand causes will speedily annihilate that race of men." Philip Freneau explained in verse what Thomas Jefferson had earlier argued in *Notes on the State of Virginia:* "Th' unsocial Indian far retreats, / To make some other clime his own."[114] One way or another, Indians inevitably would disappear.

Accompanying expectations in the 1780s of the Indians' demise was an iconographic shift. Before the Revolution, the personification of the continents had typically depicted the Americas as an Indian woman. White Americans often embraced this image of the continent as a symbol of them-

FIGURE 38. From *America Triumphant and Britannia in Distress* (1782). Courtesy Library of Congress, Prints and Photographs Division (LC-USZC4–5275)

selves when they sought to distinguish themselves as more noble and less corrupted than their European counterparts. Yet the symbolism was problematic, because the Indian could represent savagery as much as innocence. It could suggest inferiority or dependence, something entirely counter to white Americans' self-image. The ambivalence of the Indian icon limited its political utility, especially after independence. The United States needed a symbol that distanced it both from the Indian and from its former imperial master.[115]

This change in self-representation began to appear when women depicting the Americas increasingly bore the features and dress of a Greek goddess. In *America Triumphant and Britannia in Distress* (1782), for example, a woman sits on and next to two other emblems of the American nation, a snake and the continent itself on a globe (fig. 38). The juxtaposition reinforces the personification of both the nation and the continent as one. As the caption explains, "America" is "sitting on that quarter of the globe." She, like many other female depictions of the Americas, wears neoclassical garb and holds a cone-shaped liberty cap on the end of a staff. This symbol of American nationality thus also conveyed one of the country's most cherished principles. Hence, lady "Liberty."

As important as principle, the female America represented place. "Liberty" frequently went by the name "Columbia."[116] Unlike the Indian, Columbia both distinguished the Americas from Europe and linked them back to the Old World by virtue of her allusion to the ancient Roman past and her namesake, Christopher Columbus. Though Columbia never completely replaced the Indian as an emblem of America, her popularity exploded in the aftermath of the Revolution, and the new urban political and literary magazines embraced her as a symbol of both the continent and the nation.[117]

The frontispiece for the first issue of the *Columbian Magazine* (1786) celebrated the rise of Columbia (fig. 39). It shows the goddess of wisdom, Minerva, holding a spear and resting her elbow on a pedestal with a book and a globe. Columbia approaches with her children while a farmer ploughs in the background and ships set out to sea in the distant harbor. Beneath, verse explains:

> While Commerce spreads her canvass o'er the main,
> And Agriculture ploughs the gratefull plain
> Minerva aids Columbia's rising race
> With arms to triumph and with arts to grace.

Similarly, the frontispiece for the second volume of the *Columbian Magazine* (1787) shows a thirteen-pillared Greek temple with the inscription "Sacred to Liberty Justice and Peace" (fig. 40). A young, winged boy, "Concord, fair Columbia's Son," approaches his mother with a copy of the Constitution in one hand, the other pointing to the inscription above the temple. A diminutive Father Time looms in the distance, barely noticeable against the backdrop of a magnificent sunrise.[118] The historian's muse, Clio, sits next to Columbia, recording events for posterity, the relationship between political unity under the proposed Constitution and the future grandeur of the nation and the continent clear.

Though female, like most formal iconographic representations of nations in the European tradition, Columbia offered obvious allusions to Columbus. Amid the imperial rivalries of the mid-eighteenth century, British writers had elevated other explorers, particularly Cabot, to the top of the pantheon of voyagers who had made contact with the eastern seaboard. Columbus,

Independence
the reward of
Wisdom
Fortitude
and
Perseverance

FIGURE 39. Frontispiece from the *Columbian Magazine,* vol. 1 (1786). Historical Society of Pennsylvania

FIGURE 40. Frontispiece from the *Columbian Magazine,* vol. 2 (1787). Historical Society of Pennsylvania

they often noted, had only made contact with islands in the Caribbean at the time that Cabot, sailing on behalf of England, reached the North American mainland. Some suggested that when Columbus finally reached the mainland, he reached the southern continent, not the northern, which rendered British claims to North America indisputable. Cabot provided a usable past in the midst of a contest between Britain and other European nations for North America. The conception of North America as an inherent geographic phenomenon distinct from South America also meshed with the elevation of Cabot to bolster continental claims.[119]

Resistance and independence lessened the importance of Cabot's ties to Britain, and Columbus quickly became a usable hero that allowed the United States to circumvent its British past. In late 1775, the congress purchased the first five vessels for its navy. Still Britons, the congress chose to name one of them the *Cabot,* after the "Discoverer of this northern Part of the Continent." But they designated another the *Columbus,* for the "Discover[er] of this quarter of the Globe." After independence, references to Columbus quickly proliferated in printed matter. Where the number of imprints published in the colonies and the United States remained virtually the same in the 1780s as it had been in the 1770s, the number of texts containing references to the navigator increased from thirty-eight to ninety-four, an increase of 147 percent. Meanwhile, references to Cabot increased during the same period from forty-four to sixty, only 36 percent. Equally striking, "Columbus" appeared in the title of nineteen imprints before 1800, but the first did not appear until 1783.[120]

Periodicals also participated in the escalating celebration of Columbus. In the *American Museum,* "Uncas Yanke" lambasted Americans' "ingratitude to ancestors." Though Columbus "discovered the fourth part of the world," Americans had done next to nothing to commemorate him: "There is not a single province, colony, or state that bears his name—nay, not so much as a town, creek, bay, or even a small point of land." Meanwhile, "Has not Americus Vesputius, a second hand navigator, had his name given to all the discoveries of the matchless, the unrivalled COLUMBUS?" The traditional British American hero Cabot appeared in Yanke's tirade as worthy of praise but, nevertheless, merely one of "the peers of Vesputius."[121]

Despite Uncas Yanke's lament, many in the United States had already de facto named both the continent and the nation after Columbus when they referred to Columbia, and the filiopietic floodgates had only begun to open. Beginning with a trickle in the late 1760s and growing into a torrent by the 1780s, poets, songwriters, pamphleteers, and magazine editors applied the name. Alexander Hamilton's alma mater, King's College, became Columbia in 1784. The capitals of states, that of the nation, and countless other entities would soon commemorate the explorer. "Columbia" appeared in the text of 178 imprints in the 1780s, compared with only fifteen in the 1770s, while the total number of imprints published in each decade remained nearly constant. The term appeared in 1,054 more imprints before the end of the century. Columbia quickly surpassed the Indian representation of the continent and the nation in print and song. As one historian has argued, Columbia became "the most heartily adopted and commonly used allusion of the land."[122] Indeed, the success of the name stemmed in part from its ability to reference the totality of the land in a form more easily reproduced than a map.

In celebrating Columbus, Americans celebrated themselves at least as much as the man. They posited their nation as uniquely suited to the land that he had brought into their vision. Their nation's most momentous accomplishment after independence was the ratification of the Constitution. In New York, parades celebrated the event, slightly prematurely, while the state's ratifying convention still sat at Poughkeepsie. Students from Columbia joined artisans in a parade following "Columbus in his Ancient Dress." Among them, some pewterers carried a banner that included the verse:

The Federal Plan Most Solid and Secure
Americans Their Freedom Will Endure
All Arts Shall Flourish in Columbia's Land
And All her Son's Join as One Social Band.

Meanwhile, printers paraded on a horse-drawn platform that carried a working press that churned out copies of "An Ode for the 4th of July, 1788," which they distributed to the crowd. In the ode, Columbia sat on her throne and addressed her "sons," thanks to whom "rights" now extend "o'er my vast domain."[123] The United States was home to Columbia's sons, and they now determined the continent's fate.

NINE months later, the implementation of the Constitution appeared fully realized when George Washington arrived in New York City for his inauguration as the nation's first president. Jedidiah Morse timed the publication of his *American Geography* (1789) to commemorate the event. It was a work that Washington himself eagerly anticipated, and he must have approved of what he read. Morse's United States would likely someday expand across all of North America, and he defended the potential of such an empire against Buffonian aspersions. As Morse explained, "The natural genius of Americans . . . has suffered in the descriptions of some ingenious and eloquent European writers." Yet the idea that "the race of whites transplanted from Europe" would degenerate over time had been "confuted" by Thomas Jefferson, "and by the ingenuity and abilities which he has shewn in doing it, has exhibited an instance of its falsehood."

Having refuted arguments against North America's natural potential, Morse portrayed its political prospects as though governed by the inevitability of natural laws. "It is well known that empire has been travelling from east to west. Probably her last and broadest seat will be America," he opined. Exuberantly optimistic, Morse looked forward to a "period, as not far distant, when the AMERICAN EMPIRE will comprehend millions of souls, west of the Mississippi." For Morse, "The Mississippi was never designed as the western boundary of the American empire."[124]

Morse's geography paralleled writings in contemporary travel journals and personal correspondence. Jacques Pierre Brissot de Warville saw such great ardor for expansion and population growth among Americans that he thought the Spanish inevitably would be overcome: "Men who have shook off the yoke of Great-Britain, and who are masters of the Ohio and Missisippi, cannot conceive that the insolence of a handful of Spaniards can think of shutting rivers and seas against a hundred thousand free Americans. The slightest quarrel will be sufficient to throw them into a flame; and if ever the Americans shall march towards New Orleans, it will infallibly fall into their hands." Spanish efforts to cement their control of the Mississippi by attracting American settlers there with the promise of free trade through New Orleans were futile, amounting to nothing more than "the first foundation of the conquest of Louisiana, and of the civilization of Mexico and Peru." American industry would bring under cultivation lands left unimproved by the Spanish and French for more than a century.

Looking to the future, Warville saw "this whole extent of Continent, from Canada to Quito, covered with cultivated fields, little villages, and country houses." Americans expected soon to be in direct communication with Nootka Sound (in present-day Vancouver Island), because "it is probable that this place is not far from the head waters of the Mississippi; which the Americans will soon navigate to its source." Once they had explored the Mississippi, "They shall begin to people Louisiana and the interior of New Mexico." They would also see to the opening of a navigable route from the Atlantic to the Pacific via "the lake of Nicaragua."[125]

Many thought that Canada, too, sat on the precipice of incorporation into the United States. In 1788, the U.S. consul in Bordeaux wrote to Thomas Jefferson that the new Constitution would create a geopolitical

FIGURE 41. Edward Savage, *The Washington Family* (1796), Andrew W. Mellon Collection. Image courtesy Board of Trustees, National Gallery of Art, Washington, D.C.

framework completely different from Europe's. European nations spent most of their time leery of their neighbors, and their "Cord of Industry is perpetually stretcht." In contrast, America "has not a neighbor," except Canada, "the only people on the Continent to excite attention." Even Canada, however, was a plum waiting to be picked. The United States, without serious security concerns, would grow in power. When the United States was ready, Canada "ha[d] only to intimate her intentions to work the Revolution."[126]

For his part, President Washington thought that the nation now had a government in place to realize the vision of Jedidiah Morse and these others. Nine days after giving his inaugural address, Washington wrote a letter to Alexander Hamilton's father-in-law, Philip Schuyler. As one of Washington's generals, Schuyler had led the ill-fated Quebec campaign in the winter of 1775–76 that saw the demise of Richard Montgomery. The outlook had dramatically improved since those difficult days. "The clouds which have long darkened our political hemisphere are now dispersing," wrote Washington. "America will soon feel the effects of her natural advantages."[127]

During his first year in office, Washington found time and peace enough to begin posing for a portrait of the First Family. The artist, Edward Savage, would not complete the work until 1796, for he soon found himself in London studying under Benjamin West. Once Savage finished it, however, *The Washington Family* (1796) became the principal attraction in galleries in Philadelphia and New York (both venues called the "Columbian Gallery") (fig. 41).

Aside from the likenesses of the individuals portrayed, the scene was the product of the artist's imagination. Yet it was utterly appropriate. The family had gathered around a table on which lay a map of the future capital, Washington, D.C. The former general wore his Continental Army uniform and sat between his adopted grandson and granddaughter, the inheritors of the future. His right forearm rested the boy's shoulder, while the boy's hand sat, in turn, on a partially unveiled globe. Over the president's left forearm, and occupying much of the center of the painting, was a panoramic view through a window at Mount Vernon. The Potomac River—Washington's presumed conduit to the far west—flowed in the distance, as if connecting Washington and his heirs to a quarter of the globe. The president sat regally, as if having bequeathed to future generations a continental nation.[128]

With foresight born of decades of expansionism, with confidence blessed by scientific thought, Washington had gladly embraced the nation's continental destiny that he and his fellow patriots had done much to shape. His vision was, as the history of the next century would prove, just a beginning. The United States had only just begun to seize the continent.

THE CONTINENT
FROM ON HIGH

Among the highest and easternmost of the Rocky Mountains, Pikes Peak provides a picturesque backdrop to the city of Colorado Springs, Colorado. Visitors to the mountain each year number fewer than half of those to the nation's founding documents, the Charters of Freedom in the National Archives' rotunda; still, the peak draws droves of tourists—more than any other mountain in North America. An estimated half-million people reach the summit of Pikes Peak each year by foot, automobile, or cog railway. Some race up the mountain in annual events such as the Pikes Peak Marathon or the Pikes Peak Auto Hill Climb. Others enjoy the scenery as they sit comfortably in specially designed Swiss railcars for the roundtrip that lasts just over three hours. Typical rail passengers spend thirty minutes on the summit before re-boarding for the descent. During that time, many have their picture taken in front of the sign proclaiming that they are 14,110 feet above sea level. If it is cold—as it often is, even in August—they seek shelter in the Summit House Restaurant. There they can eat one of the "world famous high altitude donuts . . . made fresh at 14,000 feet!" If they are lucky, they first happened to find a coupon on the Internet, making their donut free.[1]

The first attempt by a U.S. citizen to climb Pikes Peak occurred two centuries ago and provides a reminder of how technology has annihilated distance. In 1806, Zebulon Montgomery Pike led an expedition ostensibly charged with exploring the southwestern borders of the Louisiana Purchase. Near the site of modern-day Pueblo, Colorado, he decided to make a side trip with two other soldiers and a civilian doctor "to the high point of the blue mountain, which we conceived would be one days march." After camping there, they would ascend to the "summit of the Grand Peak." But the distances proved greater than they first appeared and the going more difficult than anticipated. It took two full days just to reach the edge of the plains, and then the men were "obliged to climb up rocks sometimes almost perpendicular." After four days, the ill-clad foursome made it through waist-deep snow to the top of a minor, 10,000 foot sub-peak. Regarding their ultimate goal, Pike concluded that, under the circumstances, "no human being could have ascended to its pinical." The four men hastily retreated down a steep gully and took "shelter under the side of a projecting rock, w[h]ere we, all four, made a meal on one partridge, and a piece of deer's ribs, the ravens had left us, being the first we had eaten in that 48 hours."[2] They could only dream about free donuts.

Pike's foray toward the summit that ultimately bore his name provided just a small bit in the barrage of geographic information coming to light in the late eighteenth and early nineteenth centuries. Pike himself had just returned from an exploration of the mysterious headwaters of the Mississippi. Mapmakers no longer had to hide the region behind cartouches inserted where the river tantalizingly veered to the northwest. Nor did they sketch the northern part of America's western coast veering sharply eastward after the voyages of Cook and Vancouver roughed out the true extent of Canada and Alaska. The forbidding nature and great extent of much of the interior West became apparent when Captain Meriwether Lewis and Lieu-tenant William Clark returned to St. Louis in the same year that Pike finished his exploration of the Mississippi's headwaters. Lewis and Clark had forged their way up the Missouri River; struggled across the Continental Divide; and traveled west along the Salmon, Snake, and Columbia rivers to the Pacific. In the process, they made clear that hopes for a transcontinental water route were dead and that the formidable presence of the Rocky Mountains could not be ignored. The mortar in the geographic assumptions of the eighteenth century eroded away. The imagined continent, once seen as the natural underpinning of a national community by virtue of its man-ageable interconnectedness, no longer existed. Yet as anybody familiar with "manifest destiny" knows, geopolitical visions for the United States re-mained as vigorous as ever in the nineteenth century. Even as the continent's true contours became known, the United States expanded relentlessly.

Zebulon Montgomery Pike's life and the cultural significance of the peak that bears his name present an emblematic bridge between the old geopoliti-cal visions based on eighteenth-century continental conceptions and their reformulation into newer expansionist mindsets as the nation came to grips with geographic reality. Pike's father had served as an officer in the Conti-nental Army and honored the nation's greatest fallen hero, Richard Mont-gomery, by naming his son after him. Born in 1779, the young Pike followed in his father's footsteps and enlisted in the army at fifteen, just as the new nation was consolidating its claims to areas east of the Mississippi after a series of protracted wars with Indians. He had served at dull outposts along the Ohio River when Major-General James Wilkinson realized the tremendous potential of Pike, who by then had taught himself French, Spanish, and some basic science. Wilkinson tapped him to carry out quintessentially Jeffersonian explorations that combined science with imperialism. Pike had reached the rank of brigadier-general when, like Richard Montgomery, he died a martyr's death. During a poorly executed invasion of Canada during the War of 1812, shrapnel from an exploding British powder keg at the Battle of York (now Toronto) ripped through his torso. Although Pike's troops captured York, the United States could not hold Canada.[3]

After the War of 1812, the United States would never again invade Canada, and North America would no longer appear the same porous, yielding, and easily managed landmass that it had earlier. Yet the continent could be reinterpreted and the United States could adapt to new understandings of it. Long after the Constitution established a political system based, in part, on geographical assumptions, the legacies of the United States' continental aspirations continued to shape the nation. Old habits of the mind that equated the continent with the nation and that saw the nation's citizens as "Americans" never died, even as new evidence changed the nation's understanding of the continent's geography. Instead, the nation underwent a transportation and communications revolution that dramatically altered its relationship to space. Railroads, steamboats, canals, electric telegraphy, improvements in printing, an explosion of newspapers, and an expansion of the postal system placed less premium on the continent's being yielding and porous.[4] The United States could still become a continental nation, despite the jagged Rockies, arid Great Basin, or absent Northwest Passage.

In a far more familiar story than that told in the preceding chapters, territorial expansion, sometimes through war, continued to mark the nation's development deep into the nineteenth century. As in the eighteenth century, the acquisition of vast tracts of territory often raised the issue of Americans' political beliefs. Debate over actual and virtual representation may have quieted with the Constitution's ratification, but expansion presented challenges to other political principles. Thomas Jefferson, for example, showed an uncanny ability to repress his own deeply held beliefs about the limited powers of the government under the Constitution. When presented the opportunity, while president, to purchase the Louisiana Territory in 1803, he remarked to Madison: "The less we say about the constitutional difficulties respecting Louisiana the better."[5] Expansion followed the acquisition, and political debates surfaced. In 1820, politicians compromised on issues of moral principle to allow the establishment of the first new state in the Louisiana Territory, Missouri, as a slave state. Twenty-five years later, crystal-clear notions of geographical predestination resurfaced as rationalizations for the dubious annexation of Texas and war with Mexico, when the journalist John L. O'Sullivan pointed to the nation's "manifest destiny to occupy and to possess the whole Continent which Providence has given us."[6]

After surviving a Civil War brought on by the inability to compromise any longer on the moral issue of slavery's expansion, the nation and the continent continued to shrink. Telegraph lines and the dramatic expansion of the nation's railroad system, including a transcontinental line, proved Madison's observation in the 1790s that "whatever facilitates a general inter-communication of sentiments & ideas among the body of people, . . . is equivalent to a contraction of the orbit within wch. the Govt. is to act."[7] Gold rushes, the brutal dispossession of Indians, promises of land, and swelling numbers of immigrants in eastern cities provided the push and pull for new western settlement. By 1893, some Americans felt that this settlement was complete, that a western frontier no longer existed. The historian Frederick Jackson Turner posited "the closing of a great historic movement" and worried about how American institutions would develop without having "to adapt themselves to the changes of an expanding people—to the changes involved in crossing a continent."[8]

IN the same year that Turner first publicly lamented the closing of the frontier, a professor of English at Wellesley College, Katharine Lee Bates, traveled by train from Massachusetts to Colorado Springs to teach the summer term at Colorado College. At the end of the session, she and "strangers celebrated" with "a merry expedition to the top of Pike's Peak." Ascents of the peak were not as simple as they are today, but they had become routine. Horses and mules pulled wagons that carried Bates's party to the summit. Once there, two in her group suffered from the severe light-headedness and faintness of breath that commonly afflict those who are poorly acclimated to high altitude. Almost as soon as they had arrived at the summit, she later explained, "We were bundled into the wagons again and started on our downward plunge so speedily that our sojourn on the peak remains in memory hardly more than one ecstatic gaze."[9]

Bates translated her ecstasy into poetry. Inspired by sites on her journey west and the views from atop Pikes Peak, she wrote "America the Beautiful." Two years later, a weekly newspaper, *The Congregationalist*, published the poem to commemorate the Fourth of July. Soon, the verse became a song so popular and so inspiring that many thought it should be exalted to the status of national hymn or, because it paid homage to the nation's physical grandeur and beauty and lacked martial overtones, that it should replace the "Star Spangled Banner" as the national anthem.

It would be ironic if a song inspired by a trip up Pikes Peak ever acquired such status. Had eighteenth-century British colonists known of the ruggedness of the peak's range, of the aridity of the intermountain west, or of the geographic contours of North America in general, they would have had to reexamine their presumptions. North America, they would have realized, was not a discrete, manageable, and inherently unified entity, and history might have followed an entirely different path. But, if we are going to revere the parchments under the rotunda as our Charters of Freedom, then maybe we should pay equal homage to something that celebrates the nation's nature.

NOTES

ABBREVIATIONS

AHR   *American Historical Review*

DHFR   Mary A. Giunta et al., eds., *The Emerging Nation: A Documentary History of the Foreign Relations of the United States under the Articles of Confederation,* 3 vols. (Washington, D.C.: National Historical Publications and Records Commission, 1996).

DHRC   John P. Kaminski and Gaspare J. Saladino, eds., *The Documentary History of the Ratification of the Constitution,* 22 vols. (Madison: State Historical Society of Wisconsin, 1976–).

JAH   *Journal of American History*

JCC   *Journals of the Continental Congress, 1774–1789,* ed. Worthington C. Ford et al., 34 vols. (Washington, D.C., 1904–37).

LDC   Paul H. Smith, et al., eds., *Letters of Delegates to Congress, 1774–1789,* 25 vols. (Washington, D.C.: Library of Congress, 1976–2000).

PBF   Leonard W. Labaree et al., eds., *The Papers of Benjamin Franklin,* 37 vols. (New Haven, Conn.: Yale University Press, 1959–).

PGWC   W. W. Abbot et al., eds., *The Papers of George Washington: Colonial Series,* 6 vols. (Charlottesville: University Press of Virginia, 1983–95).

PGWCF   W. W. Abbot et al., eds., *The Papers of George Washington: Confederation Series,* 6 vols. (Charlottesville: University Press of Virginia, 1992–97).

PGWR   W. W. Abbot et al., eds., *The Papers of George Washington: Revolutionary War Series,* 12 vols. (Charlottesville: University Press of Virginia, 1985–).

PTJ   Julian P. Boyd et al., eds., *The Papers of Thomas Jefferson,* 26 vols. (Princeton, N.J.: Princeton University Press, 1950–).

WGW   John C. Fitzpatrick, ed., *The Writings of George Washington from the Original Manuscript Sources, 1745–1799,* 39 vols. (Washington: U.S. Government Printing Office, 1931–44).

WMQ   *William and Mary Quarterly,* 3rd ser.

WTP   Philip S. Foner, *The Complete Writings of Thomas Paine,* 2 vols. (New York: Citadel Press, 1945).

INTRODUCTION

1 Pauline Maier, *American Scripture: Making the Declaration of Independence* (New York: Knopf, 1997), ix–xv.

2 Thomas Paine, *Common Sense* [1776], in *WTP,* 1:24.

3 I borrow the phrase from David Lowenthal and Martyn J. Bowden, *Geographies of*

the Mind: Essays in Historical Geosophy in Honor of John Kirtland Wright (New York: Oxford University Press, 1976).

4 My phrasing here is influenced by Rogers Brubaker, *Nationalism Reframed: Nationhood and the National Question in the New Europe* (Cambridge: Cambridge University Press, 1996), 8.

5 On the imagination of islands, see John Gillis, *Islands of the Mind: How the Human Imagination Created the Atlantic World* (New York: Palgrave Macmillan, 2004).

6 Martin W. Lewis and Kären E. Wigen, *The Myth of Continents: A Critique of Metageography* (Berkeley: University of California Press, 1997), 2.

7 Colin G. Calloway, *The Scratch of a Pen: 1763 and the Transformation of North America* (New York: Oxford University Press, 2006), 20; J. H. Elliott, *Empires of the Atlantic World: Britain and Spain in America, 1492–1830* (New Haven, Conn.: Yale University Press, 2006), map 2; Richard D. Brown, *Knowledge Is Power: The Diffusion of Information in Early America, 1700–1865* (New York: Oxford University Press, 1989), 13; Richard R. John, *Spreading the News: The American Postal System from Franklin to Morse* (Cambridge, Mass.: Harvard University Press, 1995), 26; Trish Loughran, *The Republic in Print: Print Culture in the Age of U.S. Nation Building, 1770–1870* (New York: Columbia University Press, 2007).

8 Anthony Pagden, *Lords of All the World: Ideologies of Empire in Spain, Britain, and France, c. 1500–c. 1800* (New Haven, Conn.: Yale University Press, 1995); Thomas Bender, *A Nation among Nations: America's Place in World History* (New York: Hill and Wang, 2006), 44, 309n115.

9 Samuel Sewall, *Phaenomena quaedam Apocalyptica* (Boston, 1697), 2. The Virginia quotation is from Albert Bushnell Hart, ed., *American History Told by Contemporaries* (New York, 1898), 243.

10 Wayne Bodle, "The Fabricated Region: On the Insufficiency of 'Colonies' for Understanding American Colonial History," *Early American Studies* 1 (2003): 1–27.

11 Michael Zuckerman, "Regionalism," in *A Companion to Colonial America*, ed. Daniel Vickers (Malden, Mass: Blackwell, 2003), 311–33, quotation from 311.

12 Benedict Anderson, *Imagined Communities: Reflections on the Origin and Spread of Nationalism*, rev. ed. (London: Verso, 1991), 6–7, 36–46, 63–64. On fragmentation, see Loughran, *Republic in Print*. The literature on nationalism is vast. Most works on early American nationalism focus on the period of the early republic. Among these, I have found David Waldstreicher, *In the Midst of Perpetual Fetes: The Making of American Nationalism, 1775–1820* (Chapel Hill: University of North Carolina Press, 1997), most useful. Among works focusing on the period before the Constitution, I have found the following the most instructive: John M. Murrin, "A Roof without Walls: The Dilemma of American National Identity," in *Beyond Confederation: Origins of the Constitution and American National Identity,*

ed. Richard R. Beeman, Stephen Botein, and Edward C. Carter II (Chapel Hill: University of North Carolina Press, 1987), 333–48; T. H. Breen, "Interpreting New World Nationalism," in *Nationalism in the New World,* ed. Don H. Doyle and Marco Antonio Pamplona (Athens: University of Georgia Press, 2006), 41–60; Jack P. Greene, "State and National Identities in the Era of the American Revolution," in Doyle and Pamplona, *Nationalism in the New World,* 61–79. For a more general study of nationalism that I have found helpful, see Brubaker, *Nationalism Reframed* and *Ethnicity without Groups* (Cambridge, Mass.: Harvard University Press, 2004).

13 Lewis and Wigen, *Myth of Continents,* ix; Breen, "Interpreting New World Nationalism," 43; Nancy Shoemaker, *A Strange Likeness: Becoming Red and White in Eighteenth-Century North America* (New York: Oxford University Press, 2004), 6.

14 Carl Lotus Becker, *The History of Political Parties in the Province of New York, 1760–1776,* 3rd ed. (Madison: University of Wisconsin Press, 1968), 5, 22. Recent exceptions include Martin Brückner, *The Geographic Revolution in Early America: Maps, Literacy, and National Identity* (Chapel Hill: University of North Carolina Press, 2006); Marc Egnal, *A Mighty Empire: The Origins of the American Revolution* (Ithaca, N.Y.: Cornell University Press, 1988); Jack P. Greene, *The Intellectual Construction of America: Exceptionalism and Identity from 1492 to 1800* (Chapel Hill: University of North Carolina Press, 1993); D. W. Meinig, *The Shaping of America, Volume 1: Atlantic America, 1492–1800* (New Haven, Conn.: Yale University Press, 1986), 257–407.

15 *JCC; LDC.*

1. SCIENTIFIC TRENDS, CONTINENTAL CONCEPTIONS, REVOLUTIONARY IMPLICATIONS

1 Joseph J. Ellis, *His Excellency: George Washington* (New York: Vintage, 2004), 153.

2 Paul Semonin, *American Monster: How the Nation's First Prehistoric Creature Became a Symbol of National Identity* (New York: New York University Press, 2000), 6–7, 175–78; George Washington to Richard Henderson, June 19, 1788, in *PGWCF,* 6:341. Guillaume-Thomas Raynal, *Histoire philosophique et politique, des établissemens et du commerce des Européens dans les deux Indes,* 6 vols. (Amsterdam, 1770).

3 Antonello Gerbi, *The Dispute of the New World: The History of a Polemic, 1750–1900,* trans. Jeremy Moyle (Pittsburgh: University of Pittsburgh Press, 1973).

4 Drew R. McCoy, *The Elusive Republic: Political Economy in Jeffersonian America* (Chapel Hill: University of North Carolina Press, 1980); J. G. A. Pocock, *The Machiavellian Moment: Florentine Political Thought and the Atlantic Republican Tradition* (Princeton, N.J.: Princeton University Press, 1975).

5 Charles de Secondat, Baron de Montesquieu, *The Spirit of the Laws,* trans. and ed. Anne M. Cohler, Basia Carolyn Miller, and Harold Samuel Stone (Cambridge:

Cambridge University Press, 1989), 283; Peter Sahlins, "Natural Frontiers Revisited: France's Boundaries since the Seventeenth Century," *AHR* 95 (1990): 1436 (Rousseau quotation); David Hume, "On National Character," in *David Hume: The Philosophical Works* [1882], ed. T. H. Green and T. H. Grose, vol. 3 (Darmstadt: Scientia Verlag Aalen, 1964), 249; Nicholas Hudson, "From 'Nation' to 'Race': The Origin of Racial Classification in Eighteenth-Century Thought," *Eighteenth-Century Studies* 29 (1996): 256; William Doyle, *Some Account of the British Dominions beyond the Atlantic* (London, 1770), vi, 56.

6 Margaret Beck Pritchard and Henry G. Taliaferro, *Degrees of Latitude: Mapping Colonial America* (Williamsburg, Va.: Colonial Williamsburg Foundation, 2002), 45; James Gilreath and Douglas L. Wilson, eds., *Thomas Jefferson's Own Library: A Catalog with the Entries in His Own Order* (Washington, D.C.: Library of Congress, 1989), 98–107; Frances Laverne Carroll and Mary Meacham, *The Library at Mount Vernon* (Pittsburgh: Beta Phi Mu, 1977), 85; Lindsey Swift, ed., *Catalogue of the John Adams Library in the Public Library of the City of Boston* (Boston: Boston Public Library Trustees, 1917), 37, 189, 208, 214; Pritchard and Taliaferro, *Degrees of Latitude,* 43; Linda Colley, *The Ordeal of Elizabeth Marsh: A Woman in World History* (New York: Random House, 2007), xxv–xxvi.

7 David C. Jolly, comp. and ed., *Maps of America in Periodicals before 1800* (Brookline, Mass.: David C. Jolly, 1989); *Pennsylvania Gazette,* Oct. 28, 1772, June 23, 1773; *Maryland Gazette,* Feb. 4, 1762. On the spread of geographic literacy, see Martin Brückner, *The Geographic Revolution in Early America* (Chapel Hill: University of North Carolina Press, 2006), 11–12; Robert Francis Seybolt, *Source Studies in American Colonial Education: The Private School* (Urbana: University of Illinois Press, 1925), 62–68; Sara S. Gronim, *Everyday Nature: Knowledge of the Natural World in Colonial New York* (New Brunswick, N.J.: Rutgers University Press, 2007), chap. 7.

8 Edwin Wolf II, "Franklin and His Friends Choose Their Books," *Pennsylvania Magazine of History and Biography* 80 (1956): 11 (quotation), 15.

9 Edwin Wolf II, "The First Books and Printed Catalogues of the Library Company of Philadelphia," *Pennsylvania Magazine of History and Biography* 78 (1954): 45–70; *The Charter, Laws, and Catalogue of Books, of the Library Company of Philadelphia* (Philadelphia, 1757, 1764, 1770); E. A. Reitan, "Expanding Horizons: Maps in the 'Gentleman's Magazine,' 1731–1754," *Imago Mundi* 37 (1985): 54, 61–62; David S. Shields, *Civil Tongues and Polite Letters in British America* (Chapel Hill: University of North Carolina Press, 1997), 322.

10 David Kaser, *A Book for a Sixpence: The Circulating Library in America* (Pittsburgh: Beta Phi Mu, 1980), 12, 41, table I, appendix II; E. V. Lamberton, "Colonial Libraries of Pennsylvania," *Pennsylvania Magazine of History and Biography* 42 (1918): 207–12.

11 Craig Nelson, *Thomas Paine: Enlightenment, Revolution, and the Birth of Modern Nations* (New York: Viking, 2006), 54, 60; *Pennsylvania Magazine,* Jan. 24, 1775.

12 Richard D. Brown, *Knowledge Is Power: The Diffusion of Information in Early America, 1700–1865* (New York: Oxford University Press, 1989), 271; I. Bernard Cohen, *Science and the Founding Fathers: Science in the Political Thought of Thomas Jefferson, Benjamin Franklin, John Adams, and James Madison* (New York: Norton, 1995).

13 Susan Scott Parrish, *American Curiosity: Cultures of Natural History in the Colonial British Atlantic World* (Chapel Hill: University of North Carolina Press, 2006), 15 (quotation); Brooke Hindle, *The Pursuit of Science in Revolutionary America, 1735–1789* (Chapel Hill: University of North Carolina Press), chap. 8.

14 David D. Hall, "Learned Culture in the Eighteenth Century," in *The Colonial Book in the Atlantic World,* ed. Hugh Amory and David D. Hall (Cambridge: Cambridge University Press, 2000), 411.

15 Darren M. Staloff, "The Learned Class of the Eighteenth Century," *WMQ* 58 (2001): 463–72, 464–65.

16 Gary B. Nash, *The Urban Crucible: Social Change, Political Consciousness, and the Origins of the American Revolution* (Cambridge, Mass.: Harvard University Press, 1979). Data on the APS and Harvard graduates of 1772–74 come from Staloff, "Learned Class," 465, 468.

17 John Rennie Short, "A New Mode of Thinking: Creating a National Geography in the Early Republic," in *Surveying the Record: North American Scientific Exploration to 1930,* ed. Edward C. Carter II (Philadelphia: American Philosophical Society, 1999), 21–22.

18 John Adams to Abigail Adams, Aug. 13, 1776, in *LDC,* 4: 668–69.

19 Peter Heylyn, *Cosmographie in Four Bookes . . .* (London, 1652), 20; William Pemble, *A Brief Introduction to Geography . . .* (Oxford, 1675), frontispiece; Patrick Gordon, *Geography Anatomiz'd . . .* (London, 1693), preface; William Guthrie, *A New Geographical, Historical, and Commercial Grammar . . .* (London, 1770), 1; *Encyclopaedia Britannica* (Edinburgh, 1771), s.v. "geography." On the relationship between science and geography, see Margarita Bowen, *Empiricism and Geographical Thought: From Francis Bacon to Alexander von Humboldt* (Cambridge: Cambridge University Press, 1981); Robert J. Mayhew, *Enlightenment Geography: The Political Languages of British Geography, 1650–1850* (New York: St. Martin's Press, 2000), esp. 29–32.

20 Mayhew, *Enlightenment Geography,* 30–31; Lester Jesse Cappon, "Geographers and Map-makers, British and American, from about 1750 to 1789," *Proceedings of the American Antiquarian Society* 81 (1971): 244–45; James R. Masterson, "Travelers' Tales of Colonial Natural History," *Journal of American Folklore* 59 (Jan.–March 1946): 51–67, 174–88.

21 Raymond Phineas Stearns, *Science in the British Colonies of America* (Urbana: University of Illinois Press, 1970), 6; Hindle, *Pursuit of Science,* 12.

22 Heylyn, *Cosmographie,* 22, 101–2.

23 Peregrine Clifford Chamberlayne, *Compendium Geographicum . . .* (London, 1682), n.p.

24 John Ogilby, *Asia, the First Part Being an Accurate Description . . .* (London, 1673), frontispiece; Ogilby, *Africa: Being an Accurate Description . . .* (London, 1670), 1.

25 John Seller, *Atlas Minimus . . .* (London, 1679), 1, 34, 43.

26 Quoted in Martin W. Lewis and Kären E. Wigen, *The Myth of Continents: A Critique of Metageography* (Berkeley: University of California Press, 1997), 29.

27 Louis A. de LaHontan, *New Voyages to North-America,* 2 vols. (London, 1703), 1:205–6

28 Woodes Rogers, *A Cruising Voyage round the World* [1712] (New York: Dover Publications, 1970), 85, 228–29; William Douglass, *Summary, Historical and Political, of the First Planting, Progressive Improvements, and Present State of the British Settlements in North-America,* vol. 1 (Boston, 1749), 47, 51, 62–63, 220.

29 Samuel Johnson, *A Dictionary of the English Language* (London, 1755), s.v. "continent."

30 Patrick Gordon, *Geography Anatomiz'd,* 20th ed. (London, 1754), 41–42; Guthrie, *A New Geographical,* 560–61; Thomas Salmon, *A New Geographical and Historical Grammar,* 12th ed. (London, 1772), 45, 573.

31 Lewis and Wigen, *Myth of Continents,* 218n61. The authors suggest a slight trend in the nineteenth century toward viewing North and South America as separate in the United States and unified in Europe (219n75).

32 Heylyn, *Cosmographie,* 22; Chamberlayne, *Compendium Geographicum,* n.p.

33 The following discussion of geographic uncertainty and the search for the Northwest Passage draws heavily on Paul W. Mapp, *The Elusive West and the Contest for Empire, 1713–1763* (Chapel Hill: University of North Carolina Press, 2011); Glyn Williams, *Voyages of Delusion: The Quest for the Northwest Passage* (New Haven, Conn.: Yale University Press, 2002).

34 Cappon, "Geographers and Map-makers," 247–48.

35 Thomas Pownall, *A Memorial: Stating the Nature of the Service in North America . . .* [1756], reprinted as an appendix in Pownall, *The Administration of the Colonies,* 2nd ed. (London, 1765), 4.

36 Johnson, quoted in Lawrence C. Wroth, *An American Bookshelf, 1755* (New York: Arno Press, 1969), 164.

37 Guthrie, *A New Geographical,* 563; Edmund Burke, *An Account of the European Settlements,* 2 vols. (London, 1763), 2:135.

38 Thomas Anburey, *Travels through the Interior Parts of America,* 2 vols.(New York: Houghton Mifflin, 1923), 1:16.

39 Ibid., 2:205. Richard Price, *Observations on the Importance of the American Revolu-*

tion . . . [1785], in *Richard Price and the Ethical Foundations of the American Revolution,* ed. Bernard Peach (Durham, N.C.: Duke University Press, 1979), 210.

40 Arthur Dobbs to William Pitt, Jan. 21, 1760, in *Correspondence of William Pitt . . . ,* ed. Gertrude Selwyn Kimball, 2 vols. (New York: Macmillan, 1906), 2:246.

41 Pownall, *A Memorial,* 7, 9. Franklin thought in similar terms: see Joyce E. Chaplin, *The First Scientific American: Benjamin Franklin and the Pursuit of Genius* (New York: Basic Books, 2006), 228–29.

42 Pritchard and Taliaferro, *Degrees of Latitude,* 19; William P. Cumming, *British Maps of Colonial America* (Chicago: University of Chicago Press, 1974), 10.

43 On Franklin and the Gulf Stream, see Chaplin, *First Scientific American,* 175–77, 196–200, 319–25. Alexander Hamilton, *Hamilton's Itinerarium . . . ,* ed. Albert Bushnell Hart (St. Louis, 1907), 189; Thomas Jefferson to Jean Baptiste Le Roy, Nov. 13, 1786, in *PTJ,* 10:529.

44 Peter Kalm, *Travels into North America,* 2nd ed., ed. and trans. John Reinhold Forster, vol. 1 (London, 1772), 280n; Rogers, *A Cruising Voyage,* 237; "Extract from the Letters of M. de Manpertuis to the King of Prussia, on the Progress of the Sciences," *Pennsylvania Magazine* (Dec. 1775): 597. See also John Logan Allen, *Passage through the Garden: Lewis and Clark and the Image of the American Northwest* (Urbana: University of Illinois Press, 1975), 18–23.

45 John Campbell, ed., *Navigantium atque Itinerantium Bibliotheca . . . ,* 2 vols. (London, 1744–48), 2:400, 1039; Williams, *Voyages of Delusion,* 150.

46 My summary of the voyages of the 1740s draws extensively on Williams, *Voyages of Delusion.*

47 On Spanish geographic uncertainty, see Mapp, *Elusive West,* chap. 1 (Gigedo quotation); Alan Taylor, *American Colonies* (New York: Viking, 2001), 81, 454 (Galvez quotation).

48 Alison Sandman, "Controlling Knowledge: Navigation, Cartography, and Secrecy in the Early Modern Spanish Atlantic," in *Science and Empire in the Atlantic World,* ed. James Delbourgo and Nicholas Dew (New York: Routledge, 2008), 31–52; Christine Marie Petto, *When France Was King of Cartography: The Patronage and Production of Maps in Early Modern France* (Lanham, Md.: Rowman and Littlefield, 2007), chap. 3; Williams, *Voyages of Delusion,* 246–48.

49 Arthur Dobbs, "Memorial on the Northwest Passage, 1731," in *Voyages to Hudson Bay in Search of a Northwest Passage, 1741–1747, Volume 1: The Voyage of Christopher Middleton, 1741–1742,* ed. William Barr and Glyndwr Williams (London: Hakluyt Society, 1994), 35–36 (quotation).

50 Ibid., 34

51 "The Journal of Captain Christopher Middleton, 1741–42," in Barr and Williams, *Voyages to Hudson Bay,* 148–49.

52 Quoted in Williams, *Voyages of Delusion,* 149.

53 Quoted in Desmond Clarke, *Arthur Dobbs, Esquire, 1689–1765: Surveyor-General*

of Ireland, Prospector and Governor of North Carolina (Chapel Hill: University of North Carolina Press, 1957), 190.

54 Edward J. Cashin, *Governor Henry Ellis and the Transformation of British North America* (Athens: University of Georgia Press, 1994).

55 Williams, *Voyages of Delusion,* 212–14; Chaplin, *First Scientific American,* 146–47; Glyndwr Williams, *The British Search for the Northwest Passage in the Eighteenth Century* (London: Longmans, 1962), 139–42; Benjamin Franklin to John Pringle, May 27, 1762, in *PBF,* 10:85; Franklin to Pringle [1767?], in *PBF,* 14:352.

56 Pritchard and Taliaferro, *Degrees of Latitude,* 183.

57 Mapp, *Elusive West.*

58 David Armour, ed., *Treason at Michilimackinac: The Proceedings of a General Court Martial Held at Montreal in October 1768 for the Trial of Major Robert Rogers,* rev. ed. (Mackinac Island, Mich.: Mackinac Island State Park Commission, 1972), 3; Robert Rogers, *A Concise Account of North America . . .* (London, 1765), 2, 150; Norman Gelb, ed., *Jonathan Carver's Travels through America, 1766–1768: An Eighteenth-Century Explorer's Account of Uncharted America* (New York: John Wiley, 1993), 58, 225–28; Dwight, quoted in Kenneth Silverman, *A Cultural History of the American Revolution: Painting, Music, Literature, and the Theatre in the Colonies and the United States from the Treaty of Paris to the Inauguration of George Washington, 1763–1789* (New York: Thomas Y. Crowell, 1976), 231.

59 Doyle, *Some Account,* xiii (quotations), 64–87.

60 Robert F. Berkhofer Jr., *The White Man's Indian: Images of the American Indian from Columbus to the Present* (New York: Knopf, 1978), 23–24; Wilcomb Washburn, "The Meaning of 'Discovery' in the Fifteenth and Sixteenth Centuries," *AHR* 68 (1962): 2–3.

61 P. J. Marshall and Glyndwr Williams, *The Great Map of Mankind: British Perceptions of the World in the Age of Enlightenment* (London: J. M. Dent and Sons, 1982), 24.

62 Seller, *Atlas Minimus,* 1, 25, 35, 42.

63 Ogilby, *Asia,* preface.

64 Kalm, *Travels,* 80–81, 158–59, 243–55.

65 *The Journal of Nicholas Cresswell, 1774–1777* (New York: Dial Press, 1924), 269.

66 Clare Le Corbeiller, "Miss America and Her Sisters: Personifications of the Four Parts of the World," *Bulletin of the Metropolitan Museum of Art* 19 (1961): 209–23.

67 Gordon, *Geography Anatomiz'd* (London, 1693), 10.

68 Bernhardus Varenius, *Cosmography and Geography in Two Parts . . . ,* trans. and ed. Richard Blome (London, 1682), preface.

69 Karen Ordahl Kupperman, "Climate and Mastery of the Wilderness in Seventeenth-Century New England," in *Seventeenth-Century New England: A Conference Held by the Colonial Society of Massachusetts, June 18 and 19, 1982* (Boston: Colonial Society of Massachusetts, 1984), 3–37; Kupperman, "The Puzzle of

the American Climate in the Early Colonial Period," *AHR* 87 (1982): 1262–89; Robert Mountgomery, *A Discourse Concerning the Design'd Establishment of a New Colony* . . . [1717], in *The Most Delightful Country of the Universe: Promotional Literature of the Colony of Georgia,* ed. Trevor R. Reese (Savannah: Beehive, 1972), 8.

70 Robert Beverley, *The History and Present State of Virginia,* ed. Louis B. Wright (Chapel Hill: University of North Carolina Press, 1947), 59, 117, 296–97. Marion Tinling, ed., *The Correspondence of the Three William Byrds of Westover, Virginia, 1684–1776,* 2 vols. (Charlottesville: University Press of Virginia, 1977), 2:518; Joyce E. Chaplin, "Mark Catesby, a Skeptical Newtonian in America," in *Empire's Nature: Mark Catesby's New World Vision,* ed. Amy R. W. Meyers and Margaret Beck Pritchard (Chapel Hill: University of North Carolina Press, 1998), 48.

71 Joyce E. Chaplin, "Natural Philosophy and an Early Racial Idiom in North America: Comparing English and Indian Bodies," *WMQ* 54 (1997): 236.

72 John Lawson, *A New Voyage to Carolina* [1709], ed. Hugh Talmage Lefler (Chapel Hill: University of North Carolina Press, 1967), 168; Thomas Nairne, *A Letter from South Carolina* (London, 1710), 14.

73 Hans Sloane, *A Voyage to the Islands* . . . (London, 1707–25); Stephen Hales, *Vegetable Staticks* . . . (London, 1727). On shifting theories of climate, see Chaplin, "Natural Philosophy" and "Mark Catesby," 47–50; Clarence J. Glacken, *Traces on a Rhodian Shore: Nature and Culture in Western Thought from Ancient Times to the End of the Eighteenth Century* (Berkeley: University of California Press, 1967).

74 David W. Carrithers, Michael A. Mosher, and Paul A. Rahe, eds., *Montesquieu's Science of Politics: Essays on The Spirit of Laws* (Lanham, Md.: Rowman & Littlefield, 2001). Most useful in that volume are David W. Carrithers, "Introduction: An Appreciation of *The Spirit of Laws,*" 6, 10–12, 15, and C. P. Courtney, "Montesquieu and Natural Law," 57.

75 Salmon, *A New Geographical and Historical Grammar,* 430.

76 Jefferson to the Marquis de Chastellux, Sept. 2, 1785, in *PTJ,* 8:468; Thomas Jefferson, *Notes on the State of Virginia,* ed. William Peden (Chapel Hill: University of North Carolina Press, 1954), 163.

77 Hector St. John de Crèvecoeur, "What Is an American?" in Crèvecoeur, *Letters from an American Farmer* [1782] (New York: E. P. Dutton, 1962), 44–46.

78 Hudson, "From 'Nation' to 'Race,'" 255.

79 Joyce E. Chaplin, *Subject Matter: Technology, the Body, and Science on the Anglo-American Frontier, 1500–1676* (Cambridge, Mass.: Harvard University Press, 2001).

80 On memories of the war, see Jill Lepore, *The Name of War: King Philip's War and the Origins of American Identity* (New York: Knopf, 1998); Samuel Nowell, *Abraham in Arms* (Boston, 1678), reprinted in *So Dreadfull a Judgment: Puritan Responses to King Philip's War,* ed. Richard Slotkin and James Folsom (Middletown, Conn.: Wesleyan University Press, 1978), 287; Chaplin, "Natural Philosophy," 251.

81 Stearns, *Science in the British Colonies*, 526–33. See also Cohen, *Science and the Founding Fathers*, 45–49.

82 Alden T. Vaughan, "From White Man to Redskin: Changing Anglo-American Perceptions of the American Indian," *AHR* 87 (1982): 945–47; Nancy Shoemaker, "How Indians Got to Be Red," *AHR* 102 (1997): 626–27; Hudson, "From 'Nation' to 'Race,' " 254–55 (Blumenbach quotation from 255).

83 Chaplin, "Mark Catesby," 42.

84 Jorge Cañizares-Esguerra has rendered the similarities between Buffon and Linnaeus more apparent by comparing the work of Spaniards and Latin Americans with that of other Europeans in the "dispute of the New World." See Jorge Cañizares-Esguerra, *How to Write the History of the New World: Histories, Epistemologies, and Identities in the Eighteenth-Century Atlantic World* (Stanford, Calif.: Stanford University Press, 2001).

85 Ibid. Buffon, quoted in Gilbert Chinard, "Eighteenth Century Theories on America as a Human Habitat," *Proceedings of the American Philosophical Society* 91 (Feb. 1947): 31.

86 Buffon, quoted in Vaughan, "From White Man to Redskin," 946. Henry Home, Lord Kames, *Six Sketches on the History of Man* (Philadelphia, 1776), 15; Chaplin, *First Scientific American*, 83.

87 Bernard Romans, *A Concise Natural History of East and West Florida* [1775] (New Orleans: Pelican Publishing, 1961), 26, 37. Chaplin, *Subject Matter*, 321.

88 Chaplin, "Natural Philosophy," 252.

89 Burke, *European Settlements*, 2:57–58.

90 Salmon, *A New Geographical and Historical Grammar*, 618.

91 Burke, *European Settlements*, 2:96, 106–7.

92 Nathaniel Ames, "A Thought upon the Past, Present, and Future State of North America," in *The Essays, Humor, and Poems of Nathaniel Ames*, ed. Samuel Briggs (Cleveland, Ohio, 1891), 285.

93 Staloff, "Learned Class," 464–65. Benjamin Franklin, "A Proposal for Promoting Useful Knowledge among the British Plantations in America," in *PBF*, 2:381.

94 *Pennsylvania Gazette*, March 17, 1768; "A Virginia Planter" [George Mason] to the Committee of Merchants in London, June 6, 1766, in *The Papers of George Mason, 1725–1792*, ed. Robert A. Rutland, 2 vols. (Chapel Hill: University of North Carolina Press, 1970), 1:70.

95 Thomas Paine, *Common Sense* [1776], in *WTP*, 1:5, 20.

96 *PTJ*, 2:540; Doyle, *Some Account*, 57.

97 Thomas Pownall, *A Memorial Most Humbly Addressed to the Sovereigns of Europe, on the Present State of Affairs between the Old and New World* (London, 1780), 13–14, 56; the capitalization is as per the original. Cohen, *Science and the Founding Fathers*, 39–41; John A. Schutz, *Thomas Pownall: British Defender of American*

Liberty, a Study of Anglo-American Relations in the Eighteenth Century (Glendale, Calif.: Arthur H. Clark, 1951), 27.

98 James H. Cassedy, *Demography in Early America: Beginnings of the Statistical Mind, 1600–1800* (Cambridge, Mass.: Harvard University Press, 1969).

99 Benjamin Franklin, *Observations Concerning the Increase of Mankind,* in *PBF,* 4:228; *Journal of Nicholas Cresswell,* 271; Kalm, *Travels,* 313–14.

100 Cohen, *Science and the Founding Fathers,* 156; Chaplin, *First Scientific American,* 142–45, 239.

101 Franklin, *Observations,* 227, 233–34.

102 Ezra Stiles, *Discourse on the Christian Union* (Boston, 1760), 120.

103 Samuel Williams, *A Discourse on the Love of Our Country* (Salem, Mass., 1775), 22; David Ramsay, "Oration on American Independence," in *David Ramsay, 1748–1815: Selections from His Writings,* ed. Robert L. Brunhouse (Philadelphia: American Philosophical Society, 1965), 188.

104 Williams, *A Discourse,* 21–22.

105 Ibid., 23, 27.

106 David Ramsay, *An Oration on the Advantages of American Independence* (Charlestown, S.C., 1778), 14, 21.

107 François Jean, Marquis de Chastellux, *Travels in North-America, in the Years 1780–81–82,* ed. and trans. George Grieve (New York, 1828), 387; "Political Discourse, No. 9: For the Fast Day Appointed by Congress, April 1778," *United States Magazine,* May 1779, 198.

2. THE GEOPOLITICAL CONTINENT

1 Lester C. Olson, *Benjamin Franklin's Vision of American Community: A Study in Rhetorical Iconology* (Columbia: University of South Carolina Press, 2004), 33, 89.

2 Francis Newton Thorpe, ed., *The Federal and State Constitutions, Colonial Charters, and Other Organic Laws of the States, Territories, and Colonies Now or Heretofore Forming the United States of America* (Washington, D.C.: U.S. Government Printing Office, 1909), 3783, 3790; James Muldoon, "Discovery, Grant, Charter, Conquest, or Purchase: John Adams on the Legal Basis of English Possession of North America," in *The Many Legalities of Early America,* ed. Christopher L. Tomlins and Bruce H. Mann (Chapel Hill: University of North Carolina Press, 2001), 25–46.

3 Thorpe, *Federal and State Constitutions,* 1828, 1846, 3795.

4 "Plans for the Union of the British Colonies of North America, 1643–1776," comp. Frederick D. Stone, in *History of the Celebration of the One Hundredth Anniversary of the Promulgation of the Constitution of the United States,* ed. Hampton L. Carson II (Philadelphia, 1889), 439–503; Jack P. Greene, "Martin Bladen's Blueprint for a Colonial Union," *WMQ* 17 (1960): 516–30.

5 Charles M. Andrews, *The Colonial Period of American History,* vol. 4 (New Haven, Conn.: Yale University Press, 1938), 415.

6 Margaret Beck Pritchard and Henry G. Taliaferro, *Degrees of Latitude: Mapping Colonial America* (Williamsburg, Va.: Colonial Williamsburg Foundation, 2002), 19–21, 123; William P. Cumming, *British Maps of Colonial America* (Chicago: University of Chicago Press, 1974), 6–10, Burnet quotation from 9–10.

7 Warren R. Hofstra, " 'The Extension of His Majesties Dominions': The Virginia Backcountry and the Reconfiguration of Imperial Frontiers," *JAH* 84 (1998): 1281–1312, quotation from 1294–95; Greene, "Martin Bladen's Blueprint," 529.

8 Louis de Vorsey Jr., "Maps in Colonial Promotion: James Edward Oglethorpe's Use of Maps in 'Selling' the Georgia Scheme," *Imago Mundi* 38 (1986): 35–39.

9 John Robert McNeill, *Atlantic Empires of France and Spain: Louisbourg and Havana, 1700–1763* (Chapel Hill: University of North Carolina Press, 1985), 10 ("la clef de l'Amérique"), 22, 85, 214n8; W. J. Eccles, *The Canadian Frontier, 1534–1760* (New York: Holt, Rinehart and Winston, 1969), 143–50; Seymour I. Schwartz and Ralph E. Ehrenberg, *The Mapping of America* (Edison, N.J.: Wellfleet Press, 2001), 151.

10 The quotation is from a legend affixed to a map in the British Library, as quoted online at http://usm.maine.edu/maps/popple/narrative.html (viewed May 12, 2008). This is part of a site by the Osher Map Library at http://www.usm.maine .edu/maps/popple, which has informed my discussion heavily.

11 Available online at http://usm.maine.edu/maps/popple/narrative.html (viewed May 12, 2008).

12 Franklin to William Strahan, May 22, 1746, in *PBF,* 3:77; John Adams to Abigail Adams, Aug. 13, 1776, in *LDC,* 4:669. Edmund S. Morgan, *Benjamin Franklin* (New Haven, Conn.: Yale University Press, 2002), 63–65.

13 Ned C. Landsman, "The Provinces and the Empire: Scotland, the American Colonies and the Development of British Provincial Identity," in *An Imperial State at War: Britain from 1689 to 1815,* ed. Lawrence Stone (London: Routledge, 1994), 258–87; Eric Richards, "Scotland and the Uses of the Atlantic Empire," in *Strangers within the Realm: Cultural Margins of the First British Empire,* ed. Bernard Bailyn and Philip D. Morgan (Chapel Hill: University of North Carolina Press, 1991), 67–114.

14 William Douglass, *Summary, Historical and Political, of the First Planting, Progressive Improvements, and Present State of the British Settlements in North-America,* vol. 1 (Boston, 1749), 2, 4–5, 208.

15 Ibid., 209 (quotation), 234.

16 Ibid., 235.

17 Ibid., 242.

18 Benedict Anderson, *Imagined Communities: Reflections on the Origin and Spread of Nationalism,* rev. ed. (London: Verso, 1991), 47–65, area figures from 64n51.

19 Fred Anderson, *Crucible of War: The Seven Years' War and the Fate of Empire in British North America, 1754–1766* (New York: Knopf, 2000), 22–32.

20 *Pennsylvania Gazette,* May 9, 1754; ibid., May 1, 1755.

21 "A Geographical Description of those Parts of this Continent . . . ," *The Instructor,* March 20, 1755, 12.

22 *Pennsylvania Gazette,* March 11, 1756. See also *Gentleman's Magazine,* July 1754, 322.

23 Ibid., Dec. 22, 1757; see also ibid., May 16, 1754.

24 Ibid., Feb. 11, 1755, reprinted from *Maryland Gazette,* Dec. 12, 1754.

25 Excerpts of Mayhew's election sermon of May 29, 1754, reprinted in *Pennsylvania Gazette,* Aug. 29, 1754. [John Mitchell], *The Contest in America between Great Britain and France* (London, 1757), x. See also Lewis Evans, *Geographical, Historical, Political, Philosophical and Mechanical Essays . . .* (Philadelphia, 1755), 31.

26 "An Account of the Country at Present the Seat of War in North-America . . . ," *American Magazine,* Oct. 1757, 22.

27 Ibid., 22.

28 *Pennsylvania Gazette,* May 1, 1755.

29 Quoted in Andrews, *Colonial Period,* 414.

30 Robert Dinwiddie to James Hamilton, May 22, 1753, quoted in *PGWC,* 1:56.

31 Anderson, *Crucible of War,* 42–76.

32 Morgan, *Benjamin Franklin,* 82.

33 Thomas Pownall to the Earl of Halifax, July 23, 1754, in Beverly McAnear, "Personal Accounts of the Albany Congress of 1754," *Mississipi Valley Historical Review* 39 (1953): 754.

34 Timothy J. Shannon, *Indians and Colonists at the Crossroads of Empire: The Albany Congress of 1754* (Ithaca, N.Y.: Cornell University Press and New York State Historical Association), 58, 82, 197–98.

35 Albany Congress, "Representation of the Present State of the Colonies," in *PBF,* 5:374

36 Anderson, *Crucible of War,* 94–107.

37 Ibid., 135–68.

38 Richard Pares, "American versus Continental Warfare, 1739–63," *English Historical Review* 51 (1936): 450.

39 Anderson, *Crucible of War,* 208–14.

40 Joan D. Dolmetsch, *Rebellion and Reconciliation: Satirical Prints on the Revolution at Williamsburg* (Williamsburg, Va.: Colonial Williamsburg Foundation, 1976), 28.

41 The data are from a search of the Readex database *Early American Imprints, Series I: Evans, 1639–1800* on Oct. 18, 2007. Richard Merritt conducted a content analysis of colonial newspapers to gauge the use of "symbols of American community." However, his work does not encompass the full scope of continental thought. For

example, in examining what he termed "continental symbols," he excluded references to "the North American continent as a whole" and considered only those "used to denote the area comprising the American colonies." His rationale was that "this is the same sense in which the colonists themselves used the term in convening the Continental Congress and creating the Continental Army." The matter is not so simple. Richard L. Merritt, *Symbols of American Community, 1735–1775* (New Haven, Conn.: Yale University Press, 1966), 83n1.

42 *American Almanac* (Philadelphia, 1760), frontispiece; *Pennsylvania Gazette,* Nov. 19, 1761, Sept. 11, 1776.

43 *The Universal American Almanack . . . for the Year of our Lord 1761* (Philadelphia, n.d.).

44 *The Autobiography of Benjamin Franklin,* ed. L. Jesse Lemisch (New York: Signet, 1961), 107; *Universal American Almanack.* On the nationalizing effects of almanacs, see David Waldstreicher, "Rites of Rebellion, Rites of Assent: Celebrations, Print Culture, and the Origins of American Nationalism," *JAH* 82 (1995): 57–61.

45 Albany Congress, "Representation," 5:368.

46 Edmundo O'Gorman, *The Invention of America: An Inquiry into the Historical Nature of the New World and the Meaning of Its History* (Bloomington: Indiana University Press, 1961); Wilcomb Washburn, "The Meaning of 'Discovery' in the Fifteenth and Sixteenth Centuries," *AHR* 68 (1962): 1–21; Eviatar Zerubavel, *The Mental Discovery of America* (New Brunswick, N.J.: Rutgers University Press, 1992).

47 Ellis Huske, *The Present State of North-America . . .* (Boston, 1755), 1, 9.

48 "History of the War in North-America," *American Magazine,* March–April 1758, 296. See also "The History of the Colony of Massachusetts-Bay," *Royal American Magazine,* Jan. 1774, A7; "Some Account of the Colony of Virginia," *Pennsylvania Magazine,* April 1776, 186; "A Geographical Description of those Parts of This Continent, as Are Now in Dispute, with the Rights of the Several Claimants," *The Instructor,* March 20, 1755, 9; "Remainder of the Letter on Account of the French Encroachments to the Eastward, Began in Our Last," *The Instructor,* April 10, 1755, 23.

49 Claudia L. Bushman, *America Discovers Columbus: How an Italian Explorer Became an American Hero* (Hanover, N.H.: University Press of New England, 1992), 28–30. See also Samuel Nevill, *The History of North-America, from the First Discovery thereof . . . ,* vol. 1 (Woodbridge, N.J.: 1760).

50 "The Watchman: Letter V," *American Magazine,* April 1758, 350–51, 353.

51 Nathaniel Ames, "A Thought upon the Past, Present, and Future State of North America," in *The Essays, Humor, and Poems of Nathaniel Ames,* ed. Samuel Briggs (Cleveland, Ohio, 1891), 284–86.

52 Pritchard and Taliaferro, *Degrees of Latitude,* 21, 183.

53 Edmund Berkeley and Dorothy Smith Berkeley, *Dr. John Mitchell: The Man Who*

Made the Map (Chapel Hill: University of North Carolina Press, 1974); Emerson D. Fite and Archibald Freeman, *A Book of Old Maps: Delineating American History from the Earliest Days down the Close of the Revolutionary War* [1926] (New York: Dover, 1969), 180–84; *http://www.usm.maine.edu/~maps/mitchell/* (viewed on May 12, 2008).

54 J. M. Bumstead, " 'Things in the Womb of Time': Ideas of American Independence, 1633 to 1763," *WMQ* 31 (1974): 535; Lester C. Olson, *Emblems of American Community in the Revolutionary Era: A Study in Rhetorical Iconology* (Washington, D.C.: Smithsonian Institution Press, 1991), 125–99; David Waldstreicher, *Runaway America: Benjamin Franklin, Slavery, and the American Revolution* (New York: Hill and Wang, 2004), 115–44.

55 Quoted in Bumstead, "Things in the Womb of Time," 542.

56 Peter Kalm's diary entry for Nov. 2, 1748, in *Peter Kalm's Travels in North America: The English Version of 1770,* vol. 1, ed. and trans. Adolph B. Benson (New York: Dover, 1937), 139–40.

57 Quoted in Bumstead, "Things in the Womb of Time," 542.

58 Benson, *Peter Kalm's Travels,* 139.

59 Bumstead, "Things in the Womb of Time," 550; Alison Gilbert Olson, "The British Government and Colonial Union, 1754," *WMQ* 17 (1960): 31.

60 Anderson, *Crucible of War,* 344 (including quotations).

61 Ibid., 355–62.

62 Clarence W. Alvord, *The Mississippi Valley in British Politics,* vol. 2 (Cleveland, Ohio, 1917), 253–64.

63 Sir Lewis Namier, *England in the Age of the American Revolution,* 2nd ed. (New York: St. Martin's Press, 1962), 276.

64 Benjamin Franklin, *The Interest of Great Britain Considered* (London, 1760), in *PBF,* 9:62–63.

65 Ibid., 9:70.

66 Ibid., 9:93–94.

67 Ibid., 9:78.

68 Ibid., 9:90.

69 Ibid., 9:78–79.

70 Anderson, *Crucible of War,* 484–90; Stanley J. Stein and Barbara H. Stein, *Apogee of Empire: Spain and New Spain in the Age of Charles III, 1759–1789* (Baltimore: Johns Hopkins University Press, 2003), 11–12.

71 McNeill, *Atlantic Empires,* 10 (quotation), 38.

72 Anderson, *Crucible of War,* 498–501.

73 Ibid., 515–16.

74 Paul W. Mapp, *The Elusive West and the Contest for Empire, 1713–1763* (Chapel Hill: University of North Carolina Press, 2011), chap. 13.

75 Ibid., chap. 14.

76 Ibid., 416.

77 Colin G. Calloway, *The Scratch of a Pen: 1763 and the Transformation of North America* (New York: Oxford University Press, 2006), 8; Anderson, *Crucible of War*, 505–6; Mapp, *Elusive West*, chap. 15.

78 Ibid., chap. 15; Paul W. Mapp, "British Culture and the Changing Character of the Mid-Eighteenth-Century British Empire," in *Cultures in Conflict: The Seven Years' War in North America,* ed. Warren R. Hofstra (Lanham, Md.: Rowman and Littlefield, 2007), 43–50. Jack M. Sosin, *Whitehall and the Wilderness: The Middle West in British Colonial Policy, 1760–1775* (Lincoln: University of Nebraska Press, 1961), 3–26, emphasizes the quest for security as guiding British leaders.

79 "Motion on the Preliminaries of Peace," Dec. 9, 1762, in *Proceedings and Debates of the British Parliaments Respecting North America, 1754–1783,* vol. 1, ed. R. C. Simmons and P. D. G. Thomas (Millwood, N.Y.: Kraus, 1982), 417, 420–23. On East Indian interests, see Mapp, *Elusive West,* 424–425. On British politics and the downfall of Pitt generally, see Anderson, *Crucible of War,* 476–86.

80 Mapp, "British Culture," 23–59.

81 Quotation from Marc Egnal, *A Mighty Empire: The Origins of the American Revolution* (Ithaca, N.Y.: Cornell University Press, 1988), 12–13.

82 Chester E. Eisenger, "The Puritans' Justification for Taking the Land," *Essex Institute Historical Collections* 74 (1948): 131–43; Craig Yirush, "From the Perspective of Empire: The Common Law, Natural Rights, and the Formation of American Political Theory, 1689–1775," Ph.D. diss., Johns Hopkins University, Baltimore, 2004, 207–19; Robert Beverley, *The History and Present State of Virginia,* ed. Louis B. Wright (Chapel Hill: University of North Carolina Press, 1947), 9.

83 On this as the first "unequivocal British example of an Indian representing the colonies in print," see Olson, *Emblems of American Community,* 77.

84 E. McClung Fleming, "The American Image as Indian Princess, 1765–1783," *Winterthur Portfolio* 2 (1965): 65–81; Cooper Union Museum, *The Four Continents: From the Collection of James Hazen Hyde* (New York: Cooper Union Museum, 1961); Clare Le Corbeiller, "Miss America and Her Sisters: Personifications of the Four Parts of the World," *Bulletin of the Metropolitan Museum of Art* 19 (April 1961): 209–23; Olson, *Emblems of American Community,* 75–124.

85 Philip J. Deloria, *Playing Indian* (New Haven, Conn.: Yale University Press, 1998), 5. See also Robert Berkhofer Jr., *The White Man's Indian: Images of the American Indian from Columbus to the Present* (New York: Knopf, 1978), 20–21.

86 Archibald Kennedy, *The Importance of Gaining and Preserving the Friendship of the Indians to the British Interest Considered* (London, 1752), 43; Edmund Burke, *An Account of the European Settlements in America,* 2 vols. (London, 1763), 1:169; Pownall, *The Administration of the Colonies,* 2nd ed. (London, 1765), 12.

87 George Washington to Adam Stephen, Oct. 23, 1756, in *PGWC,* 8:442; George

Croghan, in *Early Western Travels, 1748–1846*, vol. 1, ed. Reuben Gold Thwaites (Cleveland: Arthur H. Clark, 1904), 144.

88 Croghan, in *Early Western Travels*, 171–72; *Pennsylvania Gazette*, May 1, 1755; William Smith, *Discourses on Several Public Occasions during the War in America* (London, 1759), 133–34.

89 Linda Colley, *Britons: Forging the Nation, 1707–1837*, 2nd ed. (New Haven, Conn.: Yale University Press, 2005), 103–5.

90 Franklin to Lord Kames, Jan. 3, 1760, in *PBF*, 9:6–7.

91 Franklin to Lord Kames, Feb. 25, 1767, in *PBF*, 14:69–70.

3. CONTINENTAL CRISIS

1 Linda Colley, *Britons: Forging the Nation, 1707–1837*, 2nd ed. (New Haven, Conn.: Yale University Press, 2005), 101–45; Richard L. Merritt, *Symbols of American Community, 1735–1775* (New Haven, Conn.: Yale University Press, 1966), 58, 147; Stephen Conway, "From Fellow-Nationals to Foreigners: British Perceptions of the Americans, circa 1739–1783," *WMQ* 59 (2002): 82–83, 100; T. H. Breen, "Ideology and Nationalism on the Eve of the American Revolution: Revisions *Once More* in Need of Revising," *JAH* 84 (1997): 13–39.

2 Edmund S. Morgan, *Inventing the People: The Rise of Popular Sovereignty in England and America* (New York: Norton, 1988), 41–44, quotation from 41.

3 On the connection between nationalism and political ideology, see T. H. Breen, "Interpreting New World Nationalism," in *Nationalism in the New World*, ed. Don H. Doyle and Marco Antonio Pamplona (Atlanta: University of Georgia Press, 2006), 41–60.

4 Fred Anderson, *Crucible of War: The Seven Years' War and the Fate of Empire in British North America, 1754–1766* (New York: Knopf, 2000), 560–62; John L. Bullion, "Security and Economy: The Bute Administration's Plans for the American Army and Revenue, 1762–1763," *WMQ* 45 (1988): 499–509; Bullion, " 'The Ten Thousand in America': More Light on the Decision on the American Army, 1762–1763," *WMQ* 43 (1986): 646–57; Eliga H. Gould, "Fears of War, Fantasies of Peace: British Politics and the Coming of the American Revolution," in *Empire and Nation: The American Revolution in the Atlantic World*, ed. Eliga H. Gould and Peter S. Onuf (Baltimore: Johns Hopkins University Press, 2005), 30–31.

5 Edmund S. Morgan and Helen M. Morgan, *The Stamp Act Crisis: Prologue to Revolution*, rev. ed. (New York: Collier, 1962), 37–38.

6 Thomas Pownall, *The Administration of the Colonies* (London, 1764), 4. On Pownall's life, see John A. Schutz, *Thomas Pownall: British Defender of American Liberty, a Study of Anglo-American Relations in the Eighteenth Century* (Glendale, Calif.: Arthur H. Clark, 1951). On how Pownall's *Administration of the Colonies*

changed over time, see G. H. Guttridge, "Thomas Pownall's *The Administration of the Colonies:* The Six Editions," *WMQ* 26 (1969): 23–25, 31–46. On Pownall's position within the British political spectrum, see John Shy, "The Spectrum of Imperial Possibilities: Henry Ellis and Thomas Pownall, 1763–1775," in Shy, *A People Numerous and Armed: Reflections on the Military Struggle for American Independence* (New York: Oxford University Press, 1976), 35–72.

7 Pownall, *Administration of the Colonies,* 6, 33.

8 Pownall, *Administration of the Colonies,* 2nd ed. (London, 1765), 36, 63–64.

9 Ibid., 7.

10 Ibid., 64.

11 Fulmer Mood, "The Origin, Evolution, and Application of the Sectional Concept, 1750–1900," in *Regionalism in America* [1951], ed. Merrill Jensen (Madison: University of Wisconsin Press, 1965), 10–11; John Mitchell, *The Present State of Great Britain and North America, with Regards to Agriculture, Population, Trade, and Manufactures* (London, 1767), 132; Mitchell, *American Husbandry* [1775], ed. Harry J. Carman (Port Washington, N.Y.: Kennikat Press, 1964), 504.

12 Morgan and Morgan, *Stamp Act Crisis,* 34–35.

13 William Doyle, *Some Account of the British Dominions beyond the Atlantic* (London, 1770), xi, and map insert entitled "A Map of all the British Dominions beyond the Atlantic." On the confusion and conflation of John and Sebastian Cabot by Britons during this period, see Peter E. Pope, *The Many Landfalls of John Cabot* (Toronto: University of Toronto Press, 1997), 43–48.

14 See, e.g., Patrick Gordon, *Geography Anatomiz'd,* 20th ed. (London, 1754), 41–42; William Guthrie, *A New Geographical, Historical, and Commercial Grammar . . .* (London, 1770), 560–61; Thomas Salmon, *A New Geographical and Historical Grammar,* 12th ed. (London, 1772), 45, 573. For a sampling of world atlases portraying North and South America as both one and two continents, see those of the David Rumsey Map Collection, available online at http://www.davidrumsey .com/atlases.html (viewed on May 12, 2008). Lewis and Wigen, *Myth of Continents,* 218n61. The authors suggest a slight trend in the nineteenth century toward viewing North and South America as separate in the United States and unified in Europe: see ibid., 219n75. For ambiguity in continental taxonomies, see Martin Brückner, *The Geographic Revolution in America: Maps, Literacy, and National Identity* (Chapel Hill: University of North Carolina Press, 2006), 80–89.

15 On the role of postwar expectations in the coming of the Revolution, see Jack P. Greene, "The Seven Years' War and the American Revolution: The Causal Relationship Reconsidered," *Journal of Imperial and Commonwealth History* 7 (1980): 85–105; Tom Hatley, *The Dividing Paths: Cherokees and South Carolinians through the Revolutionary Era* (New York: Oxford, 1995), 119–75; Anderson, *Crucible of War,* 457–71.

16 For Indian aims, see Gregory Evans Dowd, *War under Heaven: Pontiac, the Indian*

Nations, and the British Empire (Baltimore: Johns Hopkins University Press, 2002), 114–47. On the war as a qualified success for Indians, see Richard White, *The Middle Ground: Indians, Empires, and Republics in the Great Lakes Region, 1650–1815* (Cambridge: Cambridge University Press, 1991), 269–314; Dowd, *War under Heaven*, 213–48. For a concise history of Pontiac's War, see Colin G. Calloway, *The Scratch of a Pen: 1763 and the Transformation of North America* (New York: Oxford University Press, 2006), 66–91, quotation from 70. For the extremity of British tactics, see Anderson, *Crucible of War*, 542–43.

17 James H. Merrell, *Into the American Woods: Negotiators on the Pennsylvania Frontier* (New York: Norton, 1999), 282–88, quotation from 287.

18 Jane T. Merritt, *At the Crossroads: Indians and Empires on a Mid-Atlantic Frontier, 1700–1763* (Chapel Hill: University of North Carolina Press, 2003), 235–308; Daniel K. Richter, *Facing East from Indian Country: A Native History of Early America* (Cambridge, Mass.: Harvard University Press, 2001), 190. On fear and Indian war, see Peter Silver, *Our Savage Neighbors: How Indian War Transformed Early America* (New York: Norton, 2008).

19 David C. Douglas, ed., *English Historical Documents, Volume 9: American Colonial Documents to 1776*, ed. Merrill Jensen (New York: Oxford University Press, 1955), 640–43, quotations from 641–42; Daniel K. Richter, "Native Americans, the Plan of 1764, and a British Empire that Never Was," in *Cultures and Identities in Colonial British America*, ed. Robert Olwell and Alan Tully (Baltimore: Johns Hopkins University Press, 2006), 276, 291–92.

20 Woody Holton, *Forced Founders: Indians, Debtors, Slaves, and the Making of the American Revolution in Virginia* (Chapel Hill: University of North Carolina Press, 1999), 3–38, quotation from 7.

21 Quotations from ibid., 9, 32.

22 Thomas Jefferson, "A Summary View of the Rights of British America" [1774], reprinted in *Tracts of the American Revolution, 1763–1776*, ed. Merrill Jensen (Indianapolis: Bobbs-Merrill, 1967), 273.

23 Fred Anderson and Andrew Cayton, *The Dominion of War: Empire and Liberty in North America, 1500–2000* (New York: Viking, 2005), 145–46.

24 For the charters of Virginia and other colonies, see Francis Newton Thorpe, ed., *The Federal and State Constitutions, Colonial Charters, and Other Organic Laws of the States, Territories, and Colonies Now or Heretofore Forming the United States of America* (Washington, D.C.: U.S. Government Printing Office, 1909). Washington to James Wood, March 30, 1773, in *PGWC*, 9:205–7; Rufus Putnam, *The Memoirs of Rufus Putnam and Certain Official Papers and Correspondence*, comp. Rowena Buell (Boston, 1903), 53–54.

25 Washington to Thomas Johnson, July 20, 1770, quoted in Anderson and Cayton, *Dominion of War*, 146; Joel Achenbach, *The Grand Idea: George Washington's Potomac and the Race to the West* (New York: Simon and Schuster, 2004), 37–40;

Charles Royster, *The Fabulous History of the Dismal Swamp Company: A Story of George Washington's Times* (New York: Knopf, 1999), 155–56.

26 Anderson and Cayton, *Dominion of War*, 148.

27 Washington to James Tilghman, Feb. 17, 1774, and Washington to Henry Ridell, Feb. 22, 1774, in *PGWC*, 9:484, 496.

28 On the Boston Tea Party, see Benjamin Woods Labaree, *The Boston Tea Party* (New York: Oxford University Press, 1964); Alfred F. Young, "George Robert Twelves Hewes (1742–1840): A Boston Shoemaker and the Memory of the American Revolution," *WMQ* 38 (1981): 561–623.

29 Jack M. Sosin, *Whitehall and the Wilderness: The Middle West in British Colonial Policy, 1760–1775* (Lincoln: University of Nebraska Press, 1961), 239–55; David Ammerman, *In the Common Cause: American Response to the Coercive Acts of 1774* (Charlottesville: University Press of Virginia, 1974), 10–12 and passim.

30 On Dunmore's War, see Anderson and Cayton, *Dominion of War*, 150–51, 153–54; Gary B. Nash, *The Unknown American Revolution: The Unruly Birth of Democracy and the Struggle to Create America* (New York: Penguin, 2005), 167–68, 170–71.

31 Earl of Dartmouth to Earl of Dunmore, Sept. 8, 1774, as quoted in Royster, *Fabulous History*, 214.

32 Holton, *Forced Founders*, 35.

33 On migration, see Calloway, *Scratch of a Pen*, 56–59; Bernard Bailyn, *Voyagers to the West: A Passage in the Peopling of America on the Eve of the Revolution* (New York: Knopf, 1986), chap. 5. On the depression of the 1760s, see Anderson, *Crucible of War*, 588–97; Thomas M. Doerflinger, *A Vigorous Spirit of Enterprise: Merchants and Economic Development in Revolutionary Philadelphia* (Chapel Hill: University of North Carolina Press, 1986), 167–96; Marc Egnal, *A Mighty Empire: The Origins of the American Revolution* (Ithaca, N.Y.: Cornell University Press, 1988), 126–49; Gary B. Nash, *The Urban Crucible: Social Change, Political Consciousness, and the Origins of the American Revolution* (Cambridge, Mass.: Harvard University Press, 1979), 233–63. On planters, debt, and anxiety, see T. H. Breen, *Tobacco Culture: The Mentality of the Great Tidewater Planters on the Eve of Revolution* (Princeton, N.J.: Princeton University Press, 1985), 84–159.

34 George P. Anderson, "Ebenezer Mackintosh: Stamp Act Rioter and Patriot," *Publications of the Colonial Society of Massachusetts* 26 (1924–26): 15–64, esp. 9–11.

35 Jonathan Mayhew, *Two Discourses . . .* (Boston, 1759), 60–61.

36 Thomas Barnard, *A Sermon Preached before His Excellency . . . May 25th, 1763* (Boston, 1763), 42, 44.

37 Nash, *Urban Crucible*, 315, 337.

38 Morgan and Morgan, *Stamp Act Crisis*, 48–49.

39 John Dickinson, *The Late Regulations Respecting the British Colonies* (Philadelphia, 1765), reprinted in *Pamphlets of the American Revolution,* vol. 1, ed. Bernard Bailyn (Cambridge, Mass.: Harvard University Press, 1965), 672, 683.

40 Ibid., 678–79.

41 Henry Laurens, *Extracts from the Proceedings of the Court of Vice-Admiralty* (Charleston, S.C., 1769), reprinted in Jensen, *Tracts,* 187, 202.

42 Kenneth Silverman, *A Cultural History of the American Revolution: Painting, Music, Literature, and the Theatre in the Colonies and the United States from the Treaty of Paris to the Inauguration of George Washington, 1763–1789* (New York: Thomas Y. Crowell, 1976), 145–46; "The New Massachusetts Liberty Song" (Boston, 1770).

43 James Bowdoin, Joseph Warren, and Samuel Pemberton, *A Short Narrative of the Horrid Massacre in Boston* (Boston, 1770), in Jensen, *Tracts,* 209–10.

44 Quoted in Michael G. Kammen, "British and Imperial Interests in the Age of the American Revolution," in *Anglo-American Political Relations, 1675–1775,* ed. Alison Gilbert Olson and Richard Maxwell Brown (New Brunswick, N.J.: Rutgers University Press, 1970), 148–49. On the perception of a West Indian interest behind the Sugar Act, see also Morgan and Morgan, *Stamp Act Crisis,* 43–44, 50–51; Andrew Jackson O'Shaughnessy, *An Empire Divided: The American Revolution and the British Caribbean* (Philadelphia: University of Pennsylvania Press, 2000), 58–77; Agnes Whitson, "The Outlook of the Continental American Colonies on the British West Indies, 1760–1775," *Political Science Quarterly* 45 (March 1930): 56–86.

45 James Otis, *The Rights of the British Colonies Asserted and Proved* (Boston, 1764), reprinted in Bailyn, *Pamphlets,* 435.

46 Ibid., 435–36; T. H. Breen, *The Marketplace of Revolution: How Consumer Politics Shaped American Independence* (New York: Oxford University Press, 2004), 83; Brückner, *Geographic Revolution,* 76–78.

47 Dickinson, *Late Regulations,* 676.

48 *Providence Gazette,* quoted in O'Shaughnessy, *An Empire Divided,* 66.

49 Stephen Hopkins, "An Essay on the Trade of the Northern Colonies," *Newport Mercury,* Feb. 6 and 13, 1764, reprinted in Jensen, *Tracts,* 10–11.

50 Otis, *Rights of the British Colonies,* 439–40.

51 David W. Galenson, "Settlement and Growth of the Colonies," in *Cambridge Economic History of the United States, Volume 1: The Colonial Era,* ed. Stanley L. Engerman and Robert E. Gallman (New York: Cambridge University Press, 1996), table 4.9, 195.

52 This paragraph draws heavily from O'Shaughnessy, *An Empire Divided,* 81–108.

53 "A Letter from the Committee of Correspondence in Barbados, to Their Agent in London," reprinted in [John Dickinson], *An Address to the Committee of Correspondence in Barbados . . . by a North-American* (Philadelphia, 1766), v. The letter also appeared in *Pennsylvania Gazette,* May 1, 1766.

54 Dickinson, *Address to the Committee,* 1, 10.

55 Quotations from O'Shaughnessy, *An Empire Divided,* 103–4.

56 Silverman, *A Cultural History*, 220, 236–37, 374; Richard Cumberland, *The West Indian*, in *Plays of the Restoration and Eighteenth Century as They Were Acted at the Theatres-Royal by Their Majesties Servants*, ed. Dougald MacMillan and Howard Mumford Jones (New York: Holt, Rinehart and Winston, 1966), 748, 750.

57 *Pennsylvania Gazette*, June 1, 1774. John Adams writing as "Novanglus," *Boston Gazette*, Feb. 13, 1775.

58 John Aplin, *Verses on Doctor Mayhew's Book of Observations* (Providence, R.I., 1763), reprinted in Bailyn, *Pamphlets*, 280–81. Aplin was responding to Mayhew's *Observations on the Charter and Conduct of the Society* (Boston, 1763).

59 Nash, *Urban Crucible*, 245. On mortality in Massachusetts as a whole and as a "part of the common groundwork of memory for all those who served in the provincial armies," see Fred Anderson, *A People's Army: Massachusetts Soldiers and Society in the Seven Years' War* (Chapel Hill: University of North Carolina Press, 1984), 99–107, quotation from 107.

60 Anderson, *Crucible of War*, 317–24, 518–19; Thomas L. Purvis, "The Seven Years' War and Its Political Legacy," in *A Companion to the American Revolution*, ed. Jack P. Greene and J. R. Pole (Malden, Mass.: Blackwell, 2004), 114–15.

61 William Hicks, *The Nature and Extent of Parliamentary Power Considered* (New York, 1768), reprinted in Jensen, *Tracts*, 179. For the publication history of this pamphlet, see Jensen, *Tracts*, 164–65. See also Otis, *Rights of the British Colonies*, 464; Dickinson, *Late Regulations*, 690.

62 Otis, *Rights of the British Colonies*, 478; Dickinson, *Late Regulations*, 669; Jefferson, "A Summary View," 259. See also Thomas Fitch et al., *Reasons Why the British Colonies in America Should Not Be Charged with Internal Taxes* (New Haven, Conn., 1764), reprinted in Bailyn, *Pamphlets*, 404.

63 Daniel Shute, *A Sermon Preached before His Excellency . . . May 25th, 1768* (Boston, 1768), 32–33; Silas Downer, *Discourse Delivered . . . the 25th Day of July, 1768* (Providence, R.I., 1768), 4–5.

64 "Massachusettensis," *Massachusetts Gazette and Boston Post-Boy*, Dec. 19, 1774; "Novanglus," *Boston Gazette*, February 13, 1775.

65 Otis, *Rights of the British Colonies*, 478; Fitch, *Reasons*, 404; Richard Bland, *An Inquiry into the Rights of the British Colonies* (Williamsburg, Va., 1766), in Jensen, *Tracts*, 118.

66 Suffolk County Resolutions, in *JCC*, 1:32. See also John Winthrop to Richard Price, April 10, 1775, Richard Price Papers, American Philosophical Society, Philadelphia.

67 Richard Price, "Observations on the Nature of Civil Liberty, the Principles of Government, and the Justice and Policy of the War with America," in *Richard Price and the Ethical Foundations of the American Revolution*, ed. Bernard Peach (Durham, N.C.: Duke University Press, 1979), 85; Jan Ingenhousz to Benjamin Franklin, Dec. 14, 1777, in *PBF*, 25:286.

68 *Liberty: A Poem by Rusticus* (Philadelphia, 1768), 19, 21; Alexander Martin, *America: A Poem* (Philadelphia, 1769[?]), 5–6. On Columbus in American poems, see also William Livingston, *America; or, a Poem on the Settlement of the British Colonies* (New Haven, Conn., 1770), 4. *Boston Gazette,* Sept. 7, 1772, quoted in Silverman, *A Cultural History,* 227. See also Silverman, *A Cultural History,* 320.

69 As Craig Yirush has noted, "By emphasizing the labors that they had undergone in subduing what they viewed as a wilderness, the colonists were ultimately able to argue that their New World polities had independent legal and political foundations because they quite literally had been created out of nothing but the colonists labor." Craig Yirush, "From the Perspective of Empire: The Common Law, Natural Rights, and the Formation of American Political Theory, 1689–1775," Ph.D. diss., Johns Hopkins University, Baltimore, 2004, 322.

70 On colonists' views of representation generally, see Gordon S. Wood, *Representation in the American Revolution,* rev. ed. (Charlottesville: University of Virginia Press, 2008).

71 Morgan, *Inventing the People,* 141–48, quotation from 148.

72 Otis, *Rights of the British Colonies,* 442–43, 427. My interpretation of Otis draws on Bernard Bailyn, *The Ideological Origins of the American Revolution* (Cambridge, Mass.: Harvard University Press, 1967), 205–9; Lee Ward, *The Politics of Liberty in England and Revolutionary America* (Cambridge: Cambridge University Press, 2004), 331–46. On the rise of Parliamentary sovereignty in the empire, see Yirush, "From the Perspective of Empire," 250–63.

73 Bailyn, *Ideological Origins,* 209–15. Bailyn sees the "internal"/"external" distinction as "extemporized casually," and a "simple expedient" (209). I argue that it also reflects a deep-seated spatial consciousness.

74 Ibid., 216. For the moderation in Dickinson's argument, see Ward, *Politics of Liberty,* 346–50.

75 William Knox, *The Controversy between Great Britain and Her Colonies Reviewed . . .* (London, 1769), quoted in Bailyn, *Ideological Origins,* 218.

76 James Otis, *A Vindication of the British Colonies* (Boston, 1765), reprinted in Bailyn, *Pamphlets,* 564, 567.

77 *Providence Gazette,* May 11, 1765, in Edmund S. Morgan, *Prologue to Revolution: Sources and Documents on the Stamp Act Crisis, 1764–1766* (New York: Norton, 1959), 75–76.

78 Ibid., 76; *Constitutional Courant,* Sept. 21, 1765; *Proceedings of the Congress at New York* (Annapolis, Md., 1766), in Morgan, *Prologue to Revolution,* 63. For subsequent assertions of the impossibility of American representation in Parliament, see Downer, *Discourse Delivered in Providence,* 6–7; Hicks, *Nature and Extent,* 170; Samuel Adams[?], *A State of the Rights of the Colonists* (Boston, 1772), reprinted in Jensen, *Tracts,* 240–41.

79 Daniel Dulany, *Considerations on the Propriety of Imposing Taxes in the British*

Colonies (Annapolis, Md., 1765), reprinted in Bailyn, *Pamphlets,* 635. For the publication history of Dulany's pamphlet, see Bailyn, *Pamphlets,* 599. On Dulany and Buffonian formulations, see Brückner, *Geographic Revolution,* 77–78.

80 Silverman, *A Cultural History,* 33; Hicks, *Nature and Extent,* 171.

81 *Pennsylvania Journal,* March 13, 1766.

82 Pauline Maier, *From Resistance to Revolution: Colonial Radicals and the Development of American Opposition to Britain, 1765–1776* (New York: Knopf, 1972), 51–76; Nash, *Unknown American Revolution,* 45–59.

83 Christopher Gadsden to Charles Garth, Dec. 2, 1765, in R. W. Gibbes, *Documentary History of the American Revolution,* 3 vols. (New York, 1853–57), 1:8.

84 Elisabeth L. Roark, *Artists of Colonial America* (Westport, Conn.: Greenwood Press, 2003), 135–36; Silverman, *A Cultural History,* 95–96.

85 Morgan, *Inventing the People,* 243.

86 Benjamin Franklin, "On Claims to the Soil of America," in *PBF,* 20:115.

87 Jefferson, "A Summary View," 258–60, 265; *JCC,* 1:63–73. On Jefferson as a representative of the more radical thinking on the eve of the Revolution, see Ward, *Politics of Liberty,* 351–75. Yirush argues convincingly that colonists had drawn on the Lockean right to leave the government under which they live and reestablish one elsewhere long before the Revolution: Yirush, "From the Perspective of Empire."

88 Thomas Paine, *Common Sense* [1776], in *WTP,* 1:24, 29.

89 Gadsden to Garth, Dec. 2, 1765, in Gibbes, *Documentary History,* 1:8.

90 Yirush, "From the Perspective of Empire," 307–11, Adams quotation from 307–8.

91 Morgan, *Inventing the People,* 125.

92 A strong case has been made in recent years for the importance of Lockean ideas about natural rights—particularly the notion that government is the product of popular consent and exists to protect these inalienable rights—in Anglo-American political thought leading up to the Declaration of Independence. See, e.g., Breen, "Interpreting New World Nationalism," "Ideology and Nationalism," and *The Lockean Moment: The Language of Rights on the Eve of the American Revolution* (Oxford: Oxford University Press, 2001); Ward, *Politics of Liberty;* Yirush, "From the Perspective of Empire." Yirush rightly points out that natural-rights ideology had much deeper roots in the colonial American past. However, I would also argue that the heightened continental consciousness in the aftermath of the Seven Years' War, which functioned as a nascent nationalism, amplified colonists' attachment to this political ideology.

93 Otis, *Rights of the British Colonies,* 423.

94 Bland, *Inquiry into the Rights,* 123–25.

95 Josiah Quincy Sr. to Benjamin Franklin, March 25, 1775, in *PBF,* 22:3.

96 Gregg L. Lint et al., eds., *The Papers of John Adams,* vol. 9 (Cambridge, Mass.:

Harvard University Press, 1996), 157–220; Thomas Pownall, *A Memorial Most Humbly Addressed to the Sovereigns of Europe* . . . (London, 1780), 4, 12, 15–17.

97 Shy, "Spectrum."

98 Lindsey Swift, ed., *Catalogue of the John Adams Library in the Public Library of the City of Boston* (Boston: Boston Public Library Trustees, 1917), 200; John Adams to the President of Congress, April 19, 1780, in Lint et al., *Papers of John Adams*, 164.

99 Adams to Robert Livingston, June 9, 1783, quoted in James H. Hutson, "Introduction," in *Letters from a Distinguished America: Twelve Essays by John Adams on American Foreign Policy, 1780*, ed. James H. Hutson (Washington, D.C.: Library of Congress, 1978), xix.

100 Richard B. Morris, *The Peacemakers: The Great Powers and Independence* (New York: Harper and Row, 1965), 429.

101 Lint et al., *Papers of John Adams*, 158.

102 Adams, quoted in David M. Fitzsimons, "Tom Paine's New World Order: Idealistic Internationalism in the Ideology of Early American Foreign Relations," *Diplomatic History* 19 (1995): 581.

4. NATIONALISM'S NATURE

1 "Journal of Josiah Quincy, Jun., during His Voyage and Residence in England from September 28th, 1774, to March 3d, 1775," *Proceedings of the Massachusetts Historical Society* 50 (1917): 438; Joseph Galloway to Samuel Verplanck, Dec. 30, 1774, in *LDC*, 1:288

2 Galloway to Verplanck, Dec. 30, 1774, in *LDC*, 1:288; John Adams to Hezekiah Niles, Feb. 13, 1818, in *The Works of John Adams, Second President of the United States, with a Life of the Author,* ed. Charles Francis Adams, 10 vols. (Boston, 1850–56), 10:283.

3 For a sampling of scholarship on how the Continental Congress managed to oversee an improbable victory, see Merrill Jensen, *The Articles of Confederation: An Interpretation of the Social-Constitutional History of the American Revolution, 1774–1781* [1940] (Madison: University of Wisconsin Press, 1970); Jack N. Rakove, *The Beginnings of National Politics: An Interpretive History of the Continental Congress* (New York: Knopf, 1979); T. H. Breen, *The Marketplace of Revolution: How Consumer Politics Shaped American Independence* (New York: Oxford University Press, 2004); Richard B. Morris, *The Peacemakers: The Great Powers and American Independence* (New York: Harper and Row, 1965).

4 William Guthrie, *A New Geographical, Historical, and Commercial Grammar* . . . (London, 1770), viii, 561; Thomas Salmon, *A New Geographical and Historical Grammar,* 12th ed. (London, 1772), 618.

5 See, e.g., Guthrie, *A New Geographical,* 561; Salmon, *A New Geographical and Historical Grammar,* 568.

6 *Pennsylvania Gazette,* March 12, 1772.

7 Quotations from Bernard Bailyn, *The Ideological Origins of the American Revolution* (Cambridge, Mass.: Harvard University Press, 1967), 79, 135.

8 Samuel Williams, *A Discourse on the Love of our Country* (Salem, Mass., 1775), 21; John J. Zubly, *The Law of Liberty: A Sermon on American Affairs* . . . (Philadelphia, 1775), appendix.

9 Zubly, *The Law of Liberty,* ix; Williams, *A Discourse,* 23, 27.

10 "The Address of America's Genius, to the People in the American World," *Royal American Magazine,* Jan. 1774, 10; *Royal American Magazine,* Feb. 1775, 55. For America as an asylum, see Marilyn C. Baseler, *"Asylum for Mankind": America, 1607–1800* (Ithaca, N.Y.: Cornell University Press, 1998).

11 "Political Discourse, No. 9: For the Fast Day Appointed by Congress, April 1778," *United States Magazine,* May 1779, 198.

12 Jan Ingenhousz to Benjamin Franklin, December 14, 1777, in *PBF,* 25:289.

13 The section title is borrowed from Jerrilyn Greene Marston, *King and Congress: The Transfer of Political Legitimacy, 1774–1776* (Princeton, N.J.: Princeton University Press, 1987).

14 Ibid., 20–34, esp. 22.

15 On Wilson, see Craig Yirush, "From the Perspective of Empire: The Common Law, Natural Rights, and the Formation of American Political Theory, 1689–1775," Ph.D. diss., Johns Hopkins University, Baltimore, 2004, 281–91, Wilson quotations from 289–90. See also Brendan McConville, *The King's Three Faces: The Rise and Fall of Royal America, 1688–1776* (Chapel Hill: University of North Carolina Press, 2006), 250–61, Lee quotation from 256.

16 Marston, *King and Congress,* 22–25. For examples of references to "sister colonies," see Peter Force, ed., *American Archives* . . . (Washington, D.C., 1837–46), 4th ser., vol. 1, 316, 422, 440.

17 Quoted in Marston, *King and Congress,* 26–27.

18 Quoted in ibid., 26.

19 Quoted in ibid., 27.

20 McConville, *King's Three Faces,* argues ably that the colonists' loyalty to the king intensified during these years.

21 Quotation from Pauline Maier, *From Resistance to Revolution: Colonial Radicals and the Development of American Opposition to Britain, 1765–1776* (New York: Knopf, 1972), 238.

22 William Cobbett, *The Parliamentary History of England from the Earliest Period to the Year 1803,* vol. 18 (London, 1813), 696.

23 Thomas Paine, *Common Sense* [1776], in *WTP,* 1:8, 19–20, 24, 24n3. For a subtle analysis of Paine's forensic and dramaturgical strategy, see Martin Brückner, *The Geographic Revolution in America: Maps, Literacy, and National Identity* (Chapel Hill: University of North Carolina Press, 2006), 91–97.

24 Marston, *King and Congress*, 187. For apprehensions that colonial disunity in the absence of a king might lead to civil war, see 182–83; David C. Hendrickson, "The First Union: Nationalism versus Internationalism in the American Revolution," in *Empire and Nation: The American Revolution in the Atlantic World*, ed. Eliga H. Gould and Peter S. Onuf (Baltimore: Johns Hopkins University Press, 2005), 41.

25 Marston, *King and Congress*, 68.

26 Force, *American Archives*, 525, 624, 667, 700, 734.

27 Rakove, *Beginnings of National Politics*, 22–27.

28 John Adams to Joseph Hawley, Nov. 25, 1775, and John Adams to Samuel Osgood, Nov. 14, 1775, in *LDC*, 2:342, 385.

29 Rakove, *Beginnings of National Politics;* Marston, *King and Congress.*

30 Benjamin Rush, "Notes for a Speech in Congress," Aug. 1, 1776, in *LDC*, 4:601.

31 "John Witherspoon's Speech in Congress," in *LDC*, 4:585–87.

32 Arguing for the congress as a national government are Samuel H. Beer, *To Make a Nation: The Rediscovery of American Federalism* (Cambridge, Mass.: Harvard University Press, 1993); Richard B. Morris, *The Forging of the Union, 1781–1789* (New York: Harper and Row, 1987); Rakove, *Beginnings of National Politics.* Making the argument for the congress as an international compact created by sovereign states is Hendrickson, "First Union" and *Peace Pact: The Lost World of the American Founding* (Lawrence: University of Kansas Press, 2003). A lucid discussion that sees problems with both views is Jack P. Greene, "The Problematic Character of the American Union: The Background of the Articles of Confederation," in *Understanding the American Revolution: Issues and Actors* (Charlottesville: University Press of Virginia, 1995), 128–63.

33 Hendrickson, "First Union," 36–39.

34 Marston, *King and Congress*, 80–81. As Marston explains, the Albany and Stamp Act congresses were not important precedents for the Continental Congress because they were not extralegal conventions. In the former, the delegates had been convened at the urging of imperial officials. In the latter, delegates were "largely the legitimate representatives of the colonial assemblies. They believed they were acting for the entirely constitutional purpose of petitioning the king and remonstrating with Parliament" (80).

35 *LDC*, 1:25, emphasis in the original.

36 Data for the provincial resolutions and the delegates' credentials come from Force, *American Archives*, 315–16, 355–56, 416–17, 421–22, 438–40, 525–27, 606–7, 624–25, 666–68, 686–68, 700–701, 734–37, 893–98, 900–901. All data for the delegates' correspondence throughout the chapter reflect findings from a search of the Library of Congress's online version of *LDC* (http://memory.loc.gov/ammem/amlaw/lwdg.html) during June 2006. In arriving at final figures, only references in the text of documents were included, and references in the editorial notes were excluded. Also, hyphenated versions of the two-word terms are included.

37 Force, *American Archives,* 422, 526, 606, 686, 898.

38 This statement is based on a cross-listing of the names of people who used the term "Continental Congress" with their factional attributes in H. James Henderson, *Party Politics in the Continental Congress* (Lanham, Md.: University Press of America, 1974), 72–73, table 2.

39 Data from the *Pennsylvania Gazette* come from a search conducted during December 2006 of the Accessible Archives database and includes only references from the text of the newspaper and hyphenated versions of the terms. Although other colonial newspapers are searchable in electronic form, these databases require the use of character recognition software, making results unreliable. Also, a search of the *Pennsylvania Gazette* should resemble trends in other colonies, as the items from this paper were reprinted in other newspapers, and many of the items that appeared in the *Pennsylvania Gazette* first originated in materials from other colonies.

40 "Letter to the Inhabitants of Quebec," Oct. 26, 1774, in *JCC,* 1:111–12. An earlier draft of the letter is at "John Dickinson's Draft Letter to Quebec," Oct, 24–26 (?), 1774, in *LDC,* 1:242.

41 George Washington's Address to the Inhabitants of Canada, ca. September 14, 1775, in *PGWR,* 1:461–62; George Washington to Benedict Arnold, Sept. 14, 1775, in *PGWR,* 1:455–56.

42 George Washington, "Address to the Inhabitants of Bermuda," Sept. 6, 1775, in *PGWR,* 1:419–20.

43 Albert K. Weinberg, *Manifest Destiny: A Study of Nationalist Expansionism in American History* (Gloucester, Mass.: Peter Smith, 1958), chap. 1, John Adams, Samuel Adams, and John Witherspoon quotations from 19, 21–24.

44 Fulmer Mood, "The Origin, Evolution, and Application of the Sectional Concept, 1750–1900," in *Regionalism in America* [1951], ed. Merrill Jensen (Madison: University of Wisconsin Press, 1965), 22.

45 *JCC,* 5:429, 431 (quotation).

46 Paine, *Common Sense,* 1:18–21.

47 On "idealistic internationalism," see Felix Gilbert, *To the Farewell Address: Ideas of Early American Foreign Policy* (Princeton, N.J.: Princeton University Press, 1961), 36–43, 72; David M. Fitzsimons, "Tom Paine's New World Order: Idealistic Internationalism in the Ideology of Early American Foreign Relations," *Diplomatic History* 19 (1995): 569–82. On Paine's importance to U.S. diplomacy, see George C. Herring, *From Colony to Superpower: U.S. Foreign Relations since 1776* (New York: Oxford University Press, 2008), 12; Michael H. Hunt, *Ideology and U.S. Foreign Policy* (New Haven, Conn.: Yale University Press, 1987), 19–21; Lawrence S. Kaplan, *Entangling Alliances with None: American Foreign Policy in the Age of Jefferson* (Kent, Ohio: Kent State University Press, 1987), 158; Wil-

liam C. Stinchcombe, "Americans Celebrate the Birth of the Dauphin," in *Diplomacy and Revolution: The Franco-American Alliance of 1778,* ed. Ronald Hoffman and Peter J. Albert (Charlottesville: University Press of Virginia, 1981), 40.

48 Lyman Butterfield et al., eds., *Diary and Autobiography of John Adams,* 4 vols. (Cambridge, Mass.: Harvard University Press, 1961), 3:337–38.

49 Alexander DeConde, "The French Alliance in Historical Speculation," in Hoffman and Albert, *Diplomacy and Revolution,* 5; Herring, *From Colony to Superpower,* 17; Lawrence S. Kaplan, "The Treaties of Paris and Washington, 1778 and 1949: Reflections on Entangling Alliances," in Hoffman and Albert, *Diplomacy and Revolution,* 158–59; "Editorial Note," in *The Papers of John Adams,* 14 vols., ed. Robert J. Taylor et al. (Cambridge, Mass.: Harvard University Press, 1979–), 4:260–64.

50 Quoted in Mood, "Origin, Evolution, and Application," 22. The main text is in the hand of John Adams but includes notes and comments in the hands of others. See *JCC,* 5:576–89. The Committee of Congress deleted the bracketed material from the original text. See also "A Plan of Treaties," in Taylor et al., *Papers of John Adams,* 4:267–68.

51 *JCC,* 5:579–80 (quotation).

52 On Franklin's diplomatic mission to Canada, see Edmund S. Morgan, *Benjamin Franklin* (New Haven, Conn.: Yale University Press, 2002), 230–31, Franklin quotation from 231; Stacy Schiff, *A Great Improvisation: Franklin, France, and the Birth of America* (New York: Henry Holt, 2005), 17; *JCC,* 5:770; Taylor et al., *Papers of John Adams,* 4:292.

53 John Adams to George Washington, Jan. 1776, quoted in David Hackett Fischer, *Washington's Crossing* (New York: Oxford University Press, 2004), 80.

54 Mood, "Origin, Evolution, and Application," 23; *JCC,* 6:1054–58, quotation from 1057.

55 On the French armament more than Saratoga determining the timing of the French alliance, see Jonathan R. Dull, *A Diplomatic History of the American Revolution* (New Haven, Conn.: Yale University Press, 1985), 89–94.

56 For the treaties with the French, see *Treaties and Other International Acts of the United States of America,* ed. Hunter Miller, vol. 2 (Washington, D.C.: U.S. Government Printing Office, 1931), 3–47. On the treaty of alliance as a departure from the promise of 1776, see Kaplan, "Treaties of Paris and Washington," 162 (quotation). On Spanish aims, see Gregg L. Lint, "Preparing for Peace: The Objectives of the United States, France, and Spain in the War of the American Revolution," in *Peace and the Peacemakers: The Treaty of 1783,* ed. Ronald Hoffman and Peter J. Albert (Charlottesville: University Press of Virginia, 1986), 40–41.

57 Interestingly, "Confederation Congress" never gained traction as a title for the institution. A search for the term "Confederation Congress" in the online edition

of *LDC* in December 2007 yielded twenty-one items, but none used the phrase as a title. Instead, they are formulations such as "Under the Articles of Confederation, Congress. . . ."

58 Also important was colonists' shared experience as consumers, which allowed for the organization of consumer boycotts, a point brilliantly made in Breen, *Marketplace of Revolution.*

59 Jack Greene lays out these obstacles in Greene, "Problematic Character," 128–63.

60 Jensen, *Articles of Confederation,* 10n23, 12–14. Jack Rakove argues, contrary to Jensen, against the existence of strong factionalism in the Continental Congress, especially before 1777. Nevertheless, although he tries to avoid the use of labels such as radical and moderate, Rakove fails to avoid them entirely, for very real differences distinguished the delegates. Still, I agree, at least in part, with his overall argument that the delegates were able to achieve what they did thanks to shared ideology and the exigencies and constraints they faced. At the same time, what measure of consensus they achieved was braced in part by their shared meta-geographical assumptions and geopolitical vision. Rakove, *Beginnings of National Politics.*

61 In this respect, colonists were guilty of some of the same faulty logic that Wayne Bodle accuses historians of in "The Fabricated Region: On the Insufficiency of 'Colonies' for Understanding American Colonial History," *Early American Studies* 1 (2003): 1–27. Martin Lewis and Kären Wigen make a similar point: "The nation state idea—i.e., the assumption that cultural identities (nations) coincide with politically sovereign entities (states) to create a series of internally unified and essentially equal units—replicates at a smaller scale many of the errors found in continental thinking." Martin W. Lewis and Kären E. Wigen, *The Myth of Continents: A Critique of Metageography* (Berkeley: University of California Press, 1997), 7–8.

62 Lewis and Wigen, *Myth of Continents,* 9.

63 On the importance of unity appearing to emerge naturally, see David Waldstreicher, *In the Midst of Perpetual Fetes: The Making of American Nationalism, 1775–1820* (Chapel Hill: University of North Carolina Press, 1997), 2.

64 My thinking on the Declaration of Independence has been influenced most by David Armitage, *The Declaration of Independence: A Global History* (Cambridge, Mass.: Harvard University Press, 2007); Peter S. Onuf, "A Declaration of Independence for Diplomatic Historians," *Diplomatic History* 22 (Winter 1998): 71–83.

65 Paine, *Common Sense,* 1:39; Armitage, *Declaration of Independence,* 35; Gilbert, *To the Farewell Address,* 44–45.

66 Thomas Jefferson, "Notes of Proceedings in the Continental Congress" [June 7–August 1, 1776], in *PTJ,* 1:309–10. For fears of partition, see Armitage, *Declaration of Independence,* 44–46; James Hutson, "The Partition Treaty and the Declaration of American Independence," *JAH* 58 (1972): 875–96.

67 Adams and Lee, quoted in Hutson, "Partition Treaty," 891–92; Patrick Henry to John Adams, May 20, 1776, in *The Adams Papers Digital Edition,* ed. C. James Taylor (Charlottesville: University of Virginia Press, Rotunda, 2008), available online at http://rotunda.upress.virginia.edu/founders/ADMS-06-04-02-0087 (viewed on Jan. 16, 2010); Thomas Paine, *The American Crisis III,* in *WTP,* 1:80.

68 Edmund C. Burnett, "The Name 'The United States of America,' " *AHR* 31 (Oct. 1925): 79–81.

69 Dull, *A Diplomatic History,* 93; Morgan, *Benjamin Franklin,* 261–62.

5. NATIONALISM'S NURTURE

1 See, e.g., "Journal of an Officer's [Lord Adam Gordon's] Travels in America and the West Indies," in *Travels in the American Colonies,* ed. Newton Dennison Mereness (New York: Macmillan, 1916), 432, 438.

2 Jeremiah Greenman, *Diary of a Common Soldier in the American Revolution, 1775–1783: An Annotated Edition of the Military Journal of Jeremiah Greenman,* ed. Robert C. Bray and Paul E. Bushnell (Dekalb: Northern Illinois University Press, 1978), 18.

3 Ibid., 23. My account of the assault on Quebec draws from Don Higginbotham, *The War of American Independence: Military Attitudes, Policies, and Practice, 1763–1789* (New York: Macmillan, 1971), 108–15; Gustave Lanctôt, *Canada and the American Revolution, 1774–1783,* trans. Margaret M. Cameron (Cambridge, Mass.: Harvard University Press, 1967), 105–7; Robert Middlekauff, *The Glorious Cause: The American Revolution, 1763–1789* (New York: Oxford University Press, 1982), 304–8.

4 Lanctôt, *Canada and the American Revolution,* 169, 181, 191, 194, 205, 207. George Washington to the President of Congress, Nov. 11, 1778, in *WGW,* 13:223–44; George Washington to Henry Laurens, Nov. 14, 1778, in *WGW,* 13:254–57; *JCC,* 13:12–14.

5 Holly Mayer, "Canadian Continentals: Fighting for American Independence," paper presented at the Warfare and Society in Colonial North America and the Caribbean conference, Omohundro Institute of Early American History and Culture, Knoxville, Tenn., Oct. 7, 2006. Charles Carroll to Benjamin Franklin, May 7, 1781, in *PBF,* 35:26.

6 "Military memory," the historian Sarah Purcell points out, "is really at the heart of American national identity." Sarah Purcell, *Sealed with Blood: War, Sacrifice, and Memory in Revolutionary America* (Philadelphia: University of Pennsylvania Press, 2002), 6. Purcell's compelling argument can only be strengthened by expanding its temporal scope to demonstrate how memories of the Seven Years' War affected those of the Revolution.

7 Ammi R. Robbins, *Journal of the Rev. Ammi R. Robbins, a Chaplain in the American Army, in the Northern Campaign of 1776* (New Haven, Conn., 1850), 3.

8 Anthony Wayne to Colonel Joseph Penrose, Aug. 23, 1776, quoted in Thomas A. Chambers, "'American Golgotha': Patriots Comprehend the Revolution at Seven Years' War Battlefields," paper presented at the Warfare and Society in Colonial North America and the Caribbean conference, the Omohundro Institute of Early American History and Culture, Knoxville, Tenn., Oct. 7, 2006), 13; Robbins, *Journal,* 10–11.

9 Thomas L. Purvis, "The Seven Years' War and Its Political Legacy," in *A Companion to the American Revolution,* ed. Jack P. Greene and J. R. Pole (Malden, Mass.: Blackwell, 2004), 116.

10 Fred Anderson, *The War That Made America: A Short History of the French and Indian War* (New York: Viking, 2005), xix, 261.

11 Joseph Plumb Martin, *Private Yankee Doodle: Being a Narrative of Some of the Adventures, Dangers and Sufferings of a Revolutionary Soldier,* ed. George F. Scheer (Boston: Little, Brown, 1962), 5; John C. Dann, ed., *The Revolution Remembered: Eyewitness Accounts of the War for Independence* (Chicago: University of Chicago Press, 1980), 7.

12 Robert C. Alberts, *Benjamin West: A Biography* (Boston: Houghton Mifflin, 1978), 18, 21.

13 Quoted in Robert Hughes, *American Visions: The Epic History of Art in America* (New York: Knopf, 1997), 75–76.

14 Militarily, the battle over Quiberon Bay was more pivotal, yet it lacked the symbolic martyr that Quebec had provided. See Fred Anderson, *Crucible of War: The Seven Years' War and the Fate of Empire in British North America, 1754–1766* (New York: Knopf, 2000), 395. On sales of Woollett's engraving, see R. T. H. Halsey, "Prints Lived with at Mount Vernon," *Bulletin of the Metropolitan Museum of Art* 30 (March 1935): 65.

15 My interpretation of *The Death of General Wolfe* draws on Anderson, *Crucible of War,* 367; Derrick R. Cartwright, *Benjamin West: Allegory and Allegiance* (San Diego: Timken Museum of Art, 2004), 5–7; Linda Colley, *Britons: Forging the Nation, 1707–1837,* 2nd ed. (New Haven, Conn.: Yale University Press, 2005), 178–79; Hughes, *American Visions,* 70–76; Dennis Montagna, "Benjamin West's *The Death of General Wolfe:* A Nationalist Narrative," *American Art Journal* 13 (Spring 1981): 72–88; Kenneth Silverman, *A Cultural History of the American Revolution: Painting, Music, Literature, and the Theatre in the Colonies and the United States from the Treaty of Paris to the Inauguration of George Washington, 1763–1789* (New York: Thomas Y. Crowell, 1976), 175–78.

16 West, quoted in Hughes, *American Visions,* 76. William Dunlap, *A History of the Rise and Progress of the Arts of Design in the United States,* new ed. (New York, 1918), 43.

17 *Pennsylvania Gazette,* May 17, 1770.

18 Purvis, "Seven Years' War," 115; Silverman, *A Cultural History*, 12, 176, 237–38.

19 *The Rising Glory of America* (Philadelphia, 1772), reprinted in Fred Lewis Pattee, *The Poems of Philip Freneau: Poet of the American Revolution*, vol. 1 (New York: Russell and Russell, 1963), 62, 73 (quotation); John Rogers Williams, ed., *Philip Vickers Fithian, Journal and Letters . . .* (Princeton, N.J., 1900), 115; Thomas Paine, "The Death of General Wolfe," in *WTP*, 2:1083–84.

20 Paine, "A Dialogue between General Wolfe and General Gage in a Wood near Boston," in *WTP*, 2:47, 49, emphasis in the original. Paine published this piece in the *Pennsylvania Journal*, Jan. 4, 1775.

21 On the popularity of Paine and *Common Sense*, see Hugh Amory and David D. Hall, eds., *The Colonial Book in the Atlantic World* (Cambridge: Cambridge University Press, 2000), 295, 311, 518, 521.

22 Craig Nelson, *Thomas Paine: Enlightenment, Revolution, and the Birth of Modern Nations* (New York: Viking, 2006), 54, 60.

23 As one of his biographers has noted, Paine's "personal and political associations were limited to no single group; in both England and America they spanned the worlds of the upper-class salon and tavern political debates." Eric Foner, *Tom Paine and Revolutionary America* (New York: Oxford University Press, 2005), 99.

24 Adams, quoted in Pauline Maier, *American Scripture: Making the Declaration of Independence* (New York: Knopf, 1997), 31.

25 Livingston, quoted in Charles Haven Hunt, *Life of Edward Livingston* (New York, 1864), 20; Bayard Tuckerman, *Life of General Philip Schuyler, 1733–1804* (New York, 1903), 81. Thomas Paine, *Common Sense* [1776], in *WTP*, 1:23–24.

26 "Extract of a Letter from a Gentleman in London to His Friend in This City, Dated July 10, 1775," *Pennsylvania Gazette*, Sept. 13, 1775; Richard Wells, *The Middle Line; or, an Attempt to Furnish some Hints . . .* (Philadelphia, 1775), 38; Paine, *Common Sense*, 1:24.

27 James Chalmers, *Plain Truth; Addressed to the Inhabitants of America, Containing, Remarks on a Late Pamphlet Entitled Common Sense* (Philadelphia, 1776), 17; Charles Inglis, *The True Interest of America Impartially Stated in Certain Strictures on a Pamphlet Intitled Common Sense* (Philadelphia, 1776), 53; Francis Hopkinson to Benjamin Towne, Nov. 16, 1776, in *LDC*, 25:594.

28 Michael P. Gabriel, *Major General Richard Montgomery: The Making of an American Hero* (London: Associated University Press, 2002), 176–77; Purcell, *Sealed with Blood*, 25–29; Peter Silver, *Our Savage Neighbors: How Indian War Transformed Early America* (New York: Norton, 2008), 233; Silverman, *A Cultural History*, 315.

29 Purcell, *Sealed with Blood*, 30–31.

30 William Smith, *An Oration in Memory of General Montgomery* (Philadelphia, 1776), 18, 20–21, 31.

31 Thomas Paine, "A Dialogue between the Ghost of General Montgomery Just Arrived from the Elysian Fields; and an American Delegate, in a Wood near Philadelphia," in *WTP,* 2:89.

32 Ibid., 93.

33 Thomas Anburey, *Travels through the Interior Parts of America,* 2 vols. (Boston: Houghton Mifflin, 1923), 1:36, 56. The Latin phrase from Ovid's *Metamorphoses* was frequently quoted by English poets and playwrights.

34 "A Song on the Brave General Montgomery, Who Fell within the Walls of Quebec, Dec. 31, 1775, in Attempting to Storm That City" (Danvers, Mass., 1776), reprinted in *The Diary of the American Revolution, 1775–1781,* ed. Frank Moore (New York: Washington Square Press, 1967), 92–93.

35 Hugh Henry Brackenridge, *The Death of General Montgomery, at the Siege of Quebec* (Philadelphia, 1777), 27, 39–40.

36 Ezra Stiles to Richard Price, April 10, 1775, Richard Price Papers, American Philosophical Society, Philadelphia; Adams, quoted in Charles Royster, *A Revolutionary People at War: The Continental Army and American Character, 1775–1783* (Chapel Hill: University of North Carolina Press, 1979). Royster's work on the ambivalent relationship between the army and the people influences my account in this and the following section, as does E. Wayne Carp, *To Starve the Army at Pleasure: Continental Army Administration and American Political Culture, 1775–1783* (Chapel Hill: University of North Carolina Press, 1984).

37 Congress to George Washington, June 19, 1775, in *PGWR,* 1:7; General Orders, July 4, 1775, in *PGWR,* 1:54.

38 Data from the *Pennsylvania Gazette* come from a search conducted during December 2006 of the Accessible Archives database and include only references from the text of the newspaper and hyphenated versions of the terms. Although other colonial newspapers are searchable in electronic form, these databases require the use of character recognition software, making results unreliable. Also, a search of the *Pennsylvania Gazette* should resemble trends in other colonies, as the items from this paper were reprinted in other newspapers, and many of the items that appeared in the *Pennsylvania Gazette* first originated in materials from other colonies.

39 On sectional compromise, see Higginbotham, *War of American Independence,* 85. Charles Chauncy to Richard Price, July (?) 1775, in *Richard Price and the Ethical Foundations of the American Revolution,* ed. Bernard Peach (Durham, N.C.: Duke University Press, 1979), 301.

40 Fred W. Anderson, "The Hinge of Revolution: George Washington Confronts a People's Army, July 3, 1775," *Massachusetts Historical Review* 1 (1999): 44.

41 George Washington to Lund Washington, Aug. 20, 1775, in ibid., 25. See also Washington to Joseph Spencer, Sept. 26, 1775, in *PGWR,* 2:55.

42 David Hackett Fischer, *Washington's Crossing* (New York: Oxford University Press, 2004), 151.

43 Hundreds of thousands is likely a high figure, yet accurate numbers are unavailable, and numbers do not necessarily measure the pamphlet's impact. There is no doubt that the pamphlet circulated widely within the congress and the army. On *Common Sense's* dissemination, see Trish Loughran, *The Republic in Print: Print Culture in the Age of U.S. Nation Building, 1770–1870* (New York: Columbia University Press, 2007), chap. 2; Eric Slauter, "Reading and Radicalization: Print, Politics, and the American Revolution," *Early American Studies* 8 (Winter 2010): 40.

44 Paine, *Common Sense*, 31; Nelson, *Thomas Paine*, 91.

45 Fischer, *Washington's Crossing*, 138.

46 Nelson, *Thomas Paine*, 108; *WTP*, 1:49.

47 Higginbotham, *War of American Independence*, 182. For congressional attempts at reform, see Carp, *To Starve the Army at Pleasure*.

48 Fischer, *Washington's Crossing*, 143–51, quotation from 151.

49 Allen Bowman, *The Morale of the American Revolutionary Army* (Port Washington, N.Y.: Kennikat, 1964), 97; Thomas Paine, *The American Crisis I*, in *WTP*, 1:50, 54, 57; Nelson, *Thomas Paine*, 159–60.

50 Quoted in Middlekauff, *Glorious Cause*, 463.

51 Higginbotham, *War of American Independence*, 262. Pauline Maier, *From Resistance to Revolution: Colonial Radicals and the Development of American Opposition to Britain, 1765–1776* (New York: Knopf, 1972), 267n73. See also Fred Anderson and Andrew Cayton, *The Dominion of War: Empire and Liberty in North America, 1500–2000* (New York: Viking, 2005), 166–67, 178; Royster, *A Revolutionary People at War*, 114–20.

52 Higginbotham, *War of American Independence*, 262–63; *An Eulogium on General Washington Being Appointed Commander in Chief of the Foederal Army in America* (Philadelphia, 1781), 17, quoted in Purcell, *Sealed with Blood*, 35. Chapter 1 of Purcell's work presents an astute analysis of the importance of such commemoration.

53 The preceding two paragraphs draw on Higginbotham, *War of American Independence*, 264; Simon P. Newman, *Parades and the Politics of the Street* (Philadelphia: University of Pennsylvania Press, 1997), esp. 37; David Waldstreicher, "Rites of Rebellion, Rites of Assent: Celebrations, Print Culture, and the Origins of American Nationalism," *JAH* (June 1995): 37–61, esp. 51–52; *The Journal of Nicholas Cresswell, 1774–1777* (New York: Dial Press, 1924), 181; Henry Knox to Gouverneur Morris, Feb. 21, 1783, quoted in Richard R. Kohn, *Eagle and Sword: The Federalists and the Creation of the Military Establishment in America, 1783–1802* (New York: Free Press, 1975), 9; François Jean, Marquis de Chastellux, *Travels in North-America, in the Years 1780–81–82*, ed. and trans. George Grieve (New York, 1828), 72.

54 John Resch, "The Revolution as a People's War: Mobilization in New Hampshire," in *War and Society in the American Revolution: Mobilization and Home Fronts,* ed. John Resch and Walter Sargent (DeKalb: Northern Illinois University Press, 2007), 70–102; Walter Sargent, "The Massachusetts Rank and File of 1777," in Resch and Sargent, *War and Society,* 42–69.

55 Michael A. McDonnell, " 'Fit for Common Service?' Class, Race, and Recruitment in Revolutionary Virginia," in Resch and Sargent, *War and Society,* 125.

56 Gary B. Nash, *The Unknown American Revolution: The Unruly Birth of Democracy and the Struggle to Create America* (New York: Penguin, 2005), 223–32. John Shy, *A People Numerous and Armed: Reflections on the Military Struggle for American Independence* (New York: Oxford University Press, 1976), 13.

57 Robert A. Gross, *The Minutemen and Their World* (New York: Hill and Wang, 1976), 151–52, quotation from 152.

58 Charles Patrick Neimeyer, *America Goes to War: A Social History of the Continental Army* (New York: New York University Press, 1996), 21.

59 Mayer, "Canadian Continentals," 11–12, quotation from 12.

60 Shy, *A People Numerous and Armed,* 173; Nash, *Unknown American Revolution,* 216; James Kirby Martin and Mark Edward Lender, *A Respectable Army: The Military Origins of the Republic, 1763–1789* (Arlington Heights, Ill.: Harlan Davidson, 1982), 90; "Dr. John Berkenhout's Journal of an Excursion from New York to Pennsylvania, 1778," in Mereness, *Travels in the American Colonies,* 581; *Journal of Nicholas Cresswell,* 251–52.

61 Martin, *Private Yankee Doodle,* 135.

62 Ibid., 280.

63 George Washington to Alexander Hamilton, Sept. 1, 1796, in *WGW,* 35:199–200.

64 Martin, *Private Yankee Doodle,* 100.

65 Carp, *To Starve the Army at Pleasure,* 172.

66 Washington, quoted in ibid., 181. On the Pennsylvania Line mutiny generally, see Carl Van Doren, *Mutiny in January: The Story of a Crisis in the Continental Army* (New York: Viking, 1943). On New Jersey, see Neimeyer, *America Goes to War,* 152–54.

67 On the Newburgh affair, see Kohn, *Eagle and Sword,* 17–53, esp. 26–32.

68 George Washington to Nathanael Greene, Feb. 6, 1783, in *WGW,* 26:104.

69 Robert M. Calhoon, "Loyalism and Neutrality," in *Companion to the American Revolution,* 235.

70 John Shy, "Looking Backward, Looking Forward: War and Society in Revolutionary America," in Resch and Sargent, *War and Society,* 14. Chastellux, *Travels in North-America,* 24. See also Higginbotham, *War of American Independence,* 389. Carp, *To Starve the Army at Pleasure,* 14. Sargent, "Massachusetts Rank and File," 44, 63.

71 Quoted in John Keegan, *Fields of Battle: The Wars for North America* (New York: Knopf, 1996), 154.

72 *Boston Gazette*, quoted in Royster, *A Revolutionary People at War*, 116; Janet Schaw, *Journal of a Lady of Quality; Being the Narrative of a Journey from Scotland to the West Indies, North Carolina, and Portugal, in the Years 1774 to 1776*, ed. Evangeline Walker Andrews (New Haven, Conn.: Yale University Press, 1921), 190; Anburey, *Travels*, 2:1, 4.

73 Quoted in Joseph J. Ellis, *American Creation: Triumphs and Tragedies at the Founding of the Republic* (New York: Knopf, 2007), 81.

74 Adams to Abigail Adams, July 30, 1777, in *LDC*, 7:395; Adams to Abigail Adams, Aug. 23, 1777, in *LDC*, 7:533–34.

75 Adams to Edmund Jenings, July 4, 1780, in *Papers of John Adams*, 14 vols., ed. Robert J. Taylor (Cambridge, Mass.: Harvard University Press, 1977–), 9:498.

76 Adams to the Marquis de Lafayette, Feb. 21, 1779, Taylor et al., *Papers of John Adams*, 7:421–22.

77 *Pennsylvania Gazette*, Nov. 29, 1775. The piece originally appeared in the *Essex Gazette*. On the *rage militaire*, see Royster, *A Revolutionary People at War*.

78 *JCC*, Sept. 13, 1779, 15:1055–56.

79 Paine, *The American Crisis II*, in *WTP*, 1:59, 67–68.

80 Paine, *The American Crisis VII*, in *WTP*, 1:149.

81 Paine, *The American Crisis IX*, in *WTP*, 1:167.

82 Paine, *The American Crisis X*, in *WTP*, 1:192–93.

83 Paine, *The American Crisis V*, in *WTP*, 1:120–21.

84 Paine, *The American Crisis VI*, in *WTP*, 1:137; *The American Crisis X*, in *WPT*, 1:164.

85 Joan D. Dolmetsch, *Rebellion and Reconciliation: Satirical Prints on the Revolution at Williamsburg* (Williamsburg, Va.: Colonial Williamsburg Foundation, 1976), 118, 126.

86 This paragraph draws heavily on Martin Brückner, *The Geographic Revolution in Early America* (Chapel Hill: University of North Carolina Press, 2006), chap. 2, esp. 92–93, from which I take the Wells and Paine quotations. Brückner's work offers an excellent analysis of how the continent served as a useful rhetorical figure that allowed for the expression of a collective American self.

87 John Hurt, *The Love of Our Country. A Sermon, Preached before the Virginia Troops in New-Jersey* (Philadelphia, 1777), n.p.

88 "The Adventures of a Continental Dollar," *United States Magazine*, June 1779, 265.

89 Hugh Henry Brackenridge, "An Eulogium of the Brave Men Who Have Fallen in the Contest with Great-Britain: Delivered on Monday July 5, 1779 . . . ," *United States Magazine*, August 1779, 344–55, 347.

90 Anderson and Cayton, *Dominion of War,* 170–76, quotation from 170. Silver makes a similar case in his examination of Pennsylvania in *Our Savage Neighbors.* Silver also demonstrates how "whiteness" became a prevalent notion during the Seven Years' War. He documents surges in the reports mentioning "white" people in the *Pennsylvania Gazette* during both this conflict and the Revolution: see Silver, *Our Savage Neighbors,* chap. 4, appendix.

91 George Washington to Benedict Arnold, Sept. 14, 1775, in *PGWR,* 1:455; Washington's order from 1779, quoted in Nash, *Unknown American Revolution,* 346.

92 Quotation from James H. Merrell, "Declarations of Independence: Indian-White Relations in the New Nation," in *The American Revolution: Its Character and Limits,* ed. Jack P. Greene (New York: New York University Press, 1987), 198.

93 Johann David Schoepf, *Travels in the Confederation [1783–1784] from the German of Johann David Schoepf,* ed. and trans. Alfred J. Morrison (Philadelphia: William J. Campbell, 1911), 180.

94 Israel Evans, *A Discourse, Delivered at Easton . . . to the Officers and Soldiers of the Western Army* (Philadelphia, 1779), 17, 22, 39–40.

95 My summary of the Gnadenhütten massacre draws on Daniel K. Richter, *Facing East from Indian Country: A Native History of Early America* (Cambridge, Mass.: Harvard University Press, 2001), 221–23, including the "latter-day" quotation from 222. See also, esp., Silver, *Our Savage Neighbors,* 266–76, quotations from 268, 271.

96 Schoepf, *Travels in the Confederation,* 214; Paine, *Common Sense,* 1:30; Paine, "A Dialogue between the Ghost of General Montgomery," 2:92.

97 On Jefferson's duplicity in the Declaration of Independence, see Nash, *Unknown American Revolution,* 212–16. For the contention that the Revolution mirrored the Seven Years' War, with the British occupying the strategic position previously held by the French, see Anderson and Cayton, *Dominion of War,* 168–70. "America," in William Billings, *The Singing Master's Assistant, or Key to Practical Music* (Boston, 1778), n.p.

98 Quoted in Jill Lepore, *The Name of War: King Philip's War and the Origins of American Identity* (New York: Knopf, 1998), 186–87.

99 Greg Sieminski, "The Puritan Captivity Narrative and the Politics of the American Revolution," *American Quarterly* 42 (March 1990): 37. For the importance of the memory of King Philip's War, see Lepore, *Name of War.*

100 This paragraph draws from Silver, *Our Savage Neighbors,* 234–38, quotations from 235.

101 *America Invincible. An Heroic Poem in Two Books . . . to which is prefixed, a concise history of the Former wars in america* (Danvers, Mass., 1779), 28.

102 The best treatment of the Jane McCrea story is June Namias, *White Captives: Gender and Ethnicity on the American Frontier* (Chapel Hill: University of North Carolina Press, 1993), chap. 4, *Connecticut Courant* quotation from 319n2. See

also John Ferling, *Almost a Miracle: The American Victory in the War of Independence* (New York: Oxford University Press, 2007), 226–27, Gates quote from 227.

103 For the argument that McCrea's story proved pivotal at Saratoga and in the Revolution at large, see James Austin Holden, "The Influence of the Death of Jane McCrea on Burgoyne's Campaign," *Proceedings of the New York State Historical Association* 12 (1913): 249–310. Holden's argument is echoed in Ferling, *Almost a Miracle*, 226–27. For a treatment downplaying the importance of McCrea's story, at least at Saratoga, see James Kirby Martin, *Benedict Arnold: Revolutionary Hero, an American Warrior Reconsidered* (New York: New York University Press, 1997), 352–70.

104 Schoepf, *Travels in the Confederation*, 278.

105 Hugh Henry Brackenridge, *Narratives of a Late Expedition against the Indians* (Philadelphia, 1783), 32–36, quotations from 32, 36.

106 Hal T. Shelton, *General Richard Montgomery and the American Revolution* (New York: New York University Press, 1994), 175; "A Portrait Bust by Jean-Jacques Caffieri," *Bulletin of the Metropolitan Museum of Art* 24 (Jan. 1929): 14.

107 The committee's draft peace terms and the instructions to diplomats are in *JCC*, 13:240–44, 14:955–66. Gregg L. Lint, "Preparing for Peace: The Objectives of the United States, France, and Spain in the War of the American Revolution," in *Peace and the Peacemakers: The Treaty of 1783*, ed. Ronald Hoffman and Peter J. Albert (Charlottesville: University Press of Virginia, 1986), 32–34; Bradford Perkins, "The Peace of Paris: Patterns and Legacies," in Hoffman and Albert, *Peace and the Peacemakers*, 194–95.

108 Richard Henry Lee to George Washington, June 24, 1778, in *PGWR*, 15:530; John Adams to Patrick Henry, Dec. 8, 1778, in Taylor et al., *Papers of John Adams*, 7:266.

109 Thomas E. Chávez, *Spain and the Independence of the United States: An Intrinsic Gift* (Albuquerque: University of New Mexico Press, 2002); Jonathan R. Dull, *A Diplomatic History of the American Revolution* (New Haven, Conn.: Yale University Press, 1985), 107–8; Lint, "Preparing for Peace," 41.

110 Richard B. Morris, *The Peacemakers: The Great Powers and Independence* (New York: Harper and Row, 1965), 222.

111 "Notes of John Jay's Conference with James Gardoqui and Don Bernardo del Campo," Sept. 3–15, 1780, in *DHFR*, 1:109–10. Stacy Schiff, *A Great Improvisation: Franklin, France, and the Birth of America* (New York: Henry Holt, 2005), 254; Morris, *Peacemakers*, 223.

112 On the importance of Spain to the American Revolution, see Chávez, *Spain*; Dull, *A Diplomatic History*, 110–11.

113 Benjamin Franklin to John Jay, Oct. 2, 1780, in *DHFR*, 1:119.

114 Chevalier de la Luzerne to Comte de Vergennes, Feb. 11, 1780, in *DHFR*, 1:28–29, quotation from 29.

115 Lint, "Preparing for Peace," 35–39. Comte de Vergennes to Chevalier de la Luzerne, Feb. 5, 1780, in *DHFR,* 1:23; Don Juan de Miralles to Don José de Gálvez, March 12, 1780, in *DHFR,* 1:43; Chevalier de la Luzerne to Comte de Vergennes, March 13, 1780, in *DHFR,* 1:45.

116 Vergennes, quoted in Morris, *Peacemakers,* 219. On lack of French support for American territorial aims, see ibid., 66, 219–20, 308–9, 326; Perkins, "Peace of Paris," 205; Schiff, *A Great Improvisation,* 173–74. Jonathan Dull suggests that Vergennes was more indifferent to the fate of western regions than opposed to the United States' acquiring them: Jonathan R. Dull, "France and the American Revolution Seen as Tragedy," in *Diplomacy and Revolution: The Franco-American Alliance of 1778,* ed. Ronald Hoffman and Peter J. Albert (Charlottesville: University Press of Virginia, 1981), 103.

117 "Instructions to the American Peace Commissioners from Congress" (June 15, 1781), in *DHFR,* 1:199. See also "Instructions to John Jay from the Continental Congress, Feb. 15, 1781, in *DHFR,* 1:148.

118 Morris, *Peacemakers,* 439 (Livingston quotation); "Charles Thomson's Notes of Debates," Aug. 8, 1782, in *DHFR,* 1: 512–19; *JCC,* 22:459.

119 Lint, "Preparing for Peace," 31.

120 Perkins, "Peace of Paris," 196.

121 Edmund S. Morgan, *Benjamin Franklin* (New Haven, Conn.: Yale University Press, 2002), 245–51, 282; Schiff, *A Great Improvisation,* 87.

122 William Carmichael to Thomas Jefferson, Oct. 15, 1787, in *PTJ,* 12:241 (quotation); Schiff, *A Great Improvisation,* 171–72; Morgan, *Benjamin Franklin,* 292.

123 Esmond Wright, "The British Objectives, 1780–1783: 'If Not Dominion Then Trade,'" in Hoffman and Albert, *Peace and the Peacemakers,* 3–29, quotations from 15, 22; Morgan, *Benjamin Franklin,* 284–85; Morris, *Peacemakers,* 363, 429; Perkins, "Peace of Paris," 197–98.

124 "Notes of a Conversation between Benjamin Franklin and Richard Oswald" (April 18, 1782), in *DHFR,* 1:341–42; John Adams to Benjamin Franklin, April 16, 1782, in *DHFR,* 338.

125 Benjamin Franklin to John Adams, April 20, 1782, in *DHFR,* 1:356; Oswald, quoted in Wright, "British Objectives," 15.

126 Richard Oswald to Lord Shelburne, July 10, 1782, in *DHFR,* 1:462–63, quotation from 463.

127 Perkins, "Peace of Paris," 211.

128 John Jay to Robert R. Livingston, Nov. 17, 1782, in *DHFR,* 1:663. My summary of the final months of negotiations that follows draws heavily from Dull, *A Diplomatic History;* Morris, *Peacemakers;* Perkins, "Peace of Paris"; Schiff, *A Great Improvisation.*

129 In truth, argues Jonathan Dull, Russian agitations in Eastern Europe, a dwindling French treasury, and Spanish hopes to recover Gibraltar left Vergennes dispassion-

ate about many of the details discussed between Britain and the United States: Dull, "France and the American Revolution," 103.

130 Morris, *Peacemakers,* 349; Richard White, *The Middle Ground: Indians, Empires, and Republics in the Great Lakes Region, 1650–1815* (Cambridge: Cambridge University Press, 1991), 366–412.

131 Benjamin Franklin to Robert Livingston, Aug. 12, 1782, in Francis Wharton, *The Revolutionary Diplomatic Correspondence of the United States,* 6 vols. (Washington, D.C.: U.S. Government Printing Office, 1889), 5:657; American Peace Commissioners to Robert R. Livingston, July 18, 1783, in *DHFR,* 1:882–83.

132 For the severe treatments of the commissioners' work, see Perkins, "Peace of Paris"; James H. Hutson, "The American Negotiators: The Diplomacy of Jealousy," in Hoffman and Albert, *Peace and the Peacemakers,* 52–69. Examples of more charitable works include Frank W. Brecher, *Securing American Independence: John Jay and the French Alliance* (Westport, Conn.: Praeger, 2003), 219–26; Morris, *Peacemakers,* 438–59; Walter Stahr, *John Jay: Founding Father* (New York: Hambledon and London, 2005), 172–74.

133 Morris, *Peacemakers,* 321–22, 354–55.

134 Comte de Vergennes to Chevalier de la Luzerne, Oct. 14, 1782, in *DHFR,* 1:616.

135 Comte de Vergennes to Joseph Matthias Gérard de Rayneval, Dec. 4, 1782, in *DHFR,* 706; Morris, *Peacemakers,* 420–22; Perkins, "Peace of Paris," 218–19.

136 Morris, *Peacemakers,* 438–48.

137 American Peace Commissioners to Robert R. Livingston, Dec. 14, 1782, in *DHFR,* 1:717.

138 American Commissioner to Robert R. Livingston, July 18, 1783, in *DHFR,* 1:884.

6. ORDERING LANDS AND PEOPLES

1 Native Americans preceded Europeans on the continent, contributed indirectly to its intellectual construction, and came to symbolize it in European eyes. Natives also eventually and forcefully asserted the status of first Americans. But rarely, if ever, it would seem, did they think in such metageographical terms in the eighteenth century, for continental taxonomies were a relatively new European construct that hinged upon European perceptions of place. On Native Americans' fundamentally different conceptions of space—and its relationship to history—see Keith H. Basso, *Wisdom Sits in Places: Landscape and Language among the Western Apache* (Albuquerque: University of New Mexico Press, 1996); Barbara Belyea, "Amerindian Maps: The Explorer as Translator," *Journal of Historical Geography* 18 (1992): 267–77; Belyea, "Inland Journeys, Native Maps," *Cartographica* 33 (Summer 1996): 1–16; Belyea, "Mapping the Marias: The Interface of Native and Scientific Cartographies," *Great Plains Quarterly* 17 (Fall 1997): 165–84; Vine Deloria Jr., *God Is Red: A Native View of Religion,* 2nd ed. (Golden, Colo.: Fulcrum, 1994), chaps. 4 and 7; G. Malcolm Lewis, "Metrics, Geometries, Signs, and

Language: Sources of Cartographic Miscommunication between Native and Euro-American Cultures in North America," *Cartographica* 30 (Spring 1993): 98–106; Lewis, "Maps, Mapmaking, and Map Use by Native North Americans," in *Cartography in the Traditional African, American, Arctic, Australian, and Pacific Societies,* ed. David Woodward and G. Malcolm Lewis (Chicago: University of Chicago Press, 1998), 51–182; Lewis, "Native North Americans' Cosmological Ideas and Geographical Awareness: Their Representation and Influence on Early European Exploration and Geographical Knowledge," in *North American Exploration,* vol. 1, ed. John Logan Allen (Lincoln: University of Nebraska Press, 1997), 71–126; Paul W. Mapp, *The Elusive West and the Contest for Empire, 1713–1763* (Chapel Hill: University of North Carolina Press, 2011), chaps. 2, 7; Peter Nabakov, *A Forest of Time: American Indian Ways of History* (Cambridge: Cambridge University Press, 2002), chap. 5; Nancy Shoemaker, *A Strange Likeness: Becoming Red and White in Eighteenth-Century North America* (New York: Oxford University Press, 2004), chap. 1; Mark Warhus, *Another America: Native American Maps and the History of Our Land* (New York: St. Martin's Press, 1997).

2 Thomas Jefferson to Archibald Stuart, Jan. 25, 1786, in *PTJ,* 9:218. Jefferson also engaged the services of Vermont hunters, through the aid of General John Sullivan, to have a moose sent to Buffon: see Anna Clark Jones, "Antlers for Jefferson," *New England Quarterly* 12 (1939): 333–48. For a lively telling of Jefferson's quest for a moose and its importance, see Lee Alan Dugatkin, *Mr. Jefferson and the Giant Moose: Natural History in Early America* (Chicago: University of Chicago Press, 2009). On his schedule, see Dugatkin, *Mr. Jefferson,* 62, 94–95.

3 Peter Kalm, diary entry for Nov. 2, 1748, in *Peter Kalm's Travels in North America: The English Version of 1770,* vol. 1, ed. and trans. Adolph B. Benson (New York: Dover Publications, 1937), 139–40; Thomas Anburey, *Travels through the Interior Parts of America,* 2 vols. (Boston: Houghton Mifflin, 1923), 1:161; "Colonel William Fleming's Journal of Travels in Kentucky, 1783," in *Travels in the American Colonies,* ed. Newton Dennison Mereness (New York: Macmillan, 1916), 673; John Filson, *The Discovery, Settlement, and Present State of Kentucky . . .* (Wilmington, Del., 1784), 297, 306, 309, 322.

4 Translator's preface in Jacques Pierre Brissot de Warville, *New Travels in the United States of America, Performed in 1788,* vol. 1 (Dublin, 1792), iv.

5 The preceding two paragraphs draw on Richard Drayton, *Nature's Government: Science, Imperial Britain, and the "Improvement" of the World* (New Haven, Conn.: Yale University Press, 2000), chap. 3, esp. 66–67, 76–77, 80–81.

6 Alan Taylor, "Jefferson's Pacific: The Science of Distant Empire, 1768–1811," in *Across the Continent: Jefferson, Lewis and Clark, and the Making of America,* ed. Douglas Seefelt, Jeffrey L. Hantman, and Peter S. Onuf (Charlottesville: University of Virginia Press, 2005), Jefferson quotation from 35.

7 Taylor, "Jefferson's Pacific," 35–36.

8 Although the literature on both Clavigero's and Jefferson's response to Buffon is extensive, no work explicitly juxtaposes the two to reveal how their different social contexts influenced their science and, in turn, the character of their nationalism. Jorge Cañizares-Esguerra's outstanding *How to Write the History of the New World: Histories, Epistemologies, and Identities in the Eighteenth-Century Atlantic World* (Stanford, Calif.: Stanford University Press, 2001) comes closest. It sheds light on methodological and epistemological differences between "northern" Europeans and Spaniards (including creole colonists) in their responses to Buffonian formulations. As Cañizares-Esguerra argues, "The bulk of the scholarship critically addressing the epistemological and methodological proposals of the Enlightenment did not come from the British American colonies but from Mexico. Thomas Jefferson, Alexander Hamilton, and Benjamin Franklin did not offer any comprehensive methodological response to the negative views of America proposed by authors such as Buffon, de Pauw, Raynal, and Robertson" (210). With regard to Clavigero, his "constant refusal to speculate was part of his larger critique of the philosophical method of Buffon, de Pauw, Raynal, and Robertson." He sought to demonstrate "the countless tensions and contradictions incurred by these northern European authors, who, Clavigero argued, had been more interested in building systems than in cataloguing facts" (237).

9 William Peden, "Introduction," in Thomas Jefferson, *Notes on the State of Virginia,* ed. William Peden (Chapel Hill: University of North Carolina Press, 1954), xi–xix; Dugatkin, *Mr. Jefferson,* 2.

10 Dorinda Evans, *Mather Brown: Early American Artist in New England* (Middletown, Conn.: Wesleyan University Press, 1982), 62–65; John Adams, *A Defence of the Constitutions of Government of the United States of America,* vol. 1 (London, 1788), xxiii–xxiv.

11 Jefferson, *Notes,* 102.

12 Ibid., 59. For another interpretation of Jefferson's rationale, see I. Bernard Cohen, *Science and the Founding Fathers: Science in the Political Thought of Thomas Jefferson, Benjamin Franklin, John Adams, and James Madison* (New York: Norton, 1995), 77. In a slightly different context, Ronald Hatzenbuehler notes that Jefferson often wrote not about what actually existed but about "what might exist or should exist if nature were in control." Ronald L. Hatzenbuehler, *"I Tremble for My Country": Thomas Jefferson and the Virginia Gentry* (Gainesville: University Press of Florida, 2006), 74.

13 Jefferson, *Notes,* 100.

14 Ibid., 101.

15 Ibid., 102.

16 Ibid., 63.

17 On relations among sedentary Indians, non-sedentary Indians, and Spaniards, see James Lockhart and Stuart B. Schwartz, *Early Latin America: A History of Colo-*

nial Spanish America and Brazil (Cambridge: Cambridge University Press, 1983); James Lockhart, *The Nahuas after the Conquest: A Social and Cultural History of the Indians of Central Mexico, Sixteenth Through Eighteenth Centuries* (Stanford, Calif.: Stanford University Press, 1992). For King Philip's War, see Jill Lepore, *The Name of War: King Philip's War and the Origins of American Identity* (New York: Knopf, 1998). For the complexity of race relations in the southwest after the Pueblo Revolt, see James F. Brooks, *Captives and Cousins: Slavery, Kinship, and Community in the Southwest Borderlands* (Chapel Hill, N.C.: University of North Carolina Press, 2002). On the Comanches, see Pekka Hämäläinen, *The Comanche Empire* (New Haven, Conn.: Yale University Press, 2008). On Túpac Amaru, see Lillian Estelle Fisher, *The Last Inca Revolt, 1780–1783* (Norman: University of Oklahoma Press, 1966).

18 John Lynch, *The Spanish American Revolutions, 1808–1826*, 2nd ed. (New York: Norton, 1986), 299; J. H. Elliott, *Empires of the Atlantic World: Britain and Spain in America, 1492–1830* (New Haven, Conn.: Yale University Press, 2006), 170–71.

19 D. A. Brading, *Miners and Merchants in Bourbon Mexico, 1763–1810* (Cambridge: Cambridge University Press, 1971).

20 In my discussion of Clavigero's work, I take my quotations from its first English translation: Abbé D. Francesco Saverio Clavigero, *The History of Mexico . . .* , trans. Charles Cullen, 2 vols. (London, 1787). I have also included Spanish quotations in the endnotes. The Spanish versions come from Francisco Javier Clavigero, *Historia antigua de México . . .* , ed. Mariano Cuevas, 4 vols. (Mexico City: Editorial Porrúa, 1945). This work represented the first time that Clavigero's original manuscript was published in the same language he wrote it. Earlier Spanish translations were derived from the Italian translation. For a more complete publication history of Clavigero's work, see John Leddy Phelan, "Neo-Aztecism in the Eighteenth Century and the Genesis of Mexican Nationalism," in *Culture in History: Essays in Honor of Paul Radin,* ed. Stanley Diamond (New York: Columbia University Press, 1960), 769n7. Clavigero, *History of Mexico,* 2:243 ("la América es un país enteremente nuevo" from 4:89). The privileging of eyewitness accounts and Indian informants distinguished Spanish and Spanish-American works from those of northern Europeans generally: Cañizares-Esguerra, *How to Write the History.*

21 Jefferson, *Notes,* 97–98, 63.

22 Ibid., 63. On Jefferson and Logan, see Anthony F. C. Wallace, *Jefferson and the Indians: The Tragic Fate of the First Americans* (Cambridge, Mass.: Harvard University Press, 1999), 1–13.

23 Phelan, "Neo-Aztecism," 766.

24 Clavigero, *History of Mexico,* 2:327 ("Sobre la constitucion fisica y moral de los mexicanos," "Cuatro clases de hombres," "Los americanos propios, llamados vulgarmente indios," "Los europeos, asiáticos y africanos establecidos en aquellos

países," "Los hijos o descendientes de éstos, llamados por los españoles criollos," and "Las razas mezcladas, llamadas por los españoles castas," all from 4:219).

25 Ibid., 2:338 ("él forma a cada tres palabras argumentos contra todo el Nuevo Mundo por lo que se ha observado en algún pueblo o en algún individuo" from 4:236), 2:363 ("tratar a los mexicanos y peruleros como a los caribes y a los iroqueses, no hacer caso de su industria, desacreditar sus artes, despreciar en todo sus leyes, y poner aquellas industriosas naciones a los pies de los más groseros pueblos del antiguo continente, ¿no es esto obstinarse en el empeño de envilecer al Nuevo Mundo y a sus habitants, en lugar de buscar la verdad com debía según el título de su obra?" from 4:275–76).

26 Ibid., 2:419 ("Los mexicanos no tenían que hacer con la California, ni podían esperar ninguna ventaja de la conquista de un país tan distante, el mas despoblado y más miserable del mundo" from 4:366).

27 Ibid., 2:215 ("En cuanto a las otras naciones de la América, no hallando entre ellas ninguna tradición en orden a la parte por donde pasaron al Nuevo Mundo, nada podemos afirmar," and "desde la Florida hasta la parte más septetrional de la América, pasaron del septentrión de la Europa" from 4:43).

28 Phelan, "Neo-Aztecism," 767–68. On use of the term *patria*," see Jacques Lafaye, *Quetzalcóatl and Guadalupe: The Formation of Mexican National Consciousness, 1531–1813*, trans. Benjamin Keen (Chicago: University of Chicago Press, 1976), 107. The dedication did not make it into Cullen's translation, but see Cuevas's edition of Clavigero's work. Clavigero, *History of Mexico,* 1:19 ("Una historia de México escrita por un mexicano"), 23 ("como un testimonio de mi sincerísimo amor a la patria").

29 Edmund Burke to William Robertson, June 9, 1777, in *The Correspondence of Edmund Burke,* ed. George H. Guttridge, vol. 3 (Cambridge: Cambridge University Press, 1961), 350–51; William Russell, *The History of America, from Its Discovery by Columbus to the Conclusion of the Late War* (London, 1778), iv; John Adams to Benjamin Franklin, Aug. 17, 1780, in *PBF,* 33:202.

30 Drew R. McCoy, *The Elusive Republic: Political Economy in Jeffersonian America* (Chapel Hill: University of North Carolina Press, 1980). On the classical roots of this vision, see J. G. A. Pocock, *The Machiavellian Moment: Florentine Political Thought and the Atlantic Republican Tradition* (Princeton, N.J.: Princeton University Press, 1975).

31 Quoted in Phelan, "Neo-Aztecism," 766 ("No hay duda de que hubiera sido más acertada la política de los españoles si en vez de llevar mujeres de Europa y esclavos de la Africa, se hubieran enlazado con las mismas casas americanas, hasta hacer de todas una sola e individual nación" from 2:225).

32 Carroll Smith-Rosenberg, "Dis-covering the Subject of the 'Great Constitutional Discussion,' 1786–1789," *JAH* 79 (1992): 847.

33 This and the preceding paragraph draw from Patricia Seed, *Ceremonies of Possession in Europe's Conquest of the New World, 1492–1640* (Cambridge: Cambridge University Press, 1995), esp. chaps. 1, 3. For New England, see also William Cronon, *Changes in the Land: Indians, Colonists, and the Ecology of New England* (New York: Hill and Wang, 1983), esp. chaps. 4, 7.

34 For a broad comparison of the British and Spanish empires in the Americas, see Elliott, *Empires of the Atlantic World.* On the *encomienda,* see ibid., 29, 39–41. A complementary, comparative approach can be found in Stanley L. Engerman and Kenneth L. Sokoloff, "Factor Endowments, Institutions, and Differential Paths of Growth among New World Economies: A View from Economic Historians of the United States," in *How Latin America Fell Behind: Essays on the Economic Histories of Brazil and Mexico, 1800–1914,* ed. Stephen Haber (Stanford, Calif.: Stanford University Press, 1997), 260–304. Also useful for its hemispheric approach and its emphasis on the importance of the nature of indigenous societies in shaping the contours of European colonies is Lockhart and Schwartz, *Early Latin America,* esp. chap. 2.

35 Elliott, *Empires of the Atlantic World,* 12–13.

36 Alan Gallay, *The Indian Slave Trade: The Rise of the English Empire in the American South, 1670–1717* (New Haven, Conn.: Yale University Press, 2002), 294–300; Peter H. Wood, *Black Majority: Negroes in Colonial South Carolina from 1670 through the Stono Rebellion* (New York: Norton, 1974).

37 Edmund S. Morgan, *American Slavery, American Freedom: The Ordeal of Colonial Virginia* (New York: Norton, 1975), 93–94. On the importance of land as a commodity in early New England, see John Frederick Martin, *Profits in the Wilderness: Entrepreneurship and the Founding of New England Towns in the Seventeenth Century* (Chapel Hill: University of North Carolina Press, 1991).

38 "Report and Relation of the New Conversions, by Eusebio Francisco Kino, 1710," in *Spanish Exploration in the Southwest 1542–1706,* ed. Herbert Eugene Bolton (New York: Barnes and Noble, 1908), 437; Elliott, *Empires of the Atlantic,* 36–37, 272 (quotation); Dennis Reinhartz and Oakah L. Jones, "*Hacia el Norte!:* The Spanish *Entrada* into North America, 1513–1549," in Logan, *North American Exploration,* 288–89.

39 On the demographic effects of King Philip's War, see James D. Drake, *King Philip's War: Civil War in New England, 1675–1676* (Amherst: University of Massachusetts Press, 1999), 169–70. On the war's legacy for subsequent attitudes toward Indians, see Joyce Chaplin, *Subject Matter: Technology, the Body, and Science on the Anglo-American Frontier, 1500–1676* (Cambridge, Mass.: Harvard University Press, 2001); Lepore, *Name of War.*

40 Joe S. Sando, *Pueblo Nations: Eight Centuries of Pueblo Indian History* (Santa Fe: Clear Light, 1992), 63; Andrew L. Knaut, *The Pueblo Revolt of 1680: Conquest and Resistance in Seventeenth-Century New Mexico* (Norman: University of Oklahoma

Press, 1995). On Spaniards and the Indians they struggled to control in the eighteenth century, see David J. Weber, *Bárbaros: Spaniards and Their Savages in the Age of Enlightenment* (New Haven, Conn.: Yale University Press, 2005). On the Comanches, see Hämäläinen, *Comanche Empire*.

41 Anthony Pagden, "Identity Formation in Spanish America," in *Colonial Identity in the Atlantic World, 1500–1800*, ed. Nicholas Canny and Anthony Pagden (Princeton, N.J.: Princeton University Press, 1987), 57.

42 Michael Zuckerman, "Identity in British America: Unease in Eden," in Canny and Pagden, *Colonial Identity in the Atlantic World*, 146 (governor quotation); Elliott, *Empires of the Atlantic World*, 78–87; Benjamin Franklin to James Parker, March 20, 1751, in *PBF*, 4:117. This letter received a broader audience when it was published in Archibald Kennedy, *The Importance of Gaining and Preserving the Friendship of the Indians to the British Interest Considered* (London, 1752), 39–45; James Otis, *The Rights of the British Colonies Asserted and Proved* (Boston, 1764), 24. This paragraph is not intended to suggest that race mixture did not occur at all. In fact, a focal point of the chapter, Thomas Jefferson, sired children by one of his slaves: See the forum "Thomas Jefferson and Sally Hemmings Redux," *WMQ* 57 (2000): 121–210; Gary B. Nash, "The Hidden History of Mestizo America," *JAH* 82 (1995): 941–62.

43 Though the two examples that follow are more than 200 years apart, it is important to remember that Mexico was colonized a century before New England. Perfect comparisons are impossible. On the difficulties of a comparative history of the Spanish and British empires, see Elliott, *Empires of the Atlantic World*, xvi–xviii.

44 Manuel Orozco y Berra, *Noticia histórica de la conjuración del Marqués del Valle: Años 1565–1568* (Mexico City, 1853), 59–60. I was drawn to this episode by Pagden, "Identity Formation in Spanish America," 54–55.

45 Quotation from Alfred F. Young, "George Robert Twelves Hewes (1742–1840): A Boston Shoemaker and the Memory of the American Revolution," *WMQ* 38 (1981): 591–92.

46 Ibid., 591 (quotation); Philip J. Deloria, *Playing Indian* (New Haven, Conn.: Yale University Press, 1998), 32.

47 On Tea Partiers as "Mohawks," see Benjamin Woods Labaree, *The Boston Tea Party* (New York: Oxford University Press, 1964), 95, 141, 143. For newspaper accounts describing the participants as "Indians," see Francis S. Drake, *Tea Leaves: Being a Collection of Letters and Documents Relating to the Shipment of Tea to the American Colonies in the Year 1773, by the East India Tea Company* [1884], facsimile ed. (Detroit: Singing Press, 1970), lxviii–lxix, quotation from lxxi. The term "played" borrows from Deloria, *Playing Indian*.

48 Deloria, *Playing Indian*, chap. 1; Greg Sieminski, "The Puritan Captivity Narrative and the Politics of the American Revolution," *American Quarterly* 42 (March

1990): 37. See also Paul Semonin, *American Monster: How the Nation's First Prehistoric Creature Became a Symbol of National Identity* (New York: New York University Press, 2000), 199–204, for the "substitution of natural history for the new nation's antiquity" in John Filson's writings on Daniel Boone.

49 For two Indias, one "within Ganges" and the other "beyond Ganges," see Thomas Salmon, *A New Geographical and Historical Grammar* (London, 1772), 464, 479. For "India, or the Mogul Empire," and "South India," see Patrick Gordon, *Geography Anatomiz'd*, 20th ed. (London, 1754), 253, 384. By this time, Gordon had dropped the ancient practice of seeing two Indias divided by the Ganges. For these developments, see Mathew Edney, *Mapping an Empire: The Geographical Construction of British India, 1765–1843* (Chicago: University of Chicago Press, 1990), 1–16.

50 Edney, *Mapping an Empire*, 3.

51 C. A. Bayly, *Indian Society and the Making of the British Empire* (Cambridge: Cambridge University Press, 1988), 45, 58.

52 Edney, *Mapping an Empire*, 2.

53 *The Nabob: or Asiatic Plunderers. A Satirical Poem* (London, 1773), iii.

54 On Asia as a land of luxury, effeminacy, and profligacy, see Kathleen Wilson, *The Sense of the People: Politics, Culture, and Imperialism in England, 1715–1785* (Cambridge: Cambridge University Press, 1995), 274 (quotation), 278; P. J. Marshall and Glyndwr Williams, *The Great Map of Mankind: British Perceptions of the World in the Age of Enlightenment* (London: J. M. Dent and Sons, 1982). Thomas Paine, "Reflections on the Life and Death of Lord Clive," in *WTP*, 2:23; *The American Crisis IV*, in *WTP*, 1:118–19.

55 *JCC*, 9:1038; Henry Laurens to the States, December 23, 1777, in *LDC*, 8:465.

56 Richard Price, "Observations on the Nature of Civil Liberty, the Principles of Government, and the Justice and Policy of the War with America," in *Richard Price and the Ethical Foundations of the American Revolution*, ed. Bernard Peach (Durham, N.C.: Duke University Press, 1979), 118–19.

57 Benjamin Vaughan, "Memorandum," Jan. 25 and Feb. 9, 1784, in Benjamin Vaughan Papers, American Philosophical Society, Philadelphia.

58 Bayly, *Indian Society*, 119–20, 205 (quotations). On the Permanent Settlement, see ibid., 108–9, 150–51; Robert Travers, *Ideology and Empire in Eighteenth-Century India: The British in Bengal* (Cambridge: Cambridge University Press, 2007), 233–44.

59 *Oxford English Dictionary Online*, 2nd ed. (Oxford: Oxford University Press, 1989), s.v. "subcontinent."

60 Edney, *Mapping an Empire*, 16.

61 Peter Pope, "Comparisons: Atlantic Canada," in *A Companion to Colonial America*, ed. Daniel Vickers (Malden, Mass.: Blackwell Publishing, 2003), 489–507;

C. Grant Head, *Eighteenth-Century Newfoundland: A Geographer's Perspective* (Toronto: McClelland and Steward, 1976). The quotation is from J. M. S. Careless, *Canada: A Celebration of Our Heritage* (Bowmanville, Ont.: Canadian Heritage Gallery, 1997), chap. 4, available online at http://www.canadianheritage.org/books/canada4.htm (viewed on May 25, 2009).

62 My discussion of Nova Scotia draws heavily from John Grenier, *The Far Reaches of Empire: War in Nova Scotia, 1710–1760* (Norman: University of Oklahoma Press, 2008); John Mack Faragher, *A Great and Noble Scheme: The Tragic Story of the Expulsion of the French Acadians from Their American Homeland* (New York: Norton, 2005).

63 For estimates of mortality rates, see Faragher, *A Great and Noble Scheme*, 424.

64 Grenier, *Far Reaches of Empire*, 209.

65 Ibid., 207. On the congress's desire to incorporate Nova Scotia into the union, see *JCC*, 11:518.

66 Andrew Jackson O'Shaughnessy, *An Empire Divided: The American Revolution and the British Caribbean* (Philadelphia: University of Pennsylvania Press, 2000), 32. My comparison of West Indian and mainland colonists relies heavily on O'Shaughnessy's work.

67 Richard S. Dunn, *Sugar and Slaves: The Rise of the Planter Class in the English West Indies, 1624–1713* (New York: Norton, 1973), xiii.

68 David W. Galenson, "Settlement and Growth of the Colonies," in *Cambridge Economic History of the United States, Volume 1: The Colonial Era*, ed. Stanley L. Engerman and Robert Gallman (New York: Cambridge University Press, 1996), 195, table 4.9. On the unique nature of the English sugar colonies compared with Mexico and the British mainland, see Engerman and Sokoloff, "Factor Endowments," 272.

69 The quotations are from O'Shaughnessy, *An Empire Divided*, 1, 3; Janet Schaw, *Journal of a Lady of Quality; Being the Narrative of a Journey from Scotland to the West Indies, North Carolina, and Portugal, in the Years 1774 to 1776*, ed. Evangeline Walker Andrews (New Haven, Conn.: Yale University Press, 1921), 92.

70 Ibid., chap. 1, quotation from 4.

71 Jack P. Greene, "Changing Identity in the British Caribbean: Barbados as a Case Study," in Canny and Pagden, *Colonial Identity in the Atlantic World*, 266; Michael Craton, "Reluctant Creoles: The Planters' World in the British West Indies," in *Strangers within the Realm: Cultural Margins of the First British Empire*, ed. Bernard Bailyn and Philip D. Morgan (Chapel Hill: University of North Carolina Press, 1991), 314–62.

72 Trevor Burnard, "European Migration to Jamaica, 1655–1780," *WMQ* 53 (1996): 780.

73 Bernard Bailyn, *The Peopling of British North America: An Introduction* (New

York: Knopf, 1986), 9. Crèvecoeur, quoted in Bernard Bailyn, *Voyagers to the West: A Passage in the Peopling of America on the Eve of the Revolution* (New York: Knopf, 1986), 10; Thomas Paine, *Common Sense,* in *WTP,* 1:19.

74 Burnard, "European Migration to Jamaica," 780–81, 789–91. On the backgrounds of European migrants to the mainland, see Bailyn, *Voyagers,* chap. 5.

75 Bailyn, *Peopling,* 9.

76 Colin G. Calloway, *The Scratch of a Pen: 1763 and the Transformation of North America* (New York: Oxford University Press, 2006), 59.

77 Bailyn, *Voyagers,* 20.

78 Trish Loughran, *The Republic in Print: Print Culture in the Age of U.S. Nation Building, 1770–1870* (New York: Columbia University Press, 2007), 67–68.

79 Peter S. Onuf, *The Origins of the Federal Republic: Jurisdictional Controversies in the United States, 1775–1787* (Philadelphia: University of Pennsylvania Press, 1983), 21–46, 179.

80 Washington to William Grayson, June 22, 1785, in *PGWCF,* 3:69.

81 McCoy, *Elusive Republic.* On the classical roots of this vision, see Pocock, *Machiavellian Moment.* Warville, *New Travels,* xxi.

82 Jefferson, *Notes,* 164–65.

7. SEIZING NATURE'S ADVANTAGES

1 For the Federalist argument as primarily one about state formation within the limits of an American tradition wary of state expansion, see Max M. Edling, *A Revolution in Favor of Government: Origins of the U.S. Constitution and the Making of the American State* (New York: Oxford University Press, 2003).

2 George Washington, Circular to the States, June 8, 1783, in *WGW,* 26:484, 485.

3 Joseph J. Ellis, *His Excellency: George Washington* (New York: Vintage, 2004), 154–56, quotation from 155.

4 George Washington, Circular to the States, June 8, 1783, in *WGW,* 26:488

5 Carroll Smith-Rosenberg, "Dis-covering the Subject of the 'Great Constitutional Discussion,' 1786–1789," *JAH* 79 (1992): 848.

6 George Washington, Circular to the States, June 8, 1783, 488.

7 Thomas Jefferson, *Notes on the State of Virginia,* ed. William Peden (Chapel Hill: University of North Carolina Press, 1954), 64; *Massachusetts Centinel,* Dec. 14, 1785.

8 François Jean, Marquis de Chastellux, *Travels in North-America, in the Years 1780–81–82,* ed. and trans. George Grieve (New York, 1828), 168; Johann David Schoepf, *Travels in the Confederation [1783–1784] from the German of Johann David Schoepf,* ed. and trans. Alfred J. Morrison (Philadelphia: William J. Campbell, 1911), 266; John Filson, *The Discovery, Settlement, and Present State of Kentucky . . .* (Wilmington, 1784), 276, 318, 322.

9 Benjamin Hirchborn, *An Oration, Delivered July 5th, 1784 . . .* (Boston, 1784), 12,

14; John Gardiner, *An Oration, Delivered July 4, 1785* . . . (Boston, 1785), 35; Enos Hitchcock, *A Discourse on the Causes of National Prosperity* (Providence, R.I., 1786), 24.

10 Richard Price, *Observations on the Importance of the American Revolution,* 2nd ed. (London, 1785), reprinted in *Richard Price and the Ethical Foundations of the American Revolution,* ed. Bernard Peach (Durham, N.C.: Duke University Press, 1978), 177–224, quotation from 210; letter from Turgot to Richard Price, March 22, 1778, appended to Price, *Observations,* 222. On Price's vision within a larger debate over American commerce, see Drew R. McCoy, *The Elusive Republic: Political Economy in Jeffersonian America* (Chapel Hill: University of North Carolina Press, 1980), 100–104.

11 Thomas Hutchins, *An Historical Narrative and Topographical Description of Louisiana, and West-Florida* [1784] (Gainesville: University of Florida Press, 1968), 23–24, 93.

12 Morse tacked against the slight tendency in the late eighteenth century to see North and South America as two separate continents. North America, in Morse's thinking, constituted only one part of the "western" continent, or the "Continent of America," and South America constituted the other. Meanwhile the "eastern continent" comprised Europe, Asia, and Africa. Be that as it may, his treatment of North America as part of a larger American continent did not prevent Morse from ascribing to it—or Europe, Asia, and Africa, for that matter—unique characteristics as if these landmasses were discrete, coherent entities. In this respect, his writing resembled works that saw the world as having five continents instead of two and ascribed continental status to both North and South America: Jedidiah Morse, *Geography Made Easy; Being a Short, but Comprehensive System of that Very Useful and Agreeable Science* (New Haven, Conn., 1784), 21; Morse, *The American Geography* (Elizabethtown, N.J., 1789), 11.

13 Morse, *Geography Made Easy,* title page, 25, 119, 144, 189, 203. For further discussion of these maps and the popularity of Morse and geography texts in general, see Martin Brückner, *The Geographic Revolution in Early America: Maps, Literacy, and National Identity* (Chapel Hill: University of North Carolina Press, 2006), 113–20, 146–48. On Morse's nationalizing influence in the early republic, see John Rennie Short, "A New Mode of Thinking: Creating a National Geography in the Early Republic," in *Surveying the Record: North American Scientific Exploration to 1930,* ed. Edward C. Carter II (Philadelphia: American Philosophical Society, 1999), 19–50.

14 Morse, *Geography Made Easy,* 21–22.

15 Entry of October 4, 1784, in Dorothy Twohig, ed., *George Washington's Diaries: An Abridgement* (Charlottesville: University Press of Virginia, 1999), 265.

16 On the role of diplomacy in the coming of the Constitution, see Frederick W. Marks III, *Independence on Trial: Foreign Affairs and the Making of the Constitu-*

tion (Baton Rouge: Louisiana State University Press, 1973); Marks, "Power, Pride, and Purse: Diplomatic Origins of the Constitution," *Diplomatic History* 11 (1987): 303–19.

17 Alan Taylor, "The Divided Ground: Upper Canada, New York, and the Iroquois Six Nations, 1783–1815," *Journal of the Early Republic* 22 (Spring 2002): 58–61, quotation from 60; Richard White, *The Middle Ground: Indians, Empires, and Republics in the Great Lakes Region, 1650–1815* (Cambridge: Cambridge University Press, 1999), 408–33.

18 R. Douglas Hurt, *The Ohio Frontier: Crucible of the Old Northwest, 1720–1830* (Bloomington: Indiana University Press, 1996), 95–105; Eric Hinderaker, *Elusive Empires: Constructing Colonialism in the Ohio Valley, 1673–1800* (Cambridge: Cambridge University Press, 1997), 231–36; Andrew R. L. Cayton, *The Frontier Republic: Ideology and Politics in the Ohio Country, 1780–1825* (Kent, Ohio: Kent State University Press, 1986), 1–12, Washington quotation from 7.

19 George C. Herring, *From Colony to Superpower: U.S. Foreign Relations since 1776* (New York: Oxford University Press, 2008), 43–44.

20 Merrill Jensen, *The New Nation: A History of the United States During the Confederation, 1781–1789* (New York: Knopf, 1965), 114.

21 Marks, "Power, Pride, and Purse," 309–10.

22 Don Diego de Gardoqui to Conde de Floridablanca, August 23, 1785, in *DHFR,* 2:764.

23 *JCC,* 31:938–39, 947.

24 King, quoted in Eli Merritt, "Sectional Conflict and Secret Compromise: The Mississippi River Question and the United States Constitution," *American Journal of Legal History* 35 (1991): 167.

25 On the sectionalism spawned by the Jay-Gardoqui negotiations, see Joseph L. Davis, *Sectionalism in American Politics, 1774–1787* (Madison: University of Wisconsin Press, 1977), 115–26; Reginald Horsman, "The Dimensions of an 'Empire for Liberty': Expansion and Republicanism, 1775–1825," *Journal of the Early Republic* 9 (Spring 1989): 3–5; James E. Lewis Jr., *The American Union and the Problem of Neighborhood* (Chapel Hill: University of North Carolina Press, 1998), 15–17; Merritt, "Sectional Conflict"; Drew R. McCoy, "James Madison and Visions of American Nationality in the Confederation Period: A Regional Perspective," in *Beyond Confederation: Origins of the Constitution and American National Identity,* ed. Richard Beeman, Stephen Botein, and Edward C. Carter II (Chapel Hill: University of North Carolina Press, 1987), 240–43.

26 *Boston Independent Chronicle,* Feb. 15, 1787, in *DHRC,* 13:57.

27 James Madison, "Notes on the Debates in Congress," Feb. 21, 1787, in *The Documentary History of the Ratification of the Constitution Digital Edition,* ed. John P. Kaminski, Gaspare J. Saladino, Richard Leffler, Charles H. Schoenleber, and Mar-

garet A. Hogan (Charlottesville: University of Virginia Press, 2009), available online at http://rotunda.upress.virginia.edu/founders/RNCN-01-01-02-0005-0005 (viewed Jan. 16, 2010).

28 Peter S. Onuf, *The Origins of the Federal Republic: Jurisdictional Controversies in the United States, 1775–1787* (Philadelphia: University of Pennsylvania Press, 1983), 171.

29 My thinking on the Northwest Ordinance draws heavily from Cayton, *Frontier Republic*, 12–32; Cayton, "Radicals in the 'Western World': The Federalist Conquest of Trans-Appalachian North America," in Doron Ben-Atar and Barbara B. Oberg, *Federalists Reconsidered* (Charlottesville: University Press of Virginia, 1998), 77–85; Fred Anderson and Andrew Cayton, *The Dominion of War: Empire and Liberty in North America, 1500–2000* (New York: Viking, 2005), 188–91; Peter S. Onuf, "Settlers, Settlements, and New States," in *The American Revolution: Its Character and Limits,* ed. Jack P. Greene (New York: New York University Press, 1987), 171–96.

30 For the Proclamation of 1763, see Merrill Jensen, ed., *English Historical Documents, Volume 9: American Colonial Documents to 1776* (New York: Oxford University Press, 1955), 640–3. Knox, quoted in Jean H. Vivian, "Military Land Bounties during the Revolutionary and Confederation Periods," *Maryland Historical Magazine* 61 (1966): 242. On heightened expectations, see Robert C. Bray and Paul E. Bushnell, eds., *Diary of a Common Soldier in the American Revolution, 1775–1783: An Annotated Edition of the Military Journal of Jeremiah Greenman* (DeKalb: Northern Illinois University Press, 1978), xv–xvi.

31 Rudolf Freund, "Military Bounty Lands and the Origins of the Public Domain," in *The Public Lands: Studies in the History of the Public Domain,* ed. Vernon Carstensen (Madison: University of Wisconsin, 1962), 15–34; Vivian, "Military Land Bounties," 231–56.

32 Joseph Plumb Martin, *Private Yankee Doodle: Being a Narrative of Some of the Adventures, Dangers, and Sufferings of a Revolutionary Soldier,* ed. George F. Scheer (Boston: Little Brown, 1962), 281.

33 Quotation from John Resch, *Suffering Soldiers: Revolutionary War Veterans, Moral Sentiment, and Political Culture in the Early Republic* (Amherst: University of Massachusetts Press, 1999), 1.

34 Martin, *Private Yankee Doodle,* 283.

35 Charles Patrick Neimeyer, *America Goes to War: A Social History of the Continental Army* (New York: New York University Press, 1996), 160–61. See also Holly A. Mayer, *Belonging to the Army: Camp Followers and Community during the American Revolution* (Columbia: University of South Carolina Press, 1996), 19.

36 John Francis Mercer to the Public, Sept. 11, 1783[?], in *LDC,* 20:659, 660. This essay was published in *Pennsylvania Journal,* Sept. 17, 1783.

37 On contemporary criticism of the Society of the Cincinnati, see Markus Hünemörder, *The Society of the Cincinnati: Conspiracy and Distrust in Early America* (New York: Berghahn Books, 2006).

38 Cayton, *Frontier Republic,* 19, 29.

39 Minor Myers Jr., *Liberty without Anarchy: A History of the Society of the Cincinnati* (Charlottesville: University Press of Virginia, 1983), 97–98.

40 Woody Holton, *Unruly Americans and the Origins of the Constitution* (New York: Hill and Wang, 2007), 145, 219; Myers, *Liberty without Anarchy,* 87.

41 On Shays's Rebellion generally, see Robert A. Gross, ed., *In Debt to Shays: The Bicentennial of an Agrarian Rebellion* (Charlottesville: University Press of Virginia, 1993); Woody Holton, "'From the Labours of Others': The War Bonds Controversy and the Origins of the Constitution in New England," *WMQ* 61 (2004): 271–316; David P. Szatmary, *Shays' Rebellion: The Making of an Agrarian Insurrection* (Amherst: University of Massachusetts Press, 1980); Leonard L. Richards, *Shays's Rebellion: The American Revolution's Final Battle* (Philadelphia: University of Pennsylvania Press, 2002).

42 On Shays's background, see Richards, *Shays's Rebellion,* 6, 26–27.

43 Ibid., 18–19, 25–26, 79, 95, 111–13, Knox quotation from 111.

44 William Pencak, "'The Fine Theoretic Government of Massachusetts Is Prostrated to the Earth': The Response to Shays's Rebellion Reconsidered," in Gross, *In Debt to Shays,* 128–29; Sarah J. Purcell, *Sealed with Blood: War, Sacrifice, and Memory in Revolutionary America* (Philadelphia: University of Pennsylvania Press, 2002), 84.

45 Washington to James Madison, Nov. 5, 1786, in *WGW,* 29:51.

46 Charles de Secondat, Baron de Montesquieu, *The Spirit of the Laws,* trans. and ed. Anne M. Cohler, Basia Carolyn Miller, and Harold Samuel Stone (New York: Cambridge University Press, 1989), book 8, chap. 16. On the tendency of Anti-Federalists to cite Montesquieu, see Saul Cornell, *The Other Founders: Anti-Federalism and the Dissenting Tradition in America, 1788–1828* (Chapel Hill: University of North Carolina Press, 1999), 58. Thomas B. Wait to George Thatcher, Nov. 22, 1787, in *DHRC,* 4:295; "An Old Whig IV," *Philadelphia Independent Gazetteer,* Oct. 27, 1787, in *DHRC,* 13:500.

47 Sarah Knott, *Sensibility and the American Revolution* (Chapel Hill: University of North Carolina Press, 2009), 218. For a list of subscribers to *American Museum* in 1787, see *American Museum,* vol. 2, July 1787, vii–xvi. George Washington to Mathew Carey, June 25, 1788, in *PGWCF,* 6:355.

48 On Carey's life, generally, see James N. Green, *Mathew Carey: Publisher and Patriot* (Philadelphia: Library Company of Philadelphia, 1985); William Clarkin, *Mathew Carey: A Bibliography of his Publications, 1785–1824,* (New York: Garland Publishing, 1984).

49 "Thoughts on American Genius," *American Museum,* vol. 1, March 1787, 206–8,

quotation from 206; *Proposals for Printing by Subscription, The Vision of Columbus* (New York, 1787). On Barlow's rejection of Buffon, see Danielle E. Conger, "Toward a Native American Nationalism: Joel Barlow's *The Vision of Columbus*," *New England Quarterly* 72 (1999): 558–76.

50 "Remarks on 'The Happiness of America,' a Poem," *Columbian Magazine,* vol. 1, Oct. 1786, 67, 70–71.

51 Pro Republica, "Thoughts on the Present Situation of the Federal Government of the United States of America," *Columbian Magazine,* vol. 1, Dec. 1786, 171, 174.

52 Philip Freneau, "On the Emigration to America, and Peopling the Western Country," *American Museum,* vol. 1, Feb. 1787, 160; Timothy Dwight, "Columbia: A Song," *American Museum,* vol. 1, June 1787, 12.

53 Timothy Dwight, "A Valedictory Address . . . at Yale College, July 25th, 1776," *American Magazine,* vol. 1, Dec. 1787, 45–46.

54 Joel Barlow, "An Oration . . . at the Meeting of the Connecticut Society of the Cincinnati, July the Fourth, 1787," *American Museum,* vol. 2, Aug. 1787, 36.

55 Col. David Humphreys, "Address to the Armies of the United States of America" [1782], *American Museum,* vol. 1, March 1787, 232; Timothy Dwight, "Address of the Genius of Columbia to the Members of the Continental Convention," *American Museum,* vol. 1, June 1787, 561–63.

56 Dwight, "A Valedictory Address," 42, and "Columbia," 564; Barlow, "An Oration," 30.

57 "Friends and Countrymen," *American Museum,* vol. 1, April 1787, 309; *American Museum,* vol. 2, Nov. 1787, 421. See also "Remarks on 'The Happiness of America,'" 69.

58 Dwight, "A Valedictory Address," 44.

59 Ibid., 43; "Friends and Countrymen," 309; *American Museum,* vol. 2, Nov. 1787, 421; Dwight, "A Valedictory Address," 43; Thomas Hutchins, "A Description of the Mississippi River," *American Museum,* vol. 1, June 1788, 443. See also Freneau, "On the Emigration to America," 159–60; "Preface," *American Museum,* vol. 1, March 1787, 231; Dwight, "Address of the Genius of Columbia," 562.

60 For the United States as an "infant empire" and similar phrasings, see "Remarks on 'The Happiness of America,'" 67; Pro Republica, "Thoughts on the Present Situation," 172, 174; Barlow, "An Oration," 30; Dwight, "A Valedictory Address," 43.

61 Pro Republica, "Thoughts on the Present Situation," 174; "Extracts from an Oration Delivered . . . by the Late Dr. Ladd," *American Museum,* vol. 2, Oct. 1787, 333.

62 Robert A. Ferguson, "The American Enlightenment, 1750–1820," in *The Cambridge History of American Literature, Volume 1: 1590–1820,* ed. Sacvan Bercovitch (Cambridge: Cambridge University Press, 1994), 484, emphasis in original; Brückner, *Geographic Revolution,* 100.

63 "Union," *Boston Gazette,* Nov. 12, 1787, in *DHRC,* 4:220.

64 "To the Honorable Members of the Convention of Virginia," *Pennsylvania Gazette,* May 21, 1788, in *DHRC,* 9:837.

65 *Philadelphia Independent Gazetteer,* Sept. 26, 1787, in *DHRC,* 13:246. This piece had been reprinted in twenty newspapers in eight states by the end of October. *Massachusetts Centinel,* Oct. 17, 1787, in *DHRC,* 4:85. This piece had been reprinted in eight newspapers in six states by November 26.

66 *New York Journal,* May 2, 1788, in *DHRC,* 20:975. For more newspaper celebrations of cultural and artistic genius, see Kenneth Silverman, *A Cultural History of the American Revolution: Painting, Music, Literature, and the Theatre in the Colonies and the United States from the Treaty of Paris to the Inauguration of George Washington, 1763–1789* (New York: Thomas Y. Crowell, 1976), 562.

67 *Bickerstaff's Boston Almanack [for] 1788,* 4th ed. (Boston, 1788[?]), n.p.

68 Trish Loughran makes a sound case for the limited diffusion of *The Federalist* and other tracts during the ratification debate: Trish Loughran, *The Republic in Print: Print Culture in the Age of U.S. Nation Building, 1770–1870* (New York: Columbia University Press, 2007), chap. 3. Nevertheless, the nationalistic Hamilton had a wide readership in mind. For a concise summary of *The Federalist's* genesis, circulation, and reception, see *DHRC,* 13:486–94.

69 James Madison, Federalist No. 51, in *The Federalist Papers,* ed. Clinton Rossiter (New York: Signet Classic, 2001), 322.

70 Larry D. Kramer, "Madison's Audience," *Harvard Law Review* 112 (1999): 611–79. Cornell, *Other Founders,* 10, makes this point regarding Anti-Federalist tracts. On the mundane nature of most Federalist writings, see Herbert J. Storing, "The 'Other' Federalist Papers: A Preliminary Sketch," *Political Science Reviewer* 6 (Fall 1976): 215–47. For No. 10's innovative qualities, or lack thereof, see Woody Holton, " 'Divide et Impera': *Federalist 10* in a Wider Sphere," *WMQ* 62 (2005): 177. The historian Lance Banning reminds us that from its first publication through the nineteenth century, "number 10 was seldom singled out for special notice." It was only over the course of the twentieth century that scholars developed "a reductionist fixation on the absolute centrality of Federalist No. 10 to proper understanding of its author's purposes and contributions." Lance Banning, *The Sacred Fire of Liberty: James Madison and the Founding of the Federal Republic* (Ithaca, N.Y.: Cornell University Press, 1995), 205.

71 On Webster's authorship, see *DHRC,* 13:492.

72 Alexander Hamilton, Federalist No. 11, quoted in "Review of Publications," *American Magazine,* vol. 1, April 1788, 339. In the original publication, the asterisk referred the reader to "Recherches philosophiques sur les Americains."

73 Federalist No. 11, in Rossiter, *The Federalist Papers,* 85. A notable exception is Lee Alan Dugatkin, *Mr. Jefferson and the Giant Moose: Natural History in Early America* (Chicago: University of Chicago Press, 2009), 50–52.

74 Madison to Jefferson, May 12 and June 19, 1786, in *The Papers of James Madison,*

vol. 9 (Chicago: University of Chicago Press, 1975), 49, 51 ("female opossum"), 78 ("female"); and James Madison to George Washington, March 18, 1787, in *PGWCF,* 5:92. For Madison's reading of Buffon, see the editorial note in *Papers of James Madison,* 9:29–31. For Madison's scientific training, see I. Bernard Cohen, *Science and the Founding Fathers: Science in the Political Thought of Jefferson, Franklin, Adams, and Madison* (New York: Norton, 1995), 262–69. Scholars have long sought to trace Madison's intellectual influences. A useful introduction to the literature are the essays in the forum "The Madisonian Moment," *WMQ* 59 (Oct. 2002): 865–956. On the opossum as a subject of inquiry in early America, see Susan Scott Parrish, "The Female Opossum and the Nature of the New World," *WMQ* 54 (1997): 475–514.

75 This theme is developed at length in Douglass Adair, "That Politics May Be Reduced to a Science," *Huntington Library Quarterly* 20 (1957): 343–60.

76 Cohen, *Science and the Founding Fathers,* 279–80, quotation from 280. For Cohen's views on science in *The Federalist,* see ibid., 269–72. He overlooks Hamilton's explicit reference to de Pauw.

77 Federalist No. 9, in Rossiter, *The Federalist Papers,* 67.

78 James Madison, Federalist No. 14, in ibid., 95–96.

79 For the phrase "insular situation," see Alexander Hamilton, Federalist No. 8, in ibid., 64; James Madison, Federalist No. 41, in ibid., 254. Federalist No. 5, in ibid., 45, 47.

80 Federalist No. 6, in ibid., 54; Hamilton, Federalist No. 8, 62–65, quotation from 65.

81 Madison, Federalist No. 41, 254–55. On the theme of insularity, see Donald Lee Walker Jr., "Alexander Hamilton's American Empire: The Intellectual Foundations of Federalist Foreign Policy," Ph.D. diss., University of Nebraska, Lincoln, 2005, 132–34. On Anti-Federalists and defense, see Edling, *A Revolution in Favor of Government,* 90. On the geography of the United States lending itself to government with fewer means, see Edling, *A Revolution in Favor of Government,* 99, 122–23.

82 Alexander Hamilton, Federalist No. 12, in Rossiter, *The Federalist Papers,* 90; John Jay, Federalist No. 2, in ibid., 32; Hamilton, Federalist No. 11, 84.

83 Jay, Federalist No. 2, 32; Hamilton, Federalist No. 12, 88; Madison, Federalist No. 14, 98.

84 Madison, Federalist No. 51, 320, 322. My thinking in this paragraph has been heavily influenced by Banning, *Sacred Fire of Liberty,* 195–233, esp. 210–11.

85 Norman A. Graebner, "Isolationism and Antifederalism: The Ratification Debates," *Diplomatic History* 11 (1987): 337–53.

86 "A Columbian Patriot," in *DHRC,* 16:284.

87 Cornell, *Other Founders,* 12.

88 Rosemarie Zagarri, *The Politics of Size: Representation in the United States, 1776–*

1850 (Ithaca, N.Y.: Cornell University Press, 1987), 37. My discussion of representation draws heavily on Zagarri's argument on the shift from spatial to demographic representation and the resulting shift from actual to virtual representation.

89 Thomas Paine, *Common Sense*, in *WTP*, 1:27–29.

90 Thomas Paine, *The American Crisis X*, in *WTP*, 1:204; *The American Crisis XIII*, in *WTP*, 1:234.

91 Alexander Hamilton, "The Continentalist No. III," in *The Papers of Alexander Hamilton*, 27 vols., ed. Harold C. Syrett et al. (New York: Columbia University Press, 1961–87), 2:660; "The Continentalist No. I," in ibid., 2:651.

92 The best treatment of Husband is Mark H. Jones, "Herman Husband: Millenarian, Carolina Regulator, and Whiskey Rebel," Ph.D. diss., Northern Illinois University, DeKalb, 1982.

93 Husband's views have been pieced together from a variety of sources in ibid., 263–327.

94 Herman Husband, *A Dialogue between an Assembly-man and a Convention-man* (Philadelphia, 1790), 4–5.

95 Jones, "Herman Husband," 308, 321.

96 Holton, *Unruly Americans;* Edmund S. Morgan, *Inventing the People: The Rise of Popular Sovereignty in England and America* (New York: Norton, 1988), 267.

97 Madison, quoted in Gordon S. Wood, *Empire of Liberty: A History of the Early Republic, 1789–1815* (New York: Oxford University Press, 2009), 17; Holton, "Divide et Impera," 191.

98 Holton, "Divide et Impera," 189, 196.

99 Holton, *Unruly Americans*, 211.

100 Jonathan Elliot, ed., *The Debates in the Several State Conventions, on the Adoption of the Federal Constitution*, 5 vols. (Philadelphia, 1863–91), 2:243–51, 4:288. On scholars' recognition of parallels between revolutionary and Anti-Federalist rhetoric, see Edling, *A Revolution in Favor of Government*, 40. Useful discussions of Americans' thoughts on representation and the divergence of Federalists and Anti-Federalists include Holton, "Divide et Impera"; Morgan, *Inventing the People*, 274–87; Jack N. Rakove, *Original Meanings: Politics and Ideas in the Making of the Constitution* (New York: Knopf, 1997), 243. Cornell makes a persuasive case for the diversity of Anti-Federalist thought while highlighting the consistency of Anti-Federalists on certain issues, such as representation: see Cornell, *Other Founders*, 30–31.

101 Federalist No. 35, in Rossiter, *The Federalist Papers*, 210.

102 Ibid., 210–11; Gordon S. Wood, *The Creation of the American Republic, 1776–1787* (Chapel Hill: University of North Carolina Press, 1969), 471–75, 483–99, 514–18.

103 My thinking here is influenced by Morgan, *Inventing the People*, 280–82.

104 Ibid., 267–68.

105 Zagarri, *Politics of Size,* 75–76, Morris quotation from 75, Hamilton quotation from 76.

106 Noah Webster, "America," in *DHRC,* 15:195.

107 Madison, Federalist No. 14, 98–99; Jay, Federalist No. 2, 32–33. See also Hamilton, Federalist No. 12, 88.

108 Dwight, "A Valedictory Address," 44–45; *American Museum,* vol. 2, Nov. 1787, 421; Timothy Dwight, "A Valedictory Address [Concluded]," *American Magazine,* vol. 1, Jan. 1788, 99.

109 Jay, Federalist No. 2, 32; Madison, Federalist No. 14, 99.

110 *American Museum,* vol. 1, March 1787, 231–32; Curtius, "Address to All Federalists," *American Museum,* vol. 2, Oct. 1787, 384; Humphreys, quoted in "Remarks on 'The Happiness of America,'" 69; Dwight, "Address of the Genius of Columbia," 563. Virginia debate quotation from "Debates," 1788, in *DHRC,* 15:21. See also Barlow, "An Oration," 32; Knott, *Sensibility,* 235–36.

111 *American Museum,* vol. 2, July 1787, 90; William Hillhouse, "An Oration in Commemoration for General Nathaniel Greene," *American Museum,* vol. 2, Oct. 1787, 337. See also Barlow, "An Oration"; "Extracts from an Oration Delivered". On "military gratitude" between the Revolution and ratification, see Purcell, *Sealed with Blood,* 49–91.

112 Holton, "Divide et Impera," 175–211, Madison quotation from 175.

113 Jefferson, quoted in James E. Pate, "Richard Bland's Inquiry into the Rights of the British Colonies," *William and Mary Quarterly,* 2nd ser., 11 (1931): 20; Richard Bland, *An Inquiry into the Rights of the British Colonies* (Williamsburg, Va., 1766), in *Tracts of the American Revolution, 1763–1776,* ed. Merrill Jensen (Indianapolis: Bobbs-Merrill, 1967), 124–25.

114 Jacques Pierre Brissot de Warville, *New Travels in the United States of America, Performed in 1788,* vol. 1 (Dublin, 1792), 478; Freneau, "On the Emigration to America," 159.

115 John Higham, "Indian Princess and Roman Goddess: The First Female Symbols of America," *Proceedings of the American Antiquarian Society* 100, pt. 1 (1990): 54–59.

116 Ibid., 63–64.

117 On the Indian with neoclassical features, see E. McClung Fleming, "The American Image as Indian Princess, 1765–1783," *Winterthur Portfolio* 2 (1965): 81. On Columbia among the plethora of symbols of America, including the Indian woman, see Fleming, "From Indian Princess to Greek Goddess: The American Image, 1783–1815," *Winterthur Portfolio* 3 (1967): 37–66. Carroll Smith-Rosenberg offers a shrewd analysis highlighting the ambivalence of Columbia's femininity and relating it to the situation of the American subject as male in periodicals in "Dis-covering the Subject," 869–73.

118 My description of this figure as Father Time is based on Smith-Rosenberg, "Discovering the Subject," 870.

119 See Chapter 2; Claudia L. Bushman, *America Discovers Columbus: How an Italian Explorer Became an American Hero* (Hanover, N.H.: University Press of New England, 1992), 28–30.

120 John Adams, "In Congress, November and December 1775," in *The Adams Papers Digital Edition*, ed. C. James Taylor (Charlottesville: University of Virginia Press, Rotunda, 2008), http://rotunda.upress.virginia.edu/founders/ADMS-01-03-02-0016-0044 (viewed Jan. 16, 2010). The data are from a search of the Readex database *Early American Imprints, Series I: Evans, 1639–1800* on March 6, 2008. This search found 5,720 items published in the 1770s and 5,710 published in the 1780s.

121 Uncas Yanke, "On Ingratitude to Ancestors," *American Museum,* vol. 2, Oct. 1787, 400.

122 Bushman, *America Discovers Columbus,* 41–80, quotation from 57.

123 Ibid., 81–82; Silverman, *A Cultural History,* 585–86; Francis Hopkinson, *An Ode for the 4th of July, 1788* (Philadelphia, 1788).

124 On the work's timing, see Short, "A New Mode of Thinking," 34. George Washington to Richard Henderson, June 19, 1788, in *WGW,* 29:522; Morse, *American Geography,* 63, 469.

125 Warville, *New Travels,* 472–73, 480–82.

126 John Bondfield to Thomas Jefferson, March 7, 1788, in *PTJ,* 12:649.

127 George Washington to Philip J. Schuyler, May 9, 1789, in *The Papers of George Washington,* ed. W. W. Abbott et al., *Presidential Series,* 12 vols. (Charlottesville: University Press of Virginia, 1987–2002), 2:244–45.

128 Deborah Chotner, *Edward Savage: The Washington Family, an Inaugural Celebration* (Washington, D.C.: National Gallery of Art, 2005).

EPILOGUE

1 Available online at http://www.pikespeakcolorado.com/GeneralInformation.htm. For "world famous" and the coupon, see http://www.visitpikespeak.com/cafe.htm (both viewed on June 27, 2008).

2 *The Journals of Zebulon Montgomery Pike, with Letters and Related Documents,* ed. Donald Jackson, 2 vols. (Norman: University of Oklahoma Press, 1966), 1:349–51. The editor's retracing of Pike's side trip is useful: see ibid., 351n34.

3 On Pike's life, see W. Eugene Hollon, *The Last Pathfinder: Zebulon Montgomery Pike* (Norman: University of Oklahoma Press, 1949). On the War of 1812 and the psychological reclamation of virtue believed lost by the Revolutionary generation, of which Pike seems a part, see Steven Watts, *The Republic Reborn: War and the Making of Liberal America, 1790–1820* (Baltimore: Johns Hopkins University Press, 1987).

4 On the communications revolution, see Daniel Walker Howe, *What Hath God Wrought: The Transformation of America, 1815–1848* (New York: Oxford University Press, 2007).

5 Jon Kukla, *A Wilderness So Immense: The Louisiana Purchase and the Destiny of America* (New York: Knopf, 2003), 301–11, quotation from 305.

6 *New York Morning News,* Dec. 27, 1845.

7 James Madison, "Notes for the *National Gazette* Essays" (ca. Dec. 19, 1791–March 3, 1792), in *The Papers of James Madison,* vol. 14, ed. Robert A. Rutland et al. (Charlottesville: University Press of Virginia, 1983), 14:159.

8 Frederick Jackson Turner, "The Significance of the Frontier in American History," in Turner, *The Frontier in American History* (New York: Henry Holt, 1920), 1–2. Turner first presented his paper at the meeting of the American Historical Association in Chicago on July 12, 1893.

9 Available online at http://lcweb2.loc.gov/diglib/ihas/loc.natlib.ihas.200000001/default.html (viewed on June 27, 2008).

INDEX

Italicized pages indicate maps and illustrations.

Clark, George Rogers, 219, 233–34

Clark, William, 318

Clavigero, Francisco Javier: Buffon's theory dismissed by, 238–39; context of writing, 234, 236; Price compared with, 250; on space, time, and identity, 239–42

climate: as geopolitical and commercial factor, 61–62; latitudinal determinism and, 52–55; national character linked to, 60–61; racial categories in context of, 56–60; vigor and industry based on, 158; West Indies characterized by, 131

Coercive Acts. *See* Intolerable Acts (Coercive Acts, 1774)

Cohen, I. Bernard, 365n12

Collyer, Joseph, 112

colonial assemblies, 137, 141, 145. *See also* states and state assemblies

colonial charters: British-colonial relationship in, 70–71; continental taxonomies of, 87; king's granting of, 159–62; questions about, 145; territorial claims based on, 218–21; territorial claims in, 70, 117–18; types of, 67

colonial military: British disdain for, 108, 110; motives for joining, 121; Seven Years' War contributions of, 132–33. *See also* Continental Army; Seven Years' War (1756–63)

colonization: of Atlantic Canada vs. mainland colonies, 251–53; of India vs. North America, 247–51; national rivalries in, 60; of West Indies vs. mainland colonies, 253–55

Columbus, Christopher, 50, 87, 88, 135–36, 309, 312–13

Committee of Secret Correspondence, 170

Committees of Correspondence, 131, 153

Common Sense (Paine): on basis for independence, 2; context of publishing, 186–87, 189–90; on continent, 162, 187–88, 210; on Indians, 213–14; on international relations, 170–71; royal authority rejected in, 144, 187–88; royalties of, 196; style and prose of, 187

confederation: use of term, 351–52n57

congress: use of term, 165. *See also* Continental Congress

Constitution, U.S.: continental expansion and, 313–16; continental presumptions linked to, 3; metageography underlining, 285–86; Northwest Ordinance linked to, 274–75; ratification debates, 286–96; representational scheme of, 296–300, *301*, 302–7; reverence for document, 1, 260, 317, 321

Constitutional Convention: American people as authority in, 304; continental identity and representation ideas in, 260–61; delegates' goals for representation, 300, 302–3; diplomatic problems precipitating, 270–71; metageographical ideas of, 285–86; reform and continentalism in, 280–85; veterans' actions as precipitating, 275–76, 277, 278, 279, 280; wisdom of delegates touted, *287*, 287–88. *See also* Constitution, U.S.; Federalist Papers

Continental Army: appeal based on sacrifices of, 305–6; aspirations of, 193–94, 199; continent as ally of, 204–11; defeats and retreats of, 172–73, 196–97, 207–8; demobilization of, 275–78; mutiny in (1781), 202; name of, 194–95; "natural" support for, 181; Paine as voice of, 196–98; provisioning system for, 201–3; questions about, 203–4; soldiers in, 195, 197–98, 199–202; unity among reinforced by war against Indians, 211–18; victories of, 173, 198, 207, 208, 217, 218; Washington's speech to, 262. *See also* Quebec, battle of (1775); veterans of Revolutionary War

Continental Congress: activities during Paris negotiations, 222; British dismissal of, 153; colonists' sacrifices invoked in, 134–35; continental vision of, 154–55, 167–73; continent's size viewed as ally, 205–6; essential role of, 153–54; factionalism in, 273–74, 352n60; fast day of, 159; financial limits of, 201, 276; flight from Philadelphia, 197; geographer named by, 267; intellectual milieu of, 155–56; Montgomery eulogized in, 189; name of, 165–67; as national government vs. international compact, 349n32; national identity created in, 174–78; parliamentary ties rejected by, 143–44; post-1783 challenges to, 228–29; precedents limited for, 165, 349n34; territorial negotiations of, 272–75; territorial objectives of, 218–21; trade policy problems of, 270–71; unity managed in, 162–65; West Indians not invited to, 132, 253–54. *See also* Constitutional Convention; diplomacy, U.S.

continental identity: approach to, 10–13; British administrative reorganizing and, 110–13; congressional appeal to, 154–55; congressional successes in creating, 174–78; as defense against tyranny, 157–58; demobilization as attenuating, 275–78; in discourse on economic depression, 120–25, 128;

imagination's role in, 3–7; mainlanders distinguished from islanders in, 128–32; mapping vision of, 75–76, *76*, 77; metageographies' link to, 8–9; nationalism founded on, 9–10; optimism about expansion in, 262–64, *265*, 266–70; past battles and memories in, 180–86; in peace negotiations, 218–21; political representation and geography issues in, 109; post-1783 challenges to, 229; potential colonial union and, 70–71, 78–79; as precondition for revolution, 70; racial categories linked to, 56–60, 154, 181; in ratification debates, 286–96; redefinition of, 319–20; reform juxtaposed to, 280–85; reinforced by internal enemy (Indians), 211–18; representation, sovereignty, and place linked in, 136–44; representation ideas in tension with, 260–61; Seven Years' War sacrifices remembered in, 132–36, 180, 182–86, *184*; Seven Years' War settlement as boost to, 101–2; unity of Americans in, 304–7; unity of colonies in, 163–64; U.S. self-representation of, 307–9, *308, 310, 311*, 312–13. *See also* Federalist Papers; metageography

continental taxonomies: in almanacs, 86; Clavigero vs. Jefferson on, 239–40; concept of, 3–4; identities of colonists in context of, 230; India in, 247–48, 251; popularity of, 25, *26, 27*–28; potential definitions of, 284–85; in sermon, 157–58

continents: belief in balance of, 34; characteristics and traits assigned to, 18–19, 48, 50–52, *52*; comparisons of, 88–89; Doyle's view of, 47–48;

geographic features linked in, 19–24. *See also* American Revolution; continental taxonomies; degeneracy theories; science and scientific thought

European continent: American arts and sciences compared with, 282–83; American metageography compared with, 286–87; characteristics assigned to, 48, 51, *52;* hostility to British Empire in, 125; North America compared with, 88; status as continent, 47; tyranny examples in, 157

Europeans: American specimens for, 22; balance-of-power ideas of, 220–21; nationalism of, 48, 50; on nature of Americas, 18–19; racial categories of, 56–60; science and politics mixed by, 232–33; shift away from latitudinal determinism, 55

Evans, Lewis, 29–30, 78, 110

expansionism: continental aspirations lessened concerning, 172–73; continental identity linked to, 154, 283–84; expectations of, 101–2, 313–16; by exploration and purchase, 317–20; optimism about, 262–64, *265,* 266–70; Paris peace agreement and, 227–28; Plan of Union on (1754), 83. *See also* manifest destiny

Federalist Papers (*The Federalist*), 261, 288–96

Federalists, 260–61, 297, 300, 302–7

federal system: backcountry violence and support for, 307–8; Columbus iconography for, 312–13; Paine's argument for, 297–98; use of term in 1770s, 165; will of American people as authority in, 304–6. *See also* Constitution, U.S.; representation

Fenning, Daniel, 112

Fitch, Thomas, 134, 138

Florida, 99, 206, 226, 228, 272

Fort Detroit, 114, 271

Fort Duquesne, 83, 183

Fort Frontenac, 85

Fort Lee, 196–97

Fort Louisbourg, 75, 77, 85, 100

Fort Necessity, 82, 183

Fort Niagara, 75, 114, 271

Fort Pitt, 114

Fort Ticonderoga, 121, 132, 182

Fort Washington, 196–97

France: congressional negotiations and alliance with, 170–73, 177–78, 218, 219, 220–21; Louisiana territory ceded to Spain, 98–99; Paris peace negotiations of, 225–28; science and politics mixed in, 233. *See also* French in North America

Franklin, Benjamin: and almanac readers, 86; background of, 21, 23; on British Empire and future, 106–7; on Canada, 224–25; "Canada Pamphlet," 95–96, 101; circle of, 57, 110, 187, 282; on climatic diversity, 61; on colonies, 67–69; on ethnic and racial purity, 245; depictions of, *69, 287;* diplomacy and negotiations of, 172–73, 178, 218, 222–26; electrical discoveries of, 30, 64; *Experiments and Observations on Electricity,* 64; on French as check on independence, 95; on geography, 23; on Gulf Stream, 31; as influence, 22; "Join, or Die" emblem of, 68, *68,* 83, 107; on king's authority, 161; land speculation of, 116; "MAGNA Britannia" emblem of, 68, *69,* 107; negotiations with Spain, 220; on North America and empire, 77–78; on Northwest Passage, 40–41; *Observa-*

Franklin, Benjamin (*continued*)
tions on the Increase of Mankind, 63–
64, 206, 224; on Paxton Boys, 115; on
Plan of Union, 82–83; *Poor Richard's
Almanack,* 220; on population mobility, 257; on racial categories, 59, 64–
65; scientific interests of, 17, 30, 57,
64; settlement of America, 63–65; on
taxation, 138, 143
French Acadian population, 252–53
French and Indian War. *See* Seven Years'
War (1756–63)
French in North America: appropriate
place for colony of, 60; British
distrust of, 38, 40, 110; British goal of
defeat and removal of, *84,* 85; as
check on colonial independence, 91,
94, 95; feared encroachments of, 71–
73, 74–75, 78; fear of Indian alliance
with, 80–82, 105; ousted in Seven
Years' War, 46–47; territorial claims
of, 42–43, 46, 75
Freneau, Philip, 185–86, 307

Gadsden, Christopher, 142, 145
Galloway, Joseph, 153
Gast, John, 287–88, *288*
Gates, Horatio, 182, 215, 216–17
geography and geographies: arguments
for study of, 62–63; of army and
heroes, 198; continental expansion
possibilities depicted in, 264, *265,*
266–70; cultural traits and political
organizations linked to, 19–24;
definitions and uses of, 24–25; as
destiny, 208–9, 230–31; generalizations in, 155; interests in, 20–22;
island vs. mainland, 254–55; as key to
America, 23–24; limits in knowledge
of, 28–30, 47–48; political representation based in, 108–9; shift away

from latitudinal determinism, 54–55;
stability of earth (notion) in, 34; technology and distance in, 317–19. *See
also* almanacs; continents; maps and
atlases; travel narratives
George III, *106,* 107, 125, *126,* 154, 161–
62, 208
Georgia, 73–74, *74*
Germans in North America, 67, 79, 118
Gibraltar, Paris peace negotiations and,
226, 227
globes, 20, *308, 308–9, 315,* 316
Gnadenhütten massacre, 213
Gordon, Patrick, 21, 24, 28, 53, 370n49
Gordon, Thomas, 157
Great Britain: colonies compared with
founding of, 144; colonies indelibly
linked to, 68–69, *69;* expansionist
rationale of, 242–43; extralegal
conventions in, 165–66; French
declaration of war against, 77; latitudinal determinism in, 54; mainlander vs. islander attachment to, 254–
55; new kind of rule envisioned in,
105–7; North America as base for
transatlantic power of, 64–65; North
America best ruled by, 48, 50, 56–57,
60–61, 62; North American continent's size viewed from, 204; potential
new seat of government for, 141, 158;
science and politics mixed in, 233; size
of America in relation to, 2, 187; U.S.
peace with (*see* Peace of Paris [1783]).
See also British Empire; British
military; Seven Years' War (1756–63);
taxes and regulations, British
Greene, Nathanael, 196, 203, 205, 306
Guthrie, William, 24, 28, 155

Hales, Stephen, 54
Hamilton, Alexander: background of, 23,

281, 289, 312; on federal government, 298; Federalist writings described, 288–96; on king's authority, 161; on representation, 303; veteran organization and, 278; on will of American people, 304

Harris, John, 34

Hatzenbuehler, Ronald L., 365n12

Henry, Patrick, 116, 163, 164–65, 177

Heylyn, Peter, 21, 24, 25, 51, *52*

Hicks, William, 133, 140

Higginbotham, Don, 198

Hippocratic medical thought, 54, 59–60, 61

Hoare, William, 39, *41*

Holton, Woody, 120

Hopkins, Stephen, 130, 138

Hudson's Bay, 36–39, *37, 38, 40, 43, 46,* 90, *92–93*

Hudson's Bay Company, 37–38, 39

Hume, David, 20

Humphreys, David, 282–83, 305

Husband, Herman, 298–300, *301*

Huske, Ellis, 87–88

Hutchinson, Thomas, 101–2, 153, 246

immigrants and immigration: continental appropriation linked to mobility of, 256–59; distinctive nature of, 144; diversity of, 256; increased after 1763, 120; naturalization proposed for all, 79; optimism about, 262; plans to import, 118; publications for prospective, 17; settlement plan proposed for, 73–74; in West Indies vs. mainland colonies, 255–56

imperialism. *See* British Empire; expansionism; manifest destiny

independence: British military presence and, 110; colonies as empire without,

121; debates over, 176–77; de facto, 148; French alliance and, 177–78; metageographic assumptions in, 176; military key to, 181; Montgomery's death bound to ideas of, 190–91; natural as precursor to political, 158–59; obstacles to, 174–75; odds against, 203–4; post-1783 challenges to, 228–29; Pownall's view of, 111–12, 125; predictions of, 91, 94, 232

India: North American colonies compared with, 247–51

Intolerable Acts (Coercive Acts, 1774), 118–19, 131–32, 147, 154, 161, 166

Iroquois Confederacy, 80, 82, 212, 271

Jamaica, 131, 254, 256

Jamestown settlement, 243–44

Jay, John: background of, 289; diplomatic status of, 178; Federalist writings of, 288–89, 292–96; Paris peace negotiations of, 222–23, 225–27; Spain's negotiations with, 220, 221, 272–74; on war debts, 206–7; on will of American people, 304

Jefferson, Thomas: Adams's tribute to, 234–35, *235;* background of, 17, 20, 23; on Bland, 306; circle of, 187, 292–93; on colonists' suffering, 133; on Continental Army, 198; continental vision of, 239, 258–59; on declaration committee, 170; on defense of Americas, 234, 365n8; diplomatic status of, 178; on Gulf Stream, 34; on Indians, 214; land speculation of, 116, 118; Louisiana Purchase of, 319–20; and optimism about future, 263; on science and politics, 231–32, 233–34, 364n2; slaves and children of, 130, 369n42; on traits of northerners and southerners, 55; on university study,

claims envisioned in, 71–80; in Washington family portrait, *315, 316*. *See also* continental taxonomies; *and specific places*

Marston, Jerrilyn Greene, 162, 349n34

Martin, Alexander, 135–36

Martin, Joseph Plumb, 183, 201–2, 276–77, 307

Mason, George, 62, 116, 118

Massachusetts: colonial military casualties of, 132; economic depression in (1760s), 120–22; lands claimed by, 70; parliamentary acts' impact on, 119; soldiers from, 200. *See also* Boston; Intolerable Acts (Coercive Acts, 1774)

Mayhew, Jonathan, 81, 121, 132

McCrea, Jane, 216–17

McGillivray, Alexander, 272

McMurray, William, 264, *266*

Memorial to the Sovereigns of Europe (anon.), 149–50

mercantilism, 95–96, 124

Merritt, Richard, 335–36n41

metageography: concept and categories of, 8–9; Constitution and debates underlined by, 286–96; continental claims in, *84*, 85–90; continent's size and status in, 207–9; national rivalries in, 79–80; people's territory as continental in, 176; persistence in Continental Congress, 155; political identity linked to, 8–9, 70, 230–31, 283–85; shared destiny in, 163; shifted into policy, 171; systematized nature in, 58–59. *See also* continental identity

Mexico: British in India compared with Spanish in, 247–49; dismissal of, 156; Jesuits expelled from, 234, 239; map of, *44–45*; national consciousness of,

238–42; rebellion in, 245–47; Spain's interests in, 220; Spanish-Indian relations in, 242–47; U.S. war with, 320. *See also* Clavigero, Francisco Javier; Spanish in America

Middleton, Christopher, 37–38

Mississippi River: as boundary, 30; design of, 314; explorations of, 318; maps of, 31, *32–33*, 90, *92–93*, 264, *265, 266, 267;* negotiations concerning, 219–20, 272–74; Spanish control of, 221, 228

Missouri River, 90, *92–93*

Mitchell, John, 57, 78, 81, 90, *92–93*, 112, 271

Molasses Act (1733), 122. *See also* Sugar Act (1764)

Moll, Herman, 36, 39, 72

Montcalm, Louis-Joseph de, 94

Montesquieu, Baron de (Charles de Secondat), 19, 54–55, 188, 281, 289

Montgomery, Richard: in battle of Quebec, 172, 179–80; death of, 180, 181, 186–87; depictions of, *192, 193;* eulogies of, 189–91; martyrdom of, 191, 193; memorial for, 218, 306; play about, 191, *192,* 215; remembered, 318; Wolfe compared with, 182

Morgan, Edmund S., 108, 143, 145

Morris, Gouverneur, 304

Morse, Jedidiah, *268,* 268–70, 313–14, 373n12

Mountgomery, Robert, 53

Müller, Johann Sebastian, *84*

Murray, John (Lord Dunmore), 118, 119–20

music and songs: America celebrated in, 320–21; on civilizing the continent, 214; Columbus celebrated in, 312–13; continental identity reflected in, 124–25; military heroes remembered in, 186, 191

Pennsylvania (*continued*)
lands claimed by, 117–18; Paxton
Boys' attack in, 114–15, 257; refusal to
take up arms, 77, 82; soldiers from,
200. *See also* Philadelphia
Philadelphia: British takeover of, 205,
207; congress's flight from, 197;
economic depression in (1760s), 121–
22; geographic and scientific interests
in, 21–22; Independence Hall of, 260;
public library of, 22
Pike, Zebulon Montgomery, 317–19
Pike's Peak, visitors to, 317–19, 320–21
Pinckney, Charles, 273
Pitt, Moses, 27
Pitt, William, 85, 100, 102, 142–43, 157
plays and theater, 185, 191, *192,* 296
poetry and literature: America celebrated
in, 320–21; on civilizing the continent, 215–16; Columbus celebrated
in, 312–13; continental spaces in, 283–
84; on happiness of America, 282–83;
on Indians, 307; sacrifices and memories invoked in, 135–36, 185–86
Pontiac's War (1763), 114–16
Popple, Henry, 75–76, *76, 77*
Potomac River, 118
Pownall, John, 149–50, 224
Pownall, Thomas: on colonial
administration, 111–13, 146–47, 295;
on colonial unity, 82, 145; on colonies
as independent planets, 125; on commerce, 124; on Indians, 105; map
dedicated to, 30; on North America's
primacy, 63; Paine compared with,
150; Paris peace negotiations and,
224; on politics and geography, 148–
49; positions of, 110–11; on waterways, 31
Price, Richard, 31, 135, 249–50, 264
print culture: America celebrated in,

320–21; American iconography in,
307–9, *308, 310, 311,* 312–13;
availability of, 21–22; British-civilian
taunts in, 124–25, *126;* congressional
differences aired in, 273–74;
"continental" used in, 167, 194–95;
continental vision in, 305; "Join, or
Die" emblem in, 68, *68,* 83, 107; maps
in, 42, 89–90; North America
depicted in, 125, *126, 127;* Paine as
army's voice in, 196–98, 357n43;
political form and continental identity in, 281–85; racial divide reinforced in, 56–57; sense of community
and, 7–8; spatial consciousness in, *84,*
85–90. *See also* almanacs; Federalist
Papers; geography and geographies;
maps and atlases; poetry and literature; travel narratives
print culture, topics: American genius,
287; army's victories and defeats, 198–
99; British Empire map and, 75–76,
76, 77; British takeover of Canada vs.
Guadeloupe, 95–96; British taxes,
135–36; captivity narrative, 215;
climate, 61–62; colonies as continent,
187–88; colonists as Indians, 125, *128,*
209; colonists' sacrifices, 132–36;
Constitution, 286–96, *287, 288;*
continent, 88, 204, 209–11; degeneracy theories, 282–83; empire, 156;
federal government, 298; French-
Indian alliance, 80–82; imperial crisis,
187–88; Indians, 102–3, 105, 213–18;
Intolerable Acts, 131–32; king and
Parliament, 139–40, 159–62; limits of
republics, 281; McCrea's murder, 216–
17; metageography, 286; Montgomery, 191, *192;* mother America and
father Liberty, 210; New England as
nation, 274; North American con-